New England Furniture

FUNDED BY

Mr. and Mrs. George Kaufman,
the Mifflin Trust,

AND GRANTS FROM

the National Endowment for the
Humanities, the National Endowment for
the Arts, and the Ford Foundation

New England Furniture:
The Colonial Era

Selections from the
Society for the Preservation of New England Antiquities

Brock Jobe and Myrna Kaye

With the assistance of Philip Zea / Photographs by Richard Cheek

Houghton Mifflin Company   Boston   1984

Library of Congress Cataloging in Publication Data

Jobe, Brock.
   New England furniture.

   Bibliography: p.
   Includes index.
     1. Furniture — New England.   I. Kaye, Myrna.
II. Title.
NK2410.J6   1984   749.214   83-22555
ISBN 0-395-34406-9

Printed in the United States of America

M   10 9 8 7 6 5 4 3 2 1

Book design by David Ford

Marginal drawings throughout and line drawings on
pages 74, 79 and 81 are by Glenna Lang.

Preface

Furniture was not a particular concern of the Society for the Preservation of New England Antiquities when it was founded in 1910 to save "for posterity buildings, places and objects of historical and other interest." Three years later, however, the Society mounted a loan exhibition of furnishings called "The Colonial Parlor." By the end of its first decade, it was receiving gifts of seventeenth-century furniture and seeking suitable household furnishings for one of its Federal properties, the Fowler House in Danvers, Massachusetts. William Sumner Appleton, who led the Society from its founding until 1947, not only acquired appropriate furniture to "greatly improve the appearance of . . . rooms" but, in every thank-you note, asked for the provenance of the donated object. His interest in documenting an object's history remains a major goal of the organization.

The Society's collections grew like Topsy, sometimes topsy-turvy. Furniture arrived by the houseful as part of a building's contents; other times it was returned to its original setting because the house belonged to the Society. The very nature and name of the Society continue to engender donations of objects not merely with New England histories but with ties to particular houses or towns.

The Society is the repository of several comprehensive households. Some belonged to New Englanders who collected antiquities as romantic links to the past. For example, Eliza Susan Quincy (1798–1884) was the quintessential collector. A genealogist and family historian, she saw collecting her forebears' furniture as an appropriate way to honor them. By 1830, she was retrieving family items from relatives to add to the heirlooms she inherited. Eventually she filled the family homestead (now the Society's Quincy House), photographed the rooms, and compiled a history of the furniture. Her records and photographs were essential to us.

During the summer of 1975, we set out to catalogue all the furniture in the Society's collection that was of seventeenth-century design and of the William and Mary, Queen Anne, and Chippendale styles. We drove seven thousand miles, visited thirty of the Society's houses, and catalogued six hundred pieces of furniture. At summer's end, we found we were only half finished. Attics and barns, parlors and bedchambers, yielded such a wealth of furniture of the early styles that we discovered the Society's holdings were twice as large as had been assumed, some twelve hundred objects.

The next summer, we again armed ourselves with camera, tripod, film, floodlights (for examining furniture as well as photographing it), numerical blocks (a number in the photograph helped separate each chair from the rest), tape measures, knives (for cutting small wood samples for microanalysis), soft pencils (for rubbing impressions of dovetails and contours of moldings), screwdrivers (for removing hinges and table tops), and tack removers (for paring upholstery to its innermost cover), occasionally with insect repellent, and always with a picnic basket.

As we scrutinized every surface of each object, as our team moved from Stockbridge, Massachusetts, to Portsmouth, New Hampshire, from Standish, Maine, to Branford, Connecticut, we discerned designs and construction techniques peculiar to certain locales. New England, a singular region, contains many distinct regions. This collection is a unique laboratory for a study of regional variation.

Time and again New England furniture showed itself to be different from the London fashions from which it derived and distinguishable from the styles prevailing in its sister colonies. It has been studied by others as a part of English design, and we too note such relationships, but, based on the extraordinary strengths of this collection, we can also present a view of New England's towns and villages as centers of distinct design, both culturally dependent upon and independent of other locales.

The Society's collection is somewhat uneven geographically. One strong point, the many Society houses in the Portsmouth area, enabled us to discover a Portsmouth style in case furniture and in chairs. However, the Society's holdings from Connecticut and western New England are small, and in the introductory essays we include objects from other collections to help round out the story of New England furniture and to put the Society's collection in context.

The joys of the collection are many. Little of it had previously been studied or published, and every day brought new, often exciting, objects to hand. Working under 500-watt lamps on a 90-degree day was more than compensated for by finding original upholstery intact beneath layers of modern and nineteenth-century covers or by deciphering a barely legible signature that had been inscribed on an eighteenth-century desk when it was new.

Often our doubts were greater than our hopes. As we traveled to Maine to see furniture reputed to be documented to its original owner by a dated craftsman's bill, we questioned the wisdom of taking two people's time for the trip. We were wary of the ancestral connections so lovingly bestowed on much of the furniture and nurtured a robust skepticism about provenances. We doubted that we would find fine Chippendale furniture that could be tied to a patron, price, year, town, and craftsman. To our delight we found just that, furniture originally belonging to Jonathan Bowman of Pownalborough and the bill recording its purchase in 1770 from George Bright of Boston.

Over the years, the quality of the Society's holdings have grown, and during the years of our study some of the best objects were received: the Bowman furniture, the striking

Boston desk and bookcase featured in catalogue entry no. 51, and Jonathan Sayward's eighteenth-century house with its furnishings virtually intact since the Revolution.

When not examining furniture, we scrutinized the Society's extensive photographic archives, and researchers pored over probate records to discover or confirm histories. We hung the office walls with puzzlers and occasionally solved one. Having traced onto Mylar the fragmented remnants of an inscription found on a chair, we mounted the transparency like a stained-glass decoration on the office window, and suddenly one morning "Portsmouth, N.H." was clear.

We wanted to understand the furniture in its original context, so a dust-tolerant team scanned court records for all the room-by-room inventories in eighteenth-century Suffolk County, Massachusetts, indexing them all by owner, occupation, value of the estate, decade, and size of house, and gleaning many of the detailed descriptions quoted in the book. They watched for listings that documented objects in relationship to one another ("1 case of Draws Steps & Table / Glasware on the Case Draws") and noted each appearance of a new furniture term. Their work was an invaluable source of period names for many forms of furniture; it allows us to present new information on and clarification of furniture terminology.

One of our most difficult tasks was to limit the number of objects in the catalogue. The story of New Englanders and their furniture is so rich that we decided to sacrifice number in favor of detailed entries. Of the twelve hundred objects we catalogued, we include only the most interesting one hundred and forty-eight. Rarity, condition, and documentation were our primary considerations in selecting the highlights of the collection, examples that would best present New England furniture to two types of readers.

For the general reader, this is more than a catalogue. The objects illustrate the character and variety of New England furniture, illuminating the styles of living enjoyed by the owners in their several urban and rural environments. Seeing a New Englander's chair can be like seeing his brocade waistcoat or homespun shirt, hearing her accent and turn of phrase, or watching the gestures as a wealthy Bostonian or a country bumpkin seats himself and lifts his cup of tea. Furniture tells the craftsman's story as well. The introductory essays report on the careers and working patterns of artisans, the design traditions they enjoyed, the technology that was theirs, the impact of their environments on their work and lives, and, conversely, the impact of individual craftsmen on the design ethic in their environs.

For the reader knowledgeable in furniture history, the introductory essays include new information on furniture makers, and the catalogue should be a treasure house. We include an unusual number of documented objects, reproduce a few historic photographs that particularize provenance and *situ,* cite all provenances, and thoroughly describe the construction of each object to help in identifying related ones.

The catalogue entries treat more than the individual objects, for they are based on extensive comparative studies. We searched for comparable objects not only in the literature but to examine at first hand. We consulted antiques dealers and furniture historians here and abroad, were given access to many private collections, and visited more than eighty museums. We found many related objects; some are illustrated, most are footnoted. Such research helped us to assess the Society's collection and to broaden our knowledge of the objects in the catalogue. The highlights of the collection that this volume introduces to the public shed new light on the colonial furniture of New England.

Brock Jobe and Myrna Kaye

Contents

Color plates follow page 238.

Authors' Note

New England Furniture is divided into two sections. It begins with essays that treat the furniture of New England in the colonial era and introduce the craftsmen, their milieu, designs, and methods. The second part is a catalogue of the most important pieces of New England furniture in the Society's collections. (The term "New England furniture" encompasses objects made or initially owned there.)

The entries in the catalogue can be read both as a running narrative and as individual studies. They are organized first by form and within form by style. All seating forms, for example, armchairs, easy chairs, and couches, are grouped together because the similarities far outweigh the differences between armchairs and side chairs, upholstered and rush-seated chairs, single chairs and settees. Otherwise, within each category (such as case furniture or tables), the examples are presented by form in a developmental order (chest of drawers, chest of drawers on frame, chest-on-chest); within each form, the sequence of objects is dictated by a chronology of style and by design relationships.

Selecting among the many terms for furniture forms and features was a conundrum, and old terms that are unambiguous were given preference.

Dates and places of origin, given just beneath the name of the form, are as specific as possible for that particular object; they do not indicate the duration or extent of the popularity of the pattern. A craftsman's name is given in the heading only if he is known to be the maker, and attributions are made only where strong evidence proffers the name of the maker or his shop tradition.

The Society's furniture has been measured to a sixteenth of an inch; metric equivalents are given in centimeters. The measurements of objects in other collections were usually supplied by the owners.

Throughout the book, dates for the period before 1752 are Old Style, using only the new year; thus January 5, 1730/31, is written as January 5, 1731. Designations of right and left (such as the right arm of a chair) denote locations as seen by the observer. When an object has appeared with additional or contrary information in another publication, that publication is mentioned in the entry or its notes.

Footnotes, structural notes, materials, provenance, and accession information follow each entry. Newspapers, manuscripts, auction catalogues, and unpublished sources are cited in full in the footnotes; otherwise, short titles are used and complete citations can be found in the bibliography. The institutions and collections cited are listed more fully after the bibliography.

The structural notes elaborate on the general construction methods given in the third essay. Where methods of fabrication are likely to vary from object to object (for example, how a drawer bottom is affixed), the construction is fully explained. Otherwise, only those elements and joints that are distinctive or unusual are described. To facilitate comparison studies, the notes on documented objects are more detailed. Significant repairs and changes to the original structure are always given, usually as part of the condition of each object. Under MATERIALS, the woods printed in italics have been microanalyzed.

The figure numbers beginning with roman numerals (I-2, II-3, III-4) refer to illustrations in the three introductory essays. The subjects of catalogue entries are designated by their number (box no. 1, chest no. 5). Secondary illustrations in the catalogue — details of the object, comparable items, the object *in situ* — bear letters after the entry number (1a). Small details that would be difficult to picture, such as the contour of a molded edge, are drawn in the margin.

Categorizing furniture by style was secondary to placing it in a continuum of evolving design. However, names for styles are useful. For the sake of simplicity and familiarity, some style periods are designated in traditional terms — William and Mary, Queen Anne, and Chippendale. Style names are customarily identified with a historical era (Queen Anne refers to the reigning years of a sovereign), but here they are used less to pinpoint time than to signify a design aesthetic popular at a particular period.

The styles of the seventeenth century in America include the molded work (chest no. 5), the carved style (box no. 2), and the applied geometric designs (chest no. 6) generally associated with medieval, renaissance, and mannerist design. With cane chairs such as chair no. 82, the William and Mary style arrived in New England and remained current through the first third of the eighteenth century, long after both monarchs had died.

The Queen Anne style (chair no. 94) designates a set of characteristics that took hold of the New England aesthetic in about 1730 and remained in vogue into the 1760s. The Chippendale style (chair no. 111), introduced by the middle of the century, flourished through the 1770s and 1780s, remaining fashionable in the hinterlands into the nineteenth century. There our survey of New England furniture of colonial design ends, omitting the Windsor style, which did not become truly popular in New England until after the Revolution.

The study of furniture requires a special terminology for the joints and parts. The joints are named, described, and illustrated in the essay on construction methods (III-8, III-9, and III-10), and the terms used for furniture parts appear in illustrated references herewith. Craftsmen's terms have been favored, but modern terminology is occasionally used. These labeled pictures are not a guide to the most authentic or even the best terms; they are merely designed to serve the reader as a handy guide to the terms used in this book.

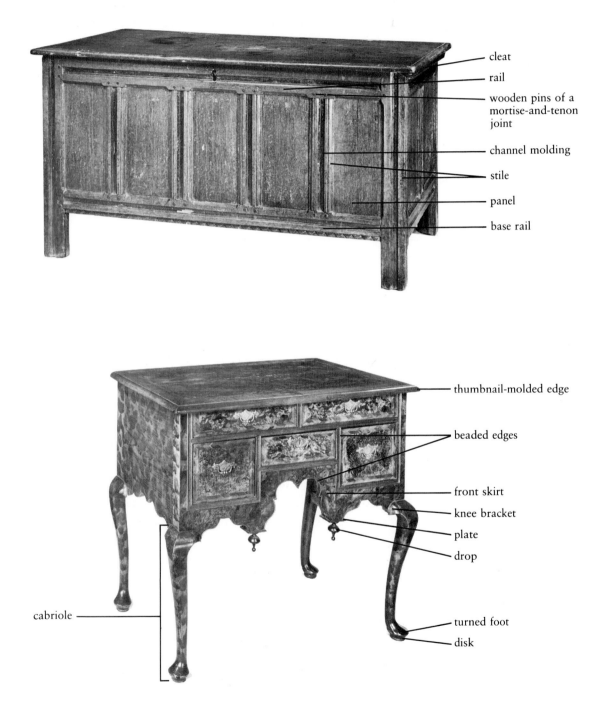

cleat

rail

wooden pins of a mortise-and-tenon joint

channel molding

stile

panel

base rail

thumbnail-molded edge

beaded edges

front skirt

knee bracket

plate

drop

cabriole

turned foot

disk

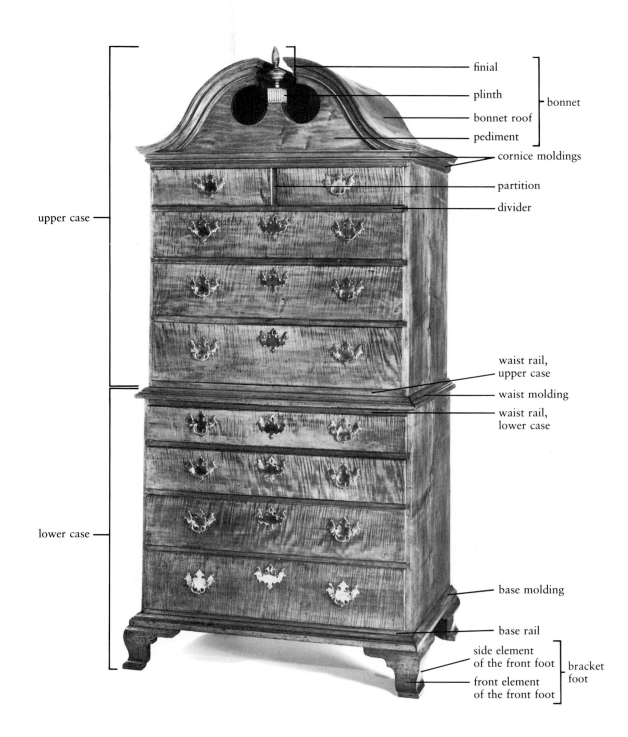

upper case

lower case

finial

plinth

bonnet roof

pediment

bonnet

cornice moldings

partition

divider

waist rail,
upper case

waist molding

waist rail,
lower case

base molding

base rail

side element
of the front foot

front element
of the front foot

bracket
foot

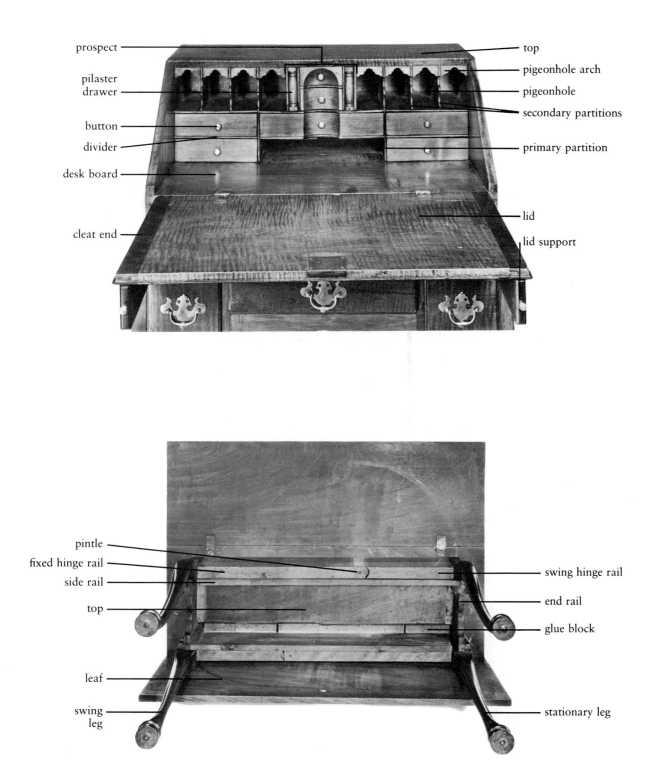

prospect — top

pilaster drawer — pigeonhole arch

— pigeonhole

button — secondary partitions

divider — primary partition

desk board —

cleat end — lid

— lid support

pintle

fixed hinge rail — swing hinge rail

side rail — end rail

top — glue block

leaf

swing leg — stationary leg

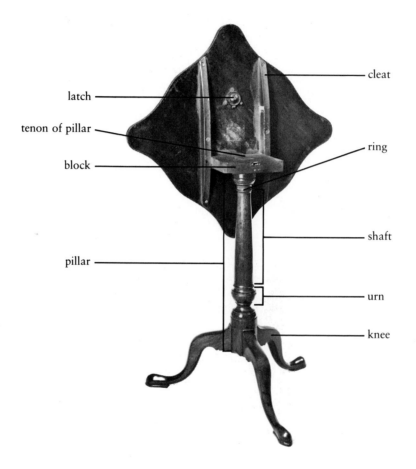

latch

tenon of pillar

block

pillar

cleat

ring

shaft

urn

knee

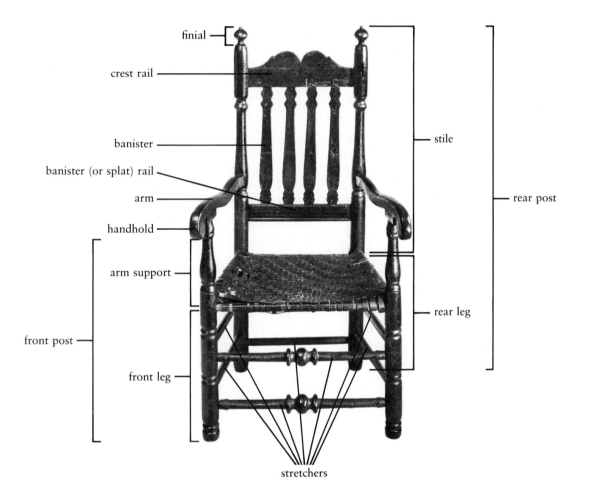

finial

crest rail

banister

banister (or splat) rail

arm

handhold

arm support

front post

front leg

stile

rear post

rear leg

front post

stretchers

shoulder ———————————— crest rail

stile ——————————

splat ——————————

splat shoe ——————————

loose seat ——————————

knee bracket ——————————

knee ——————

front seat rail

medial stretcher ——————————

block

disk ——————

turned foot

Part One / Essays

I. Urban Craftsmen and Design

Brock Jobe

The history of New England furniture begins with two important facts: the landscape offered an unlimited supply of raw materials and the Great Migration of settlers created a significant demand for finished products. "The land affords [a] good store of woods," wrote William Wood in 1634.[1] Large stands of oak, chestnut, maple, butternut, ash, cherry, poplar, cedar, and "sky-towering" pine grew throughout the region. Settlers were soon felling trees and sawing or riving them into boards, clapboards, and pipestaves. By the middle of the seventeenth century, many towns had sawmills where white pine timbers were sawn into boards quickly and inexpensively.[2]

Although fishermen had established temporary outposts earlier in the century and a small band of Pilgrims had ventured to the area in 1620, it was the Great Migration that truly settled New England. Between 1630 and 1643, about twenty thousand English men and women emigrated from their homeland.[3] London tradesmen, East Anglian weavers, Yorkshire farmers, and West Country yeomen arrived at ports such as Boston or Charlestown (across the Charles River from Boston), then moved on along the coast or rivers to establish dozens of towns, many of which are identified on a map of 1702 (I-1). The immigrants usually brought only the chests, boxes, or trunks that held their personal belongings and turned to the artisans among them to build their houses and to furnish them.

Virtually every town had a carpenter or joiner capable of performing both tasks. Larger seaports, however, attracted sizable groups of woodworkers and offered them increased opportunities. Furniture craftsmen were needed to do the finish work on vessels as well as houses, to outfit ships' cabins as well as household interiors. The ports also gave craftsmen the opportunity to export their wares and, by purchasing vessels, to engage in widespread mercantile ventures. Furthermore, in harbor towns, tradesmen could easily acquire the imported materials they needed for their work. Hardware and upholstery goods came from England, black walnut from the Middle Colonies, and mahogany from the West Indies.

By far the most prosperous seventeenth-century seaport was Boston, the "Metropolis of New England" (I-2).[4] Founded on a hilly peninsula jutting into Massachusetts Bay, the town benefited from an excellent harbor, which became crowded with wharves, shipyards, houses, and shops. The merchants who had profited from provisioning immigrants during the 1630s invested in shipping and shipbuilding in the 1640s, endeavors that ensured the success of the community.[5] Visitors found Boston "full of good shopps well furnished with all kind of Merchandize," and by 1690 the population had surpassed 6000.[6] Its artisans greatly outnumbered those in other towns and included many with specialized skills rarely practiced elsewhere in seventeenth-century America. Some forty silversmiths, for example, worked or apprenticed in Boston before 1700, whereas there were fewer than a dozen in the next largest American port, New York.[7]

Boston remained New England's major urban center in the eighteenth century. Its population exceeded 16,000 by 1740; mercantile fortunes were amassed by such men as Peter Faneuil, Thomas Hancock, and Charles Apthorp; production at local shipyards rose sharply; and craft activity as a whole continued to expand.[8] In 1750, a traveler from the West Indies admitted that "the Artificers in this Place Exceed Any upon ye

I-1. "An Exact Mapp of New England and New York." London, 1702. Engraving; H. 11½ (29.2); W. 14¼ (37.0). Massachusetts Historical Society. *The map first appeared in Cotton Mather's history of New England, Magnalia Christi Americana.*

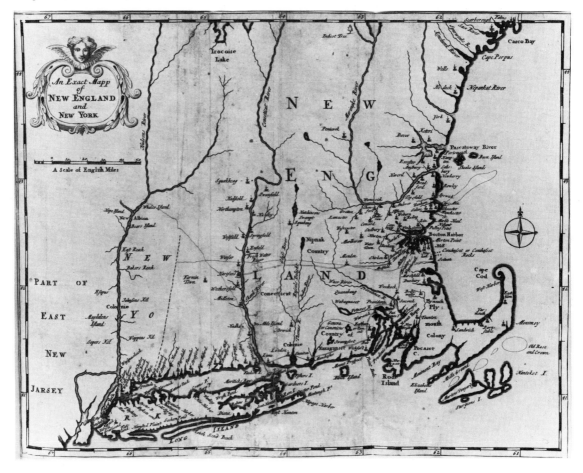

Continent."[9] However, the same writer found that the trade of Boston was "upon the decline."[10] Merchants in Philadelphia and New York no longer turned to Boston importers for English wares but dealt directly with overseas suppliers. Traders in smaller New England communities took over regional markets that the Boston merchants had controlled. By the time of the Revolution, nine towns had concentrated settlements of more than 3000 people: Portsmouth in New Hampshire, Newburyport, Salem, Marblehead, and Boston in the Massachusetts Bay Colony, Newport and Providence in Rhode Island, and Norwich and Hartford in Connecticut.[11] Though smaller, Charlestown also functioned as an urban community because of its proximity to Boston. And all the towns except Marblehead served rapidly growing inland populations.

The northern towns of Portsmouth, Newburyport, Marblehead, and Salem prospered from the shipbuilding and fishing trades. In Newburyport alone, more than seventy

I-2. "The Town of Boston in New England by John Bonner 1722." Drawn by John Bonner, engraved by Francis Dewing, Boston, 1722. Engraving, first state; H. 16¹³/₁₆ (42.7); W. 23 (58.4). I. N. Phelps Stokes Collection, Prints Division, New York Public Library.

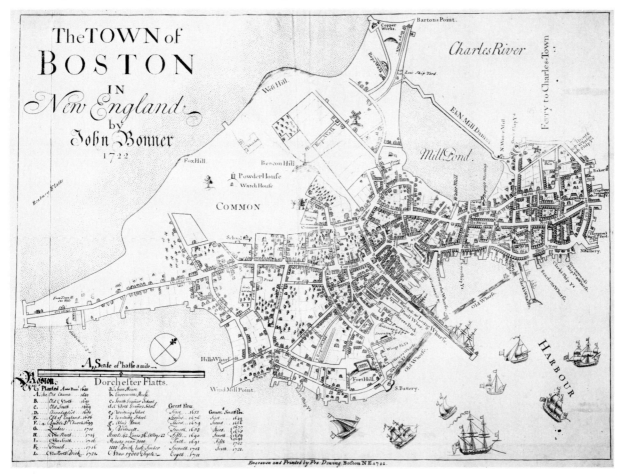

vessels were under construction in a single year, 1766; in Marblehead, according to an account of 1744, residents operated ninety fishing sloops and kept more than two hundred acres of land covered with fish flakes for drying cod.[12] Portsmouth gained added prominence as the capital of New Hampshire and was the center of the lumber trade of northern New England.

In Rhode Island, Newport and Providence were the centers of commerce. Newport (I-3) enjoyed a fine natural harbor and, during the early eighteenth century, many highly skilled artisans settled on Easton's Point, just north of Long Wharf. By 1774, Newport's 9000 residents included some of the shrewdest and most successful merchants in New

I-3. "A Plan of the Town of Newport in Rhode Island . . ." Drawn by Charles Blaskowitz, engraved by William Faden, London, 1777. Engraving; H. 14¾ (37.5); W. 21 (53.3). Newport Historical Society. *Many craftsmen resided on Easton's Point, an area north of Long Wharf and just left of center on the plan.*

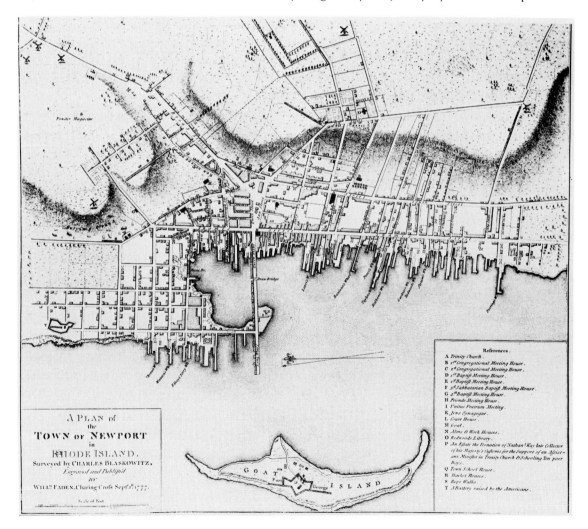

England, men who profited from slave trading and privateering in addition to more common mercantile pursuits.[13] Traders such as Godfrey Malbone and Abraham Redwood maintained stately country seats and handsome townhouses and funded the construction of public buildings, including the library and market designed by Peter Harrison, "an ingenious English gentleman" who moved to Newport in 1738.[14]

Growing inland markets and an enterprising group of merchants led by the Brown family enabled Providence, at the head of Narragansett Bay, to develop rapidly during the latter half of the eighteenth century, and after the Revolution it became more prosperous than Newport.[15]

No single town in Connecticut dominated colonial commerce the way Boston, Newport, and Portsmouth did in their respective regions. Instead, by 1775, the river towns of Norwich and Hartford had become important regional trading centers. Norwich, at the headwaters of the Thames River, served the eastern hinterlands; Hartford, below the falls of the Connecticut River, served the Connecticut River valley. New London, with a well-protected deepwater harbor at the mouth of the Thames, was the port of entry for much of Connecticut's commerce but was smaller than its inland rivals.[16]

During the seventeenth and eighteenth centuries, the nine largest towns in New England supported an estimated twelve hundred furniture craftsmen, a total probably exceeding that for all the rest of New England.[17] The number of workmen varied considerably from one community to another. The majority, not surprisingly, were in the region's two major centers, Newport and Boston. At least 105 artisans lived in Newport; Boston had 562, a remarkable number that reflected the town's economic importance.[18] Boston's craft population rose gradually for a century and a half, but Newport's grew rapidly late in the colonial era. Between 1745 and 1775, both towns had almost equal numbers of furniture craftsmen, Newport with 56 cabinetmakers, Boston with 64.[19]

Within each community, the craftsmen tended to live close to one another. In Boston, most resided along Back, Middle, Ann, and Union streets in the North End or near Fort Hill in the South End. In Charlestown, one thoroughfare was dubbed Joiner's Street because of the numerous woodworkers living there. The houses of Newport's artisans were crowded along the waterfront at Easton's Point.[20]

Shop space was generally limited; some craftsmen worked in their homes. Thomas Foote of Boston used a second-floor chamber as his shop.[21] Most individuals, however, built small structures next to their homes or rented rooms in waterfront buildings. The shop of Christopher Townsend, a successful Newport cabinetmaker, is one of the few to survive (I-4). It adjoins his house and contains a single room, 12 by 24 feet.[22] Most urban shops were probably similar in size, and only a few men could work together in such cramped quarters. Thomas Wood, a prominent Charlestown craftsman, had "Tools for four hands" in his shop in 1775.[23] The Boston chairmaker Joseph Putnam outfitted his establishment with seven workbenches, the largest number found in a colonial

I-4. The House and Shop of Christopher Townsend, 74 Bridge Street, Newport, 1725–1750. Photograph, 1890–1900. Newport Historical Society.

inventory but a far cry from the thirty-two benches in the mid-eighteenth-century shop of the London cabinetmaker Samuel Norman.[24]

To man these small workrooms, master craftsmen took on apprentices and occasionally hired journeymen, both traditional procedures in the English guild system. But New England had no guilds of furniture makers. Working arrangements were loosely defined and often temporary. The craftsmen's sons learned their fathers' trades without the formality of apprenticeship agreements. Parents who wished to put out their sons to tradesmen had to secure indentures, a task that sometimes proved difficult. During the spring of 1744, the Reverend Ebenezer Parkman of Westborough traveled to Boston "to obtain a good place to bind my son Thomme out a' Prentice."[25] He convinced Joshua Emms, a goldsmith, to take on his son, but the arrangement was short-lived. After just forty-five days, the boy returned home and Parkman again went seeking an indenture. "I was full of Concern about my Son Thomme," he wrote, "my hopes all blasted respecting his living with Mr. Emms. . . . I sought to Mr. Skelling the Carver [Simeon Skillin, a noted Boston carver], but in vain — to Mr. Samuel Jarvis, but not direct Success."[26] Parkman eventually placed Tom with a saddler in Grafton, but that arrangement also ended quickly. After serving three more saddlers, Tom finally completed his apprenticeship on October 12, 1750.

Though not as structured as in England, the apprenticeship system remained a significant feature of craft life in colonial New England (see page 67). It enabled masters to obtain workmen and made it possible for young men to learn a craft and ultimately set out on their own. This process ensured a continuity in design details and construction techniques within a particular area and, through the migration of trained apprentices, encouraged the transfer of motifs and methods from one town to another.

Urban ports offered young boys a wide range of crafts from which to choose. Walking along the waterfront in Boston or Newport, prospective apprentices saw the shops of dozens of specialists, shops that could only exist in urban settings. Among them were numerous branches of the furniture trade. By 1660 Boston had joiners, turners, and upholsterers, by 1690 cabinetmakers and chairmakers as well, and during the eighteenth century, carvers, japanners, chair caners, Windsor chair makers, picture frame carvers, and looking glass makers. Within the general areas of cabinetmaking and chairmaking were further subdivisions of labor. By the late seventeenth century, some craftsmen focused on the production of inexpensive slat-back chairs with rush seats (chair 78a); others made joined frames that upholsterers covered with fabric or leather (I-5).[27] While nowhere in New England did the degree of specialization rival that of London, the diversity of craftsmen in the larger communities set them apart from rural areas, where versatile woodworkers engaged in farming, carpentry, repair work, coopering, and the production of farm implements in addition to furniture.

The careers of two urban craftsmen — one a turner, the other an upholsterer — illustrate the character of specialized crafts, the interdependence of specialists, and the opportunities for large-scale production. Turners made a wide variety of lathe-turned

I-5. Side Chair. Boston, 1660–1690. Maple and oak; H. 34¼ (87.0); W. 18 (45.7); SEAT D. 15 (38.1); SEAT H. 18⅛ (46.0). Wadsworth Atheneum. *One of the best-preserved examples of a popular Boston type, the chair retains its original black leather upholstery, missing only the leather strip and brass nails that ornamented the front seat rail. During the eighteenth century, the chair may have belonged to John Edwards of Trumbull, Connecticut.*

ware such as stair balusters and handles as well as large quantities of chairs composed primarily of turned parts. By its very nature, turned work was ideally suited to mass production, for craftsmen could easily turn the same form again and again. In 1672, a Boston turner was able to produce fifteen chair frames a week.[28]

John Underwood (1704–1758) is one of the few eighteenth-century Boston turners whose activities can be traced in detail.[29] The son of a turner, he apparently was apprenticed to his father. By 1733, he was working on his own but still residing with his family and often serving as a journeyman in his father's shop. An excerpt from a bill of February 6, 1733, reveals the assortment of furniture forms and decorative details that Underwood produced for the cabinetmaker Nathaniel Holmes:

To turning 2 handel	[£]0: 1:6
To Piller & Balls & 4 Draps [Drops] & Colloms	0: 7:6
To 4 Draps and 4 Bead [Bed] posts	0: 4:0
To 4 Legs and 2 Draps	0: 7:8
To too Sets of Piller & Balls & one Table	0:15:0
To 6 Draps & one Collom & 4 Legs	0: 3:6
To one Table & Draps	0: 3:1
To 4 Legs & one Table	0: 5:0[30]

Underwood was a specialized craftsman, to be called upon by the cabinetmaker for individual elements: pillars and balls for legs and feet on William and Mary cases and drops to embellish the skirts of dressing tables and high chests. In addition to doing this piecework, he worked in his father's shop, constructing great quantities of lathe-turned slat-back chairs probably similar to chair no. 79. Between 1734 and 1746 he supplied 6180 chairs, an average of 475 chairs per year, receiving two shillings per chair for his labor.[31]

Like many other craftsmen, Underwood attempted to supplement his income by running a tavern. In 1743, the town selectmen granted him permission to operate as a retailer. His efforts, however, provided only a marginal income; throughout his life he was in debt, and at his death his assets were not sufficient to pay his creditors, a common occurrence among urban artisans.

In contrast, many upholsterers achieved considerable affluence by combining the activities of merchants and craftsmen. As merchants, they continually acquired a variety of imported textiles and dry goods to use in their own shops and to sell to customers; as craftsmen, they supervised the fabrication of beds and seating furniture in their shops, relying on the skills of several workmen to carry out the many facets of production.

Upholstery was solely an urban trade. Only in the largest colonial ports could upholsterers obtain imported materials, find the necessary specialists, and secure a sufficient number of wealthy clients. During the colonial period in New England, one town was a focal point for the craft: Boston supported fifty-six upholsterers; no other community had more than a dozen.[32]

The majority of Boston upholsterers came from well-established families of the middle and upper strata of society. Such family ties were invaluable to young tradesmen, who had to purchase expensive textiles on credit at the start of their career. The most prosperous upholsterers gained substantial incomes; their wealth, in fact, exceeded that of artisans in other branches of the furniture trade. The upholsterer Thomas Fitch left a personal estate of more than £3000 (excluding real estate) at his death in 1736. William Downe, William Gray, and Samuel Grant assembled comparable fortunes. All four enhanced their social and political status as well. Downe, Fitch, and Grant served as town selectmen, Gray as town auditor.[33]

Fortunately, four business ledgers kept by Samuel Grant (1705–1784) survive to document the career of a prominent Boston upholsterer.[34] Grant began to work in his own shop, the Crown and Cushion on Union Street, in 1728. He practiced his trade there for over half a century, and his son Moses Grant continued the business into the nineteenth century. For Samuel Grant, the sale of textiles and dry goods provided more income than upholstery work did. In the year 1730, for example, he earned £1888 from the sale of merchandise and £530 from his craft.

Grant managed numerous and complex shop activities. Workmen performed such diverse tasks as hanging wallpaper and making covers for chairs, tables, and desks. Producing a fully outfitted high post bed required the efforts of a chairmaker to construct the bedstead, a carver to embellish the headboard or cornice, a sailmaker to fashion a canvas bottom for the bedstead, and, working in Grant's shop, a journeyman to make mattresses, a bolster, and pillows, and a seamstress to assemble the bed hangings.[35] For the upholstery of seating furniture, a major source of income for Grant, he turned to chairmakers for chair frames and employed journeymen to do the actual upholstery work. Grant's chair production was significant; from 1729 through 1738, he sold 2006 chairs, 138 stools, 49 couches, 44 easy chairs, and made 66 cushions and 182 seats for chairs.

By far the mainstay of Grant's production in the early years of his career was what we call the Boston chair (chair no. 91). Made of maple and upholstered in black leather, the chairs were sold in large quantities for export to towns up and down the coast and in the West Indies. In the 1730s, one merchant alone bought 400 leather chairs from Grant, and Grant himself shipped more than 125 chairs to New York and Philadelphia.[36]

Although he continued to produce this form throughout the first half of the eighteenth century, Grant also oversaw the construction of expensive seating furniture in the newest fashion. By 1732, he was offering chairs in the Queen Anne style with solid splats, cabriole legs, and round feet; in 1734, he recorded his first sale of chairs with compass (i.e., rounded) seats and claw feet; and in 1746, he sold chairs with Marlborough (i.e., straight) legs.[37] These early references to stylish features show that Grant, the exporter of mass-produced chairs for the many, was also catering to the elite of New England and working in the vanguard of fashion.

Specialists like Grant and Underwood fulfilled important roles in the urban furniture

I-6. *The Income of Joseph Lindsey of Marblehead, 1739–1764.*

	Income in £*	Percentage of Total
Furniture	322: 0:8	38.2
Furniture repair	10:12:0½	1.3
Coffins	12: 7:4	1.5
House and ship work	320:12:0¼	38.0
Lumber	15: 7:7	1.8
Surveying lumber	27: 7:6¼	3.3
Barter goods	76: 2:9¾	9.0
Miscellaneous goods and services	58: 4:8¾	6.9
Total	842:14:8½	100.0

The income is listed in devalued Massachusetts Lawful Money. On March 31, 1750, Massachusetts devalued its currency, setting an exchange rate of £1:0:0 Lawful Money for £7:10:0 Old Tenor. All Old Tenor charges in the account book were converted to Lawful Money at that rate.

trade. However, the most significant contributions to the trade were made by cabinet-makers, or shop joiners, as they were sometimes called. These workmen made case furniture, tables, and often chairs, offering their patrons considerable choice in design and amount of ornament. Cabinetmakers also performed many miscellaneous tasks; their degree of versatility depended on their skills, ambition, and environment. The business papers of three shop joiners active in the middle of the eighteenth century — Joseph Lindsey of Marblehead, John Cahoone of Newport, and Nathaniel Holmes of Boston — reveal a range of working patterns in the trade.

Though born in Lynn, Massachusetts, and among the fourth generation of Lindseys to reside there, Joseph Lindsey (1714–1764) had moved to Marblehead by 1739, when he married Rebecca Henley and set to work as a joiner. Lindsey achieved a measure of success in his trade: he garnered sufficient income to purchase his own dwelling, but he was not one of Marblehead's wealthier craftsmen.[38] His account book records many of his activities from 1739 until his death.[39]

Lindsey earned more than 38 percent of his income from the production of furniture and related wooden wares such as ships' lanterns (I-6). His goods were varied, and for the most part he sold them only to the residents of Marblehead. His work for the merchant Jacob Fowle ranged from a "Case of Draws and Chamber Table" (a high chest and matching dressing table), costing £13:15:8, to a knife box, candle box, and warming pan handle, each at less than £0:4:0.[40] Lindsey seems to have made little, if any, furniture for export on Marblehead vessels. However, he did occasionally outfit the cabins of newly built craft. In 1759 Jeremiah Lee, the town's most prosperous merchant, bought six chairs and a table from Lindsey for the ship *Vulture*.[41]

Lindsey used imported black walnut and mahogany as well as native woods in his

work. He did his own upholstery, undoubtedly because there was no upholsterer in Marblehead, but limited such efforts to "bottoming" chairs; for example, in 1751 he billed Robert Hooper for "4 Black walnut Chears and Bottoming 4:0:0."[42] There is no evidence that he constructed or covered more ambitious forms such as an easy chair or couch.

Lindsey's income from work on houses ("My Part of finishing ye Back Part of y^r House") and ships ("Work on board Scuner Sarah") almost equaled that from furniture.[43] Such an arrangement was typical of craftsmen in small urban centers. In the major seaports of Boston and Newport, artisans were able to be more specialized. Ship joiners worked on vessels, house joiners on buildings, and cabinetmakers on furniture. Lindsey took on several workmen to assist him in his craft. Between 1754 and 1764 he had at least six hands. Three were apprentices: his son Nathaniel, his nephew Joseph Lindsey (a son of his brother Ralph, of Lynn), and a boy named John. Three were journeymen: Stanford Flack, Benjamin Hill (sometimes identified as Servant Benjamin), and a man named Madison. Flack and Hill boarded with Lindsey; in all likelihood, the apprentices did as well.

Lindsey's other income, almost 24 percent of his total earnings, came partly from sources related to woodworking. He repaired furniture, made coffins, and, for much of his career, served as a measurer of lumber for the town of Marblehead.[44] He performed such miscellaneous services as carting wood and working on highways. His earnings were minimal from the sale of the goods (foodstuffs, wine, and textiles) received in exchange for his work, an indication that Lindsey, though living in a commercial center, made little attempt to become a trader in order to supplement his income. There is also no record of his acquiring shares in any Marblehead shipping (though his brother Ralph was a ship's captain). Lindsey lived by the skills of his craft alone.

His counterpart in Newport, John Cahoone (ca. 1725–1792), pursued a different path.[45] Cahoone was established as a shop joiner by 1749. Like Lindsey, he enjoyed a moderately successful career. The inventory of his personal estate, recorded shortly after his death, totaled £65:18:8, an average figure for Newport cabinetmakers. Cahoone's activities for a ten-year period, 1750 through 1759, are well documented in his account book, preserved in the Newport Historical Society. The book records only credit sales but nevertheless offers a good look at the general characteristics of Cahoone's business (I-7).

Cahoone derived more than 56 percent of his income from the sale of furniture, the majority of that coming from sales for export. Cahoone's reliance on the export trade is typical of the experience of many Newport craftsmen. A writer in 1849 offered this reminiscence of cabinetmaking in the town:

> All the cabinetmakers on Bridge and Washington Streets, employed a large number of hands, manufacturing furniture, for which a ready market was found in New York and the West Indies. The stores of David Huntington and Benjamin Baker were also on the

point; both these men were extensively engaged in manufacturing furniture, which they shipped to New York, and the West Indies . . . Benjamin Peabody, cabinetmaker . . . carried on a large trade with Surinam.[46]

In order to maintain a sizable output in an efficient manner, Cahoone employed at least three journeymen and an apprentice during the 1750s. The bulk of the wares produced by his shop were plain desks and tables for export.[47] A typical account in 1751 records the purchase of three cedar desks, a tea table, and a mahogany table by Isaac Steele, a Newport merchant.[48] Steele probably had these wares cased for shipment and placed aboard one of his vessels destined for southern and West Indian ports.

Steele paid for the furniture with a hogshead of rum and a barrel of sugar. Cahoone resold these goods, and such transactions represented his second largest source of income, almost a third of his earnings for the decade. Unlike Lindsey, Cahoone was active in the trading economy around him, gaining income from several mercantile ventures. In 1749, he and two fellow cabinetmakers chartered a sloop to sail to North Carolina. He also speculated in real estate in Newport. As one studies Cahoone's dealings, a picture emerges of an entrepreneur risking the capital earned through his craft in the hope of achieving wealth. His endeavors, however, were modest in scale. Cahoone lacked sufficient capital to play a major role in the bustling economy of Newport.

Nathaniel Holmes (1703–1774) of Boston was far more successful in taking advantage of a seaport environment.[49] Holmes had opened his own cabinet shop near the Mill Bridge in Boston by 1725. Three years later he married Mary Webber, the daughter of a lumber dealer and sawmill owner, a connection that served his business interests. During the next decade he expanded his trade by employing workmen from outside Boston.

In 1735, Holmes purchased a distillery on Back Street and began hiring vessels to carry his goods up and down the coast. For five years he prospered through the production of both rum and furniture. His rum business and carrying trade proved so profitable that after 1740 he abandoned his cabinetmaking operation, built a sugar baking house, and shipped sugar, molasses, and rum on his own sloops and schooners to Newfoundland, the Middle Colonies, and the South. Holmes owned dwellings on Back, Charter, Middle, and School streets in Boston as well as a farm in Malden, Massachusetts, and land in Falmouth (now Portland) and Kennebeck, Maine. He achieved greater affluence than any other Boston cabinetmaker during the colonial period and left an estate valued at almost £4000. His career indicates that a craftsman could become wealthy, but only by changing occupations could he amass a fortune.

Surviving documents permit a detailed analysis of Holmes's furniture business, for during the 1730s Holmes served as a middleman for numerous craftsmen in Boston and the surrounding towns. He supplied them with food, clothing, brassware, lumber, and glue; they made furniture that they delivered to Holmes, who sold it to private customers in Boston or, like Cahoone, to ship captains for export.

I-7. The Credit Income of John Cahoone of Newport, 1750–1759.

	Credit Income in £*	Percentage of Total
Furniture for the local market	2,739:17:10	20.5
Furniture for the export market	4,778:16: 8	35.7
Miscellaneous joinery	286: 4: 0	2.1
Repairs and services	200:16: 0	1.5
Coffins	160: 7: 0	1.2
Rum	684: 1: 3	5.1
Lumber	147:14: 1	1.1
Barter goods	4,383: 9: 4	32.8
Total	13,381: 6: 2	100.0

The income is listed in inflated Rhode Island currency. In 1763, the exchange rate of Rhode Island currency was set at £1:0:0 Lawful Money for £23:6:8 Old Tenor.

Of the ten joiners and cabinetmakers Holmes employed, only four worked in Boston: Robert Lord, Richard Woodward (who boarded with Holmes), Thomas Johnson, and Thomas Sherburne (who helped manage the business in 1736 and 1737). John Mudge and Jacob Burdit lived and worked in Malden, Thomas and Chapman Waldron in Marblehead, and James Hovey in either Plymouth or Boston; the home of Timothy Gooding, Jr., has not been located. Most of these men were between twenty-one and twenty-eight years of age, and Holmes probably helped them at the start of their careers when they needed credit to purchase household and shop goods. Holmes used the specialized services of three turners (including John Underwood) and a japanner, all from Boston. The japanner's work involved gilding carved shells and japanning entire cases.

Holmes's papers record that between 1733 and 1739 his workmen constructed 338 pieces of furniture for him. Unfortunately, only a portion of the business is documented in the bills and receipts, and we have no information on how much furniture Holmes built himself. Nor do we have complete accounts for each craftsman's work. Apparently the total number of objects far surpassed that recorded in the papers.

As in the Cahoone shop, desks and tables constituted the great majority of the work. The 62 desks and 225 tables were 85 percent of the documented items. Many of the desks were decorated with an inlaid star, a fashionable detail popular on Boston work of the 1730s.[50] The remaining furniture included desks and bookcases, chests of drawers, high chests, dressing tables, a bureau table, a chest-on-chest, a tea chest and frame, and a tankard board.

Of the three urban cabinetmakers, Lindsey was the most versatile craftsman, constructing a variety of furniture — chairs, case furniture, and miscellaneous small items. Cahoone and Holmes limited the number of forms they produced, but they made these items in volume either by employing journeymen or by commissioning tradesmen working in their own establishments. All three depended on the mercantile economy of the New England seaports. The shipbuilding industry in Marblehead provided Lindsey with considerable business, and coastal trading afforded Cahoone and Holmes the opportunity to make objects for a burgeoning export trade. For Holmes, the commercial environment also offered the means to make the leap from craftsman to merchant successfully.

The forms that Lindsey, Cahoone, and Holmes crafted, the patterns that Underwood turned, the bed hangings that Grant fashioned, were all based on English precedents. Designs reached New England in three ways: immigrant craftsmen, pattern books, and imported furniture.

During the seventeenth century, immigrant craftsmen had by far the greatest influence. Hundreds of woodworkers from towns throughout England crossed the ocean in the Great Migration. In New England these craftsmen continued to make furniture much like that they had made in their homeland, and their work reflects the diversity that existed in English regional design of the period. In Boston, a group of artisans from London apparently fashioned the handsome case furniture ornamented with broad bev-

I-8. Chest of Drawers with Doors. London, 1640–1670. Oak and exotic woods. Present location unknown; illustrated in Macquoid, *History of English Furniture,* 1:231.

I-9. Chest of Drawers with Doors. Attributed to the Russell-Gibbons Shops, New Haven, Connecticut, 1660–1690. Oak, black walnut, red cedar, and pine; H. 36⅜ (92.4); W. 44⅜ (112.7); D. 22¾ (58.0). Museum of Fine Arts, Boston.

eled moldings and columnar split spindles (chest no. 6) that closely resembled contemporary London examples. Two London craftsmen, William Russell and William Gibbons, settled in New Haven in 1640.[51] They too made furniture in a decorative style modeled on London work, which can be seen by comparing a London chest of drawers with doors (I-8) with a New Haven example (I-9). Two Ipswich, Massachusetts, joiners, William Searle and Thomas Dennis, had emigrated from the Exeter area of southwest England in about 1660 and continued to ornament furniture (box no. 1) with the carved leaf and vine patterns, grotesques, and strapwork common on furniture in southwest England.[52]

More than a dozen distinct regional traditions in English furniture have been identified in New England, some coexisting in a single town.[53] Thomas Mulliner, a skilled artisan trained by his father in Ipswich, England, traveled to New Haven in 1639.[54] Though he later moved to neighboring Branford, he continued to produce furniture for residents of New Haven. His decorative scheme, represented on a carved chest of the 1640s (I-10), corresponded to that of work in Ipswich, England, and differed significantly from that of the London artisans in New Haven (I-9).

In New England the geographical extent of English furniture traditions varied considerably. The same style could appear in two towns many miles apart because both had immigrants with similar backgrounds. Often, however, a specific pattern of ornament was limited to a single town (or small group of adjoining towns) and remained a common element of local design for many years. John Thurston left Suffolk, England, for Massachusetts in 1637, eventually settling in Medfield and training several apprentices. He and his workmen perpetuated a form of Suffolk carved ornament until the end of the

I-10. Chest with Drawer. Attributed to Thomas Mulliner (married 1625, d. after 1658), New Haven, Connecticut, 1639–1649. *White oak;* H. 33 (83.8); W. 51 (129.5); D. 23 (58.4). Home Sweet Home Museum. Photograph, Robert Blair St. George. *The chest was acquired by Thomas Osborne, a New Haven tanner who removed to East Hampton, New York, in 1649.*

I-11. Cupboard. Duxbury, Massachusetts, 1660–1690. *Red oak, maple, white cedar,* and *white pine;* H. 58¾ (149.2); W. 49½ (125.7); D. 23½ (59.7). Henry Francis du Pont Winterthur Museum. *The cupboard descended in the Tracy family of Duxbury.*

seventeenth century.[55] One particular decorative scheme had a wide sphere of popularity, and by the 1680s the style had spread throughout the Plymouth Colony from Scituate to Yarmouth.[56] Its English antecedents are unclear; possibly craftsmen from southeastern England were responsible for its introduction. The style, well illustrated by a joined cupboard from Duxbury (I-11), combines distinctive turnings and applied moldings with such details as "sawtooth" serrations and paired gouges.

Immigration slowed to a trickle in the last quarter of the seventeenth century and remained so for the rest of the colonial period. Those craftsmen who did emigrate were influential conveyors of English design. The Wiltshireman Robert Salmon, who settled in Stratford, Connecticut, in 1719, probably played a major role in the development of the so-called crown chair (II-1), a form that enjoyed immense popularity along the Connecticut coast for much of the eighteenth century.[57] Similarly, the arrival of the London upholsterer Henery Golden in Portsmouth in 1763 probably contributed to the sudden appearance there of stylish upholstered chairs.

By 1725, immigrant craftsmen represented only a small fraction of the urban work force; most furniture makers were second-, third-, or even fourth-generation New Englanders. Many were linked by kinship: sons worked for fathers; unrelated apprentices married daughters of masters. The Frothingham family of Boston and Charlestown included sixteen woodworkers in the course of four generations.[58] In Newport, the

I-12. Side Chair. Boston or Salem, 1765–1775. Mahogany, maple, and white pine; H. 38¼ (97.2); W. 23⅝ (60.0); SEAT D. 17½ (44.5); SEAT H. 17¼ (43.8). Massachusetts Historical Society.

I-13. Design for a Chair. Manwaring, *The Cabinet and Chair-Maker's Real Friend and Companion*, pl. 9. Boston Athenaeum. *The Athenaeum's copy was owned by Thomas Dawes (1731–1809), a Boston brick mason and architect.*

Goddards and Townsends, relatives through marriage, had nineteen furniture craftsmen among their combined families in four generations.[59] Such ties fostered the development of tightly knit craft enclaves in urban areas.

These craftsmen, lacking the immigrants' firsthand experience with English design, could turn to pattern books or imported furniture for inspiration. In 1754 Thomas Chippendale, a London cabinetmaker, published *The Gentleman and Cabinet-Maker's Director*, the first of several pattern books to reach America. Copies of the *Director* are known to have been in Salem, Boston, and Newport.[60] During the 1760s, books by the Society of Upholsterers, William Ince and John Mayhew, Robert Manwaring, and John Crunden, as well as a new edition of the *Director*, were published in England and imported into America.[61] A Boston newspaper of 1767, for example, advertised Manwaring's *Cabinet and Chair-Maker's Real Friend and Companion* and Crunden's *Joyner and Cabinet-Maker's Darling or Pocket Director* and his *Carpenter's Companion*.[62]

However, this flurry of publications during the third quarter of the eighteenth century had surprisingly little impact on New England craftsmen. Only one design was derived from a pattern book; a Massachusetts chair (I-12) features a back that closely parallels a plate in Manwaring's *Real Friend and Companion* (I-13). Even the carved details of the back were carefully copied by the craftsman. After the Revolution, pattern books assumed greater importance in New England, and the publications of George Hepple-

I-14. Side Chair. Samuel Walker, London, 1763. *Mahogany* and *beech;* H. 37⅜ (94.9); W. 22 (55.9); SEAT D. 17⁵⁄₁₆ (44.0); SEAT H. 17 (43.2). Private collection. *The chair is one of a set purchased in England by Nathaniel Barrell of York, Maine.*

I-15. Side Chair. Portsmouth, 1763–1780. *Mahogany, maple,* and *white pine;* H. 37⁷⁄₁₆ (95.1); W. 22³⁄₁₆ (56.4); SEAT D. 17⁵⁄₁₆ (44.0); SEAT H. 17⁵⁄₈ (44.8). Old Gaol Museum. *The chair was originally owned by Nathaniel Barrell of York, Maine.*

white and Thomas Sheraton reached the region in more substantial numbers than previous works.

The infrequent use of pattern books in pre-Revolutionary New England is puzzling. Elsewhere in America, cabinetmakers seem to have considered the books helpful. Southern furniture makers, particularly those in Williamsburg, Norfolk, and Charleston, modeled several of their works on Chippendale's patterns.[63] In New England, however, imported furniture was a far more significant source of foreign designs.

Some English products were shipped in great quantity: London cane chairs, during the first quarter of the eighteenth century, and looking glasses, throughout the colonial era. Though these did not serve as prototypes to be copied in their entirety, they were important design sources. Cane seating "Lately arrived from England" (such as couch no. 81 and chairs no. 82–84 and 90) provided New England chairmakers with the latest proportions, with stylish models for turned finials, legs, and stretchers, and with fashionable samples of carved feet and scrolled handholds (compare the English and American armchairs 86a and b).[64] The looking glasses, which arrived in America by the case, had few emulators here. Yet details such as a central finial of a carved bird may have inspired the carving on top of desk no. 51.

In addition to wares imported in volume, small groups of items were ordered by merchants for their own use. Surviving letters to London agents are sprinkled with requests for household furnishings; descriptions are usually brief and emphasize acquiring objects "of the newest fashion" and "at the cheapest rate." The choice of a particular item lay in the hands of the English factor. "As you are [the] best Judge I leave it to you to purchase it where you think proper," concluded the Bostonian Thomas Hancock in 1738, when asking his London agent, Francis Wilkes, to buy him a tall case clock for his new stone mansion.[65] Wilkes's selection obviously pleased Hancock, for shortly after the arrival of the clock he thanked his agent, noting "the Clock I like well."[66] The elegant clockcase, veneered in figured walnut, may have inspired similar Boston cases.[67] Yet none matched the opulence of Hancock's clock, which originally was crowned by carved and gilt figures representing fame, peace, and plenty.

Some wealthy New Englanders bought furniture while visiting London to establish business relationships or to meet with overseas agents. During a visit in 1748, Josiah Quincy apparently acquired his mahogany settee (no. 107). Nathaniel Barrell, a young Portsmouth merchant, traveled to England in 1760 and remained there for three years.[68] Just before his return, he purchased from Samuel Walker, a London cabinetmaker and upholsterer,

To 6 Mohogany Chairs ye Seats cov^d wth Crimson Damask @ 22/ [I-14]	6:12:—
To a Mohogany Writing Table	4: 4:—
To a Large Sconce Glass	4: 4:—
To a Pair of Carv'd Sconces	10:6
To Painting the Glass & Sconces	6:—
To a Packing Case & to Matts	10:6
To 2 Pair of Wilton Bedside Carp^{ts}	1:10:—
To a Moh^y Night Table wth a pan Bason & Bottles	3:10:—
To a Matt for D^o	1:—
To a Mah^y Biddey	1: 2:—
To a Matt for D^o	1:—[69]

Barrell had the furniture shipped to York, Maine. There, in a house built for him by his father-in-law, Jonathan Sayward, three items on the bill — the chairs, sconce glass, and carved sconces — remained until recent years.[70] The glass and sconces hung together in one of Barrell's parlors, the most impressive articles in a modest interior. Their richly carved ornament in the Chinese taste was far grander than that on most imported glasses. The chairs (I-14) are stylish examples of a popular English design.[71] Barrell apparently found the design appealing for he obtained from Walker a second set of chairs, identical in every respect except that the backs were plain instead of carved.[72] Barrell bought a third set locally (I-15), commissioning a Portsmouth chairmaker to copy the carved version. The craftsman adopted every detail of the London models but the upholstery. His carving, however, is flatter than Walker's.

Barrell's two sets of carved chairs document the transfer of a specific design from England to America. Once the Portsmouth maker had taken measurements and patterns from one of Barrell's London chairs, he could easily construct copies for other patrons as well. The survival of several similar chairs from Portsmouth indicates that the pattern became a standard part of the repertory of the town's craftsmen.[73]

In Boston, the effect of expensive English wares on local design was especially pronounced. Craftsmen probably learned of the bombé through an English example, such as the mahogany clothes press owned by Charles Apthorp of Boston (I-16). The earliest dated Boston bombé, a desk and bookcase (I-17 and I-17a) made by Benjamin Frothingham in 1753, closely follows the contour of the English case. Both display a swelled base with straight-sided drawers. (The Boston desk originally had a beaded molding attached to the drawer divider below the top drawer, a common English detail.) Frothingham, a fourth-generation Bostonian trained by his father, must have become acquainted with the bombé form through an import.

I-16. Clothes Press. England, 1740–1758. Mahogany, white oak, and deal; H. 97 (246.4); W. 46¾ (118.7); D. 25½ (64.8). Museum of Fine Arts, Boston. *The press belonged to Charles Apthorp (1698–1758), a Boston merchant.*

I-17. Desk and Bookcase. Benjamin Frothingham (1734–1809), Boston or Charlestown, 1753. Mahogany, red cedar, and white pine; H. 97⅜ (247.3); W. 44½ (113.0); D. 24⅝ (62.5). Diplomatic Reception Rooms, U.S. Department of State. *The desk and bookcase was probably made for John Sprague, a Charlestown doctor.*

London tea tables (I-18 is a japanned example) influenced the shape of tables made in Boston (I-19). Chair design, however, displays the greatest dependence on English furniture. Every popular splat pattern on Boston chairs in the Chippendale style is derived from an English example (compare English chair 109a with Boston chairs no. 109, 110, and 111). Even a chair (I-20) that at first appears to have a pattern book as its source (I-21) is probably based on an actual English chair (I-22).

The Massachusetts chair (I-20), though resembling English ones, can be clearly distinguished from foreign examples. Its overall appearance is more delicate; it has a thinner crest rail, slimmer bands within the splat, narrower seat rails, and flatter carving. Its knee brackets, knee carving, and claw-and-ball feet follow patterns common in the Boston area in the 1760s and 1770s. Its secondary woods, birch and maple, are typical of eastern Massachusetts work. This combination of features separates the chair not only from its English counterparts but also from examples made in other areas of New England. Its traits are seen in furniture from only one region: coastal Massachusetts from Boston to Salem.

During the eighteenth century, craftsmen in each urban community favored certain woods, designs, and construction techniques. These preferences, perpetuated by apprentices, became in time the hallmarks of a local style. Some products differed noticeably from their counterparts made elsewhere. A blockfront desk and bookcase from Newport contrasts dramatically with a Boston version. Yet some designs, particularly of chairs, varied little from town to town. Newport craftsmen fashioned chairs in the Queen Anne style that are almost indistinguishable from the work of Boston artisans (see chairs no. 94 and 95).

A sampling of documented furniture from New England's nine major pre-Revolutionary towns affords a general view of urban regional characteristics. Boston, because of its long-standing prominence in the furniture industry, is treated first, followed by Salem, Marblehead, Newburyport, and Portsmouth, towns whose products often resemble Bos-

I-17a. Desk Interior. *Detail of the Frothingham desk and bookcase (I-17).*

I-18. Tea Table. London, 1730–1745. H. 27 (68.5); W. 35¼ (89.5); D. 23 (58.0). Ham House, Victoria and Albert Museum.

I-19. Tea Table. Boston, 1735–1765. Mahogany and white pine; H. 27 (68.6); W. 29⁷⁄₁₆ (74.8); D. 20¾ (52.7). Gore Place.

I-20. Side Chair. Boston or Salem, 1760–1785. Mahogany, maple, and birch; H. 37¹⁵⁄₁₆ (96.4); W. 23¾ (60.3); SEAT D. 17⅝ (44.8); SEAT H. 16½ (41.9). Private collection, Milwaukee, Wisconsin.

I-21. Design for a Chair. Chippendale, *The Director,* 1st ed., 1754, pl. 12. Society for the Preservation of New England Antiquities Library.

I-22. Side Chair. England, 1750–1775. Mahogany. Present location unknown. Photograph, courtesy, Israel Sack, Inc., New York.

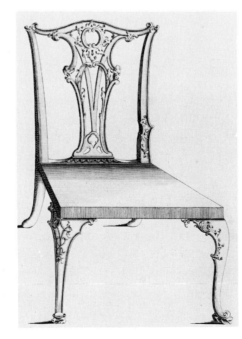

ton work. Southern New England design begins with Newport, then turns to Providence, Norwich, and Hartford.

The craftsmen of Boston produced an enormous quantity of stylish furniture. Their finest case furniture of the 1730s and 1740s displays dazzling ornament. Many pieces are decorated with japanning (plate 3); others feature figured veneers, inlaid stars and stringing, carved and gilded shells, and urn finials with twisted flames (I-23). During the second half of the century, shaped façades predominated; the blockfront (I-24), bombé, serpentine, and reverse serpentine all gained favor. Veneers were rarely used, and carving was generally limited to a few specific details, such as the rosettes and pilasters on the upper section of a desk and bookcase or the shells on a high chest. Turned urns with twisted flames remained common, but occasionally corner finials of carved urns with pierced flames and central finials of carved birds were made for the most elegant objects.

Boston craftsmen repeatedly used certain design motifs in their work. Two patterns of bracket feet were especially popular; on the first, a cyma curve leads into a pronounced spur (chest no. 15), on the second, a half-round appears above a small spur (chests no. 18 and 19). A central drop of a simple outline was often applied to the front base molding. One common shape of drop ended in two small half circles (desk and bookcase no. 50); another was embellished with a stylized shell (chest no. 15). Particular patterns of desk interiors were also favored. On desks of the second quarter of the eighteenth century, a central door is flanked by pilastered document drawers and eight pigeonholes above two tiers of drawers (I-17a). Later desks (I-24a) often have only four pigeonholes and a column of drawers at each end; carved shells ornament the uppermost drawers and central door. These interiors may also be "stepped" (i.e., the lower tier of drawers projects beyond the rest of the interior).

The most sophisticated piece of case furniture was the desk and bookcase. On Boston examples, the bookcases were fitted with a complex array of shelves, drawers, and pigeonholes. Craftsmen favored door panels with arched tops during the 1740s and 1750s (I-17), but later they surrounded the panels with serpentine edges (I-24). The finest Boston bookcases have mirrored glass panels (desk and bookcase no. 50), a fashionable English feature rarely seen elsewhere in New England.

Boston artisans were quick to adopt English designs but slow to relinquish them. A card table (I-25), apparently owned by the merchant Peter Faneuil, corresponds in appearance and construction to English examples of the same period. A generation later, Benjamin Frothingham made a card table (I-26) that, except for its squared edges and claw-and-ball feet, differs little from Faneuil's table.

Boston chairs in the early Queen Anne style are related in proportion, leg design, and stretcher pattern to English cane chairs of the 1720s (chair no. 90).[74] Later Queen Anne chairs are less vertical, have wider splats, and sometimes feature compass seats (III-24). Chippendale chairs often retain such traditional features as cabriole legs and turned stretchers (chair no. 109). The cabriole usually has a squared edge on the knee and ends in a round foot with a tall pad or a claw-and-ball with prominent knuckles and long

I-23. High Chest. Boston or Charlestown, 1735–1745. Black walnut and white pine; H. 88¼ (224.2); W. 43¼ (109.9); D. 22 (55.9). Private collection. Photograph, courtesy, Israel Sack, Inc., New York. *The chest closely resembles one inscribed by its maker, Ebenezer Hartshorne, in 1739, now at the Museum of Fine Arts, Boston.*

I-24. Desk and Bookcase. Boston, 1765–1785. Mahogany and white pine; H. 95 (241.3), W. 41¾ (106.0), D. 24¾ (62.9). Museum of Fine Arts, Boston. *The desk and bookcase descended in the Low family to Mrs. Foster Low, who sold it in 1849 to Micah Cutler of Boston.*

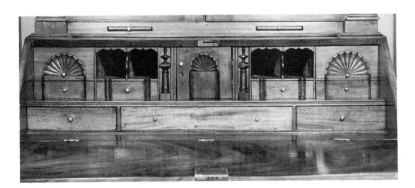

I-24a. Desk Interior. *Detail of the Low family desk and bookcase (I-24).*

I-25. Card Table. Boston, 1735–1742. Mahogany and white pine; H. 26½ (67.3); TOP W. 36⅞ (93.7); TOP D. CLOSED 16⅛ (41.0), OPEN 32¼ (81.9). Bayou Bend Collection, Museum of Fine Arts, Houston. *The table is one of a pair owned by Peter Faneuil (1700–1742), a Boston merchant.*

I-26. Card Table. Benjamin Frothingham (1734–1809), Charlestown, Massachusetts, 1765–1785. Mahogany, *yellow pine*, and *white pine*; H. 28 (71.1); TOP W. 34⅛ (86.7); TOP D. CLOSED 16¾ (42.5), OPEN 33½ (85.1). Henry Francis du Pont Winterthur Museum.

I-27. High Chest. Salem, Massachusetts, 1765–1790. Mahogany and white pine; H. 90⅛ (228.9); W. 40⅝ (103.2); D. 22⅛ (56.2). New England Historic Genealogical Society. *An early owner of the chest, William Sanderson Roberts (m. 1829), probably inherited it from his ancestors, the Sanderson family of Salem.*

I-28. Desk. Salem, Massachusetts, 1765–1790. Mahogany and white pine; H. 44 (111.8); W. 44 (111.8); D. 23 (58.4). Private collection. Photograph, courtesy, Israel Sack, Inc., New York. *The desk, originally made for the Derby family of Salem, descended to the Rand family, also of Salem.*

talons. The stretchers are more attenuated than those on earlier chairs. Marlborough legs and straight stretchers became a popular alternative to the cabriole base. Boston craftsmen often embellished both legs and stretchers with a bead (chair no. 113). While much fashionable seating had loose seats, over-the-rail upholstery enjoyed far greater popularity in Boston than elsewhere, no doubt because of the town's numerous upholsterers. These artisans produced a significant quantity of ambitious upholstered forms, and the number of easy chairs, couches, sofas, and settees made in Boston probably exceeded the combined output of the other eight urban centers in pre-Revolutionary New England.

Though the furniture of Salem, Marblehead, and Newburyport resembles Boston work, differences can be identified, especially in case furniture. The best examples from these towns are exceedingly well made, their craftsmanship often surpassing that of Boston. Veneering remained a popular form of decoration in Essex County longer than it did in Boston; Essex cabinetmakers may well have continued to use figured veneers

I-29. Chest-on-Chest. Salem, Massachusetts, 1765–1795. Mahogany and white pine; H. 88¼ (224.2); W. 40¾ (103.5); D. 21½ (54.6). Essex Institute. Photograph, Helga Studio; courtesy, *Antiques*. *The chest closely resembles a chest-on-chest attributed to Abraham Watson of Salem* (Boston Furniture, *fig. 76*).

I-30. Side Chair. Salem, Massachusetts, area, 1755–1785. Mahogany, maple, and white pine; H. 38½ (97.8); W. 21½ (54.6); SEAT D. 17⅜ (44.1). SEAT H. 17 (43.2). Colonial Williamsburg Foundation. *The chair descended in the Dane family of Andover, Massachusetts.*

on stylish cases into the 1760s. Shaped façades had considerable appeal. Salem workmen adopted every Boston case shape but added feet and drops of more ambitious design.

Of the three North Shore communities, Salem had by far the largest number of craftsmen.[75] Their products survive in quantity and often feature distinctive details. Many Salem dressing tables (dressing table no. 32) and high chests (I-27) have skirt outlines of reverse curves instead of the flattened arches of their Boston counterparts. Small carved pinwheels and pierced diamonds sometimes embellish the skirts, and occasionally flat, stylized leaf carvings similar to those on Newport furniture ornament the legs. Salem desks (I-28) and chests of drawers (I-29) are also recognizable. Their feet have broad, bold brackets, and the central drop is often a skillfully cut scallop shell or a thin ogee arch. Desk interiors can vary in design from Boston examples (I-24a). Several Salem desks have six pigeonholes, swelled knobs capping the pilasters, and an arched panel on the central door. Salem cabinetmakers also favored arched panels for bookcase doors, rarely choosing the serpentine shape so popular in Boston. Twisted flame finials enjoyed widespread popularity throughout Essex County (I-27), yet in Salem, other patterns such as one with a ball at the top and a bell-shaped base (I-29) were also made.

Fashionable Salem chairs (I-30) in the Queen Anne and Chippendale styles resemble Boston examples. A few features — for example, a pattern of scored lines on round feet or an awkward transition from squared knee to rounded leg — have been associated with Essex County craftsmanship but may well also be characteristic of Boston. Skilled chairmakers resided in each of the four urban communities in Massachusetts and occasionally migrated from one town to another (see page 385). Their products can rarely be ascribed to a particular place.

Little documented furniture from Marblehead and Newburyport has survived. The Marblehead work is similar to that from Boston and Salem, and, to date, few specific details of Marblehead craftsmanship have been discerned. Were it not, in fact, for a

I-31. Chest of Drawers. Ebenezer Martin (ca. 1735–1800), Marblehead, Massachusetts, 1791. Black walnut and white pine; H. 34 (86.4); W. 40 (101.6); D. 21½ (54.6). Private collection. Photograph, Helga Studio; courtesy, Bernard and S. Dean Levy, Inc., New York.

I-32. Desk and Bookcase. Attributed to Abner Toppan (1764–1836), Newburyport, Massachusetts, 1795. Mahogany and white pine; H. 95¼ (241.9); W. 45½ (115.6); D. 25¾ (65.4). Newburyport Public Library. *According to a bill of sale, now lost, this desk and bookcase and a chest-on-chest were made by Toppan for the Bannister family of Newburyport in 1795.*

Marblehead maker's mark on a reverse serpentine chest of drawers (I-31), one could only attribute it to eastern Massachusetts.

Newburyport case furniture, while similar to that of other coastal centers, has certain distinguishing characteristics. Craftsmen ornamented many pieces with carved pinwheels or sunbursts (I-32). On desks, they sometimes installed a pair of pigeonholes instead of a central door (desk no. 47). Decorative moldings were often cut along the top edges of drawer sides (see page 208); the contours were far more elaborate than the single or double bead that decorated the drawers of elegant chests from Boston or Salem. In the past, far too many objects were ascribed to Newburyport. Armchairs with paired volutes at the base of the arm supports (chair no. 119) were once considered the work of Joseph Short; however, that attribution cannot be documented, and the chairs are now considered to be from Portsmouth.

Portsmouth furniture of the 1730s and 1740s differs dramatically from that made later in the century. The earlier products are distinctive variations of Boston work. John Gaines, who moved to Portsmouth from Ipswich, Massachusetts, in 1724, constructed chairs (I-33) related in many details to examples from eastern Massachusetts.[76] Yet the unusual pierced carving in the crests, the bold outline of the splats, and the exaggerated curve of the Spanish feet separate Gaines's chairs from their Boston counterparts.

One Portsmouth cabinetmaker, Joseph Davis, served his apprenticeship in Boston. A documented dressing table (I-34) reveals his reliance on a popular Boston design, the blockfront, but the overall appearance of the dressing table (as well as two others and a high chest attributed to Davis) varies from that seen in eastern Massachusetts.[77] Davis used flat angular blocking, wide fluted pilasters, and slender cabriole legs with ridges across the feet to create an ambitious whole of diverse details.

Other Portsmouth craftsmen also produced blockfront furniture; usually the blocking is sharply defined at the corners, flat across the surface, and rather shallow in profile (chests no. 16 and 17). One maker of blockfronts, working during the third quarter of the century, more closely followed Boston models than did Davis. A desk and bookcase (I-35) by this unknown artisan displays a typical Boston blocking pattern and foot design. However, this piece, like Davis's dressing table, is not a copy of Boston work; it has several distinguishing features: a plain desk interior (I-35a), simple cove moldings at the base and cornice, and elaborate arches on the door panels.

During the 1760s, new forms in the Chippendale style were both imported to Portsmouth and made by local craftsmen.[78] The best-known furniture from Portsmouth is a group of six china tables (I-36), a kettle stand, and a side table; each has molded or fretwork legs, carved brackets, and (except for the side table) arched stretchers culminating in a pierced finial.[79] Recent research efforts have tied other handsome tables (I-37) and numerous Marlborough chairs with intricate splats (I-15, chairs no. 119–121) to Portsmouth as well. The sudden appearance of these items, differing noticeably from most Boston chairs and tables, suggests the arrival of skilled English artisans. It is tempting to assume that an English chairmaker immigrated to Portsmouth in 1763,

I-33. Side Chair. Attributed to John Gaines III (1704–1743), Portsmouth, 1728–1743. Maple; H. 40¼ (102.2); W. 20½ (52.1); SEAT D. 14⅛ (35.9); SEAT H. 18¼ (46.4). Macpheadris-Warner House. Photograph, Douglas Armsden. *Charles Brewster wrote in 1858 that the chair was made by his ancestor John Gaines in 1728 and descended from Gaines's daughter to the Brewster family.*

I-35. Desk and Bookcase. Portsmouth, 1745–1760. Mahogany and white pine; H. 93⅛ (236.5); W. 43¾ (111.1); D. 23¾ (60.3). Society for the Preservation of New England Antiquities. *The desk and bookcase descended in the Gerrish family of Kittery, Maine, and may have belonged originally to Sir William Pepperrell (see chest no. 16). It entered the Society's collections as this book went to press. The lower 3⅜ inches of the feet are replaced.*

I-34. Dressing Table. Joseph Davis, Portsmouth, 1740–1760. Black walnut and white pine; H. 30½ (77.5); W. 36½ (92.7); D. 23½ (59.7). Dietrich Brothers Americana Corporation.

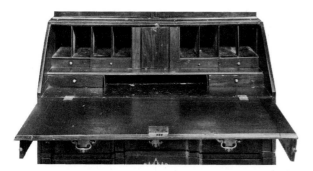

I-35a. Desk Interior. *Detail of the Gerrish family desk and bookcase (I-35).*

I-36. China Table. Portsmouth, 1760–1780. Mahogany and white pine; H. 28¾ (73.0); W. 36¹/₁₆ (91.6); D. 22⅜ (56.8). Museum of Art, Carnegie Institute. Photograph, Carl M. Martahus. *The table was owned by the Reverend Mr. Stephen Chase (d. 1805) of Portsmouth.*

I-37. Pembroke Table. Portsmouth, 1770–1795. Mahogany, maple, and white pine; H. 27 (68.6); W. 31 (78.7); D. CLOSED 21 (53.3), OPEN 38 (96.5). Private collection. Photograph, courtesy, Israel Sack, Inc., New York. *The table was owned by Richard Hart (ca. 1733–1820), a Portsmouth merchant.*

arriving at the same time as Henery Golden, the London upholsterer.[80] The work of this unidentified chairmaker (and that of others who adopted his style) closely follows English examples and is, in design and construction, the most English of all New England Chippendale furniture.

In southern New England, the finest furniture was made by the craftsmen of Newport. Their products display an originality of design and quality of workmanship unmatched in the other urban areas. Newport cabinetmakers took pride in their craft, for they signed or labeled far more examples than artisans did elsewhere. A sequence of documented furniture illustrates many attributes of their work. A high chest by Christopher Townsend (I-38) has such distinctive traits as square-edged legs ending in pointed "slipper" feet, narrow knee brackets, and a skirt outlined with reverse curves and originally punctuated at the center by a drop (on more elaborate furniture, a carved

I-39 (top). Card Table. John Townsend (1732–1809), Newport, 1762. Mahogany, maple, chestnut, and white pine; H. 27⅛ (68.9); TOP W. 35¼ (89.5); TOP D. CLOSED 18¼ (46.4), OPEN 36½ (92.7). Private collection.

I-38. High Chest. Christopher Townsend (1701–probably 1787), Newport, 1748. Black walnut, chestnut, and white pine; H. 70 (177.8); W. 38½ (97.8); D. 20 (50.8). Private collection. Photograph, Will Brown.

I-40 (bottom). Card Table. John Townsend, Newport, 1770–1795. Mahogany, maple, chestnut, and tulipwood; H. 27¼ (69.2); TOP W. 33⅞ (86.0); TOP D. CLOSED 16⅞ (42.9), OPEN 33¾ (85.7). Metropolitan Museum of Art.

shell is often substituted for the drop). The cabriole portion of each leg is a separate element that fits into the lower case, a common practice in Newport but rarely seen elsewhere.

Two card tables by John Townsend exhibit other Newport characteristics. The first

(I-39), dated 1762, features large front feet with undercut talons on elongated balls, round rear feet, and a stylized pattern of knee carving. The deep rails and projecting panel at the center of the front rail give the table a boldness strikingly different from the delicacy of contemporaneous Boston tables (I-26). The second Townsend example (I-40) illustrates the fashion current in late-eighteenth-century Newport. Square in outline and supported by straight legs, the table is a dramatic foil to the baroque exuberance of the craftsman's earlier work. The ornament is typical of Marlborough furniture from Newport: stop fluting on the legs, fretwork brackets, and cross-hatching on the rails (on chairs, cross-hatching often appears on the splat; see chair no. 122).

Newport chests (II-6) and desks (I-41) differ significantly from those made in Boston, Salem, and other centers in northern New England. Newport cases often have three drawers instead of four, façades are usually straight or blocked, and base moldings are bolder. On chests of drawers, cornice moldings are more complex in shape and tops are securely fastened in a sophisticated manner (see page 85). Bracket feet are far more common than claw-and-ball, and one simple pattern of bracket (chest-on-chest no. 26) surpassed all others in popularity. Carved shells of a striking design often decorate blockfront cases. On the most elaborate shells, curved lobes radiate from C-scrolls filled with stop-fluted petals.

Newport's grandest form was the block-and-shell desk and bookcase. Apparently few were made, for only about a dozen survive.[81] They are stunning sculptural monuments, overwhelming in scale yet integrated in design. A bold pattern of blocking unifies the desk façade, lid, and bookcase, and an array of stylish ornament enhances the form. One example (I-41 and I-41a), made by John Goddard in 1761, displays such unmistakably Newport characteristics as stop-fluted quarter columns along the edges of the bookcase, raised panels in the pediment, and fluted plinths and finials. Its interior follows a common Newport plan, quite distinct from those on Boston desks (I-24a). Instead of document drawers, thick partitions faced with channel moldings flank the central door; rows of three, rather than two, pigeonholes appear; and the front edges of the partitions separating the pigeonholes are boldly curved instead of slightly curved or straight. As in most Newport desks, the interior of the Goddard secretary is not stepped.

Seating furniture was produced in great quantity in Newport, but it is difficult to identify because many examples, especially those in the Queen Anne style, closely resemble Boston products. Such features as flat stretchers, beaded edges on the knees, and shell-carved crests, long considered trademarks of Newport manufacture, were adopted by Massachusetts craftsmen.[82] Yet a few Newport forms are recognizable. One group of chairs (I-42) is capped by bowed crests with pointed ears. A contemporary group is more massive in appearance (I-43), having square rear legs, thick compass seats, and large claw-and-ball feet reminiscent of those on the John Townsend card table (I-39). A third group (chair no. 122) is in a later Chippendale style and features straight (often stop-fluted) legs, intricate splats, cross-hatching on the crests, and molded ears. Few

I-41. Desk and Bookcase. John Goddard (1724–1785), Newport, 1761. Mahogany, red cedar, tulipwood, and white pine; H. 97 (246.4); W. 45³⁄₁₆ (114.8); D. 26 (66.8). Museum of Art, Rhode Island School of Design. *In the early nineteenth century, the desk and bookcase was inscribed "Made by John Goddard / 1761 & Repeard By / Thomas Goddard 1813." Although the central portion of each finial is the reverse of the typical Newport pattern, the finials have not been altered and appear to be original.*

I-41a. Desk Interior. *Detail of the Goddard desk and bookcase (I-41).*

other Chippendale chair designs from Newport have been identified.[83] Apparently craftsmen continued to make examples with rounded crests and vase-shaped splats through much of the century.

Newport's northern neighbor, Providence, supported a sizable number of furniture makers. In 1757, six of its artisans prepared a list of prices for joinery work, the earliest known document of its kind.[84] These men offered a wide variety of case furniture and tables, most of which resembled Newport cabinetry to judge by a desk and bookcase (I-44) attributed to Grandall Rawson, one of the artisans who signed the price list. The shells on the desk lid copy those on Newport examples, and the quality of construction equals that of the best furniture by John Goddard or John Townsend. Many Providence woodworkers had close ties with Newport; for example, William Proud, a successful pre-Revolutionary turner, was the brother of the Newport chairmakers John and Joseph Proud.

In Norwich, Connecticut, craftsmen also adopted many stylish elements of the New-

I-42 (above left). Side Chair. Newport, 1750–1775. Black walnut and maple; H. 38¼ (97.2); W. 22 (55.9); SEAT D. 16¾ (42.5); SEAT H. 17 (43.2). Private collection. *The chair descended in the Davenport family of Newport and Middletown, Rhode Island.*

I-43 (above right). Side Chair. Newport, 1750–1775. Mahogany and cherry; H. 38 (96.5); W. 22 (55.8); SEAT D. 16 (45.5); SEAT H. 17 (43.2). Newport Restoration Foundation. Photograph, Helga Studio. *The chair descended from Ellen Townsend, a granddaughter of the cabinetmaker John Townsend (1732–1809), to the Sheffield family of Newport.*

I-44. Desk and Bookcase. Attributed to Grindall Rawson (1719–1803), Providence, 1760–1785. Cherry, chestnut, tulipwood, and white pine; H. 100¼ (254.6); W. 38⅝ (98.1); D. 23¼ (59.1). Private collection. *The desk and bookcase was originally owned by Amos Atwell of Providence.*

port design. A desk from the Norwich area (I-45 and I-45a) displays the same three-drawer format and shell carvings seen on Newport examples; however, the design of its feet and interior as well as its overall construction clearly tie it to southeastern Connecticut. There, cabinetmakers often added a series of scrolls to decorate the base molding and ornamented the bracket feet with a pair of wavelike spurs, usually outlined with a bead. Their desk interiors frequently have a center drawer flanked by document drawers and rows of four pigeonholes above pairs of small drawers. Elaborate examples may be stepped and the façade of the lower middle drawer cut with grooves at the corners of the concave blocking.

The influence of Massachusetts design can be seen occasionally in Norwich work. A

I-45 (top). Desk. Norwich, Connecticut, 1760–
1790. Cherry and white pine; H. 47¾ (121.3); W.
44¹⁵/₁₆ (114.1); D. 25¾ (65.4). Mabel Brady Garvan Collection, Yale University Art Gallery.

I-45a (bottom). Desk Interior. *Detail of the Norwich desk (I-45).*

I-46. Chest-on-Chest. Norwich, Connecticut, ca.
1784. Mahogany, tulipwood, and white pine; H.
80½ (204.5); W. 38¼ (97.2); D. 20 (50.8). Fred-
erick K. and Margaret R. Barbour Collection, Connecticut Historical Society. *The roof of the pediment is lined with pages from the* Norwich Packet
for June 10, 1784.

I-47. Side Chair. Norwich, Connecticut, 1750–1760. Maple; H. 41¼ (104.8); W. 21 (53.3); SEAT D. 15 (38.1); SEAT H. 16½ (41.9). Wadsworth Atheneum. *The chair was probably acquired by Deborah Lothrup Gardiner Putnam (1717–1777) of Norwich when she married John Gardiner in 1754. The worsted plush upholstery is original.*

I-48. Side Chair. Norwich or New London, Connecticut, 1790–1805. Mahogany and white pine; H. 38½ (97.9); W. 21 (53.5); SEAT D. 16 (40.5); SEAT H. 17¼ (43.5). Cincinnati Art Museum.

serpentine chest-on-chest (I-46) is reminiscent of furniture from the Boston area in its carved shell, urn and flame finials, and overall restraint. Yet this documented example of 1784 displays several fashionable Norwich details: double spurs on the feet, chamfered pilasters on the upper case, and fluted plinths (also seen on Rhode Island furniture).

Few Norwich chairs in the Queen Anne style survive. One example (I-47) is based on Boston models but has side stretchers of an unusual pattern. Straight-legged chairs in the Chippendale style are far more numerous. The most popular design (I-48) has a pierced splat with two circular scrolls, or "eyes." The splat is related to a common Massachusetts pattern (I-30), and the overall form often features such Boston attributes as simple fretwork brackets at the front and a beaded edge on each stretcher (chair no. 123). The shape of the crest, however, is unique to the Norwich area; the rounded ears jut well beyond the stiles and are sometimes decorated with spiral carving.[85]

For most of the eighteenth century, Hartford was one of several central Connecticut communities supporting small groups of furniture craftsmen. Windsor, Wethersfield, and Glastonbury each had skilled woodworkers, and their products are difficult to separate from those of Hartford. However, after the Revolution, Hartford's expanding economy attracted many artisans, and by the 1790s the town had become the center of the

I-49. High Chest. Wethersfield or Hartford, Connecticut, 1750–1782. *Mahogany, white pine, and
tulipwood;* H. 70 (177.8); W. 37½ (95.3); D. 19⅞
(50.5). Brooklyn Museum. *The chest belonged to
Thomas Belden (1732–1782) of Wethersfield.*

I-50. High Chest. Attributed to Eliphalet Chapin
(1741–1807), East Windsor, Connecticut, 1771–
1795. Cherry and white pine; H. 87 (221.0); W.
39½ (100.3); D. 18 (45.7). Wadsworth Atheneum.

furniture industry on the Connecticut River. In 1792 its craftsmen organized a Society
of Cabinetmakers and wrote a Table of Prices in order to regulate the prices they charged
the public.[86]

Queen Anne and Chippendale furniture from the Hartford area is related stylistically
to that from such diverse communities as Philadelphia, New York, Norwich, Newport,
Boston, and Salem. Because of the plethora of influences, designs vary considerably. Two
Hartford-area high chests, for example, illustrate dramatic differences. The stiff, slender
legs, undulating skirt, and drawer arrangement of the first (I-49) are characteristic of
Hartford-area work. On some examples, a small ogee arch decorates the center of the
skirt much like that on Salem high chests; others feature a double bead in place of the
arch.[87] The second chest (I-50), attributed to Eliphalet Chapin of East Windsor, resembles
stylish Philadelphia furniture in its general proportions, leg and foot design, skirt shape,
and latticework pattern in the pediment. Chapin worked in Philadelphia for four years.
Once back in Connecticut, he modified his Pennsylvania sources. His furniture is more
delicate, and his carved details — the asymmetrical cartouche and vine ornament on the

I-51. Side Chair. Wethersfield or Hartford, Connecticut, 1750–1770. *Cherry* and *maple;* H. 41⅛ (101.8); W. 19⅝ (49.8); SEAT D. 17 (43.1); SEAT H. 16½ (41.8). Museum of Fine Arts, Boston. *The chair, originally one of a set of twelve, may have been acquired by Ezekiel Porter (1707–1775) of Wethersfield and descended to his son-in-law Thomas Belden (1732–1782). The needlework upholstery is original.*

I-52. Side Chair. Eliphalet Chapin (1741–1807), East Windsor, Connecticut, 1781. *Cherry, white oak,* and *white pine;* H. 38⅜ (97.5); W. 22⁷⁄₁₆ (57.0); SEAT D. 16⅝ (42.2); SEAT H. 16⅜ (41.6). Mabel Brady Garvan Collection, Yale University Art Gallery. Photograph, Joseph Szaszfai. *According to a bill of sale, now lost, this chair is part of a set purchased by Alexander King in 1781. The original upholstery survives beneath the modern leather outer covering.*

I-53. Side Chair. East Windsor or Hartford, 1771–1790. Cherry and pine; H. 38 (96.5); W. 21 (53.3); SEAT D. 17 (43.2); SEAT H. 16⅜ (41.6). Connecticut Historical Society. Photograph, Paul Koda. *The chair probably descended in the family of George Belden, a Hartford cabinetmaker. The seat retains all of its original upholstery except for the outer covering.*

drawers — are striking adaptations of Philadelphia rococo motifs. Like his fellow craftsmen in the Hartford area, he selected cherry for even his most elegant articles.

Some chairs from the Hartford area reflect the influence of Philadelphia furniture. By the 1760s, a craftsman was making stylish Queen Anne chairs with compass seats and narrow splats (I-51). Unlike most New England chairs, these lack stretchers and feature chamfered rear legs reminiscent of the "stump" legs common in Philadelphia. The seat construction echoes a Philadelphia technique; the front legs are tenoned into the seat rails. Chapin's chairs (I-52) closely resemble a later style of Philadelphia work, featuring interlaced scroll splats and shell-carved crests. Numerous chairs of diverse splat patterns (I-53) are related in construction to Chapin's work.[88] Yet all were probably not produced in one shop. Chapin undoubtedly trained apprentices, who spread the style throughout the Hartford region. His cousin Aaron Chapin, for example, worked with Eliphalet for several years and then moved from East Windsor to Hartford in 1783.[89] Other design traditions also gained popularity in the Hartford area. Rush-seated chairs based largely on Boston work were common throughout Connecticut.[90] These feature solid splats, yoke crests, turned legs, and Spanish feet (chair no. 92).

Craftsmen in the Hartford area, though influenced by a variety of sources, sometimes created bold and inventive designs. A desk and bookcase by George Belden of Hartford (III-6) is a stunning example in which the swelled façade of the lower case is capped by a blocked drawer in the bookcase. Belden's secretary is part of a large group of Hartford-area work that includes more conventional chests of drawers with serpentine fronts, quarter columns, and bracket feet with a single spur, somewhat similar to the feet on Rhode Island case furniture.[91] All are linked by a distinctive form of foot construction, in which a vertical support behind the bracket foot is attached to a large horizontal block with a curved inner edge.[92]

New England furniture craftsmen have left a remarkable legacy. Thousands of examples of their work, from sophisticated bombé desks to simple slat-back chairs, reside in houses and museums across the country. Many of their shop accounts survive; in addition, public records such as wills and inventories provide insight into their careers. Here, relying on both artifacts and documents, I have examined the working patterns, the sources of design, and some of the regional traits of their work.

The separation of craftsmen into urban and rural categories is sometimes difficult. During the seventeenth century, only Boston was of sufficient size to qualify as an urban center, yet in New Haven, a much smaller community, immigrants from London worked in an urban style. John Gaines III lived in Portsmouth, an eighteenth-century urban community; his brother Thomas, also a furniture craftsman, lived in Ipswich, Massachusetts. To label one an urban craftsman and the other a rural one is deceptive, for their work was probably similar. On occasion, rural and urban artisans worked together. During the 1730s, Nathaniel Holmes of Boston employed several men in outlying towns to make furniture. Prosperous rural cabinetmakers sometimes sought to market their wares in nearby seaports. After the Revolution, Luther Metcalf operated a large shop in Medway, Massachusetts, producing furniture that was carted to Providence to be finished and sold by his business partner (see entry 23).

Though the differences between rural and urban workers are at times hard to identify, the significance of the urban environment to all New England is clear. Urban craftsmen were the most specialized and most prolific manufacturers of furniture in the region. They were aware of English design, and their products, especially those from Portsmouth and Boston, display the greatest reliance on foreign fashion. Changes in style were often seen first in their work and, through it, were disseminated to rural areas.

Not all craftsmen in urban centers had equal skill or influence. Certain individuals strongly affected local taste. Eliphalet Chapin introduced one striking version of the Chippendale style to the Hartford area; an English immigrant brought another to Portsmouth. Through such urban masters, the colonial furniture of New England achieved a complexity and richness unsurpassed in America.

1. Wood, *New England's Prospect,* 38.

2. The best accounts of the establishment of sawmills in New England and their importance to the furniture trade are Candee, "Merchant and Millwright," and Forman, "Mill Sawing in Seventeenth-Century Massachusetts."

3. Allen, *"Vacuum Domicilium:* The Social and Cultural Landscape of Seventeenth-Century Massachusetts," 2–3.

4. Maverick, "Brief Description," 237.

5. Rutman, *Winthrop's Boston,* 178–90.

6. Maverick, "Brief Description," 238; Nash, *Urban Crucible,* 2, 409; Shattuck, *Report,* 3.

7. Roe and Trent, "Robert Sanderson," 480, 487–88.

8. According to a census of 1742, Boston's population was 16,382; Shattuck, *Report,* 3–4. The economic growth of Boston during the first half of the eighteenth century is described in Henretta, "Economic Development," 79, 81; Nash, *Urban Crucible,* 54–57, 115, 117–18.

9. Birket, *Some Cursory Remarks,* 24.

10. Ibid., 23.

11. Cappon, *Atlas of Early American History,* 22, 97–98.

12. Coffin, *Merrimac River Shipping,* 10; [Hamilton,] *Gentleman's Progress,* 118.

13. According to a census taken in 1774, Newport's population was 9209; *Century of Population Growth,* 14.

14. Burnaby, *Travels Through the Middle Settlements,* 83. For a thorough assessment of Harrison's career, see Bridenbaugh, *Peter Harrison.* Malbone and Redwood's residences are described in Downing and Scully, *Architectural Heritage of Newport,* 37–41.

15. The mercantile activities of the Brown family are chronicled in Hedges, *The Browns of Providence Plantation.*

16. The colonial economies of Norwich, Hartford, and New London as well as of the smaller towns of New Haven and Middletown are discussed in Daniels, *Connecticut Town Growth,* 145–51.

17. This estimate is derived from manuscript sources and a review of the following secondary sources on furniture making in urban centers.

For Portsmouth: Burroughs, "Furniture Widely Made in New Hampshire," 6, 7, 14, 15.

For Newburyport, Salem, and Marblehead: Belknap, *Artists and Craftsmen of Essex County;* Forman, "Seventeenth-Century Case Furniture of Essex County" and "Salem Tradesmen and Craftsmen Circa 1762"; and Swan, "Newburyport Furnituremakers."

For Boston: Forman, "Boston Furniture Craftsmen," and Kaye, "Eighteenth-Century Boston Furniture Craftsmen."

For Newport and Providence: Garrett, "Newport Cabinetmakers," "Providence Cabinetmakers," "The Goddard and Townsend Joiners," and "The Goddard and Townsend Joiners of Newport"; Ott, "Recent Discoveries Among Rhode Island Cabinetmakers" and "More Notes on Rhode Island Cabinetmakers"; and Vibert, "Market Economy and the Furniture Trade of Newport," 91–93.

For Norwich and Hartford: Kane, "Joiners of Seventeenth-Century Hartford County"; Kihn, "Connecticut Cabinetmakers"; and Myers and Mayhew, *New London County Furniture,* 106–32.

18. These totals exclude upholsterers.

19. Vibert, "Market Economy and the Furniture Trade of Newport," 23.

20. Jobe, "Boston Furniture Industry, 1720–1740," 9; Vibert, "Market Economy and the Furniture Trade of Newport," 46.

21. Accounts of losses in the Boston fire of March 20, 1760, Thomas Foot Account, Boston Public Library.

22. A plan of Townsend's shop appears in Downing and Scully, *Architectural Heritage of Newport,* pl. 95.

23. Accounts of losses from the burning of Charlestown, June 17, 1775, Thomas Wood Account, Boston Public Library.

24. Accounts of losses in the Boston fire of March 20, 1760, Joseph Putnam Account, Boston Public Library; Kirkham, "Samuel Norman," 508.

25. [Parkman,] "Diary of Ebenezer Parkman," 175.

26. Ibid., 189.

27. Specialization in the chairmaking industry continued in the eighteenth century; Jobe, "Boston

Furniture Industry, 1725–1760," 103–6.

28. Forman, "Boston Furniture Craftsmen, 1630–1730," 9:3–4.

29. Jobe, "Boston Furniture Industry, 1725–1760," 96–98.

30. Bill, John Underwood to Nathaniel Holmes, Boston, bills 1728–59, vol. 8, Bourn Papers, Baker Library, Harvard University.

31. Anthony Underwood's Estate Accounts, docket 9182, Suffolk County (Mass.) Probate. See also Jobe, "Boston Furniture Industry, 1725–1760," 125, n. 259.

32. Biographies of these upholsterers appear in Forman, "Boston Furniture Craftsmen, 1630–1730," 11:1–8; Jobe, "Upholstery Trade of Colonial Boston."

33. The careers of Fitch and Grant are discussed in detail in Jobe, "Boston Furniture Industry, 1720–1740," 24–27; for information on Downe and Gray, see Jobe, "Upholstery Trade of Colonial Boston."

34. Account Book, 1728–37, Massachusetts Historical Society; Account Book, 1737–60, American Antiquarian Society; Petty Ledger, 1755–62, Boston Public Library; Petty Ledger, 1762–71, Boston Public Library. In addition, a receipt book for the years 1731 to 1740 is at the Bostonian Society.

35. Grant's petty ledgers record that the following persons assisted him in the production of beds during the 1750s and 1760s: George Bright, Abraham Hayward, Edmund Perkins, Sr. and Jr., Henry Perkins, and Clement Vincent for bedsteads; Joseph Beath, Simeon Skillin, and John Welch for carved work; Thomas Kemble and the firm of Kemble and Greenwood for bed bottoms; John and Elizabeth Grant for mattresses; and Elizabeth Kemble, Sarah Flagg, Katherine Stanton, and Elizabeth Russell for bed hangings. For additional information on these workers, see Jobe, "Upholstery Trade of Colonial Boston."

36. The merchant was Peter Faneuil; see Jobe, "Boston Furniture Industry, 1720–1740," 33.

37. Ibid., pp. 42–47; Samuel Grant, Account Book, August 20, 1746, p. 507, American Antiquarian Society.

38. The dates of Lindsey's birth and marriage are listed in the Lindsey family genealogical files, Marblehead Historical Society. For Lindsey's purchase of a dwelling, see Perley, "Marblehead in the Year 1700, No. 3," 245.

39. The account book is probably incomplete. Charges for the years 1739 to 1746 are far less frequent than those afterward, suggesting that this may be the second of two books kept by Lindsey.

40. Joseph Lindsey, Account Book, 1739–64, March 8 and May 16, 1760, November 23, 1757, November 1755, p. 9, Joseph Downs Manuscript Collection, Winterthur Museum Library.

41. Ibid., June 2, 1759, and January 6, 1760, p. 12.

42. Ibid., February 1759, p. 9; June 20, 1755, p. 6.

43. Ibid., May 30, 1751, p. 4.

44. The account book is filled with references to "survaing" boards brought by ship to Marblehead. A typical account reads "To Survaing 5036 feet of Boards out of Wire and Lind[sey]." The names refer to ships under the command of Captains Wire and Ralph Lindsey, Joseph's brother; ibid., May 17, 1757, p. 7.

45. Cahoone's career is discussed in detail in Vibert, "Market Economy and the Furniture Trade of Newport," pp. 26–46.

46. Thomas Hornsby, "Newport, Past and Present," *Newport Daily Advertiser*, December 8, 1849, p. 2.

47. Though no documented examples of Cahoone's work are known, his furniture undoubtedly resembled that of other Newport makers. A straight-front desk made in 1753 by one of Cahoone's workmen, Jonathan Swett, is probably representative of the plain forms Cahoone crafted; Vibert, "Market Economy and the Furniture Trade of Newport," 30–37, 50, 52. For an illustration of the desk, see Carpenter, "Discoveries in Newport Furniture and Silver," 47.

48. Vibert, "Market Economy and the Furniture Trade of Newport," 30.

49. Holmes's career is discussed in detail in Jobe, "Boston Furniture Industry, 1720–1740," 13–24.

50. A documented desk with star inlay in Ellesin, "Collectors' Notes," is probably similar to those made for Holmes.

51. Kane, *Furniture of the New Haven Colony*, 81, 84; *New England Begins*, 3:524–25.

52. *New England Begins*, 3:514–19.

53. Trent, "New England Joinery," 501.

54. Kane, *Furniture of the New Haven Colony*, 11, 78; *New England Begins*, 3:519–21.

55. St. George, *The Wrought Covenant*, 56; also St. George, "Style and Structure in the Joinery of Dedham and Medfield."

56. St. George, *The Wrought Covenant*, 25–27.

57. Trent, *Hearts & Crowns*, 39–44.

58. Jobe, "Boston Furniture Industry, 1720–1740," 11.

59. Garrett, "The Goddard and Townsend Joiners of Newport," 1153–55.

60. The estate inventory of Nathaniel Gould, a Salem shop joiner, included a copy of "Chipendales Designs" valued at £1:8:0; Forman, "Salem Tradesmen and Craftsmen Circa 1762," p. 78. A copy of the third edition of the *Director* at the Boston Athenaeum bears an eighteenth-century inscription, "Boston 1768," on the title page; unfortunately the name of the owner has been erased. A copy of the third edition, at the Museum of Fine Arts, Boston, descended in the Goddard family of Newport and may well have belonged to the cabinetmaker John Goddard.

61. *Household Furniture in Genteel Taste; The II^d Edition of Genteel Household Furniture;* Ince and Mayhew, *Universal System of Household Furniture;* Manwaring, *Cabinet and Chair-Maker's Real Friend and Companion* and *The Chair-Maker's Guide;* and Crunden, *Joyner and Cabinet-Maker's Darling* and *The Carpenter's Companion.*

62. *Boston News-Letter,* January 8, 1767, p. 1.

63. See Gusler, *Furniture of Williamsburg,* 3, 66–67, 75–79, 115–16, 123, 129, 151–53. The files at the Museum of Early Southern Decorative Arts include photographs of several Charleston chairs modeled on Chippendale's designs.

64. *Boston News-Letter,* May 9, 1715, p. 2.

65. Thomas Hancock to Francis Wilkes, Hancock Letterbook, December 20, 1738, p. 58, New England Historic Genealogical Society.

66. Ibid., July 10, 1739, p. 67.

67. A related but less ornate Boston clock, with works by Benjamin Bagnall, is illustrated in Fairbanks, "American Antiques in the Collection of Mr. and Mrs. Charles Bybee, Part 2," 77.

68. Barrell had arrived in London by May 1, 1760, and "came home by York from London" on May 17, 1763. See Jonathan Sayward Diary, 1760–97, two-volume transcript of the original diary at the American Antiquarian Society, 1:6, 33, Society for the Preservation of New England Antiquities.

69. The bill, dated March 26, 1763, is included in a group of Barrell family papers owned privately.

70. For an illustration of the sconce glass and carved sconces, see Morse, *Furniture of the Olden Time,* 380.

71. Similar English examples appear in Kirk, *American Furniture,* 269–70.

72. The plain chairs, though not documented by a bill of sale, are sufficiently similar in appearance and size to the carved ones to warrant an attribution to Walker. Every surviving chair from the two sets has such distinctive features as mahogany strips nailed to the inside of the rear seat rails to support the loose seats and shoes and rear rails constructed of one piece of wood. Only two chairs from the plain set are known; they remained in the Barrell House until 1978, when a descendant of Nathaniel Barrell donated them to the Old Gaol Museum.

73. The similar chairs include a carved example at the Western Reserve Historical Society in Cleveland and an uncarved pair at the Moffatt-Ladd House in Portsmouth; Giffen, "The Moffatt-Ladd House, Part 1," 117–18.

74. For Boston examples in the early Queen Anne style, see Fairbanks and Bates, *American Furniture,* 95; Jobe, "Boston Furniture Industry, 1720–1740," 44; and armchair 92a.

75. In 1762, Salem was the home of seventeen furniture makers: thirteen were shop joiners, three chairmakers, and one a chairmaker and painter; Forman, "Salem Tradesmen and Craftsmen Circa 1762," 65.

76. Comstock, "Ipswich Account Book," 188; Brewster, *Rambles About Portsmouth,* 2:355–56.

77. The related dressing tables and high chest are shown in Morse, *Furniture of the Olden Time,* 34; Cooper, *In Praise of America,* 213–14; Lockwood, *Colonial Furniture,* 3rd ed., 1:103.

78. The best-known imported furniture is a set of two settees, six armchairs, and a stool in the Chinese Chippendale style. Three of the chairs, a settee, and the stool are on display at the Moffatt-Ladd House in Portsmouth (Giffen, "Moffatt-Ladd House, Part 1"), two chairs and the other settee are at Colonial Williamsburg, and the sixth chair is privately owned.

79. The stand, side table, and one of the china tables are privately owned. For an illustration of the stand, see Biddle, *American Art,* 46. Other china tables are owned by the Warner House Association (Wendell, "The Macpheadris House in Portsmouth," 713), the Metropolitan Museum (Comstock, *American Furniture,* no. 373), and the Department of State (Cooper, *In Praise of America,* 142–43). A china table was sold at auction in 1929 and shown in the same year in the Girl Scouts Loan Exhibition (*Loan Exhibition of Eighteenth and Early Nineteenth Century Furniture,* no. 653). Its present location is not known.

80. Golden announced the opening of his shop in the *New Hampshire Gazette,* July 29, 1763, p. 2.

81. The group includes two at the Museum of Fine Arts, Boston (Hipkiss, *Eighteenth-Century American Arts,* 30–32; Randall, *American Furniture,* 84–86), two at the Rhode Island School of Design (I-41 and Landman, "Pendleton House," 934, 936), one at the Yale University Art Gallery

(Cooper, "Purchase of Furniture by John Brown," 339), one at Bayou Bend (Warren, *Bayou Bend,* 69), one at the Winterthur Museum (Downs, *American Furniture,* no. 232), one at the Metropolitan Museum (Schwartz, *American Furniture,* 63), one at the Rhode Island Historical Society (Cooper, *In Praise of America,* 160, 169), one originally owned by Nicholas Brown of Providence and now belonging to his descendants, and another example owned privately.

82. The Boston upholsterer Samuel Grant sold chairs with "Flat Strech^{rs}" in the 1740s; Samuel Grant, Account Book, 1737–60, February 3, 1742, p. 261. Boston chairs with beaded edges on the knees include one in Jobe, "Boston Furniture Industry, 1720–1740," 44, and a related example at the Museum of Fine Arts, Boston, that descended in the Eliot family of Boston. For information on Boston chairs with carved shells, see notes 2 and 3 for entry 99.

83. Kirk illustrates one other Chippendale pattern (*American Chairs,* 140, no. 183).

84. The agreement is reprinted in *John Brown House Loan Exhibition,* 174–75.

85. Other Norwich chairs with a similar crest pattern but different splat designs include a pair of slat-back chairs with their original needlework seats at the Connecticut Historical Society (*Connecticut Chairs,* 43), a similar slat-back chair with its original horsehair seat at the Connecticut Historical Society, and a chair with a pierced splat once owned by Jabez Huntington of Norwich (Kirk, *Connecticut Furniture,* no. 246).

86. The Table of Prices is reprinted in Lyon, *Colonial Furniture,* 3rd ed., 267–70.

87. See, for example, a high chest probably owned by Joshua Wells of Wethersfield in the eighteenth century; Benes, *Two Towns,* 49.

88. Fales, *Furniture of Historic Deerfield,* 56–58; Kirk, *Connecticut Furniture,* 130–35.

89. Richards, "Furniture of the Lower Connecticut River Valley," 2, 4, 18–19.

90. Examples with Hartford-area provenances include a set of five originally owned by Ezekiel Porter of Wethersfield, now in the Brooklyn Museum.

91. See, for example, Randall, *American Furniture,* 40–41.

92. Bulkeley, "George Belden and Erastus Grant," 77, 79.

II. Rural Craftsmen and Design

Philip Zea

In rural America, cyclical patterns of production, exchange, and consumption define the life of the people. Since furniture is needed for eating, sleeping, and impressing the neighbors, these household items stand as microcosms of cultural attitudes about fashion and method. A chair, like the person sitting on it, holds clues to the environment in which it was produced. The furniture and business records of rural New England joiners reveal the impact of the environment and an agricultural economy on fashion and life's expectations in the "back of beyond."

By the middle of the seventeenth century, coastal towns had become prosperous commercial centers, drawing on hill towns and forests for raw materials to exchange for imported goods. But wagons of produce and manufactured items were not alone on New England roads. Ideas about fashion and taste, affordability and adaptation, were also carried by newcomers to the frontier, hoping to make their surroundings like home. Meanwhile, land speculators aimed to realize their investments as quickly as the pine stumps and log huts could be cleared away. As memories of back home faded, relationships with new neighbors, prosperity, and local pride created new reference points and altered the concept of acceptable taste.

Jonathan Chase, who lived in the Connecticut River town of Cornish, New Hampshire, was supplying his neighbors with the little extras they had enjoyed in their previous homes within three years of the town's settlement. In 1768 and 1769, Chase's customers bartered for chocolate, ginger, knee buckles, spelling books, fine thread, mohair, and silk.[1] Such goods were carried to the New Hampshire Grants in canoes up the Connecticut River, a better highway than the rutted paths along its flood plain. Chase and others used this natural trade route in their dealings with merchants downriver in Massachusetts and Connecticut.[2]

The lay of the land, the resulting political boundaries, and the religious differences among the first settlements created three spheres of influence in New England before the end of the seventeenth century. They were anchored by Boston, Newport-Providence, and Hartford.[3]

Boston was the primary commercial center of Massachusetts Bay and Cape Cod, the Merrimack and Piscataqua River basins, and coastal Maine.[4] The longshore currents, which assure careless waders a trip "Down East" to Maine, form an oceanic trade route between Boston and northern New England. The fresh tributaries of this salty river carried Boston's exports and ideas into Worcester County, downwind to Salem and Newburyport in Essex County, north along the Merrimack River to the Scotch-Irish settlements in southern New Hampshire, around Cape Ann to Portsmouth, and farther down the Maine coast to growing towns like Falmouth (now Portland).[5] The citizens of these regional trade centers emulated Boston airs (although they may not have admitted it publicly) and conveyed their provincial interpretations of acceptable taste to the people in the surrounding hill towns, who in turn molded fashion to accommodate their budgets and sense of style.

Although Boston was New England's largest port, it was not the only clearinghouse of ideas and imports in the five northern colonies. Many immigrants traveled directly to other colonies in New England and did their utmost to ignore the Boston "wags" in their trade with Great Britain and the other English colonies. For example, Thomas Salmon left Wiltshire, England, before 1719 and settled in Stratford, Connecticut. Salmon owned a number of joiner's and turner's tools and, at his death in 1750, was recognized as "ye ingenius Architect" of Stratford's Anglican church. Salmon trained a number of apprentices and initiated the shop tradition that furnished southern Connecticut houses with "crown" chairs (II-1) until the 1820s.[6]

Newport and Providence, Rhode Island, were the trade and style centers for New England's southeastern sector.[7] The rivers and coastal trade wove a network of economic exchange that included towns like Dartmouth, Massachusetts, and New London, Norwich, and Colchester in the Thames River valley of eastern Connecticut.

After the annexation of the New Haven Colony to Connecticut in 1664, the towns of Milford, New Haven, and Guilford joined Hartford's sphere of influence, which grew in western New England during the eighteenth century to include Windsor and Litchfield, Connecticut, and Springfield and Hadley, Massachusetts.

Later, New England's northwestern territory farther up the Connecticut Valley was thrown open to speculation and settlement after the end of the French and Indian Wars in 1760.[8] The rapid growth of the New Hampshire Grants and the distance to the sea discouraged the growth of large towns of great economic influence.[9] Nevertheless, the prospering citizens of Walpole, Hanover, and Haverhill, New Hampshire, and Windsor, Vermont, built fine houses and read local newspapers before the War of 1812.

These definitions of economic and cultural regions within New England strain our modern perception of society. The act of turning on a television reduces our acceptance of a few hundred square miles as a cultural region. A walk from Hanover to coastal New Hampshire, a distance of one hundred miles, would help us to understand the secession of the eastern towns in the upper Connecticut Valley from New Hampshire during the latter years of the Revolution.[10] The settlers' economic, political, and cultural allegiances were bound to their transplanted Connecticut cousins across the river in Vermont, not to a government two valleys away. The cultural differences between regions were more distinct before trains and automobiles conquered the landscape.

II-1. Armchair. Stratford or Milford, Connecticut, 1745–1775. Maple and ash; H. 47½ (120.6); W. 25½ (64.8); SEAT D. 17¼ (43.8); SEAT H. 17⅛ (43.5). Historic Deerfield. Photograph, Helga Studio. *The armchair was produced in the style of the shop tradition begun by Thomas Salmon in Stratford.*

In his study of New England dialect, Hans Kurath substantiates the existence of thirteen separate regions, for those who think, work, and trade together are bound to speak alike.[11] These regions are eastern and York County, Maine, eastern New Hampshire, the Merrimack Valley, Essex County, the Boston area, the Plymouth area, the Worcester area, Rhode Island, eastern Connecticut, the lower and upper Connecticut Valley, and western Vermont. They are separated by topographical features, are perceived as the next frontier during the course of colonial New England history, are roughly a day's ride or sail from their neighbors, are marked by different speech idioms, and have distinctive attitudes about the construction and decoration of furniture.

By examining the fashion consciousness of consumers and the working patterns of rural tradesmen, we can recognize the furniture made in these regions. Versatility, vital for success in an agricultural economy, governed the aspirations and skills of rural joiners, who engaged in a division of time rather than a division of labor. The skills of these farmer-tradesmen were seasonally directed at other tasks, and their furniture is marked by imitation, exaggeration, native woods, and a wide range of workmanship. Their cabinetwork often embodied loose-fitting copies of furniture designs popular in the commercial centers. Although the trade routes brought imported goods and a concept of current fashion to upland New England, the seasonal repetition of agriculture reinforced time-honored expectations and made rural folks conservative in their stylishness. So-called Queen Anne chairs, for example, were made in rural towns well into the nineteenth century, two generations after their popularity had faded in the cities.

Utilitarian and conservative furniture was used by urban householders.[12] Conse-

II-2. Chest with Drawer. Springfield, Massachusetts, area, 1700–1710. *White oak, beech,* and *yellow pine;* H. 34 (86.4); W. 49½ (125.7); D. 19¼ (48.9). Henry Francis du Pont Winterthur Museum. *The chest was made for Priscilla Warner of Enfield, Connecticut, and descended in the Meacham family.*

quently, "city-country" is not the seam to rip when defining furniture. "High style" and "urban" are not synonymous. A more natural delineation lies on a scale between the vernacular and the sophisticated as defined by the originality, modernity, and visual success of design, the sources of the material used, and the training, construction techniques, and working patterns of the cabinetmakers.

The impact of urban taste and its connotations of innovation and wealth were tempered by the confidence of rural joiners. Through repetition, renaissance motifs like flowers and vines became ingrained in the culture of rural New England. The joiners who made the vine-carved Hadley chests in western Massachusetts in about 1700, several generations after settlement, drew from a heritage of designs popular in the northwest of England (II-2).[13]

Paint was also used on furniture to provide both well-to-do farmers and the poor with civilized and colorful surroundings. The application of expensive pigments did not necessarily undersell the cost or stylishness of carved decoration. When John Marsh of Hadley died in 1725, he left the substantial estate of £1249:2:11. His inventory included "A Carved work Chest 30ˢ" and "A floward Chest 32ˢ."[14] Since *carved* was not used

II-3. Cupboard. Hadley, Massachusetts, area, ca. 1715. Oak and yellow pine; H. 61⅛ (155.3); W. 50 (127); D. 21¼ (54.0). Greenfield Village and the Henry Ford Museum. *Hannah Barnard (1684–1717) was the second wife of John Marsh of Hadley.*

II-4. Desk and Bookcase on Frame. Hartford County, Connecticut, 1750–1800. Cherry and white pine; H. 87¼ (221.6); W. 39 (99.1); D. 21½ (54.6). Greenfield Village and the Henry Ford Museum.

II-5. High Chest. Saybrook or Guilford, Connecticut, 1710–1725. Tulipwood, white pine, and ash; H. 54⅝ (138.7); W. 40⅛ (101.9); D. 21⅛ (53.7). Henry Francis du Pont Winterthur Museum.

to describe the second chest, it was probably painted and may have resembled the colorful cupboard inscribed "HANNAH BARNARD," Marsh's second wife (II-3). The "flow-ard Chest" was appraised at two shillings more than the carved chest and was the second most expensive of the six domestic chests listed in the inventory. The façade of the cupboard, a highly urban form, conveys a classical sense of balance in its geometric design and moldings. Similarly, the classical demand for fluted pilasters on a later Connecticut Valley desk and bookcase was abandoned for stylized sunflowers from the region's cultural index of accepted design (II-4). The inclusion of decorative motifs from the immediate environment, which serve the same visual function as formal architectural devices, shows that imagination was not a pawn for ignorance but a separate, vital entity in the construction of upland furniture.

The regional differences in New England furniture are emphasized by a painted high chest (II-5) made in the Guilford-Saybrook area of coastal Connecticut in about 1715, the approximate date of Miss Barnard's cupboard. The high chest's sophistication suggests a relationship between the proximity of the frontier and the rate of changing taste. It was built entirely of native woods and in the modern form of a high chest in a town closer to the coastal trade and the fashion pulses of Anglo-American commerce. Oak, the favored wood in the joined furniture of the seventeenth century, was abandoned in its construction. The high chest is a tapestry of the environmental pressures of the time. The baroque design is highlighted by foliate scrolls around the drawer edges, imitating herringbone inlay. The balanced ornamentation calls to mind the effect of crotched veneer, and the oversized tulips on the sides of the upper case, a regional decorative motif, create the same impact as the jackal and birds on the sides of some japanned Boston high chests of drawers.[15] The ornamental roses, thistles, fleurs-de-lis, and crowns on the drawer fronts were derived from the British royal coat of arms. Although these motifs had been used for years, the chest may celebrate the union of England and Scotland in 1708. English ceramics of the period commemorated the event and may have served as prototypes for a decorative painter in distant Connecticut.[16] Despite the goals of the maker, the chunky legs, simple arched skirt with painted trees, and squat proportions bring the chest back to earth as a document of high-style aspirations and the environment of coastal Connecticut during the early eighteenth century.

Design ideas were occasionally carried into the hinterland with little damage to the original concept. The blockfront design epitomized by a chest of drawers made by John Townsend at Newport in 1765 (II-6) is the analogue and probable prototype for a chest of drawers made for the Day family of Colchester and Moodus, Connecticut, between 1770 and 1790 (II-7).[17] The primary wood of the Newport chest is imported mahogany; the secondary wood, tulipwood. The Day chest was constructed solely of native woods: cherry, chestnut, and tulipwood. The Townsend chest is a sculptural unit. All of its parts are melded together by the careful balance of lines and planes over its façade. With concessions to form, utility, fashion, and consumer preference, Townsend approached furniture making as an art form.

By comparison, the Day chest is a conglomeration of visual units all vying for attention. The blocking is suspended on the façade, whereas on the Townsend chest it springs logically from the base molding. The feet of the Day chest are exaggerated in size and contour and are not visually united to the case in the way the line rising from the instep of each front foot of the Townsend chest becomes the outside border of the blocking. The cornice of the Day chest is classical in inspiration but not in detail, and the fluted pilasters are architecturally nonsensical. They rise from imaginary bases and reach for

II-6. Chest of Drawers. John Townsend (1732–1809), Newport, 1765. Mahogany and tulipwood; H. 34½ (87.6); W. 36¾ (93.3); D. 19 (48.3). Metropolitan Museum of Art.

II-7. Chest of Drawers. Colchester, Connecticut, 1770–1790. Cherry, chestnut, and tulipwood; H. 35⅜ (89.8); W. 40¼ (102.2); D. 20 (50.8). Antiquarian & Landmarks Society of Connecticut. *The chest descended in the Day family of Colchester and Moodus.*

unseen capitals, but they do frame a well-proportioned rectangle and offset the strong horizontal thrust of the cornice, drawers, and base molding. The inaccurate attention to architectural precedent is best seen by the inclusion of a dentil course in the base molding of the Day chest, where it visually creates a cornice for the feet, dividing the façade into two distinct units.

The barter of raw materials for manufactured goods supported the economy of New England towns. The success of the barter system relied upon trust, liberal credit, and long-term agreements in an economy lacking hard cash but strengthened by the homogeneity of farm life. Since accounts were settled when mutually convenient, ledgers were kept to remember debits and credits from one season to the next.

Most farmers prospered beyond subsistency in established rural towns. Surpluses were produced and shipped to regional trade centers. Further investment followed in land and production, and small cottage industries grew to meet people's needs and to fill working time during slack seasons. Although most transactions were settled in barter, farmers slowly made improvements in their estates, adding value to their initial property investments. A social structure of "haves" and "have-nots" evolved in farming communities, and ideas about displaying prosperity to best advantage followed.

Diversity in the working patterns of the farmer-artisan carried him beyond subsistence farming. No one could afford to make and barter a single product for supplemental income because of few potential customers and because the farmer-artisan could not market his wares widely. While the Boston tradesman was forced by competition to perfect a single, year-round specialty in a large, bustling marketplace, the rural joiner mustered a livelihood from several activities within a local agricultural economy dependent on the weather for prosperity. Rural tradesmen centralized their marketing procedures and specialized, not in a product, but in a material.

Wood was the plastic of a world before industrial chemistry: it was plentiful, cheap, versatile, durable, and attractive. Each community needed someone capable of efficiently transforming wood into functional and attractive forms. Business acumen and a sensitivity to the fashion consciousness of the local elite characterized the best cabinetmakers.

During the 1690s, Boston became the center of the new fashion for cabinetry. With King William's War, the first conflict in New England determined by European politics, England asserted new colonial responsibilities and commerce thrived. British bureaucrats arriving in the Puritan commonwealth brought the London style with them. The accepted taste in furniture in polite circles sprang from the enlightened, revolutionary concept of dovetailed construction, outdating the heavy joined furniture of oak. The new method called for dovetailed boards, veneered surfaces of exotic woods, and the evolution of lathe-turned spindles from applied decoration to functional legs on case pieces. Classicism demanded a stage, not a firm foundation.

The skills of veneering and dovetailing bypassed the traditional joiner. As the market for furniture framed like houses diminished, urban joiners specialized in housewrighting.[18] The lavish style of the early baroque, however, was generally beyond the means of upland farmers. Few people working in an agricultural economy could afford the specialized skills of an urban cabinetmaker, and the new tastes were alien to their heritage of Anglo-Saxon design and to the ethos of farm life. With the development of decorative painting, the woodworking skills of the traditional joiner or carpenter were sufficient in upland New England for a while longer.

Little is known about the rural joiners of the seventeenth century. Personal accounts are rare, but their houses, furniture, and legal documents show that they were farming artisans. The inventories of New Hampshiremen who died before 1700 owning such woodworking tools as chisels and augers reveal that 30 percent of the average joiner's estate was invested in animals, farm implements, and produce, 45 percent in land and buildings, and just 4 percent — less than a fifth of the worth accorded his furnishings and kitchen utensils — in joiner's tools.[19]

Edward Clarke, for example, lived on an island in the Piscataqua River between New Hampshire and Maine and was in his prime when he drowned in 1675.[20] His inventory shows that his house was comfortably furnished and offers a rare glimpse "In yᵉ Shopp" of a seventeenth-century rural joiner. The appraisers found:

32 chissells & gouges   10^s hamers 4^s [£]00:14:00
a power brace & 3 bitts   18 planes & joynter 30^s 01:11:06
2 hansaws 4^s 1 drawing knife 2^{s}6^d 00:06:06
2 ades 2^s a thwart saw — a holdfast 18^d 00:06:06
2 bettles & 4 wedges 8^s spade 18^d 00:09:06
5 augers 6^s 1 ax 2^{s}6^d old iron 12^d 00:09:06
old iron & old warn tooles 5^s 00:05:00
2 wainscot chairs unfinis't 8^s a grinstone 10^s 00:18:00
1 chist new 6^s 00:06:00
                                5:06:06

And out in the barn were:

5 hamers 5^s 3 augers 6^s 2 chissels 2 plaine stockes 4^s [£]00:15:00
iron crow 18^d a p'cell of nales & old iron & chest 7^s 00:08:06
a pitch fork 18^d 00:01:06
35 lite windows 1^s a peece   01:01:00
1 window of 2 lites 2^s 00:02:00
2 windows of 3 lites 3^s a peece   00:09:00
a p'cell of sheepes wooll 10^s 00:10:00
a p'cell of hew'd timber   00:12:00
2 cannoos   01:00:00
2 cowes 4 lb a peece   a bull 2 lb   14:00:00
1 calfe 10^s one hors 3 lb   03:10:00
two sheepe & 3 lambs   01:10:00
2 shotes & a sow & piggs   02:00:00
                           £ 25:19:00

At the time of his death, Clarke had invested 9 percent of his estate in animals and farm implements, 14 percent in furnishings and kitchen utensils, 73 percent in land and buildings (he owned forty-eight acres and the "island where he lived"), and 3 percent in his woodworking tools. His inventory shows that Clarke, who constructed buildings and furniture, farmed to keep body and soul together.

The men who made furniture in rural New England applied their skills to much more than one trade. William Mather (1766–1835) of Whately, Massachusetts, supported his family as a cabinetmaker (II-8), housewright, brickmaker, mason, glazier, wheelwright, distiller, land speculator, and farmer, and served the community as town clerk, assessor, treasurer, and captain of the militia.[21] Mather's estate ranked sixteenth of 154 in 1810.[22] Jonathan Colton Loomis of Whately, who worked with Mather as a journeyman cabinetmaker, also labored as a weaver and clockmaker.[23]

Mather's account book supplies insight into the geographic and economic domains of a rural handyman in a Connecticut Valley town. Between 1808 and 1825, Mather dealt with more than 230 people, 35 of whom lived outside the town. Only 7 customers came from towns not bordering Whately, but 104 of his patrons shared their surnames with at least one other customer. As a part-time farmer, Mather's low overhead and the low

II-8. Chest with Drawers. Attributed to William Mather (1766–1835), Whately, Massachusetts, area, 1790–1820. White pine; H. 45 (114.3); W. 37¾ (95.9); D. 18½ (47.0). Historic Deerfield. Photograph, Helga Studio. *The chest is identical to one in the collections of Historic Deerfield that was owned by a niece of William Mather.*

cost of lumber made his varied services available to most members of the community.

A newcomer would despair of displacing an established artisan like Mather in a small, homogeneous town short on specie. Well known in the community, he maintained positions in local government, the church, and in military affairs. Underselling him was impossible. Everyone in town was familiar with what he could do and at what price. The personal tone of rural business life explains why formal advertisement was unnecessary. Mather's relationship with his neighbors is recorded in accounts such as that with Asa Dickinson on July 11, 1812, "to a Coffin for Miss Dickinson in the 67 yr of her age $2.50."[24] A joiner's work, although unsigned, was recognized by the community.

Solomon Sibley (1769–1856) was a woodworker who lived in the southern Worcester County town of Ward (now Auburn), Massachusetts.[25] Little is known of Sibley's family life. Tax records show that at best, he coped with genteel poverty. In 1797, only 28 percent of his neighbors were taxed less than Sibley.[26] Four years later, Sibley paid a Minister's Tax of $1.13 when the average tax bill was $2.45 and 42 percent of his neighbors were taxed less.[27] In 1805, Sibley's property was appraised at $400.[28] The average appraisal was $379.04, and 59 percent of Ward's property owners had lower evaluations. That year Sibley owned $8 worth of produce, a horse, four cows, and a hog, but no oxen.

More a carpenter than a cabinetmaker, Sibley performed a variety of woodworking and farming jobs to fill the daylight hours (II-9). He is recorded as a furniture maker because a chest of drawers manifests more skill and thought than a hay rake and because furniture production accounted for the largest portion of his earnings. But that portion was only 28 percent of the total. As an active person in a rural setting, Sibley's work as a craftsman was eclipsed by his farm life.

The seasons of the year demanded diversity. Sibley made furniture in the winter and spring, leaving outside carpentry work for the late spring and autumn (II-10). He worked in the fields during the summer. Sibley also made hoes, rakes, and scythe snaths through the warmer months to coincide with the needs of his neighbors.

A chest-on-chest that descended in Sibley's family (and is attributed to him) (II-11) puts flesh on our impressions of his abilities and the functional needs and artistic expectations of his neighbors.[29] The chest, originally stained red, relies upon an elaborate bracket base to mask its simplicity. The two bottom drawer fronts conceal a single drawer, and the frame of the upper case was constructed differently from the lower case, although there is little doubt that the two sections were originally intended for one another. The dovetailing is irregular, and the mass of the lower chest could support a slightly larger upper case for better balance in overall design. But Sibley could not develop his skills through daily repetition, although the potential for excellence may have been there.

Rural tradesmen were as closely tied to shifts in local commerce as we are to fluctuations in the stock market or to the closing of a local factory. John Wheeler Geer (1753–1828) lived in the eastern Connecticut town of Preston and began to keep his account

II-9. *Distribution of Income: Solomon Sibley of Ward, 1793–1823*

Activity	Income	% of Total	Years
Furniture making	$210.95	27.7%	1793–1809
Carpentry (housewrighting, painting, and glazing)	168.65	22.2	1798–1818
Rake making	154.83½	20.3	1793–1823
General construction (yokes, carts, harrows, &c.)	96.07	12.1	1799–1821
Repair work	54.04½	6.8	1793–1823
Agricultural labor	40.01	5.3	1799–1819
Rental of horse, oxen, and cart	30.81	4.0	1802–1818
Cutlery	3.82	.4	1800–1823
Cooperage	3.04	.4	1796–1817
	$760.24	99.2%	

II-10. A Rural Tradesman's Composite Year: Solomon Sibley of Ward, 1793–1809

	Jan	Feb	Mar	Apr	May	June	July	Aug	Sept	Oct	Nov	Dec
A												
B												
C												
D												
E												
F												
G												
H												
I												
J												

KEY:

A. Furniture making. B. General construction (yokes, carts, harrows, &c.). C. Repair work. D. Carpentry (including housewrighting, painting, and glazing). E. Cooperage. F. Cutlery. G. Hoe making. H. Hay rakes (manufacture and repair). I. Grain cradles, scythe snaths & nibs, fork handles. J. Agricultural labor.

book at the age of twenty-one.[30] A year later (1775), Geer's estate was number 132 of 215 entries.[31] On September 3, 1778, he married Sally Denison.[32] By 1790 Geer was deriving 27 percent of his recorded earnings from furniture making and 24 percent from the rental of land, draft animals, and vehicles. He credited 17 percent of his earnings to carpentry, 11 percent to unskilled labor, 8 percent to produce, and 4 percent to housewrighting. Geer adapted to the woodworking demands of his neighbors, the agricultural year, and the trials of the Revolution. But war and inflation did not diminish his furniture making. Geer bartered 58 percent of the furniture that he made during his career between 1775 and 1781.

The postwar depression was another matter. In 1784, 1789, and 1794, Geer did not barter any furniture. He traded only 34 percent of the furniture that he made between 1782 and 1802. Although he occasionally made pieces of furniture for his neighbors through 1816, the financial woes of the 1780s forced him to alter his formula for making a living. In 1788 Geer bought the Oliver Sisson farm and a number of surrounding properties.[33] His family, which included five sons, turned to farming, a profitable choice. By 1791, his property ranked fifty-fifth among 126 estates.[34] He owned a horse, seven cows (no oxen), six acres of tillage, nineteen acres of mowing and open pasture, five acres of bog, and twenty-eight acres of brush pasture and was the wealthiest of his immediate family.[35] The value of his farm grew each year, and by 1796, it had increased

II-11. Chest-on-Chest. Attributed to Solomon Sibley (1769–1856), Ward (Auburn), Massachusetts, 1790–1810. Maple, chestnut, and white pine; H. 76¾ (194.9), W. 39½ (100.3); D. 20 (50.8). Old Sturbridge Village. *The chest-on-chest descended in the family of Solomon Sibley.*

II-12. Chest-on-Chest. Attributed to John Wheeler Geer (1753–1828), Preston, Connecticut, 1775–1800. Maple, white pine, and tulipwood; H. 86⅛ (218.8); W. 43¾ (111.1); D. 20⅞ (53.0). Lyman Allyn Museum. *The chest-on-chest descended in the family of Geer's brother David. Its drawer construction is identical to that of a chest with drawer signed by John Wheeler Geer.*

from £51:2:6 to £202:02:0.[36] Seven years later, Geer's estate ranked second in a partial listing.[37] In 1803, Geer earned only 7 percent of his livelihood from his furniture, and carpentry amounted to only 20 percent. He derived 56 percent of his recorded earnings from produce and another 11 percent from farm labor.

Although Geer was an accomplished cabinetmaker (II-12), his business was a casualty

II-13. The House and Shop of Samuel Wing, Sandwich, Massachusetts, photograph ca. 1900. Old Sturbridge Village. *Entrance to the shop was gained through the door at the extreme left of the ell. The view of the house, which was built in the late seventeenth century, and surrounding fields illustrates the bond between the Wing family and agriculture.*

of his prosperity. There were at least eight other furniture makers working in Preston during Geer's adult life.[38] After the market tightened, Geer reshuffled his priorities and, in later years, turned to weaving and shoemaking.

A generation later Samuel Wing (1774–1854) supplemented his small farming operation in Sandwich, on Cape Cod, as a woodworker (II-13).[39] Local patrons called upon him for turning and repair work; he made very few case pieces. The market did not warrant a large investment in time and materials, and he was involved in a variety of activities (II-14–16). Wing's commitment to any one of them was founded on the ageless need to make a living. Like most tradesmen in an agricultural economy, Wing could not afford to specialize. He relied upon diversity and change as he tried to fill his working time to best advantage.

Wing's account book reveals that he had nearly concluded his career as a furniture maker by 1808.[40] Perhaps Jefferson's Embargo Act of 1807 caused Wing to change his course. Responding to the British impressment of American sailors, Jefferson believed that the United States could starve Britain into respecting American sovereignty. The embargo forbade ships flying the Stars and Stripes to sail into foreign waters and banned certain English goods. Yankee shipping was strangled in the process. Boston merchants

II-14. *Occupational Change: Furniture Production, 1800–1809, Samuel Wing of Sandwich*

	1800	1801	1802	1803	1804	1805	1806	1807	1808	1809
A	■	■	■	■	■	■	■	■	■	
B	■	■	■	■	■	■	■	■	■	
C			■	■	■	■	■	■	■	
D			■	■	■	■	■			
E		■	■	■	■	■	■	■	■	
F		■	■	■	■	■				
G		■	■	■						

KEY:

A. Tables. B. Chairs. C. Bedsteads. D. Chests. E. Desks. F. Trunks. G. Clockcases.

II-15. *Occupational Change: General Woodworking and Other Services, 1800–1809, Samuel Wing of Sandwich*

	1800	1801	1802	1803	1804	1805	1806	1807	1808	1809
A			■	■	■	■	■	■		
B			■	■	■	■	■			
C						■	■	■	■	
D								■	■	■
E						■	■	■		
F				■	■	■				
G			■	■						

KEY:

A. Turning tool handles and parts. B. Carpentry and mending. C. Boatmaking (15 boats). D. Shinglemaking (56,500 shingles). E. Sale of paint goods. F. Rental of horse and cart. G. Shoemaking (95 prs.). (Quantities are totals for the decade.)

II-16. *Occupational Change: Agricultural Transactions, 1800–1809, Samuel Wing of Sandwich*

	1800	1801	1802	1803	1804	1805	1806	1807	1808	1809
A	■	■	■	■	■	■	■			
B			■	■	■	■	■			
C	■	■	■	■	■	■	■	■	■	■
D	■				■	■	■			

KEY:

A. English hay (3,972 lb.). B. Beef (849½ lb.) and pork (114 lb.). C. Lumber (29,000 ft.). D. Apples (18 bu.) and potatoes (37 bu.). (Quantities are totals for the decade.)

were forced to turn their vessels to the less profitable coastal trade.[41] Samuel Wing took advantage of the cheap transportation and enforced dependence on local industry by developing a lumber trade. The same trade system made fashionable Boston furniture more accessible to his customers.

The career changes of Geer and Wing scour away most of the romanticism attached to early craftsmanship. Like today, prosperity depended upon a steady stream of similar contracts, not on a desire for self-fulfillment. For Geer and Wing, the time arrived to find something better to do.

Many furniture makers who worked in agricultural communities or small coastal towns, however, did not reflect the characteristics typical of rural joiners such as Mather, Sibley, Geer, and Wing. Those who pursued atypical careers before the War of 1812 show the impact of special environmental conditions on their training and working patterns.

John Gaines II (1677–1748) and his son Thomas I (1712–1761) were turners in the Essex County, Massachusetts, town of Ipswich (II-17). Their account book, between 1707 and 1761, documents the careers of two tradesmen in the same small coastal community during the first half of the eighteenth century.[42] John II made 1183 chairs, deriving 62 percent of his recorded earnings between 1707 and 1725 from furniture, mostly chairs.[43] He credited another tenth of his earnings to his making buttons, fans, and handles and his carpentry, and 12 percent to the barter of produce. His unskilled labor and the rental of draft animals and farm implements amounted to 9 percent, leaving a miscellany of 5 percent.

The large volume of chairs and the probable consignment of furniture to ships' captains in the coastal trade afforded Gaines an urban level of specialization. The production of chairs accounted for 53 percent of his livelihood; only 35 percent of Gaines's recorded earnings were unrelated to his trade as a turner.[44] However, he sold only a tenth of his furniture during the fertile months of June through September, when he and his neighbors were actively farming. John II was bound to the seasonal economy of Ipswich.

Despite the population growth and an improvement in the standard of living, Thomas Gaines I maintained the same balance of work activities in Ipswich as had his father. Between 1750 and 1755, the younger Gaines derived 69 percent of his recorded earnings from furniture making, 7 percent more than his father. Only 4 percent of his earnings were the product of carpentry, 6 percent less than John II, but 14 percent came from unskilled agricultural labor and the rental of animals and vehicles, 5 percent more than his father. He too gained 12 percent of his earnings by trading produce.[45] Thomas bartered only 17 percent of the recorded value of his furniture during the warm summer months, and he traded only a fifth of the value of his produce between the fertile months of April and September. There is no difference in the financial histories of the Gaineses; Thomas derived 57 percent of his earnings throughout his career from the barter of chairs, only 4 percent more than John II.[46]

II-17. Side Chair. Attributed to John Gaines II (1677–1748) or Thomas Gaines I (1712–1761), Ipswich, Massachusetts, 1720–1745. Maple and white pine; H. 46 (116.8); W. 18¼ (46.4); SEAT D. 12 (30.5); SEAT H. 16¼ (41.3). John Whipple House, Ipswich Historical Society. *The chair descended in the Appleton family of Ipswich.*

Before the Revolution, cabinetmakers in coastal towns speculated by making furniture for trade in the South and in the West Indies.[47] The Revolution snapped these trade routes and brought depression to many urban artisans. Lemuel Tobey (1749–1829) was such a tradesman in the small port of Dartmouth, Massachusetts. He was twenty-four years old in 1773, and was beginning to establish himself as a cabinetmaker when talk of rebellion filled the taverns.[48]

The years 1773 and 1774 were relatively good ones for Tobey.[49] Of his goods and services, valued at least at £196:11:4, 68 percent was derived from furniture making, 14 percent from venture cargo. Tobey recorded the sale of maple, mahogany, walnut, and cedar furniture in his ledgers. Only 4 percent of his earnings were from repair work and woodworking unrelated to furniture. The value of his field labor was 1 percent. Tobey's remaining earnings, at least 26 percent of his credits in 1773 and 1774, came from marketing lumber and fish.

Then came the shot heard 'round the world. Tobey initially augmented his income by making cartridge boxes, but rebellion burst into war, and colonial governments began to press their citizens for more taxes and produce to sustain the military. As inflation tightened its grip during 1776 and 1777, Tobey's goods and services earned him only £87:17:0. (Perhaps he spent some time away from his shop in the army.) Tobey's earnings from cabinetmaking dropped to 57 percent. His Majesty's Navy put a stop to coastal trade, and Tobey recorded only one mahogany table as venture cargo. His carpentry and agricultural labor plummeted to only a few shillings. Apparently his neighbors were doing their own chores, saving their resources for the tax collector. However, the volume of Tobey's repair work (3 percent), produce (34 percent), and miscellaneous earnings (4 percent) all rose as people began to make do with what they had and to concentrate on the necessities of life.

On September 5, 1778, the British burned Dartmouth.[50] Tobey's daybook for the months between 1778 and 1780 is missing. There may have been little to record; commerce was at a standstill, and inflation was uncontrolled. The theater of war, however, had moved south. During 1780 and 1781, Tobey valued his goods and services at £35:5:10. Cabinetmaking again amounted to two thirds of his earnings, but the worth attached to his furniture was only £23:12:6. Tobey's carpentry (5 percent), repair work (9 percent), and miscellaneous labor (10 percent) all increased, probably because he was forced to expand his earning power and because patching was all that his neighbors could afford. But Tobey's sale of produce slumped to only 8 percent of his total income as Cornwallis's surrender approached. The war had taken its toll, and everyone in New England's towns felt the pinch of commercial stagnation. Although Dartmouth was a small port, Tobey's high degree of specialization clearly marked him as an urban tradesman with too much sail when the storm struck.

In 1766, a young joiner named Samuel Gaylord, Jr. (1742–1816), began to keep regular accounts in the Connecticut Valley town of Hadley, Massachusetts.[51] Like the Gaineses, who specialized as turners, Gaylord at first glance also lacked one hallmark of the typical farmer-artisan: he did little farming. Instead, Gaylord worked for prosperous farmers, trading his skills as a joiner (II-18) for produce. Despite this partial independence from farming, Gaylord was a rural cabinetmaker in the farmer-artisan tradition.[52] He applied his woodworking skills to tasks choreographed by the annual needs of his neighbors and by the caprice of the weather.

Gaylord was briefly married to Submit Dickinson of Hatfield in 1766.[53] Four years later he married Penelope Williams, who bore him eight children before 1789; Gaylord provided well for them. In 1770, the newlyweds' estate was appraised at £45:10:0, fifty-eighth on a list of 104 taxable properties.[54] The average evaluation was £48:9:0. At the age of twenty-eight years, Samuel Gaylord, Jr., was firmly lodged in Hadley's broad middle class.

Gaylord's establishment as a joiner, however, followed a course guided more by necessity than choice. During 1767 and 1768, he derived 13 percent of his recorded earnings from furniture making. Miscellaneous woodworking, repair work, and unskilled labor amounted to only 3 percent. Sixty-nine percent of his livelihood came from housewrighting and related carpentry. Cabinetmaking was only a sideline, but he sold 77 percent of his furniture from December through April. He recorded no earnings from contracting during January through March, when it was too cold to work outside on buildings, and during June and July, when he tilled his garden and the fields of his neighbors.

II-18. Side Chair. Attributed to Samuel Gaylord, Jr. (1742–1816), Hadley, Massachusetts, 1775. Maple; H. 42½ (107.9); W. 20½ (52.1); SEAT D. 16⅛ (41.0); SEAT H. 18½ (47.0). Porter-Phelps-Huntington House Museum. *Gaylord remodeled the house of Charles Phelps, called Forty Acres, in 1775 and 1786. Gaylord also made the "banister" chairs for Phelps in 1775. The banisters in the front hall are quite similar in feeling to the turned elements of this chair, which descended in the Phelps family.*

Ten years later Gaylord had drastically altered the balance of his work activities. In 1777 and 1778, a time of financial disaster for Lemuel Tobey and other urban tradesmen, Gaylord gleaned 44 percent of his livelihood from cabinetmaking, but his contracting work plummeted to 14 percent. Perhaps uncertainty about the future and the major expense of house raising was prohibitive during the inflationary years of the Revolution. However, unlike Dartmouth, where maritime commerce was disrupted by the Royal Navy, the inland towns of the Connecticut Valley prospered as cattle-raising centers for the war effort.[55] Gaylord adjusted the focus of his skills. General woodworking, which included the construction of farm implements, rose to 25 percent, and repair work nudged its way to 7 percent of his recorded earnings. Whereas before Gaylord had kept the warmer months free for housewrighting and field work, now his furniture accounts were more evenly distributed throughout the seasons of the prosperous years during the Revolution. He produced 60 percent of his cabinetwork during June of 1777 and 1778 alone.

By 1787 and 1788, Gaylord's division of working time had stabilized. He credited 47 percent of his recorded earnings to cabinetmaking, only 3 percent more than during the war years. Contracting held at 17 percent of his livelihood, perhaps because of the postwar depression and the collapse of the cattle market. General woodworking and repair work fell to 14 percent, but his bartering of produce rose from practically nothing to a tenth of his earnings. Gaylord's children were old enough to do heavy chores, and he may have put them to work. The seasonal distribution of his cabinetmaking accounts returned to its prewar balance. He traded 91 percent of his furniture during the cooler months of January through April.

Like Lemuel Tobey, Gaylord's working patterns were altered by the Revolution. Different economic circumstances in another region, however, allowed Gaylord to exercise his flexibility as a rural joiner and to apply his chisels to different tasks within his trade. Between 1763 and 1790, Gaylord made no fewer than 1982 finished objects in his shop (independent of contracting jobs). As in Geer's case, the decade after 1773, when he tackled two thirds of these items, was the most productive. With the exception of 1777, the year of Burgoyne's invasion from Canada and the greatest military threat to the Connecticut Valley, Gaylord found himself in an agricultural economy that was drawing substantial credit (albeit inflated) into the system through the sale of produce to the government. The failure of the British to crush the colonial rebellion lay in their inability to upset the standard of living in rural towns.[56]

Most rural New England towns were characterized by extensive cousinage. (Scratch one cousin, and they all bleed.) Yankee independence quietly included the approbation of the family, which kept town meeting democracy running smoothly by laying the foundation for compromise and an understanding of the greater good, or else.[57] The lessons learned were that no one prospers alone in a small town and that only a fool would overlook the line of steady customers in church or at town meeting. Assured of food, company, and a bed under the eaves, members of large families often capitalized on a built-in division of labor and committed their work time to one basic medium, such as wood. They marketed their goods more widely because more hands were turned to the task, and they became less sensitive to the demands of the agricultural year as individuals.

In New Hampshire, the Dunlap family of cabinetmakers was led by the brothers John (1746–1792) and Samuel (1752–1830). At least eleven of their sons, grandsons, and cousins also followed the joiner's trade (see page 170). They worked, often together, in the small Merrimack Valley towns of Chester, Goffstown, Bedford, Henniker, Salisbury, and Antrim, which were largely settled by people of Scotch-Irish descent.[58] Familiar with their religion, customs, and tastes, the Dunlaps supplied New Hampshire's Scotch-Irish with distinctive furniture. Their unique decorative motifs, like the "flowered ogee" molding, and the volume of surviving pieces of furniture from the Dunlap school show that they hit upon a successful formula and capitalized upon it (II-19, chest no. 25, high chest no. 42).

The Dunlap style was perpetuated by both family members and apprentices. Although the lure of land and opportunity in the American wilderness undermined the traditional rigidity of Europe's guild system in the colonies, many craftsmen in rural New England formalized their training agreements with adolescent boys.[59] The customary instruction period of seven years was usually shortened. William Houston (1755–1830) of Bedford was apprenticed to John only from March 1775 to July 1776, according to his indenture of apprenticeship.[60] Houston closely emulated his master's sense of scale and use of decorative motifs. He signed his name on a chest-on-chest (II-19), although he may not have been the sole creator. A slight variation in furniture construction may indicate the work of two men, not the sloppiness of one.

Many apprenticeships, particularly to family members, were less formal. But whether begun formally or casually, they did not always succeed. Samuel Willard wrote to Judge James Hooker of Guilford, Connecticut, on June 8, 1738, regarding Hezekiah May of Wethersfield and an apprentice:

> . . . my Ward has been of very unstedy Disposition & I have mett with Great Deal of Dificulty Relateing to him; about two years agoe I thought he chose the trade of Joyner:
> . . . Constantly, he chose Mr May of Weathersfield & was with him about six months (I think) but stedy Business & strict government being what he could never bear; He Ran away from him; for no other Reasons as ever I could Learn w[he]n he came to me again he attempted to set up for himselfe, but with some Dificulty I Reduced him to my Care again . . . he has a mind to learn the trade of Shoe makeing.[61]

II-19. High Chest. William Houston (1755–1830), probably working in the shop of Major John Dunlap, Bedford, New Hampshire, ca. 1780. Maple and white pine; H. 83¼ (211.5); W. 41⅞ (106.4); D. 20¹⁵/₁₆ (53.2). Henry Francis du Pont Winterthur Museum. *The high chest of drawers is inscribed "Willᵐ Houston" and "J Miller 1780."*

The personality of the master and the cultural environment were transmitted to the work of his apprentices, becoming a highway for the development, travel, and evolution of fashion trends. Eliphalet Chapin (1741–1807) was a cabinetmaker who worked in East Windsor, Connecticut. After his training, Chapin left Connecticut and worked as a journeyman in Philadelphia during the late 1760s.[62] The differences between the furniture in vogue in Pennsylvania during Chapin's three years there and acceptable fashion back home in the land of steady habits were distinct. A side chair made by Chapin in 1781 at East Windsor, after his return from Pennsylvania, reflects the impact of both environments upon his work (I-52). The qualities of Philadelphia craftsmanship are seen in Chapin's use of rounded back posts below the seat rail, tenons extending from the rear of the side seat rails completely through the back posts, and round corner blocks constructed of two pieces of pine.[63] Nevertheless, Chapin used cherry as a primary wood and pared away the elaborate and expensive carving often seen on Philadelphia furniture.

Chapin did not make his stylish furniture for his own satisfaction as much as for that of his customers. The upper strata of citizens north of Hartford patronized Chapin and other cabinetmakers because they believed that their woodworking skills best portrayed their social station. The craftsman, or "mechanick," as early tradesmen were called, had to be responsive to the fashion consciousness of his customers. John Chester of Wethersfield wrote to Joshua Huntington of Norwich on July 4, 1782, that he

> was in hopes to have procured those articles at least some cheaper. They still appear to me to be very unreasonably high considering the scarcity of hard Cash. The Chairs we will have, but as for the other articles. . . . If we can procure them *Cheaper* we *shall,* and I think we *can,* unless Mahogany is much dearer than I am aware. Huntington [Felix, of Norwich (1749–1822)] has rather raised the price of Bureaus. I understand [from] you he asked £7 for one swell'd and trimmed [serpentine front with brass pulls]. £6 is certainly higher for a plain one without trimmings.[64]

Just as today, the eighteenth-century consumer pursued the best value in the marketplace. The cabinetmaker responded to his customers' needs and, once a bargain had been struck, produced a useful piece of fashionable furniture.

Today a sense of regionality persists in New England, but the cultural distinctiveness of those regions in the "back of beyond" has dissipated. Even before the thundering arrival of the machine age, vernacular furniture reflected a change in the cultural and economic climate sustained by cabinetmaker and customer. Men like Richard Ransom (1740–1811) of Lyme, Connecticut, announced this change in the May 15, 1767, *New-London Gazette* when he became the first Connecticut joiner to advertise.[65] Slowly, urban marketing procedures and specialization spread up the valleys. In 1792, "at a meeting of the Cabinet-makers, held in the City," Hartford furniture makers agreed to a detailed price list and price fixing.[66] Four years later, "the House-Joiners and Cabinetmakers" in rural Hampshire County, Massachusetts, met at Hatfield in the Connecticut Valley to compose separate price lists.[67] Rural conservatism persisted, however, and

II-20. Chest of Drawers. S. (G.?) Stedman, Norwich, Vermont, 1800–1820. Cherry, mahogany cross-banding, tulipwood, and white pine; H. 34⅞ (88.6); W. 41⅝ (105.7); D. 20⅛ (51.1). Henry Francis du Pont Winterthur Museum.

many woodworkers, like William Mather, did not specialize in either trade. Furthermore, among the itemized furniture forms were older designs, such as high chests with "scroll'd heads," already abandoned by the urban enthusiasts of neoclassical furniture.

The impact of a changing New England is visible in a chest of drawers (II-20) "Made by S [G?] Stedman / Norwich / Vt" in about 1810 in the new "French" style, with flared feet, veneered surfaces, and inlay. The chest is constructed of cherry and decorated with variegated inlay, both popular in Connecticut. But it incorporates a swelled façade popular on Boston chests of the mid-eighteenth century, similar to contemporary French provincial furniture. The hybrid chest is "trimm'd" with brasses stamped with the nation's new symbol.

The methods of manufacture and transportation improved after the War of 1812, and rural furniture makers found a larger audience and a call to specialize. Industrialization weakened the grip of the agricultural year, and the trades of cabinetmaking and carpentry grew apart in rural New England as cabinetmaking and joinery had in the urban centers a century before. Rural New England cabinetmakers turned to manufacturing furniture for Americans rather than for their Yankee friends and neighbors.

1. Chase Papers, 1732–1800, Ledger 1, 1–50, New Hampshire Historical Society.

2. Ibid., 28, 30, 51.

3. Jorgensen, *Guide to New England's Landscape*, 15–61; Andrews, *Colonial Period of American History*, 1:249–99, 462–519, 2:1–194; Clark, *Eastern Frontier*, 334–59; [Sewall,] *Diary of Samuel Sewall*, 256–58, 319n–21n, 829–32, 854–55;

Dwight, *Travels in New England*, 1:217–27, 346–79, 2:1–195, 253–333.

4. Van Deventer, *Emergence of Provincial New Hampshire*, 12–15, 28–30, 75–77, 130–31, 159–78; Andrews, *Colonial Period of American History*, 1:297–99. New Hampshire was governed by Massachusetts between 1641 and 1680 and again between 1689 and 1692. Between 1698 and 1741,

New Hampshire was governed as a separate royal province, but shared royal governors with Massachusetts. The Plymouth Colony was annexed to Massachusetts in 1691.

5. Clark, *Eastern Frontier*, 97–98, 101, 116.

6. Ibid.; Trent, *Hearts & Crowns*, 39–43; Forman, "Crown and York Chairs."

7. Bridenbaugh, *Fat Mutton and Liberty of Conscience*, 93–126.

8. Zea, "New Hampshire Grant Town," 1–30.

9. Daniell, *Experiment in Republicanism*, 52; Belknap, *History of New Hampshire*, 61–62, 153, 191–92.

10. Daniell, *Experiment in Republicanism*, 145–62.

11. Kurath, *Linguistic Geography of New England*, 1–18.

12. Evans, "Unsophisticated Furniture Made and Used in Philadelphia and Environs," 151–203.

13. Kirk, "Sources of Some American Regional Furniture," 790–98; Gilbert, "Regional Traditions in English Vernacular Furniture," 43–77; Kane, "Seventeenth-Century Furniture of the Connecticut Valley," 79–122.

14. John Marsh's inventory, September 1725, Hampshire County (Mass.) Probate, 4 (1708–80): 138–40. Marsh's will, June 5, 1725, ibid., 4:134. Judd, *History of Hadley*, 91–92; Fales, *American Painted Furniture*, 20–23. A cupboard was not included in the inventory of Marsh's estate.

15. Rhoades and Jobe, "Recent Discoveries in Boston Japanned Furniture," 1082–91; Fales, "Boston Japanned Furniture," 49–69; Hill, "History and Technique of Japanning," 59–84. The high chest of drawers made by John Pimm and perhaps japanned by Robert Davis has such jackals and birds on its sides.

16. Warren, "Were the Guilford Painted Chests Made in Saybrook?," 1–10; "Connecticut Cabinetmakers, Part 1," 126–27; Fales, *American Painted Furniture*, 24. The high chest of drawers may have been made and painted by Charles Gillam, who died in 1727.

17. Bjerkoe, *Cabinetmakers of America*, 216–18; Myers and Mayhew, *New London County Furniture*, 75.

18. Forman, "Urban Aspects," 15–20.

19. *New Hampshire Provincial Probate Records*, 1–4 (1649–1713), New Hampshire State Archives and Records Management Division, Concord. These figures must be qualified. Most of the men in the sample died after their most productive years. They may have lived with their children during their old age, altering the composition of their household contents. The tools in each inventory may have gone untouched for years.

20. Edward Clarke's inventory, June 17, 1675, *New Hampshire Provincial Probate Records*, 1 (1655–98): 157–59; *Probate Records of New Hampshire*, 167–68.

21. Zea, "William Mather"; Temple, *History of Whately*, 191.

22. Crafts, *History of Whately*, 306.

23. Jonathan Colton Loomis, Account Book, 1806–22, Joseph Downs Manuscript Collection, Winterthur Museum Libraries.

24. Mather Account Book, 30.

25. Sibley Account Book, 1793–1840, Old Sturbridge Village Research Library.

26. State Tax Inventory of Ward, 1797, Town Hall, Auburn, Mass.

27. "Minister's Tax for the Year 1801," Town Hall, Auburn, Mass.

28. "Valuation of the Year 1805," Town Hall, Auburn, Mass.

29. The chest-on-chest stood in the Sibley House at Auburn until 1971.

30. Myers and Mayhew, *New London County Furniture*, 58–59, 118. Geer's account book (1774–1816) is in the Connecticut Historical Society Library.

31. Phillips, *Griswold*, 341–43.

32. Geer, *Geer Genealogy*, 28–29, 48.

33. Norman, *Meet Our Craftsmen*, 13–16.

34. Grand List of the First Society of Preston, 1791; Town Vault, Preston, Conn.

35. Tax Inventory of Preston, 1791, Town Vault, Preston, Conn.

36. Ibid., 1796.

37. Highway Tax List of 1803 (incomplete), Preston Town Papers, Connecticut Historical Society Library.

38. Norman, *Meet Our Craftsmen*.

39. Harlow, "Shop of Samuel Wing," 372–77.

40. Wing Account Book, 1800–09, Old Sturbridge Village Research Library.

41. Morison, *Oxford History of the American People*, 373–75.

42. Gaines Account Book, 1707–61, Joseph Downs Manuscript Collection, Winterthur Museum Libraries.

43. Hendrick, "John Gaines II and Thomas Gaines I," 78. It should be noted that a ledger may not contain complete accounts. There was little reason to record transactions settled immediately.

44. Ibid., 67.

45. Hendrick found in his analysis of the Gaineses that John II derived 22 percent of his

earnings from the barter of produce, but that Thomas's surplus produce accounted for only 5 percent of his livelihood. Twenty-six years of Thomas's work is recorded in the ledger; his father made entries for forty-two years. The present study considers the careers of the two Ipswich men at roughly the same age.

46. Hendrick, "John Gaines II and Thomas Gaines I," 95–96.

47. Ott, "Exports of Furniture," 135–41.

48. *Dartmouth Vital Records*, I:277.

49. Daybooks (1773–78, 1780–82) of Lemuel Tobey of Dartmouth, Mass., Old Sturbridge Village Research Library.

50. Ellis, *History of New Bedford*, 109–41.

51. Gaylord Account Book, 1763–90, Henry N. Flynt Library, Historic Deerfield.

52. Samuel Gaylord, Jr.'s in-law Eliakim Smith was also a cabinetmaker in Hadley before his death in 1775.

53. Judd, *History of Hadley*, 55.

54. Ibid., 69.

55. Sheldon, *History of Deerfield*, 2:705–6.

56. Shy, "The American Revolution," 126, 128–29, 142, 144–45, 149, 154.

57. Zuckerman, *Peaceable Kingdoms*, 72–84.

58. Parsons, *Dunlaps*, 2–4, 33–35; *Plain & Elegant*, 17–18, 90–93, 112–13, 144; Dibble, "Major John Dunlap," 50–58.

59. Bridenbaugh, *Colonial Craftsman*, 129–41.

60. Parsons, *Dunlaps*, 53; *Plain & Elegant*, 50–51, 147.

61. Samuel Willard to James Hooker, Saybrook, June 7, 1738, "Connecticut Cabinetmakers, Part 2," 2.

62. Bjerkoe, *Cabinetmakers of America*, 59–62. A privately owned letter documents Chapin's presence in Philadelphia.

63. Kirk, *Connecticut Furniture*, 131.

64. John Chester to Joshua Huntington, Wethersfield, July 4, 1782, Huntington Papers, Connecticut Historical Society Collections, 20 (1923): 159–60, 171.

65. "Connecticut Cabinetmakers, Part 2." According to Houghton Bulkeley, Ransom was the earliest Connecticut furniture maker to advertise.

66. Ibid., 34–36; Montgomery, *American Furniture*, 19–26, 488. The original imprint is deposited at Watkinson Library, Trinity College, Hartford.

67. Fales, *Furniture of Historic Deerfield*, 286. The original imprint is deposited at the Historical Society of Pennsylvania.

III. Construction Methods and Materials

Philip Zea

The methods and materials used by furniture craftsmen in the American colonies can be discerned through a clear and consistent examination of the appearance, the joints, and the surfaces of their furniture. Practical attention to an object's components is at the heart of the New Englander's retort to his new neighbor, who, having watched the old-timer lead a horse with a logging chain into the woods, asked, "Why are you dragging that chain?" "Eva try to push one?" the Yankee replied. Similarly, an analysis of a piece of furniture leads to an understanding of its design, assembly, and function.

The chairmaker had to build a chair that would support the sitter. The cabinetmaker had to assemble the parts of a chest into a system for storing clothes. With a firm understanding of their tools and their materials — for example, the fixed set of properties inherent in each species of wood — craftsmen followed a logical and efficient course through the processes of design, selection of lumber, assembly, and finishing. Long before smoke curled from the first factory of the Industrial Revolution, the construction of furniture relied on design plans, efficient procedures, and multiplication of parts.

The principles of furniture design were based on those of architecture. "Of all the Arts which are either improved or ornamented by Architecture," wrote Thomas Chippendale, "that of CABINET-MAKING is not only the most useful and ornamental, but capable of receiving as great assistance from it as any whatever."[1] Many joiners and cabinetmakers used drafting tools to lay out plans for house frames, interior woodwork, and furniture. The surviving plans of cabinetmakers (III-1) show that they perceived a piece of furniture as a unified assemblage of parts. In a way, furniture makers were architects whose plans allowed form and function to coexist. They designed each piece of furniture with both scale and construction in mind; failure meant that the object could either look ugly or topple to the floor.

Many of the furniture maker's most successful products assumed architectural proportions. The design of a tall clock (III-2) corresponds to that of a Tuscan column.[2] The clockcase was conceived as a column divided into eight parts or circles. The diameter of one circle defined the width of the case, and the diameter of two circles the height of the hood (or entablature). The diameter of a circle from the midpoint of the hood plotted

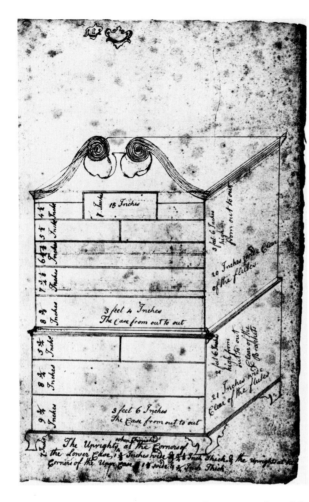

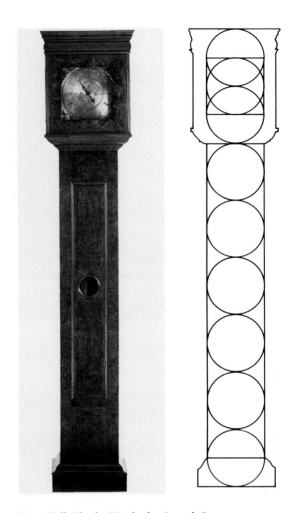

III-1. Design for a Chest-on-Chest. Samuel Mickle, drawn in the shop of Jonathan Shoemaker, Philadelphia, ca. 1766. Philadelphia Museum of Art.

III-2. Tall Clock. Works by Joseph Lawrence, possibly Long Island, New York, 1710–1730. Walnut and tulipwood; H. 90⅜ (229.6); W. 17⁹/₁₆ (44.6); D. 11³/₁₆ (28.4). Henry Francis du Pont Winterthur Museum. *The clock mechanism is not original to the case, although the two were combined at an early date.*

the height and width of the face. The system of proportions varies from joiner to joiner, thus forming — even when the identities of the joiners are not known — a partial signature of a shop at a particular time.

The production of identical tables and chests in a shop sprang from fixed concepts of the right way to execute a design. Efficiency demanded consistency, and consistency was derived from templates, marking gauges, and calipers, tools that assure the "workmanship of certainty."[3] Freehand work, like carving, manifests the "workmanship of risk." Such embellishment is time-consuming, expensive, and threatens total loss with a false move. Carefully planed drawer bottoms or chamfered glue blocks were also extra touches of quality, which cost the craftsman more hours. Time was a factor in design and

III-3. Unfinished Windsor Chair Seats. The shop of Samuel Wing (1774–1854), Sandwich, Massachusetts, 1800–1810. White pine. Old Sturbridge Village. Photograph, Henry Peach.

workmanship even in a barter economy. The step-by-step implementation of furniture design is evident in the sequence of unfinished Windsor chair seats (III-3) made by Samuel Wing at Sandwich, Massachusetts, in about 1800.

Apprenticeships perpetuated consistency and over time established a shop tradition that put a hallmark on local fashion. This phenomenon is best illustrated by the work of two pewterers (III-4). The cann on the right was made by Joseph Danforth in Middletown, Connecticut, in about 1780. It is almost identical to the cann on the left, which was made by Samuel Pierce of Greenfield, Massachusetts, in about 1795. Pierce is believed to have apprenticed to Danforth and thus to have been influenced by his master's sense of design and his molds. Together, the two canns illustrate a preference for a particular pattern in the Connecticut Valley.

Although the designs of early furniture and other decorative arts reflect regional tastes, there are many gray areas because shop production varied with the peregrinations of journeymen and apprentices and with changes in fashion. Today, people may look at a chest and call it Frothingham or Chapin, meaning that the proportions, materials, and details of the chest relate to the documented work of a known shop. However, many such attributions are cavalier. Numerous men and boys passed through shops in busy market towns. Benjamin Frothingham and Eliphalet Chapin did not construct from scratch every object made from their templates or copies of their templates. As a result, their products contain measures of both conformity and idiosyncrasy.

The appearance of a particular design combined with distinctive construction methods is important evidence for identifying the origins of furniture. Yet two shops in the same town might sell markedly different cabinetwork. For example, a chest of drawers (III-5) made in Hartford in about 1790 by John Wells incorporates features normally associated with eastern Massachusetts and New Hampshire furniture (I-31). A desk and bookcase (III-6) inscribed "George Belden Hartford May 6, 1791" is quite different from the Wells chest but is virtually identical to a desk and bookcase that was made some forty miles away by Erastus Grant of Westfield, Massachusetts.[4] Belden and Wells, though working simultaneously in Hartford, were not trained in the same shop tradition; Belden and Grant, as their furniture suggests, were.

III-4 (top). Pewter Canns. *Left:* Samuel Pierce (1767–1840), Greenfield, Massachusetts, 1792–1810. H. 5¹¹/₁₆ (14.4). *Right:* Joseph Danforth, Sr. (1758–1788), Middletown, Connecticut, 1780–1788. H. 5¹¹/₁₆ (14.4). Historic Deerfield. Photograph, Bob Laramie.

III-5 (bottom). Chest of Drawers. John Wells (1769–1832), Hartford, 1790–1800. Mahogany grain painting on birch and white pine; H. 33½ (85.1); W. 38⅝ (98.1); D. 19¾ (50.2). Connecticut Historical Society.

III-6. Desk and Bookcase. George Belden (1770–1838), Hartford, 1791. Cherry and white pine; H. 83¼ (211.5); W. 42½ (108.0); D. 20¼ (51.4). Wadsworth Atheneum. Photograph, Joseph Szaszfai.

The confusing plurality of shop traditions is complicated by the American penchant for seeking greener pastures and by the desires of paying customers. A chest of drawers (III-7) illustrates the adaptability of tradesmen as they traveled. The chest is constructed of cherry and white pine, a combination often found in Connecticut furniture. The fluted quarter columns and the overall proportions of the chest also point to Connecticut

III-7. Chest of Drawers. Thomas Bliss (1767–1839) and John W. Horswill, Charlestown, New Hampshire, 1798. Cherry and white pine; H. 35 (88.9); W. 41⅛ (104.5); D. 21 (53.3). Private collection. Photograph, Bill Finney; courtesy, New Hampshire Historical Society. *Bliss and Horswill worked in partnership for only four months, December 1797–March 1798.*

origins. A detail generally inconsistent with the work of Connecticut cabinetmakers in the eighteenth century is the use of glue blocks to reinforce the drawer bottoms; this practice is normally associated with coastal shops in Massachusetts and Rhode Island. However, the chest was made in the upper Connecticut River valley at Charlestown, New Hampshire, in 1798 by the firm of Thomas Bliss and John W. Horswill. Their label states that they were "of Boston," where Bliss was born in 1766. Horswill is believed to have come from Rhode Island.[5] The chest shows that Bliss and Horswill, as master cabinetmakers, superimposed local design preferences and materials on their knowledge of furniture technology acquired in the Boston and Narragansett Bay areas.

Cabinetmakers knew that the properties of wood varied from species to species; that the shrinkage, flexibility, durability, malleability, attractiveness, and weight of each wood gave it different technical advantages. We call the woods that cabinetmakers used for exterior surfaces of furniture primary. The woods that form the interior construction elements, such as drawer bottoms and glue blocks, are called secondary. The principal primary hardwoods in New England furniture are ash, birch, cherry, mahogany, maple, oak, poplar, and walnut; each was available in several varieties. Ash was a favorite wood of turners in the seventeenth century because it was sturdy and easily worked on a lathe when freshly cut, or green. Burled ash was sometimes used as a colorful veneer on William and Mary furniture. In the eighteenth century, ash was occasionally a secondary wood. Birch, although subject to warping, served as a primary wood in northern New England and was often stained to imitate mahogany. Cherry was used extensively by cabinetmakers in Connecticut and along the Connecticut Valley because wide boards were plentiful. It was easily worked with planes and chisels and finished to an attractive red color or stained mahogany. Mahogany was exported to New England from the West Indies and, because of its expense, was used almost exclusively by cabinetmakers in seaports. Maple, plentiful throughout New England, was the most versatile of furniture woods. It was attractive, reacted well to most tools because of its tight grain, and resisted scarring. Oak, both red and white, was widely used by seventeenth-century joiners. They were able to split, or rive, the wood into usable shapes instead of sawing it, thus saving time. Poplar, lightweight and relatively free of knots, was favored as a primary wood in the early eighteenth century and was always painted. Black walnut, imported from the southern colonies, was a durable wood that took a good, dark finish. Walnut moldings were applied to the stylish joined furniture of the late seventeenth century and walnut veneers ornamented William and Mary case furniture. Walnut remained the principal decorative wood in urban centers during the first half of the eighteenth century and a common primary wood in seaports until the Revolution. Many of these woods, particularly ash, maple, oak, and poplar, were also used as secondary woods in New England furniture.

Among secondary woods, the ubiquitous eastern white pine was the most popular. This conifer was plentiful, lightweight, easily sawn, easily glued, and available in wide boards. A considerable amount of furniture was made entirely of white pine and was painted. Hard yellow pine, called pitch pine, was used as a secondary wood throughout inland New England. In the Connecticut Valley, it was often used as a primary wood and painted. Although a conifer, yellow pine is tough and straight-grained but somewhat unattractive. Red cedar, straight-grained and lightweight, were used for applied moldings on some early joined furniture in New England. The imported red cedar was insect-resistant; it was occasionally used for drawer linings and in some instances as a primary wood by Boston cabinetmakers. Chestnut was favored as a secondary wood in southern New England, particularly in Rhode Island and occasionally in some Boston-area work. It planes easily when green, is very strong, and does not expand or contract greatly with changes in the weather. Beech, a tight-grained wood, was sometimes used in eastern New England as a secondary wood. Tulipwood, lightweight, easy to work, and knot free, was employed as a common secondary wood in southern New England.

Joiners and cabinetmakers throughout the Northeast benefited from the great variety of trees. Virtually everything, from agricultural implements and fuel to buildings and furniture, was made of wood. Each species had at least one desirable property and was put to good purpose. Inconsistency or an exotic use of woods in furniture is not always an indication of modern repair and replacement. A handy billet on the woodpile was turned into that final baluster or became that last drawer bottom. In a dressing table from York, Maine (no. 33), one drawer bottom is elm, normally used for wagon tongues and bridge flooring because of its hard, twisted grain; the applied skirt bead on its companion high chest (no. 37) is sumac, selected for its flexibility.[6]

Sawn boards and planks (more than 1½ inches thick) were stockpiled to cure slowly in the open air, though some woods, such as ash, chestnut, and oak, were worked when somewhat green. The lumber was cut into furniture parts and assembled by craftsmen

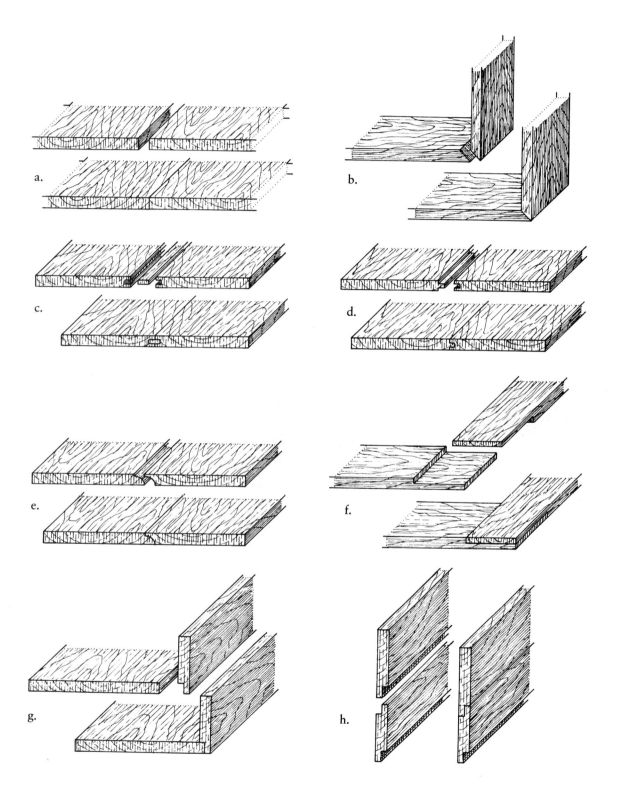

III-8. Simple Joints: (a) Butt; (b) Miter; (c) Spline; (d) Tongue-and-Groove; (e) Rule; (f) Lap; (g) Rabbet; and (h) Double Rabbet.

using simple, sliding, or locking joints, often reinforced with animal glue, nails, or wooden pins. Simple joints — the butt, miter, spline, tongue-and-groove, rule, lap, rabbet, and double rabbet — require a binding agent to secure them and generally are made more quickly and inexpensively than sliding or locking joints. Two butted boards (III-8a), their edges simply flush, may form the back of a chest. Two mitered boards (III-8b) can form a bracket foot, with the vertical seam along the corner. In a spline joint (III-8c), a spline, or thin strip of wood, acts as an independent tongue that fits simultaneously into corresponding grooves cut in two butted or mitered boards. The mitered corners of early looking glass frames were often secured with glued splines. On some chests from the Plymouth Colony, the joint reinforces the butted bottom boards. The tongue-and-groove joint (III-8d) also appears in seventeenth-century drawer bottoms of two or more boards, assuring that cracks will not appear as the wood ages and shrinks. During the first four decades of the eighteenth century, this joint was favored for drop-leaf tables but was replaced by the rule joint (III-8e), which minimized the gap between a table top and its leaf in the closed position. The lap joint (III-8f) appears at each corner of the stretchers of a William and Mary high chest. Cross stretchers are also usually lapped. The rabbet (III-8g) and double rabbet (III-8h) joints involve the passing of a rabbet plane over the edge of a board to create a square lip to receive the edge of another board (which in the case of a double rabbet is also lipped). The rabbet joint is the principal joint in pine furniture and is common on case backs and drawer bottoms of hardwood cabinetry. The double rabbet joint also appears occasionally on a case back along the common edges of its boards. Like the tongue-and-groove joint, it prevents gaps from developing as the wood shrinks.

Sliding joints, or housed joints, as they are sometimes called, are used chiefly to secure two perpendicular boards. In a dado joint (III-9a), the end of one board slides into a groove in another board. Often the end is beveled to fit into a narrow groove. Joiners used the dado joint to frame a panel; the beveled edges fit into grooves along the rails and stiles, allowing the panel to remain in place despite shrinkage. The joint is also seen in drawer construction where the edges of the bottom fit into grooves in the drawer front and sides. A sliding dovetail (III-9b) or shouldered dovetail joint (III-9c) often fastens drawer dividers to the sides of a chest or desk; a dovetail, a fanlike tenon, is cut on each end of the divider and fits into a notch, sawn and chiseled into the front edge of the case side. On eastern Massachusetts furniture, the dovetails are usually covered with a thin facing strip, glued and tacked into place. Blind dovetails (III-9d) join the legs to the shaft of a three-legged candlestand: a single dovetail cut along the vertical edge of a leg slides into a corresponding groove in the base of the shaft.

Locking joints are the mortise-and-tenon (both rectangular and round), dovetail, and mitered dovetail. These joints usually fastened two parts at right angles. For example, the frame of a joined chest is made of mortised-and-tenoned rails and stiles. A rectangular tongue or tenon is sawn at one end of a board and fits into a slot in another board (III-10a). The slot or mortise is begun with a small auger or a bit and brace (drill) and

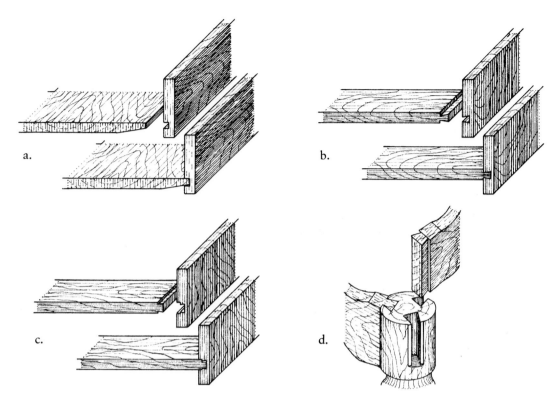

III-9. Sliding Joints: (a) Dado; (b) Dovetail; (c) Shouldered Dovetail; and (d) Blind Dovetail.

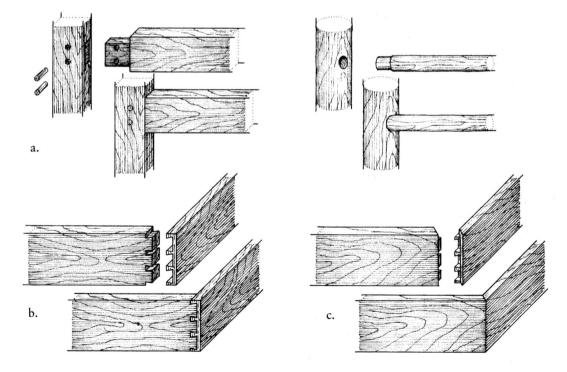

III-10. Locking Joints: (a) Mortise-and-Tenon (rectangular and round); (b) Dovetail; and (c) Mitered Dovetail.

completed with chisels. The mortise and tenon are glued and pinned together. Round mortise-and-tenon joints incorporate the same principle, but were the province of turners, who cut round mortises with augers and forced oversized tenons into them. Drawers were usually dovetailed together (III-10b). A row of fanlike tenons were cut along an end of a board to interlock with corresponding notches on another board. Sometimes nails reinforced the dovetails. Mitered dovetails (III-10c) took additional time to execute and were seldom used. They sometimes joined the top and side of a desk or the elements of a bracket foot. The joint unites two rows of dovetails and is mitered at the outer corner.

Using these joints, craftsmen created every type of furniture needed by their customers. Case furniture (chests of various types, desks, and cupboards) was designed as a series of boxes within boxes. Tables and chairs are boards or seats supported by lightweight frames of vertical stiles and horizontal rails. In constructing these forms, cabinetmakers had to devise: a system for rigidity, or a plan for assuring that the object retained its shape; a system for support in relationship to the floor; and a system for accessibility. Experience with the problems inherent in woodworking led craftsmen to perfect their systems of assembly.

In the seventeenth century, most householders owned chests of either board or joined construction. Board chests, like the one inscribed "HT/1673" (III-11), were relatively inexpensive to make.[7] These chests were built of sawn pine boards nailed along their rabbeted edges. The sides of six-board chests extended to the floor. The façades were often ornamented with punchwork or incised moldings and the chests were almost always painted. Their simple, nailed construction has proven less durable than the framed assembly of joined chests over the years.

Joined chests (no. 5) were made of oak by joiners, who also built houses and who constructed their furniture of rails and stiles that were mortised and tenoned together to frame panels. The stiles supported the object and defined its height. Drawers in joined chests, often made of nailed boards an inch in thickness, were side-hung; that is, a groove was cut in each drawer side to ride on a slat nailed between each front and rear post (III-12). The design and decoration of joinery were determined by the visibility of structural members and the properties of oak, an easily riven wood not readily worked into curved shapes or carved with fine detail.

Joinery required special tools. When the probate inventory of Benjamin Barrett of Deerfield, Massachusetts, was taken in 1690, his tools included:

To 1 Square 2ˢ rule 2:6 handsaw 5ˢ holdfast 4:0 1 plow [plane] 3:6			16:6
To 3 Creasing [molding] plaines 5:0 1 Joyntʳ 5:0 2 Smoothing planes 4:0			14:0
To 1 open Rabbitt [plane] 2:6 3 round planes 3:0 2 hollow plaines 2:0			
3 chizels 4:0			11:6
To 1 gouge 1:0 Compass Saw 1:6 1 auger 1:6 3 augers 4:6			8:6
To 1 Shave 2:0 1 fro 2:0 other small Tooles £1 1 plane 1:0			£1: 5:0
old crosscut Saw 2:0[8]			

III-11. Board Chest. Wethersfield, Connecticut, area, 1673. Yellow pine and tulipwood; H. 22 (55.9); W. 45⅞ (116.5); D. 16⅜ (41.6). Wadsworth Atheneum, gift of William B. and Mary Arabella Goodwin. Photograph, E. Irving Blomstrann. *The chest is inscribed "HT/1673" and probably was made and owned by Henry Treat, a Wethersfield joiner.*

III-12. Detail, Joined Chest with Drawer 7a. Boston area, 1700–1720. Historic Deerfield. *The groove in the drawer side runs on a supporting slat.*

These tools, similar to those illustrated by Joseph Moxon (III-13), were precisely the ones required to make a joined chest. Barrett used the crosscut saw to cut the oak to appropriate lengths. He used the froe to rive the billets of oak into desired widths. The holdfast secured the parts on his bench while he measured them with his rule and trimmed them with his handsaw. To dress the panels, drawer parts, and lid, Barrett chose the smoothing planes to make flat surfaces, the jointer plane to give the parts of the chest straight edges, and the creasing planes to incise molded patterns in the rails and stiles. The rabbet plane was used to make the boards for the drawer and chest bottoms fit tightly. Barrett's plow plane shaped the grooves in the edges of the rails and stiles to receive the panels. He used an auger to drill holes for the mortises, which were finished to rectangular shapes with chisels. With the compass saw, Barrett made the corresponding tenons. The augers also drilled the holes into which wooden pins were driven to bind the mortises and the tenons together. The square assured that the joints were plumb. Barrett used the gouge to ornament the façade of the chest.

By 1700, a revolutionary change was occurring in furniture construction in the colonies.[9] Following trends in northern Europe and England, the craft of the cabinetmaker replaced that of the joiner in making fashionable furniture. Cabinetmakers constructed each case of dovetailed boards. Usually the top and bottom were dovetailed to the sides; the back (usually two or three horizontal boards) was nailed into place. Shallow drawer

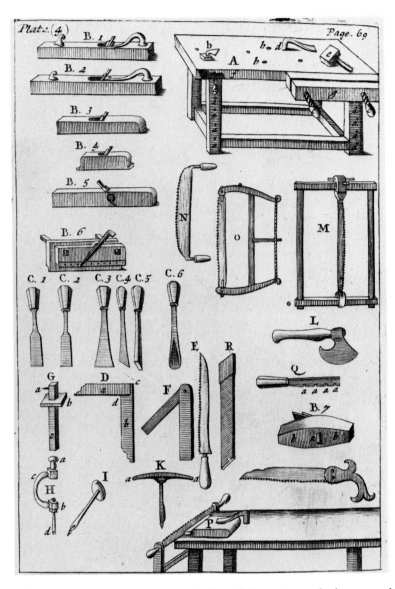

III-13. "Joiner's Work." Moxon, *Mechanick Exercises*, 3rd ed., 1703, pl. 4. Collection of Printed Books, Henry Francis du Pont Winterthur Museum Library. *The jointer plane (B.2) and smoothing plane (B.4) were used to dress rough boards. The rabbet plane (B.5) and plow plane (B.6) created lips and grooves for fitting boards together. The brace and bit (H), gimlet (I), and auger (K) made holes of various sizes. Chisels (C.1–5) and gouges (C.6) were used to make mortises and ornamental carving. In the absence of water-driven sawmills, two men used the pit saw (M) to cut planks and boards along the grain of the log. The whip saw or crosscut saw (N) cut wood across its grain. The frame saw (O) was used to cut precise shapes and, like many tools, was made in a range of sizes. Various gauges and squares (D, F, G, and R) regulated workmanship at the bench, where boards were temporarily fixed in place with a vise (A.g) or hold-fast (A.d).*

dividers were dovetailed to the case sides (III-9b), making the case more rigid. Dovetailed drawers slid between the dividers. The result was lightweight, often flimsy furniture of vertical, vaguely classical proportions, sometimes ornamented with highly figured veneers.

The tools in Barrett's shop were no longer adequate to make stylish furniture. When William Howell died in Boston on December 31, 1717, his shop contained many of the tools that Barrett had owned in Deerfield a generation earlier as well as "2 Phillisters [planes] 1:6 . . . & one tooth Plain . . . 1 fine Saw 3:0 . . . 1 Finereing Hammer & Pinchers 2:0 . . . 2 Glew Potts 4:0 . . . 12 Pillers for a Chest of Drawers 9:0."[10] Howell, a cabinetmaker, owned the tools necessary to his trade. He used a fillister plane, with its adjustable fence, to groove drawer sides and fronts to receive the drawer bottoms. Howell made veneered furniture, so he needed the "fine" saw to cut flitches or sheets of veneer and perhaps to cut dovetails. With the toothing plane, Howell scored the front of each drawer front, creating a rough surface. A thin coat of hot hide or fish glue was applied to the drawer front and to the back of the veneer and was allowed to become tacky before the two surfaces were joined. Howell hammered the veneer from the center outward to drive air from the joint and to form a tight bond. He then clamped each drawer front between pine boards to distribute the pressure until the glue was dry.

The twelve pillars in Howell's probate inventory were turned legs, probably intended for two fashionable high chests of drawers. They typify William and Mary furniture and were particularly unsound because the legs were not integral parts of the dovetailed lower case. Instead, they were tenoned into blocks glued to the case (see entry 29). Later in the century, the fashionable cabriole legs of high chests and dressing tables were mortised and tenoned to the sides of the case. Many Rhode Island cabinetmakers continued to construct dovetailed cases and to brace the cabriole legs independently within the case.

The tops of low chests of drawers were attached in a variety of ways. Throughout rural New England, the top was secured with wooden pins driven into the upper edges of the sides and back of the chest. In urban furniture, the joints were concealed to provide an unbroken surface. In Rhode Island workshops, two horizontal boards were dovetailed to the case sides, and the top was often affixed to these horizontal boards with screws driven from the underside or with dovetail keys.[11] Glue blocks were sometimes applied to the interior juncture of the sides and top. In eastern Massachusetts, the top was usually secured to the upper edge of the case side by a blind dovetail (III-14). The underside of the top was grooved to slide onto the case sides and was occasionally plugged at the back of the chest.

The strips of base molding on dovetailed chests generally were mitered at the corners and joined to chests with glue and nails. In eastern Massachusetts, the front base molding on blockfront and oxbow cases was often attached to the front edge of the case bottom

III-14. Back of Chest of Drawers No. 18. Boston, 1760–1780. *The groove in the underside of the top receives the top of the case side.*

III-15. Front Foot of Desk No. 49. Boston area, 1785–1805. *A bracket foot and supporting glue blocks.*

by a large dovetail (chest no. 20, detail 20a). The base molding was thicker than the case bottom and, except on bombé cases, was flush with the interior and overhung below, giving a layered effect beneath the case (chest no. 20, detail 20b). The blocks supporting the base molding were under the case. The bottom drawer ran directly on the bottom of the chest. In Rhode Island work and in bombé cases from eastern New England, the layered effect was visible within the case. The base molding was flush with the underside of the chest. The supporting blocks were within the case. The bottom drawer rode on supports placed behind the base molding (chest-on-chest no. 26, detail 26a).

Early dovetailed chests of drawers were supported by turned feet that were simply let into drilled holes in the bottom of the case. The tenon of each foot, often visible within the chest, was either square or round and was usually wedged. The later bracket feet of stylish New England chests of drawers were glued and nailed to the bottom of the base molding. On some cases, the base molding and bracket feet were a single unit cut from one board. The bracket feet were supported by a system of vertical and horizontal glue blocks (III-15). Carved claw feet were usually mortised and tenoned into the bottom of the case and supported by flanking brackets and horizontal glue blocks (III-16).

Drawer construction differed from place to place. Cabinetmakers joined the fronts, sides, and backs of drawers with dovetails, occasionally in combination with nails. Quality varied considerably. Newport dovetails have thin necks and were sawn precisely; Boston dovetails are coarse and often irregular. Bottoms were attached in several ways. A bottom could be nailed or wood-pinned to a rabbeted edge on the front and to the flush edges of the sides and back (an earlier method). Often bottoms were attached to

III-16. Front Foot of Desk and Bookcase No. 51. Boston, 1770–1790. *A claw-and-ball foot and supporting glue blocks.*

III-17. Rear Corner of a Drawer of Chest of Drawers No. 15. George Bright, Boston, 1770. *The drawer bottom is nailed to a rabbeted drawer side.*

III-18. Rear Corner of a Drawer of Desk and Bookcase No. 51. Boston, 1770–1790. *The drawer bottom fits in a groove in the drawer side.*

rabbeted sides as well as fronts (III-17). Many bottoms were driven from the rear of the drawer into grooves in the sides and front and nailed to the back (III-18).

Most drawers in New England case furniture were supported within the case by narrow strips of pine nailed to the case sides, sometimes in a shallow groove (III-19). Drawer stops were generally applied to the case sides at the back or occasionally to the drawer dividers. Sometimes in western New England, protruding rear dovetails served as drawer stops.

A desk is a variation on a chest of drawers. Cabinetmakers met the needs for a writing surface and for the secure storage of small objects in standard ways during the eighteenth century. The lids of desks were hinged horizontally to double as a work area when open and as a lockable door when closed. The lid was supported by two vertical boards that, when not in use, slid into the case at either end of the upper drawer. Consequently, the upper drawer of a desk was usually narrower than the others. The lid, like many table tops of a single board, was fitted with cleats at each end to retard warping. Occasionally, the cleats were cut diagonally at their upper ends.

Interior desk drawers are of thinner-gauge wood and are often built differently from the large drawers below the lid. Interior drawers are more apt to run directly on their bottoms because their contents weigh so little. The bottoms are sometimes attached with wooden pins, a practice that does not reflect a scarcity of iron brads or sprigs (small nails) but suggests a sound understanding of wood. Wooden pins expand and contract with the parts they unite at the same rate, diminishing the chance of splitting. The parts

III-19. Chest of Drawers No. 15 with the Drawers Removed. George Bright, Boston, 1770. *Note the horizontal drawer supports and the vertical drawer stops at the back of the case.*

of interior drawers are particularly thin and liable to split around nails. The drawers and pigeonholes are supported by thin partitions of wood that are driven from the back into grooves in the sides and top of the case.

Table surfaces require sturdy but portable frames. In seventeenth-century tables, rails and stretchers were mortised and tenoned to four stationary legs. In about 1700, drop-leaf tables with elaborately turned legs and stretchers supplanted heavily framed tables without leaves. The benefit of a drop-leaf table lay in its light construction and mobility. The table had four stationary legs and usually two pivoting supports for the leaves (see table no. 59). Tongue-and-groove joints, or in later tables rule joints, disguised the gap between the common edges of the fixed top and leaves. In the closed position, the pivoting fifth and sixth legs fit neatly into notches in the stretcher base of the table. Gate-leg tables often had drawers.

In later drop-leaf tables, cabinetmakers reduced the number of legs to four; two legs are stationary and two, at diagonal corners, pivot to support the leaves without the added strength of the stretcher base (table no. 60). A fixed hinge rail was nailed to each side rail and joined to a swing rail with a pintle hinge secured with a wooden pin (detail 63a). The side and end rails were dovetailed together at the corners behind the swing legs. The tops of early drop-leaf tables were attached with wooden pins driven through the surface into the upper edges of the frame. The mahogany or walnut tops of later tables were generally secured with glue blocks or with screws driven into the underside of the top from notches in the rails of the table frame. Tables with only two stationary legs were usually made without drawers, assuring a stronger joint between the end rails and the side rails.

The growing popularity of genteel pastimes like tea drinking, card playing, reading, and doing fancy needlework led to the development of specialized tables. Most tables and stands incorporated four legs mortised and tenoned to connecting rails. The mobile pedestal table (III-20), however, offered different technological challenges. Tripod tables with either hinged or fixed tops (the smaller examples usually have fixed tops) became popular in the 1760s. The three legs, the replication of which was assured by a template, were joined to the base of the lathe-turned shaft with deep, blind dovetails (III-9d), which fit into long mortises and were often reinforced with a metal brace. The top of the pillar was cut to form a square tenon that fit through a block and was secured with wedges. On hinged-top tables, the block was cut on one edge to form pintles. Each pintle fit into a cleat that was screwed to the underside of the top. On small candlestands with fixed tops, a single wide cleat received the pillar's tenon and was then nailed or screwed to the underside of the top. Square, round, or shaped tops were cut out with a saw; to create a raised edge on a round top, the disk was turned on a lathe to remove wood from the center portion.

Chairs are technologically and aesthetically the most demanding furniture form to execute. The seating unit must retain its shape, support the sitter comfortably, incorporate lightness for mobility, and look stylish. Heavy "wainscot" armchairs were constructed by joiners following the same principles as for joined chests, using rectangular mortises and tenons. Turners practiced other skills and owned a number of expensive, specialized tools. When William Crockford died in Boston in 1756, his shop contained at least 75 turning chisels and gouges, 20 "Mortar Turning Tools," 50 rasps and files, a variety of augers, bitts, and chucks, and five lathes of various sizes.[12] When making chairs, Crockford and other turners were guided by principles that we might call mass production. Lathes assured the speedy manufacture of decorative, interchangeable parts. Crockford turned dozens of banisters or stretchers with his long-handled chisels and gouges before he assembled a single chair. His probate inventory also lists "1 Bundle of Rungs, & Ferrils 2:6 . . . 17 Maple Bannisters 2:0, 14 Beach do 2:4 . . . 12 pr Screen Handles 8:0, 12 Bow handles for platters 6:0 . . . 28 Chaffen dish handles 2:4 . . . Sundry patterns of turn^d Bannisters & other Things 1:0:0 . . . 1 Doz^n & 8 Bannisters unturned 1:11:6, 3 Doz^n & 10 turned do 1:15:10, 2 Stand Tops turned 4:6."

To turn a chair leg, Crockford probably held a marking gauge with nails spaced along its length against a billet of wood as it revolved on the lathe. The resulting marks told him where to shape the balusters, rings, and tenons and where to drill the mortises. Most of the tenons in turned chairs are round and depend upon the shrinkage of green wood around them to make a tight fit. To make two banisters for a chair back, Crockford used a single billet, which he split and glued together with a pine shim between each half. Turning the desired shape, he soaked the billet to separate the halves along the seam. Each banister is a little less than half round.

Only a few parts of a turner's chair (III-21) were not turned on a lathe. The crest, banister rail, and arms were laid out with templates and sawn. The crest and rail have

III-20. Rear View of Tilt-Top Stand No. 76. Boston or coastal Essex County, 1775–1800.

III-21. Armchair. Southern New Hampshire or northeastern Massachusetts, 1725–1775. *Soft maple* and *ash*; H. 46⅛ (117.2); W. 21¾ (55.2); SEAT D. 16⅞ (42.9); SEAT H. 15½ (39.4). Mabel Brady Garvan Collection, Yale University Art Gallery.

rectangular tenons; Crockford's inventory also lists two "Tennant [tenon] Saws 9:0" and a "Douvtail Saw 4:0." The seat rails and often the side and rear stretchers were made with a drawknife because the simple round shape of these parts was quick work with this tool and because a thin billet would whip while revolving on a lathe.

Turned chairs were assembled at the crest and seat in two ways. The crest was either fastened into mortises in the stiles (III-21) or the crest itself was mortised to receive the tops of the turned stiles (III-22). The front seat rail was either fastened into mortises in the front posts (III-22) or the front corners of the seat frame were mortised to receive the tops of the front legs (III-23). Turned chairs with mortised crests and seat rails, popular in coastal Connecticut and New York, imitated the effect of visual uniformity seen in many chairs made by cabinetmakers.

The cabinetmaker's chair (III-24) was made contemporaneously with the turner's chair. The philosophy behind the two types, however, is different. Each set of cabinetmaker's

III-22. Side Chair. Western Connecticut, 1780–1820. Maple; H. 40 (101.6); W. 16½ (41.9); SEAT D. 14¼ (36.2); SEAT H. 16½ (41.9). Historic Deerfield. Photograph, Philip Zea.

III-23. Side Chair. Western Massachusetts or Connecticut, 1750–1800. *Soft maple;* H. 43⅞ (111.4); W. 18¹⁵⁄₁₆ (48.1); SEAT D. 13¼ (33.7); SEAT H. 17⅛ (43.5). Society for the Preservation of New England Antiquities.

chairs was commissioned by a specific customer, not assembled quickly from stockpiled parts. For uniformity, the cabinetmaker relied largely on templates rather than marking gauges. He constructed chairs of sawn and carved parts, with few if any turned elements. Expensive handwork was applied to unify the joined elements of the chair visually. For example, the stiles, crest, and splat look like a unit because the crest sits atop the vertical members, and the edges of these parts were shaved to a continuous contour. The cabinetmaker did use a lathe to turn the stretchers and the disk portion of the feet, but most of the mortises and tenons are rectangular, including the tenons of the turned side stretchers (III-25). By cutting a rectangular mortise, the cabinetmaker removed less wood across the grain of the ankle, making the joint stronger. Only the tenons of the medial and rear stretchers of the chair are round. Chairs with straight Marlborough legs (no. 113) have no turned elements and hence no round mortises and tenons.

The construction of the cabinetmaker's chair recalls the rectangular mortise-and-tenon

III-24. Side Chair. Boston area, 1735–1750. Black walnut and maple; H. 39⅝ (100.6); W. 21½ (54.6); SEAT D. 17½ (44.5); SEAT H. 16½ (41.9). Marblehead Historical Society. *The chair retains its original black leather upholstery except for the addition of a modern strip on the edge of the front and side seat rails.*

III-25. Lower Leg and Stretcher of Side Chair No. 94. Boston area, 1735–1760. *The side stretcher joins the front leg with a rectangular mortise-and-tenon joint.*

joints of the joiner. Each end of the stylish splat simply rests in a mortise (pins would encourage splitting). The lower end rides in a shoe, often a separate element, that is nailed with small sprigs to the rear seat rail. The front legs extend to the top of the seat and receive the tenons of the seat rails. The other ends of the side rails are tenoned into the stiles. In some Connecticut work, the tenon passes through the stile and is visible from the back of the chair in a manner seen on Philadelphia chairs (III-26). The joints securing the seat rails are often reinforced with blocks, which vary in shape and application. On chairs from eastern Massachusetts and New Hampshire, for example, the corner blocks are of one triangular piece, with the grain horizontal (III-27). On some Connecticut chairs, the blocks are of two rounded pieces with a vertical grain (III-28). Instead of corner blocks, diagonal braces, set in slots in an English manner, reinforce the seat frames of some upholstered chairs (detail 119b). New England chairs with compass seats feature rounded front rails and side rails shaped like S-curves, whose

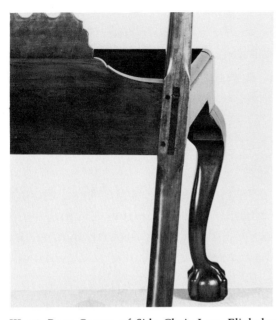

III-26. Rear Corner of Side Chair I-52. Eliphalet Chapin, East Windsor, Connecticut, 1781. *The tenon of the side seat rail passes completely through the stile.*

III-27. Front Corner of the Seat of Side Chair No. 118. Portsmouth area, 1760–1775. *A triangular corner block.*

III-28. Front Corner of the Seat of Side Chair I-52. Eliphalet Chapin, East Windsor, Connecticut, 1781. *A two-part rounded corner block.*

III-29. Seat of Side Chair No. 99. Newport, 1750–1765. *The seat rails of a compass seat.*

added width precludes the need for additional bracing (III-29). Knee brackets are decorative as well as functional and are glued and nailed to the legs and seat rails.

After the craftsman constructed a piece of furniture, he applied a coating to the surface to protect the wood and to enhance the design. A variety of paints, clear finishes, and ornamental treatments were available. Today, original finishes on furniture are rarely found, and when furniture with original paint or varnish is discovered, grime obscures the visual effect intended. The gleaming furniture depicted in eighteenth-century portraits documents highly polished surfaces in dimly lit rooms and a passion for rich color. Early trade manuals provided recipes for producing these surfaces.[13]

Paint was used throughout the seventeenth and eighteenth centuries to unify objects made of several woods, to cover mundane woods like oak, ash, hickory, and pine, to imitate more exotic materials, and to provide color inside houses. Popular paint colors were derived from metals and earths. These pigments included lamp black, red lead, venetian red, vermilion, white lead, verdigris, umber, and yellow ocher. They were generally ground and suspended in linseed oil with a drier of lead oxide or magnesium dioxide. Inexpensive pigments such as brick dust, distemper paints (pigments ground into hot water and glue), and milk-based paints were not part of the color scheme of colonial New England furniture.

Three types of clear finishes were applied to New England furniture in the eighteenth century: oil, wax, and varnish.[14] Such finishes heightened the rich, swirling grain of hardwoods like mahogany and walnut and brightened the translucent oil-based stains applied to hardwoods like maple, birch, and cherry. Oils — animal, vegetable, and mineral — were used to darken the visible surfaces of furniture and to provide a shiny, protective coating. Linseed oil was the most popular because it was inexpensively produced from local flaxseed. A lead oxide was added to quicken drying, and turpentine was used to thin the brown mixture. Linseed oil was boiled to improve its gloss. Several coats of oil were wiped onto the surface of furniture until the wood was saturated. Prolonged rubbing hardened the oil, making the surface shine. Unfortunately, linseed oil darkens wood over time and is damaged by moisture, heat, alcohol, and soap.

Some cabinetmakers favored a wax finish, which is inert and does not oxidize or crack. Although wax smudges, the surface is easily renewed. Beeswax, sometimes mixed with turpentine and varnish, was the most popular wax. Widely available, it was particularly favored for light-colored woods because of its clarity. Thomas Sheraton described its application in 1803: "The cork is rubbed hard on the wax to spread it over the wood, and then they take a fine brick-dust and sift it through a stocking on the wood, and with a cloth the dust is rubbed till it clears away all the clammings [sticky residue]."[15]

Most professional cabinetmakers experimented with varnishes in their search for a tough, clear finish. Like medieval alchemists, they tinkered with ingredients and scrawled their recipes. There were innumerable formulas with varying procedures for heating and refining varnish. Basically, natural resins and gums were combined with a solvent and were sometimes tinted. Most resins were drawn from trees or plants; others, like lac, were left by insects.

There were three kinds of varnish. The most common was made from resins dissolved in linseed oil, with an additive to promote drying. Soft resins, distilled from turpentine, were often combined with linseed oil. A more satisfactory varnish was derived from copal, a hard tropical resin, which was liquefied with linseed oil at high temperatures. The second type of varnish relied on turpentine as the principal medium for dissolving the resins. The resulting varnish, however, was of poor quality and threatened life and limb when it was heated during its preparation. The third type of varnish featured resins dissolved in alcohol, which was normally distilled from poor-grade wine or rum. During the eighteenth century, the most common alcohol-soluble resin was sandarac, a translucent resin derived from a cypress-like African tree. The use of shellac (a derivative of lac) as a clear finish was limited in the colonial period because of the difficulty in removing a natural reddish-brown dye. It was suitable, however, for japanning, which did not require a clear surface. In either case, all alcohol-based varnishes lacked hardness and were not resistant to heat, water, and spiritous beverages.

The most decorative finish was simulated lacquerwork, called japanning (high chest no. 36, plate 4). In Boston, specialized tradesmen, japanners, applied a ground of black paint or red heavily streaked with black. Coats of varnish followed. Raised figures depicting Oriental scenes or exotic creatures were formed with gum arabic and whiting and were highlighted with metallic dust. The bright, contrasting surface was then covered with successive coats of varnish and polished to give visual depth to the decoration.

After applying a finish to their chairs, cabinetmakers turned to upholstery. Although requiring few additional tools, upholstery was a trade distinct from furniture making. One of the most complete accounts of an eighteenth-century Boston upholstery shop lists only "Sundry hamm[rs] gimlets, Pincher [pincers], Shears" and "2 Iron goose," a type of smoothing iron.[16] Yet, with these items and a supply of needles, thread, pins, and tacks, upholsterers transformed chair frames into attractive, comfortable furniture. Their methods were typical of upholsterers in England and elsewhere in America.

The upholstery of a loose-seat frame was a simple task. Upholsterers nailed girt web, a narrow twill strip of linen, to the top of one rail, stretched it across the frame with a pair of pincers, and nailed it to the opposite rail. Usually upholsterers wove two webs running front to back with one or two running side to side. They nailed a piece of coarse linen cloth over the webbing (III-30a) and added a layer of stuffing, choosing from such materials as marsh grass, tow, wool, and curled horsehair. Horsehair, the costliest of the group, was generally used only in small amounts on top of other materials.[17] Upholsterers often placed a second piece of linen over the stuffing and nailed it to either the edge or the bottom of the seat frame (III-30b). An outer cover, nailed to the bottom of the frame, completed the upholstery.

III-30. Loose Seat from Side Chair. Boston, 1755–1775. Cherry seat frame; w. 19⅞ (50.5); D. 15¼ (38.7). On loan to the Society for the Preservation of New England Antiquities. *The seat retains its original underupholstery: (a) strips of girt web and*

a linen bottom nailed to the seat frame (b) with layers of marsh grass and curled hair added and a layer of linen nailed to the edges of the frame. An outer covering nailed to the bottom of the frame would have completed the upholstery.

Over-the-rail upholstery, while similar to that for loose seats, required two additional steps. First, upholsterers had to build up and precisely shape the contour of a seat. Often they applied a roll of marsh grass between projecting corners of the front legs (chair no. 133, detail 133b) to ensure a firm contour for the seat.

The installation of brass nails was the last step. Throughout the seventeenth and eighteenth centuries, upholsterers embellished over-the-rail upholstery with rows of brightly polished brass nails. The cast nails were available in several sizes. Large ones, 9/16 to ¾ inch in diameter, became especially popular during the second half of the eighteenth century. In New England, nailing patterns consisted of either a single row (chair no. 113) or a double (III-24). Craftsmen ornamented the common Boston leather chair (III-31) with a double row on the chair back and seat, with only a single row along the sides of the seat, and none across the seat back.

Despite a fashion for crisp contours in upholstery, loose-fitting slipcovers also enjoyed popularity during the eighteenth century (chair no. 133, detail 133c). Often they were simply draped over seats finished in white linen. Such covers, commonly made of printed cotton or furniture check (a lightweight cloth usually woven of cotton and linen), were appropriate for stylish seats. In 1755, a patron purchased from the Boston upholsterer Samuel Grant "covers of fine check" for "6 walnutt chairs carv'd tops knees & bares claw feet stuffd in canv^s."[18]

Upholsterers also covered couches, easy chairs, lolling chairs, back stools, and sofas. A couch of the form now called a daybed (III-32) needed a long feather cushion for its cane or canvas bottom and a small matching pillow for its back. Upholstered couches

III-32. Couch. Lebanon, Connecticut, area, 1765–1790. Cherry; H. 39⅝ (100.6); W. 39 (99.1); SEAT D. 71¼ (181.0); SEAT H. 17⅜ (44.1). Jonathan Trumbull House. *The couch belonged to Jonathan Trumbull (1710–1785) of Lebanon. It retains its original canvas bottom: a large linen panel laced to linen strips.*

III-31. Side Chair. Boston, 1725–1740. Maple and oak; H. 43⅞ (111.4); W. 18⅜ (46.7); SEAT D. 14¾ (37.5); SEAT H. 18¾ (47.6). Wilton, Richmond, Virginia. *The chair retains its original black leather upholstery.*

(such as 81a), sofas, and chairs with upholstered backs were all handled in a similar manner. For example, the method for upholstering the seat of an easy chair followed the sequence for covering a side chair upholstered over the rails. The upholstery of the back resembled the treatment of a loose seat with the addition of stitches sewn through the layers to hold the stuffing in place (chair no. 101, detail 101a). The wings usually had no webbing (III-33); upholsterers merely nailed on a piece of linen (sometimes two) and nailed a roll of marsh grass along the edge of the wing. After stuffing the wing, another piece of linen was nailed on. The final covering (III-34) was cut out with patterns and nailed or sewn in place. The seams were covered with a silk binding or brass nails. A thick feather cushion completed the upholstery.

The greatest achievement for an upholsterer was the assembly of a fully outfitted high-post bed. The form consisted of four parts: bedstead, bottom, mattresses with bolster and pillow, and hangings. The posts and rails were usually joined with large bolts that passed through the posts and were screwed to nuts set inside the rails. The screw holes were hidden by brass covers. The bottom was made of either interlaced rope or "sacking," a large panel of canvas laced to pins in the bed rails or to narrow strips of canvas

III-33. Easy Chair. Boston or Salem, 1760–1780. Mahogany, maple, and white pine; H. 45¼ (114.9); W. 34 (86.4); SEAT D. 22¾ (57.8); SEAT H. 14⅛ (35.9). Henry Francis du Pont Winterthur Museum. *The chair retains its original underupholstery on the back and wings.*

III-34. Easy Chair. Boston, 1740–1765. Black walnut, maple, and white pine; H. 48 (121.9); W. 35¼ (89.5); SEAT D. 24 (61.0); SEAT H. excluding cushion 14⅛ (35.9). Brooklyn Museum. *The chair retains its original red stamped worsted upholstery.*

nailed to the rails (III-35). For expensive beds, upholsterers made two mattresses: the bottom, a quilted pad stuffed with wool, and the top, a tick filled with as many as forty pounds of feathers.

Bed hangings, the most expensive component, were composed of valances, tester cloth, curtains, a headcloth, a counterpane, and bases (III-36). Sets were sometimes imported from England, but in most cases, New England upholsterers assembled the hangings using English materials and patterns. Before the Revolution, worsteds were the most common fabrics for beds; printed materials and woven check became popular in the latter half of the century. It was customary for the curtains to completely enclose the bed. There were two common methods for mounting the curtains. One was to suspend them from metal rings that ran on rods below the tester. Another method was to tack the curtain to a tester or cornice and raise it in drapery fashion (detail 140d) by pulling a cord that ran through loops in the back of the curtain and over pulleys in the tester. The cord could be wrapped tight around cloak pins screwed into the bedposts. Even after purchase and installation, upholsterers were often called upon to oversee the maintenance of beds and the seasonal changes of hangings in the homes of the wealthy.

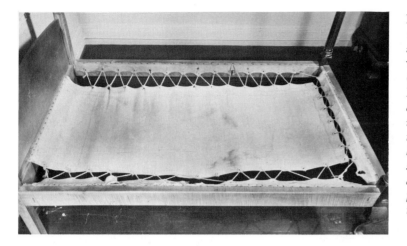

III-35. Bedstead. Boston area, 1760–1780. Mahogany, maple, and white pine; H. 83⅜ (211.8); W. 48½ (123.2); D. 71¼ (181.0). Concord Antiquarian Museum. *The bed, though reduced in width by 6 inches, still retains its original canvas bottom. The bottom is nailed to the head rail and laced to canvas strips that are nailed to the side and foot rails. Linen tape reinforces the strips to prevent their tearing at the nails.*

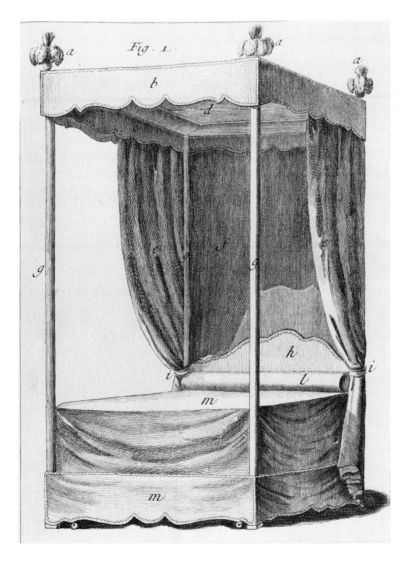

III-36. Design of a Bed. Diderot, *Recueil de Planches*, 1771, "Tapissier" section, pl. 6, fig. 1. Society for the Preservation of New England Antiquities Library. *This view, appearing in a volume of plates that accompanied Diderot's* Encyclopédie, *illustrates the major elements of a high-post bed: (a) finial of ostrich feathers; often a wooden cornice was installed instead; (b) outside valance; (c) inside valance; (d) tester cloth; (e) curtain; (f) headcloth; (g) bedpost; (h) headboard; (i) tieback; (l) bolster; (m) counterpane; (n; incorrectly labeled as m) base; usually its outline matched that of the valance.*

Today, an understanding of early design and construction helps us appreciate the aesthetics of our forebears and recognize original workmanship. Are the proportions of the object consistent? Do they reflect seventeenth- or eighteenth-century thinking? Does close examination of each surface and joint show that the object was constructed in a predictable, sequential manner with early tools? The answers to these questions, in an archaeological way, lead to perceptions of a society, a precursor to our own, whose need for furniture documents the economy, taste, and home life of New England more than two centuries ago.

1. Chippendale, *Director,* 1st ed., 3.

2. See, for example, the Tuscan column delineated in Salmon, *Palladio Londinensis,* pl. 26, "Composite Order."

3. Pye, *Nature and Art of Workmanship,* 7–10.

4. Bulkeley, "Belden and Grant," 72–81.

5. *Plain & Elegant,* 124–27.

6. For more information on the appearance and properties of wood, see Hoadley, *Understanding Wood,* and Saltar, "New England Timbers."

7. Hosley and Zea, "Decorated Board Chests," 1146–51.

8. Benjamin Barrett's inventory, vol. 2, p. 61, Hampshire County (Mass.) Probate.

9. Forman, "Urban Aspects," 17–27.

10. William Howell's inventory, old series, vol. 26, pp. 33–35, Suffolk County (Mass.) Probate.

11. Lovell, "Boston Blockfront Furniture," 81–89.

12. William Crockford's inventory, old series, vol. 51, pp. 546–50, Suffolk County (Mass.) Probate.

13. The first volume printed in America that dealt solely with finishes for wood was *The Cabinet-Maker's Guide: or, Rules and Instructions in the Art of Varnishing, Dying, Staining, Japanning, Polishing, Lackering and Beautifying Wood, Ivory, Tortoise-shell and Metal,* published in Greenfield, Mass., by Ansel Phelps in 1825, a reprint of a work published in London by Knight and Lacey in 1818.

14. The comments on clear furniture finishes in this essay are largely derived from Mussey, "Transparent Furniture Finishes in New England."

15. Sheraton, *Cabinet Dictionary,* 289.

16. Thomas Baxter's 1758 inventory, old series, vol. 45, p. 540, Suffolk County (Mass.) Probate.

17. The time-consuming process that made curled hair expensive was described in *Godey's Lady's Book and Magazine* (February 1856): 156–57: "Curled hair, for stuffing sofas, chairs, etc., is prepared from the short black or gray hair of a horse. The first process is to card it. . . . Tipping is the next process performed; it is done by a boy, who, with a cane in each hand, tosses the hair into a tolerably regular tuft or top, which he beats on the top to consolidate it. One of these tops is then attached to a wheel, which makes the hair into a tight curl or rope by rapid rotation; another top is then placed in the loose ends of the first, and spun in with it; a third is placed on that, and so on, until a dense rope is formed of considerable length. This rope is tied into a bundle, and steeped in cold water for three or four hours, and then, still wet, put into a hot oven for about twenty-four hours, the heat of the oven being gradually let down; when taken out, the rope is slightly untwisted, and then the hairs are separated by towsing, or pulling to pieces. After this latter process, the hair will possess that springy character which fits it so admirably for stuffing cushions, sofas, etc."

18. Samuel Grant, Account Book, November 11, 1755, p. 808, American Antiquarian Society.

Part Two / Catalogue

Case Furniture

1 / Box

1663–1680
Ipswich, Massachusetts
Attributed to William Searle or Thomas Dennis
H. 7³/₁₆ (18.3); W. 25⁵/₈ (65.1); D. 16⁷/₈ (42.9)

During the seventeenth century, boxes with carved façades were common furnishings in the best rooms of houses. They appear in numerous New England inventories, often in conjunction with chests because boxes customarily sat on chests. At the time of his death in 1695, Isaac Curtis, a Roxbury, Massachusetts, farmer, had in his parlor his wearing apparel, bed, cupboard, table, chair, chest, and "a chest & box."[1] Today, collectors identify the form as a Bible box; however, documents of the period suggest that boxes also provided safe, lockable storage for family papers, writing implements, and valuables.

The Society's collection includes two excellent examples made in coastal Massachusetts during the second half of the seventeenth century. This one is firmly tied through its provenance and style of carving to Ipswich. During the 1880s, the Ipswich artist Arthur Wesley Dow (1857–1922) acquired it from the estate of William Leatherland (1790–1870), whose family had lived in Ipswich since at least 1708, when an earlier William Leatherland married Elizabeth Perkins.[2] Even without this history, one would associate the box with Ipswich because of its decoration. The strapwork and foliage carving on the front is very similar to that on three pieces of furniture that descended in the Dennis family of Ipswich: the President's Chair at Bowdoin College (1a), a wainscot chair in the Essex Institute, and a deed box (1b).[3]

Since 1937, when Lyon published his findings, furniture historians have attributed these objects to Thomas Dennis (1638–1706), a joiner who was working in Ipswich by 1668.[4] More recent research by Park disclosed a close association between Dennis and an earlier Ipswich joiner, William Searle (1634–1667).[5]

Searle was born in Ottery-Saint-Mary in Devonshire, England, and married Grace Cole there in 1659. He immigrated to New England and was living in Ipswich by 1663, when he sold land in that town to Thomas Dennis of Portsmouth, New Hampshire.[6] Searle died in 1667, and the next year his widow married Dennis. Surviving accounts reveal that Dennis inherited through his wife an assortment of furniture from Searle's

1

estate, including "a box with a draw to it," probably the Dennis family deed box (1b), and "on great char," one of the two wainscot chairs cited above.[7] Thus, some of the Dennis family furniture was probably made by Searle.

The strapwork pattern on this box is derived from a design seen on the most ornate English furniture of the early seventeenth century, furniture that has been pinpointed by related stone sculpture, plaster ornament, and interior woodwork to the Exeter region of Devon.[8] This area, whose decorative work was unequaled in all England at the time, includes Ottery-Saint-Mary.

Searle learned his craft in the environs of Exeter and would have been familiar with this regionally popular strapwork motif. Dennis too probably trained in Devon. "Dennis" (a common name in the area) and "Searle" appear in lists of those engaged in carpentry in Exeter during the first quarter of the seventeenth century.[9]

Because of the interest in carved furniture from Ipswich, scholars have long appreciated the Society's box, but have assumed that it always appeared in its present form. It did not.

The box originally had a drawer below it and probably stood on small feet. The Dennis family deed box illustrates the rare box-with-drawer form. The clearest indications for the original form of the Society's box are two vertical holes in the front, remnants of the locking device that secured the drawer (see *Notes on Structure and Condition*).

1b. Deed Box. Attributed to William Searle, Ipswich, Massachusetts, 1663–1667. Oak; H. 14⅜ (36.5); W. 25¾ (65.4); D. 17⅜ (44.2). Collection of H. Ray Dennis, Jr.

1a. Joined Armchair. Attributed to William Searle (1634–1667) or Thomas Dennis (1638–1706), Ipswich, Massachusetts, 1663–1680. White and red oak; H. 45¼ (114.9); W. 25¾ (65.4); D. 17⅜ (44.2); SEAT H. 16⅛ (40.9). Bowdoin College Museum of Art, gift of Ephraim Wilder Farley, 1872.

1. Cummings, *Inventories*, 74.
2. Lyon ("Oak Furniture, Part 2," 301) records Dow's acquisition of the box. Leatherland family information, *Vital Records of Ipswich*, 2:274, 614.
3. These three Dennis family items are figures 1, 2, and 4 in Lyon, "Oak Furniture, Part 1," and numbers 474, 475, and 477 in *New England Begins*, vol. 3. The same strapwork appears on a chest that descended in the Staniford family of Ipswich; St. George, "Staniford Family Chest."
4. Lyon, "Oak Furniture, Part 1."
5. Park, "Thomas Dennis," 42–43.
6. Lyon, "Oak Furniture, Part 1," 231.
7. Quoted in Park, "Thomas Dennis," 43.
8. Wells-Cole, "Oak Bed at Montacute."
9. Conversation with Wells-Cole, 1979.

NOTES ON STRUCTURE AND CONDITION: The back of this nailed box is undecorated; each side originally had a central oval boss. The two-board top is secured to the back with its original cotter-pin hinges. The left cleat is original, the right an old replacement. A molding is applied at the base of the front; the corresponding side moldings are missing. Related moldings can be seen on the Dennis family deed box. The interior has a till on the left side.

The box originally had a drawer (or two side-by-side drawers), which could be locked from above by two rods passing through vertical holes in the box's front board into notches in the top edge of the drawer front. Similar devices exist on some seventeenth-century furniture, including the Short family dressing chest, dated 1692, now at the Winterthur Museum; a similar piece at the Museum of Fine Arts, Boston; and two large chests, one inscribed "PK/1699" and the other "AW," at the Museum of Fine Arts, Boston.

The box was cut just above the drawer sometime before it was acquired by Dow. The bottom is four tongue-and-groove boards running front to back. Seven original forged nails secure the bottom to the front. Originally additional nails, passing through the side moldings, helped hold the bottom.

MATERIALS: *Red oak*. Original cotter-pin hinges; replaced lock.

PROVENANCE: The box may have come to the Leatherland family of Ipswich through Mary Leatherland Dennis, the widow of Thomas Dennis, Jr. (1733–1760). It descended in the Leatherland family to William (1790–1870), from whose estate it was acquired by Arthur Wesley Dow, an uncle of the donor.

ACCESSION: 1961.18   A gift of Mrs. Wilton L. Putnam

2 / Box

1670–1690
Hingham-Scituate area, Massachusetts
H. 9½ (24.1); W. 25½ (64.8); D. 15¹⁵⁄₁₆ (40.5)

The Society's other seventeenth-century box is of the standard New England form: a nailed six-board box, each plane a single board. Whereas box no. 1 is exclusively oak, a more common arrangement of woods is seen here: four boards — the front, sides, and back — are riven oak; the bottom and top are sawn white pine.

This box never had applied moldings such as those on the preceding example. It originally looked much as it appears today except that the bottom board, now worn flush, protruded in front to simulate a base molding. All the ornament is on the façade: a decorative escutcheon and two carved, foliage-filled lunettes with additional sprigs in the spandrels.[1]

2

The carving is an important clue in attributing the box to coastal Massachusetts south of Boston. The floral lunette was a popular English motif. Related furniture can be documented to Dorset and Norfolk,[2] and the motif remained part of the design vocabulary of immigrant craftsmen in New England. Four chests from the New Haven area have the motif.[3] More closely comparable to the Society's box is a group of furniture, including a joined chest, a box-on-frame, and seven examples of a form (2a) variously termed "chest on frame" (by Nutting), "chest-on-frame with drawer" (by Fales), and "chamber table" (by Forman, who believed these to be the "toilet tables" and "chamber tables" mentioned in seventeenth-century inventories).[4]

Because of the similarity of the turnings on the legs of the chamber tables and on the arm supports of a wainscot armchair from seventeenth-century Hingham, St. George has attributed the group of pieces to the Hingham-Scituate area.[5] The Society's box, which descended in the Briggs family of Scituate, reinforces that attribution.[6]

Among this small group of carved furniture, the work on the Society's box is notable. It alone has a band of punchwork squares above and at the sides of the lunette pattern. The quality of the foliage carving on this box and on the joined chest is somewhat better than that on the rest of the group. Small dots terminate some of the veins on the leaves, and the foliage appears less constricted than the crowded leaves on the chamber table drawer fronts.

2a. Chamber Table. Hingham-Scituate, Massachusetts, area, 1650–1690. Oak and white pine; H. 32⅞ (83.5); W. 27¼ (69.2); D. 16¾ (42.5). Henry Francis du Pont Winterthur Museum.

1. The iron lock and escutcheon are of a type usually associated with trunks. Randall refers to four boxes with similar escutcheons in *American Furniture*, no. 3. One of these, the palmette-carved box at the Metropolitan Museum, is figure 21 in St. George, "Style and Structure."

2. Examples of the motif on Dorset furniture are figures 5c, 6a, and 6c in Wells-Cole, "Oak Furniture in Dorset." The motif can also be seen on interior paneling at Scoulton, Norfolk; Wells-Cole to authors, March 8, 1979.

3. Kane, *Furniture of the New Haven Colony*, nos. 2–5.

4. The chest was sold at auction, "Collection of the Late Dr. James W. Marvin," Sotheby Parke Bernet, sale 4156, September and October 1978, lot 304. The box-on-frame is privately owned. The present location of six of the chamber tables is known: the Winterthur Museum (two); the Metropolitan Museum (no. 117 in Nutting, *Pilgrim Century*, rev. ed.); the Philadelphia Museum (Nutting, *Pilgrim Century*, 1st ed., 88); Historic Deerfield (Fales, *Historic Deerfield*, 164); and a private collection. The seventh example was owned by Henry Wood Erving in 1913 (Lockwood, *Colonial*

Furniture, rev. ed., 1:215). Conversation with Forman, 1979.

5. St. George, *The Wrought Covenant,* 61–64; and St. George to the authors, March 10, 1979.

6. Stephen H. Nash to the authors, March 16, 1977. When the box was in the Nash collection, it was illustrated (no. 185) in the *Harvard Tercentenary Exhibition.*

NOTES ON STRUCTURE AND CONDITION: The box's boards are quite thin for New England work of the seventeenth century. The front is ¾ inch thick, the sides ⅝ inch, the back and bottom ½ inch. The frame is nailed together in typical seventeenth-century-box fashion with forged rose-headed nails.

The lid, an eighteenth-century replacement, retains its original cleats, forged nails, and one original cotter-pin hinge. Except for the replaced lid, the box is in excellent condition. It has an old coat of dull red paint. The replacement lid never was lockable, and no till was ever present.

MATERIALS: *Red oak; white pine* top, cleats, and bottom. The iron lock and escutcheon are original; the escutcheon's right slot is for a key, the left for a hinged hasp. Both iron hinges are replaced; the older is original to the eighteenth-century lid.

PROVENANCE: The box, which descended in the Briggs family of Scituate, supposedly held the Briggs Bibles well into the twentieth century. It was purchased (with the Bibles) by Chauncy C. Nash, whose paternal grandmother was a Briggs, and inherited by the donors.

ACCESSION: 1971.374   A gift of Mr. and Mrs. Stephen H. Nash in memory of Chauncy C. Nash

3 / Box

1750–1770
Boston
H. 8⅝ (21.1); W. 23½ (59.7); D. 11½ (29.2)

In the eighteenth century, new, specialized furniture, such as the desk, dressing table, and chest of drawers, provided many small places for storage, thus supplanting the once

ubiquitous box. The few extant eighteenth-century boxes feature handsome primary woods, brass hardware, and well-shaped feet instead of the decorative carving that distinguished their seventeenth-century counterparts.[1]

This box is typical of the craftsmanship of its era. The case is dovetailed at the sides rather than nailed like seventeenth-century boxes. The lid is attached with small brass butt hinges instead of the earlier iron cotter-pin hinges. As with a large eighteenth-century case, an applied ogee molding frames the base, straight bracket feet support the case, and rococo brasses grace the front and sides.

This box is the only item in the Society's furniture collection made of red cedar. Though not a common wood in American furniture, it was used in the Boston area during the eighteenth century. Samuel Burnell, a Boston cooper, owned "1 cedar box" and "a large cedar chest" in 1735.[2] In 1760 Thomas Foot, a Boston cabinetmaker, listed among his shop goods "36 foot Cedar Logs," and in 1776 Thomas Wood, a cabinetmaker in nearby Charlestown, included six cedar desks in an inventory of recently completed furniture.[3]

Red cedar, shipped to Boston from Bermuda, was comparable in price to imported black walnut; it cost less than the prestigious imported mahogany, more than the native hardwoods — maple, birch, and cherry.[4]

The history of the box indicates a Boston origin. It belonged to Oliver Brewster (ca. 1757–1812), a prominent Boston merchant and public official, whose initials appear in an old ink inscription on the bottom of the box.

1. Another New England eighteenth-century box is illustrated in *Israel Sack Collection,* 1:161.

2. Samuel Burnell's estate inventory, old series, vol. 32, p. 184, Suffolk County (Mass.) Probate.

3. Accounts of losses in the Boston fire of March 20, 1760, Thomas Foot Account, Boston Public Library; accounts of losses from the burning of Charlestown, June 17, 1775, Thomas Wood Account, Boston Public Library.

4. The shop inventory of Benjamin Salisbury, a Boston cabinetmaker, records the value of these woods in 1760. Cedar and black walnut boards were appraised at 3 shillings per foot, mahogany boards at 6 shillings per foot, and maple and pine boards at 6 pence per foot; accounts of losses in the Boston fire of March 20, 1760, Benjamin Salisbury Account, Boston Public Library.

NOTES ON STRUCTURE AND CONDITION: The bottom is nailed into the rabbeted lower edges of the front and back and to the flush lower edges of the sides. The ogee base molding is glued and nailed to the case. The feet are backed by vertical and flanking horizontal blocks. The top is edged with an ogee curve at the back. Cleats are fastened to the top with the original forged finishing nails. There is no till.

The front of the right cleat is recut. The feet are well worn; originally the box stood slightly higher. Small portions of the front feet have been pieced. The box was refinished in 1976.

MATERIALS: *Red cedar; white pine* bottom. Original brass hardware and steel lock.

PROVENANCE: The box was owned by Oliver Brewster of Boston, inherited by his son Oliver (1811–1868), and presented to the Society by the latter's only child, William (ca. 1858–1933).

ACCESSION: 1929.496   A gift of William Brewster

4 / Tea Chest

ca. 1758
England
H. 6¹¹⁄₁₆ (17); W. 10½ (26.7); D. 6³⁄₁₆ (15.7)

This handsome English tea chest has a well-documented American history. On August 16, 1759, John Scollay, a Boston importer, sold and shipped to Jonathan Sayward:

1 Easy Chair & packing	£4:18:6
1 doz Scythes	2:13:4
1 Copper Coffeepott	0:13:4
1 doz Ivory Handle Knives & forks	1: 2:–
1 Tea Chest	2: 8:–[1]

The bill (4a) survives as a loose insert in Sayward's almanac-diary in the collection of the American Antiquarian Society; the tea chest survives in Sayward's house in York, Maine.

The house still contains most of the furniture purchased for it by Sayward (1713–1797), a prosperous merchant of York, which was then part of Massachusetts. Prominent in civic as well as commercial affairs in York County, Sayward served in Boston as York's representative in the provincial Massachusetts legislature (1766–1768) and later was judge of probate for the county.

Fifteen pieces of his furniture are included in this book.[2] Among them are looking glass no. 146 and the tea chest, both made in England. Most tea chests used in eighteenth-century American homes were imported by merchants such as Scollay from English cabinetmakers, many of whom specialized in the form. One such specialist — Richard Holmes, at the sign of the Tea Chest in London — advertised that he made looking glasses, frames, tea trays and "Tea Chests for Exportation."[3]

The Society's chest is a good example of English cabinetwork of the period. The substantial sum paid Scollay for the chest, almost half the price of the "Easy Chair," indicates its value and quality. The mahogany case is veneered with figured panels of dense, dark mahogany inlaid with brass stringing on its four sides and top in a pattern reminiscent of door panels on London clothes presses and bookcases of the 1740s.[4] The case has vertical beads of mahogany at the corners and rests on small, modified ogee-bracket feet.

The interior arrangement follows a common English formula, and each of the three compartments retains its original tin canister (4b). The two flanking canisters held different types of teas; their tops served as measures.[5] The central container was used for sugar. The chest has a lock to ensure safe storage of the costly imported teas.

The tea chest was only one of an elegant assortment of specialized articles associated with the fashionable eighteenth-century social custom of tea drinking. Tea tables, tea boards or trays, tea sets, teaspoons, and more were considered necessary accouterments for the proper serving of the beverage.

4

4a. Bill. John Scollay to Jonathan Sayward. American Antiquarian Society.

4b

Because tea was prepared and sipped in the parlor, the tea equipment was kept there, often providing the principal decorative embellishments for the best rooms of wealthy New Englanders. In 1763 the "Setting Parlour" of Robert Oliver of Dorchester contained a tea chest, waiters, and a tea table set with tea china.[6] In the same year Benjamin Prat's middle parlor in his Milton home included two japanned waiters, a tea chest, "Tea Geer," and "a Mahogony Tea Board & coarse set of blue & white China."[7]

Sayward's tea chest seems always to have been kept in the southwest parlor. It is not among the tea equipment Sayward willed to his widow, Elizabeth, to be used "during her Widowhood" in the part of the house he left to her, the northwest end.[8] The tea chest remained in the southwest parlor for the use of Sayward's grandson and heir, Jonathan Sayward Barrell. Sayward's great-granddaughter Mary, who owned the house from 1857 to 1884, kept the tea chest in the "bofat," the parlor's built-in corner cupboard, with other small and valued objects.[9]

1. Scollay to Sayward, Boston, August 16, 1759, bill folded into Sayward's interleaved almanac-diary of 1760; Sayward Papers, American Antiquarian Society.

2. Sayward's other objects are: chest of drawers no. 21, dressing table no. 33, high chest no. 37, tall clock no. 54, drop-leaf tables no. 59 and 62, tea table no. 68, card table no. 69, side chairs no. 96, 112, and 118, corner chair no. 100, easy chair no. 101, and looking glass no. 146.

3. Holmes's trade card is illustrated in Heal, *London Furniture Makers*, 84.

4. See, for example, the labeled case pieces by Giles Grendy in Edwards and Jourdain, *Georgian Cabinet-Makers*, 144–45.

5. Roth, "Tea Drinking in 18th-Century America," 89.

6. Cummings, *Inventories*, 191.

7. Ibid., 199.

8. Manuscript copy of the 1793 will of Jonathan Sayward, Sayward Papers, Society for the Preservation of New England Antiquities.

9. "Copy of Inventory of Estate of Mary Barrell," a manuscript copy of the 1884 York County (Me.) Probate; Sayward Papers, Society for the Preservation of New England Antiquities.

NOTES ON STRUCTURE AND CONDITION: Because the box was made to be viewed from all sides, its rear feet are finished and the back is veneered and inlaid with brass like the top, front, and sides. The carcass is dovetailed, and a vertical bead is inserted at each corner. The bottom is glued to the chest; the base molding, mitered at the corners, is glued to the bottom. The feet have no support blocks.

The chest is in superb condition. The interior of the lid has its original velvet lining and silk braid.

MATERIALS: Mahogany veneer on *mahogany*. Original brass inlay, handle, and hinges; original lock and tinned sheet-iron canisters.

PROVENANCE: The box was willed by Jonathan Sayward with his house to his grandson Jonathan Sayward Barrell, then left to the latter's unmarried daughters Elizabeth and Mary, and by Mary to her nephew George Octavius Barrell (1848–1900). It was purchased in 1900 by a relative, Elizabeth Cheever Wheeler.

ACCESSION: 1977.212   A gift of the heirs of Elizabeth Cheever Wheeler

5 / Chest

1680–1700

Scituate-Marshfield area, Massachusetts

H. 27⅝ (70.2); W. 52¾ (134); D. 20⅝ (52.4)

Seventeenth-century New Englanders needed large locked containers for the storage of bulky items, primarily textiles, which were exceedingly valuable. Michael Metcalfe, a farmer in Dedham, Massachusetts, kept in his bedchamber "a joyned Chest with 6 p.ʳ of Sheets, 12 napkins, 3 pʳ of pillowbeers, 2 Table Cloths and a Towell."[1]

Many seventeenth-century chests were, like Metcalfe's, "joyned." Their rails and stiles, grooved to hold the panels they framed, were fastened at every juncture with a mortise-and-tenon joint. In tribute to the mortise and tenon, the chests were called "joined chests"; the men who made them, "joiners"; and their craft, "joinery."

The chest, the principal furniture in seventeenth-century households, was either joined, the more valuable type, or of six-board construction (III-11), nailed at the corners like some boxes (no. 1 and 2). Dovetailed chests did not become popular in America until the following century.

Although joined chests were commonplace, one with a façade of five panels was not. Usually joined chests had three front panels; a few had four. This chest is one of only four known American examples with a five-panel façade.[2] One, which descended in the Little family of Marshfield, is similar to the Society's but lacks the serrated chip carving

5

on the edge of the lower front rail and the paired notches on the lower side rails (5a).

In the 1920s, Nutting identified a large body of joinery — more than twenty chests and cupboards (I-11) — all sharing several design characteristics: (1) a serrated edge, often on the lower front rail; (2) an incised sawtooth pattern (see 5b, the top of the till), an echo of the serrated edge; (3) paired notches on rails of secondary importance; (4) the use of riven white cedar boards for the bottom (Nutting mistakenly referred to the wood as pine); and (5) applied ornament.[3] (The Society's chest has all these features except applied ornament.) Nutting attributed the group to Plymouth, although one piece was found in an attic in Scituate.[4]

In recent studies, St. George further defines this furniture, attributing it to distinct communities in southeastern Massachusetts and placing this chest among a group made in the prosperous North River towns of Marshfield and Scituate.[5] St. George finds the incised sawtooth pattern, which decorates the till lid (5b), on the board furniture of that area.[6] He notes that fine construction, evident throughout the Society's chest, is characteristic of Scituate-Marshfield joinery.

This chest, with a history in the Boston area, has a Scituate connection. It descended in the family of Peleg Bronsdon (1854–1931) of Milton, Massachusetts.[7] Peleg's grandmother Nancy Wade Damon Bronsdon (1789–1860), who died in Milton, was born in Scituate, the fifth generation of Scituate's Damon family.[8] Apparently the chest migrated to the Boston area through Nancy Damon Bronsdon. Although her family included woodworkers, attributing this chest to a Damon cannot yet be done. For now it must suffice that the maker of this well-designed and finely constructed chest was a skillful joiner of the Scituate-Marshfield area.

1. Cummings, *Inventories*, 71.

2. One, in the Connecticut Historical Society, appears in *Seymour Collection*, 17. Another, at the Smithsonian Institution, is shown in the "The Greenwood Gift," 120. The third, at the Winslow House in Marshfield, descended in the Little family; St. George, *The Wrought Covenant*, no. 1.

3. Nutting, *Pilgrim Century*, rev. ed., 60, 65–66, 71–72, 199–200, 205–6, nos. 24–28, 197–99. Other examples of the Plymouth group appear in Randall, *American Furniture*, nos. 8, 19; Lockwood, *Colonial Furniture*, rev. ed., vol. 1, figs. 22–24; Fales, *Historic Deerfield*, fig. 488; *Antiques* 56 (August 1949): 105 and Andrus, "American Furniture," 167; and Sack, *Fine Points of Furniture*, 110. A discussion of white cedar in Massachusetts is in Emerson, *Report on the Trees*, 1:114–17.

4. Nutting, *Pilgrim Century*, rev. ed., 65, no. 26.

5. St. George, *The Wrought Covenant*, 26.

6. Ibid.; see the sawtooth decoration on figures 23–26.

7. Stephen H. Nash to the authors, March 16, 1977; an informative account of Bronsdon's life is in *The Milton Record*, November 14, 1931, pp. 1, 8.

8. St. George, *The Wrought Covenant*, 81.

NOTES ON STRUCTURE AND CONDITION: The joined chest has fourteen riven oak panels. Forged nails fasten the bottom, four front-to-back boards, to the carcass. The top is held with its second set of cotter-pin hinges. Remnants of the original hinges survive in the top rail. The right cleat is fastened to the top with forged nails; the left is missing. The ogee edges of the stiles match those on the till.

The chest is in excellent condition. The molded edges of the stiles and rails are still crisp. The feet are barely worn. A nineteenth-century layer of tan paint was removed by a previous owner to reveal the original black paint still on the deep channel moldings of the rails and stiles and on the serrated edge of the lower front rail.

5a

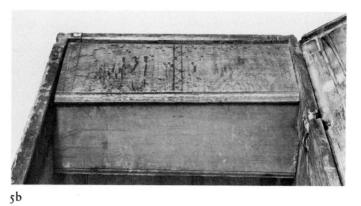

5b

MATERIALS: *Red oak; northern white cedar* chest bottom, till side and bottom; *white pine* top and cleat. Replaced iron hinges and lock.

PROVENANCE: The chest descended in the family of Peleg Bronsdon, from whom it was purchased in the early 1920s by Chauncy C. Nash. It descended to the donors.

ACCESSION: 1971.372   A gift of Mr. and Mrs. Stephen H. Nash in memory of Chauncy C. Nash

6 / Chest with Drawers

1635–1670
Boston
H. 26⅛ (66.4); W. 47⅝ (121); D. 21½ (54.6)

This Boston chest, older than the preceding Scituate chest, is newer in form and in style. The old form, a chest accessible from the top only, is difficult to use because items stored deep within are hard to reach. The newer form, the chest with drawers, solves the problem. Drawers — bins or compartments so called because they were *drawn* out through the front of the chest — were placed in one or two tiers at the bottom of chests, where they were most needed.

What survives here is a chest with what appears to be two side-by-side drawers but is really one case-wide drawer. The chest originally had two drawers, one above the other, but lost its lower drawer and feet long ago. The drawing (6a) shows the chest as it would have originally appeared (see *Notes on the Drawing*).

Some of the stunning splendor of the original can be imagined from the remnant and the sketch. Here on an American case piece is the elaborate decoration — the applied

6

ornament and varied woods — fashionable at the same time in London. This chest is so early and so elegant an example of the new style that even with the present coat of brown paint masking its original color and without its lower drawer, base molding, and feet, the remnant is of outstanding importance in the history of American furniture. When Forman first saw it, he called it "the most important eastern Massachusetts chest in captivity."[1]

The decoration on the chest represents a major departure from the flat, stylized carving so popular in seventeenth-century New England and seen on boxes no. 1 and 2. The carved boxes illustrate the continued popularity of sixteenth- and early-seventeenth-century English design traditions; the chest is an urban American version of contemporaneous London fashion — the new style of bold contrasts in shapes, texture, and colors.

Contrasting shapes were provided by applied moldings, bosses, triglyphs, and split spindles; contrasting textures, by varied woods as well as by the applied elements; contrasting colors, by different woods and paint. The maple split spindles were originally painted black to simulate ebony. The moldings were made of red cedar, the flat insets on the front panels of black walnut. The carcass of cream-colored oak showed through within the panels' L-shaped corners and on the stiles and rails. Thus ebonized spindles, bosses, and triglyphs stood out from oak stiles and top rail; red cedar moldings formed the boundaries between dark black walnut and light oak. Amid this play of color, the applied shapes caused shadows, creating even more variations.

6a. Re-creation of the Original Appearance of Chest No. 6. Drawing, Corinne Pascoe.

This robust style began on the European continent. Early in the seventeenth century, Dutch craftsmen boldly employed contrasting woods in geometric patterns, and the style was soon available in London. Immigrant Dutch woodcarvers and stonemasons, their sons and apprentices, worked in the multicolored geometric and architectural style, plying their trades in Southwark, across the Thames from London, because as foreigners they were forbidden to settle within the city limits.[2] By 1647, they developed a distinct Southwark style, featuring inlays of exotic woods, mother of pearl, and ivory.[3] Two London or Southwark products, a chest of drawers dated 1653 and a chest with drawers dated 1661 (6b), illustrate the design vocabulary and motifs used by the joiner who made chest no. 6 — paired spindles, applied moldings, and most notably the turned ring inset with four keystones and bordered by an octagon.[4]

Five known examples of Boston furniture in this high style survive: the chest shown here, a chest of drawers with doors, a chest of drawers, and two chests, each with one drawer.[5] All have similar applied ornament, although only the Society's chest has the especially stylish feature of the applied ring. All the chests have dovetailed drawers (6c). All use woods imported to New England (black walnut and red cedar in this chest), although the chest of drawers and the chest of drawers with doors use the most exotic woods.

The Boston craftsmen who made these chests were trained in London or Southwark. The dovetailed drawer construction characteristic of the group was a common feature of London work and is seen in Boston and New Haven, where London craftsmen settled; elsewhere in New England joiners were nailing drawers together.[6] The Boston furniture uses the same decorative woods as London or Southwark examples. The fine manner in which the Boston furniture is finished, even on the inside surfaces, indicates London training. The turned ring on the Society's chest illustrates the furniture maker's thorough knowledge of excellent English examples.

The 1661 English chest (6b) is strong evidence for similarly dating this example and for assuming that Europe's fashionable geometric style reached Boston in about 1660 in the person of an immigrant craftsman. But Forman's extensive research of joiners working in Boston in the seventeenth century does not reveal the name of any London-trained man who came to Boston in the midcentury.[7] Several London and Southwark woodworkers came to Boston in the early years of the settlement: joiners Ralph Mason (in 1634), John Davis (1635), and Henry Messinger (by 1641), and turners Thomas Edsall (in 1635) and Robert Winsor (by 1644).[8]

6b. Chest with Drawers. England, 1661. Oak, exotic woods, and mother-of-pearl; H. 42 (106.7); W. 53 (134.6); D. 22 (55.9). Present location unknown; illustrated in Macquoid, *History of English Furniture*, 1:233. *A lower drawer is missing, and the base is a replacement. The chest is dated in the middle of the surviving drawer.*

Whether this chest and the related examples are of 1635–1640 vintage, as the settlement of joiners from London to Boston may suggest, or whether some unknown immigrant brought the style to Boston closer to the 1661 date of the English example, awaits further documentation and dating of joinery styles in London. Whenever it was made, in about 1640 or 1660, the Society's chest with its ring decoration is a direct link to high-style London fashion and marks the migration of a major style from Europe to America in the hands of a joiner who was making stylish furniture in London one year and similar pieces in Boston the next.

6c

1. Conversation with Benno M. Forman, 1976.

2. Forman, "Continental Furniture Craftsmen," and Whinney, *Sculpture in Britain*, 13–14.

3. Jourdain, *English Decoration and Furniture*, 225, fig. 310.

4. The 1653 chest appears in Smith, *Catalogue of English Furniture*, no. 602, and Hayden, *Chats on Old Furniture*, frontispiece. Hayden illustrates it with earlier replaced feet.

5. Forman, in "Urban Aspects," discusses three of the group — a chest of drawers with doors in the Garvan Collection at the Yale University Art Gallery, a chest of drawers of similar size in the Museum of Fine Arts, Boston, and a chest with a single drawer in a private collection — and cites a fourth identical to the latter. Also see Forman, "Joined Chest," and *New England Begins*, vol. 3, nos. 481, 493.

6. Trent, "New England Joinery," 501, 503.

7. Forman, "Joined Chest," 177–79.

8. Ibid., 179. Also see *New England Begins*, vol. 3, no. 481.

NOTES ON STRUCTURE AND CONDITION: The joined carcass has a four-panel back. The lower side panels have been cut. The bottom of the chest compartment consists of seven front-to-back boards, three of which are replaced. The top — four narrow butt-jointed oak boards — and the cleats are original. The nails that held the cleats have been replaced with screws. The top lifts on wood pintles that go through the cleats into the upper rails of the sides. One pintle is original. The slats to support the drawer are missing, and the drawer now runs on its replaced bottom.

Most of what survives on the chest is original. The façade retains almost all its applied decoration. The moldings are held with glue; the central ring with glue and four clenched nails. The only replacements are the upper oval boss on the left front stile, the horizontal members of the small applied square in the center of the left front panel, and the drawer knobs. The till is original. The craftsman's attention to detail is epitomized by the finishing touch in the chest interior of ogee-molded edges cut on the rear stiles.

NOTES ON THE DRAWING: The drawing is based on a suggested pattern for restoration by Forman. He re-created the original appearance of the Society's chest after studying its surviving elements and the related chest of drawers with doors.

First, the original number of drawers was ascertained. If the chest originally had only one drawer, there probably would be side rails at the level of the present bottom front rail. If it originally had three drawers, it would have had two pairs of vertical side panels. Only if it had two drawers was the configuration of the side panels explainable.

The façade for the lower drawer was copied from the chest's existing drawer because such repetition was standard. The feet, molding, and drawer knobs were adapted from the chest of drawers with doors because it is of the same style, of the same era and origin, and closest to the Society's chest in elegance.

MATERIALS: *Red oak; black walnut* applied flat insets; *red cedar* applied moldings; *maple* spindles and bosses; *white pine* chest and till bottoms. The case never had metal hinges or a lock.

PROVENANCE: James L. Little (d. 1914), a collector, had the chest in his Brookline, Mass., home. Little's son eventually sold it to George McMahon, a Boston antiques dealer, from whom it was purchased by the Society.

ACCESSION: 1940.55   Museum purchase

7 / Chest with Drawer (drawer missing)

1700–1720
Coastal Massachusetts, possibly Boston
H. 30⅞ (78.4); W. 44⁷⁄₁₆ (112.9); D. 19¼ (48.9)

The preceding chest was an early, rare, and elegant example of what was called in period documents a chest with drawer (or drawers). During the eighteenth century, the form became New England's common and humble blanket chest. This chest (whose drawer has been lost) is typical of the very early eighteenth century, when the transformation from rare to commonplace, from elegant to humble, was under way. This is a vernacular example of what was once an avant-garde form; it features a modified and inexpensive version of the geometric style.

Like its high-style predecessor (drawing 6a), this chest has a façade of panels whose expanse is broken up with moldings and insets. (The corner insets have been lost.) The central panel continues, in elongated form, the octagonal shape seen in chest no. 6. The amount of applied decoration on this chest, however, is far less. Painted dots simulate applied bosses. There are no triglyphs or spindles.

Each flanking panel has an "arch" created with straight moldings, reminiscent of English prototypes, with curved arches supported by realistic pilasters (see I-10, an American version). Under these "arches," painted trees grow in painted soil; similarly located foliage on stylish English prototypes is carved or inlaid with exotic woods.

No costly woods are used on this chest for contrasts in color. Instead, inexpensive pigment supplies color to native woods. The entire piece was painted red, then the moldings, feet, and channel-molded grooves were painted black, as were the dots, trees, and mounds of earth.

The construction is simple. A base molding, such as that in drawing 6a, never skirted this example. But the primary simplification results from the availability of native white pine in broad mill-sawn planks. Using pine planks, a New England joiner could make chests easily and quickly.

7

The top of the chest is a single pine board instead of the multiboard oak top of chest no. 6. The panels are sawn pine; riven oak was used on the two preceding examples. The back has a single panel; chest no. 6 has four back panels. Each side has a single pine panel in place of the three side panels on the older chest. The fielded side panel — deeply beveled on four sides with a molding plane — is a nicety easily cut in soft pine. Fielded paneling on interior walls and doors appeared in New England in the early eighteenth century and no doubt was introduced at about the same time in furniture.[1]

This chest is one of a large group of similarly designed case furniture. Four related chamber tables with fielded side panels and twelve other chests with similar elongated front panels and fielded side panels — most with ball-turned front feet — form a group closely related in construction and panel design.[2] Two chests, one at the Wadsworth Atheneum and one at Historic Deerfield (7a), are so remarkably similar to the Society's in structure, moldings, and even in painted decoration that they can be attributed to the same shop.[3]

The lack of documentation on the related chests and chamber tables makes pinpointing their origin impossible at this time. Existing provenances suggest coastal Massachusetts

7a. Chest with Drawer. Coastal Massachusetts, possibly Boston, 1700–
1720. Red oak, maple, and white pine; H. 30½ (77.5); W. 44½ (113.0);
D. 18¾ (47.6). Historic Deerfield.

from Boston to Newbury, and several cases have been found in the Ipswich area.[4] The
large number of related objects probably indicates an urban origin, possibly Boston,
where much more furniture was made than elsewhere in the colony; the craftsmen of
Boston far outnumbered those of other coastal communities. The simplified style and
construction of this furniture suggest stock items, produced in quantity in urban shops.

Chests of this type remained in fashion for over a quarter of a century, from the 1680s
through the first decade of the eighteenth century. The thin, vertical appearance of this
chest and the presence of fielded panels suggest that such chests are late examples of the
geometric style and one of the last examples of New England joinery.

1. For an illustrated history of interior wall
paneling, see Cummings, *Framed Houses*, 168–90.

2. The twelve chests are in: the Connecticut Historical Society (*Seymour Collection*, 25); Historic
Deerfield (Fales, *Historic Deerfield*, 179); three at
the Ipswich Historical Society (one is in Singleton,
Furniture of Our Forefathers, 1:213); the Elizabeth
Perkins House, York, Me.; the Rhode Island School
of Design (Kettell, *Pine Furniture*, no. 21); the
Rowley Historical Society; the Wadsworth Atheneum (Nutting, *Pilgrim Century*, rev. ed., no. 69);
and three in private collections (one is in ibid., no.
53; one in "Fine Early American Furniture Gathered by Jacob Margolis," Anderson Galleries, sale

2207, December 1927, lot 89; and one in *Antiques* 79 [January 1961]: 76). The four chamber tables are in: the Henry Ford Museum (Bishop, *American Furniture*, 14); the Winterthur Museum (Forman, "Urban Aspects," 14); and two in private collections (one is in Morse, *Furniture,* 18; the other, in Nutting, *Pilgrim Century*, rev. ed., no. 120). These four are similar to a large group of chamber tables, some of which even have painted foliage related to the Society's piece but which also have flat side panels.

3. The chest at the Wadsworth Atheneum is missing its drawer.

4. Three chests now owned by the Ipswich Historical Society have been in Ipswich at least since the nineteenth century. Another, owned by the Rowley Historical Society, has been in that neighboring town as long. A fifth chest, at the Connecticut Historical Society, was acquired in Cambridge, Mass., early in the twentieth century.

NOTES ON STRUCTURE AND CONDITION: Originally the chest had a single case-wide drawer below the paneled façade. (The drawer on Historic Deerfield's example is nailed together [III-12].) Supports for the drawer remain on the inside of the stiles. Ap-plied moldings are held with hide glue and clenched nails. Originally flat triangular insets, all of which have been lost, were glued at the corners of the panels. One strip of molding on the center panel is replaced. Six front-to-back boards (four of pine, two of oak) form the bottom of the chest. The chest retains its original feet: flattened balls in front and extensions of the stiles in back. Each front foot is round-tenoned into a hole in the bottom of the stile and held with glue. The top was attached to the back with two cotter-pin hinges. Remnants of these hinges are visible in the top and back. Two cleats, now missing, were nailed to the underside of the top. The right side of the chest interior has a till.

MATERIALS: *Red oak; maple* feet; *white pine* top, panels, moldings, till, and four bottom boards. Replacement iron hinges; the lock is missing.

PROVENANCE: The chest was found in Maine by Roger Bacon, a New Hampshire antiques dealer, and sold to the donor in 1959.

ACCESSION: 1961.186   A gift of Mrs. Bertram K. Little

8 / Chest with Drawers

1730–1750
Coastal Massachusetts
H. 41¾ (106); W. 36 (91.4); D. 18⅛ (46)

In the last years of the seventeenth century and the early years of the eighteenth, furniture construction underwent a revolutionary change: joinery gave way to cabinetry. Producing chests of joined frames filled with panels was superseded by the new craft, in which cases were made of large boards used as flat surfaces and fastened at each right angle with a row of dovetails. Drawers were similarly dovetailed. This chest is an example of cabinetry: large, precisely cut dovetails secure the case sides to the case bottom (8a), and the drawer fronts and backs are dovetailed to the drawer sides.

Exactly when the new craft was introduced in New England is unknown. "John Clark, cabinetmaker" is listed in court records as a newly admitted resident of Boston in 1681.[1] No more is known of him, and the term "cabinetmaker" does not appear again in the seventeenth-century court records of New England. The first cabinetmaker known to have worked at his craft in Boston was John Brocas (Broccas).[2] Brocas was in Boston by 1696, had a shop on Union Street in the late 1730s, and practiced his trade from at least 1701 until his death in 1740.[3]

A cabinetmaker's stock in trade, the chest of drawers, was the fashionable form when this top-loading chest with three drawers was made, and it was originally finished to look like a chest of six drawers. Three simulated drawers were outlined on the chest façade with applied moldings (now missing), which corresponded in contour to the

8

drawer dividers between the real drawers. Dovetailed chests of drawers featured drawers graduated in size, with the deepest on the bottom, a pattern reflected here in the real and imaginary drawers.

To enhance the illusion of six drawers, brasses were applied to the upper "drawers" at considerable cost. In the 1730s, the Boston cabinetmaker Nathaniel Holmes paid £1:9:8 for a desk set (eight handles and five escutcheons) of common brasses and £2:5:0 for a set of fine brasses.[4] During the same era Holmes paid a workman £2:10:0 for crafting a desk.[5] This chest required far less woodwork than a desk and more brasses (twelve handles and six escutcheons). Its brasses originally cost as much as, or possibly more than, the cabinetry.

Adding to the chest's appearance as a chest of drawers is the lipped molding on top. It is shaped like a cornice molding on a chest of drawers and is applied to mask the front edge of the lid.

This chest, of later manufacture than one might guess at a glance, can be dated by the quality of its dovetails, which are quite precise, and by the style of its brasses. Although the time of its origin can be specified, the locale remains elusive. Except for maple feet, this red painted chest is all pine. Painted pine furniture was made in urban and rural areas alike; red was a favored color. The absence of unusual provincial woods and the quality of the workmanship suggest a coastal rather than an inland shop. Abraham Foster, a Boston cabinetmaker, owned "3 Pine Chests" in 1796.[6]

Despite its worn condition, this chest is important to the Society's collection. Dovetailed chests of six drawers with ball feet and single-arched moldings around the drawer openings are rare. This example, emulating a rare type, is truly distinctive.

1. Forman, "Urban Aspects," 17.

2. Ibid., 18.

3. Kaye, "Furniture Craftsmen," 273. The 1696 date for Brocas in Boston is from Forman, "Urban Aspects," 18.

4. Bill, Joseph Scott to Nathaniel Holmes, January 20, 1736, Accounts Current 1727–38, vol. 6, Bourn Papers, Baker Library, Harvard University. See January 22, 1734, entry for the 1:9:8 set and an earlier, undated January entry for the "fine" brasses.

5. Bill, John Mudge to Nathaniel Holmes, January 6, 1738; Joseph Downs Manuscript Collection, Winterthur Museum Libraries.

6. Abraham Foster's inventory, docket 20582, Suffolk County (Mass.) Probate.

NOTES ON STRUCTURE AND CONDITION: The back (three horizontal boards) and the front are nailed to the sides. The top is hinged to the back with

8a

cotter-pin hinges. Moldings are applied at the front of the lid and the base. Side moldings at the lid and base are missing. The drawer bottoms fit into grooves in the front and sides. The original ball feet, round-tenoned into holes in the bottom board, have suffered severe woodworm damage. Two feet were salvaged for use in front; reproductions were made for the back.

A twentieth-century coat of red paint covers the original red paint. The chest never had a till.

MATERIALS: *White pine;* maple feet. Original brass escutcheons and handles; original cotter-pin hinges (once augmented with butt hinges). It never had a lock.

PROVENANCE: The donor acquired the chest in 1938 from Edward C. Wheeler, Jr., of Boston, an early collector of American antique furniture.

ACCESSION: 1956.135   A gift of Mrs. Bertram K. Little

9 / Chest with Drawers

1735–1755
Southeastern Massachusetts or Rhode Island
H. 42¼ (107.3); W. 37¹⁄₁₆ (94.1); D. 16⅞ (42.9)

This is another chest with drawers (two real ones) disguised as a chest of drawers. Again, moldings and brasses feign drawers, and again, a lipped molding on the lid aspires to a cornice.

Unlike the preceding chest, however, this case is not cabinetry but nailed board construction, the simple skill used on boxes no. 1 and 2. The craftsman who made it knew how to make a dovetail; he dovetailed the drawers and did it quite well. He chose not to dovetail the case because a dovetailed case requires that the sides terminate where they join the bottom board. Instead he continued the sides below the bottom board to form the feet. The technique was a traditional way of making feet on simple furniture — on chests (III-11) and on chests with drawers. Here, however, the extension feet do not stand alone. Therein lies the unusual feature of this chest, for the craftsman augmented the side extension feet with front elements. The effect is that the chest appears to stand on bracket feet, a more sophisticated base than extension feet and standard on chests of drawers. The bracket-like feet add to the illusion that this is a chest of drawers.

True bracket feet (chest no. 10) are formed of boards mitered at the corners and glued to the underside of a base molding. Like true bracket feet, the feet here are mitered. And this chest has a base molding. But the added front elements are not glued to the underside of the base molding; they fit into notches in the bottom.

The unusual feet may be a clue to the chest's origin. Unfortunately, the authors do not know of a similarly constructed example that is documented. This chest's recent history associates it with southeastern Massachusetts.

Of particular delight is the chest's excellent condition. It has all of its applied moldings, its original brasses, its original red paint under a second coat of red, scarcely a dent, and its well-preserved original feet.

9

NOTES ON STRUCTURE AND CONDITION: The chest bottom fits into grooves in the sides and is fastened by forged nails that go through the base molding, through the sides, and into the bottom. The bottom and a narrow rail inside the case behind the front base molding are both notched to receive the front elements of the feet.

The cornice molding is nailed to the front and sides of the top and mitered at the corners. The base molding is of the same configuration and is similarly secured and cornered. An applied double-arched molding borders the two simulated drawers and forms the "divider" between them. The double-arched bead on the drawer divider is not applied.

The drawers are joined with wide but even dovetails. Original L-shaped nails reinforce most of the dovetails. Each bottom is nailed to the rabbeted edge of the drawer front and to the flush edges of the side and back. There never was a till.

MATERIALS: *White pine.* The lock is an early addition; all the brass hardware is original. The top escutcheon was moved higher when the lock was inserted.

PROVENANCE: The chest was purchased at auction in Marshfield, Mass. It reportedly came from an eighteenth-century house, the Morton estate, on the border of Pembroke and Hanson, Mass.

ACCESSION: 1958.57   Museum purchase

10 / Chest with Drawers

1750–1775
Eastern Massachusetts
H. 34¼ (87); W. 37⅝ (95.6); D. 18¹⁵⁄₁₆ (48.1)

The chest with drawers remained popular as a storage unit for textiles. Samuel Pierce of Dorchester kept "Five Table Cloths 9/ [shillings]. Six best pillow Cases 12/ two Coarse d°. 2/. four Napkins 5/. 18 Towells 10/ one pair of sheets 8[/]" in "a Chest with two draws" in his first-floor bedchamber in 1768, and in 1802 Jonathan Hamilton of South Berwick, Maine, kept "7 Homespun Blankets" and a "Lot Blankets and Quilts" in a chest in the chamber above his kitchen.[1]

Unlike chests no. 8 and 9, this is a blanket chest with no pretensions to a more stylish form. Yet it is a chest with distinction. The dovetailed construction is neatly done, both where the case bottom joins the sides (10a) and at the corners of the drawers. The top

10

edges of the drawer sides are stylishly molded, a feature often seen on finer cases but seldom on chests with drawers. The outline of the bracket feet is rather intricate. While many blanket chests lacked brasses and locks (chest no. 9 had no lock for a while), this one originally had brass handles and escutcheons (removed long ago) and two locks (which survive). The chest is in excellent condition; its original red paint remains beneath a second coat of red.

No history of ownership or inscription helps to determine the origin of the chest. However, the construction offers clues. The contour of the top edges of the drawer sides and the arrangement of support blocks for the feet (10a) are often seen on case furniture made in eastern Massachusetts in the second half of the eighteenth century.

1. Cummings, *Inventories*, 221–24, and Jonathan Hamilton's inventory, docket 8215, York County (Me.) Probate.

NOTES ON STRUCTURE AND CONDITION: The three-board back is neatly attached; the uppermost board is double-rabbeted to the sides and nailed in place. The top is secured at the back with cotter-pin hinges. Forged finishing nails hold the cleats to the top. Each drawer bottom fits into grooves in the front and sides. There never was a till.

The right rear foot and its support blocks are replaced; the left rear foot (10a) is missing a vertical block behind the rear element.

MATERIALS: White pine. Original cotter-pin hinges and iron locks.

PROVENANCE: The chest was found in the attic of the Society's Boardman House, Saugus, Mass.

ACCESSION: 1975.181   Donor unknown

10a

11 / Chest of Drawers

1670–1700
Boston area
H. 38⅜ (97.5); W. 38¾ (98.4); D. 22¾ (57.8)

> Lower Room . . .
> A chest with drawrs underneath 15 [shillings]
> A chest of drawrs 20 . . .
> — Boston estate inventory, 1700[1]

This chest (plate 1) is a chest *of* — not merely *with* — drawers, a form unknown in England at the time the Pilgrims emigrated. Before the seventeenth century, no English term existed for "drawer" or "chest of drawers." A 1599 Spanish-English dictionary had to resort to "a great chest, or standerd with drawing chestes, or boxes in it."[2] In the mid-seventeenth century, however, elegant English households had "chests of drawers," and the term appears occasionally in American inventories of the same era.[3] Early in its etymological history, "chest of drawers" probably included other furniture with drawers, such as cupboards, cabinets, and armoires.

By the end of the seventeenth century, New England household inventories frequently list chests of drawers. In 1700, Joshua Gardner of Muddy River (on the periphery of Boston) had in his parlor a feather bed and trundle, two tables, twelve chairs, a small trunk, a desk, a framed stool, and "a chest of drawrs and a Case of drawrs."[4] Although the men who took the inventory perceived some difference between a "chest" and a "case" of drawers, that distinction is lost. Probably the "case" was what we call a "high chest" (for an example, see 29a). Or possibly the "chest" was joined, like this chest, while the "case" was cabinetry.

Chests of drawers as well as chests and chests with drawers were used to hold textiles. The new form provided the advantage of increased accessibility to the stored items and, possibly even more important, a fixed top permanently available as a stand for boxes and other small articles. In 1704 Zechariah Long, a mariner, kept "a sett of Glasses on a Chest of Drawers" in his Boston house.[5]

This chest has four drawers, each decorated to look as if it had two panels. The case is joined, and the sides are genuinely two panels; each drawer front, however, is a board with applied moldings simulating panels. This geometric style was previously seen in chest no. 6.

A comparison with the earlier chest (drawing 6a) makes apparent the relationship of this chest *of* drawers to that chest *with* drawers. Both stand on turned feet and have two lower drawers with panel-like façades. The configuration of the two upper drawers in this chest is also derivative. The top rail of chest no. 6 has become the thin, minimally

11

ornamented top drawer. The largest and most elaborately decorated area on the chest with drawers has been translated here into the largest, most decorated drawer.

In the last years of the seventeenth century, the third drawer from the bottom, so prominent on this chest, lost the importance it inherited from forebears like chest no. 6. Furniture makers tried various drawer configurations in chests of drawers. Two of the configurations were large drawers on top and bottom (chest no. 13) and four equal drawers (chest no. 12).

More than a dozen American chests of drawers with façades similar to this one's survive, and where provenances exist, they are tied to Boston.[6] The Society's chest differs in several details from others in the group. This is a single case; all but three of the others are really two cases, one atop the other, each with two drawers and one side panel. The two-panel sides on the Society's chest emulate the sides of the stacked variety. The top on the Society's chest is most unusual. All of the other chests but one have overhanging tops with quarter-round or ogee moldings beneath the overhang. This top does not overhang; a coved cornice is attached to its edges. The feet on this chest have a sharper outline than those on related ones. The presence of tulipwood as a secondary wood is noteworthy, for it was seldom used as far north as Boston.

Some of the chests of drawers in this group are made of oak; others, like the Society's, are of black walnut, a wood coming into fashion in America in the 1670s.[7] Chest no. 6 illustrates an early and modest use of walnut as an embellishment on an oak case; this example illustrates the extensive use of walnut after 1670.

This chest exemplifies late-seventeenth-century joinery in other ways as well. The moldings are typical of the less flamboyant geometric style of the 1670s and 1680s. The flat side panels also typify the work of the period; in the early eighteenth century, joined chests of drawers would feature fielded side panels, sometimes with applied moldings (chest 13b).

1. Nathaniel Thayer's inventory, old series, vol. 14, p. 305, Suffolk County (Mass.) Probate.

2. Minsheu, *Dictionaire*, translates *caxón*.

3. Lyon, *Colonial Furniture*, 73, has a Plymouth reference, and an Essex County reference is in Forman, "Seventeenth-Century Case Furniture," 136. Dated English examples are figures 3 and 4 in Macquoid and Edwards, *Dictionary*, vol. 2.

4. Cummings, *Inventories*, 83–84.

5. Long's inventory, old series, vol. 15, p. 234, Suffolk County (Mass.) Probate.

6. Related chests of drawers include: (1) a walnut chest sold at auction in 1977, which appears identical even to the brasses; (2) a walnut chest in a private collection with similarly constructed feet; (3) a walnut chest at the Lexington Historical Society with a Boston-area provenance; (4) a chest similar to the preceding one (*Antiques* 116 [August 1979]: 213); (5) a privately owned chest of oak that descended in the Pierce family of Dorchester (now part of Boston); (6) one almost identical to the Pierce chest (Norman-Wilcox, "American Furniture," 282); (7 & 8) another, similar to the Pierce chest and a related straight-footed version, both of single-case construction and in the Wadsworth Atheneum; (9) a straight-footed version at the Milwaukee Art Center; (10) a chest advertised in *Antiques* 78 (August 1960): 99; (11) a one-piece oak chest found in Malden, just north of Boston, which was at the Wayside Inn in Sudbury, Mass., when illustrated in Morse, *Furniture*, rev. ed., 18–19; (12) a more elaborate version at the Museum of Fine Arts, Boston, which belonged to the collector Hollis French of Boston before 1913; (13) a chest found in Dedham, Mass., now in the Seymour Collection at the Connecticut Historical Society; (14) a somewhat related one owned by H. W. Erving when illustrated as figure 46 in Lockwood, *Colonial Furniture*, rev. ed., vol. 1; and (15) a chest owned by Morris Schwartz (Nutting, *Furniture Treasury*, vol. 1, no. 226). A related chest with two drawers was owned in Boston (Nutting, *Pilgrim Century*, rev. ed., no. 51).

7. English chests of drawers with this drawer configuration date from the 1660s and, like the cupboards and cabinets from which they originated, are seldom of walnut. See Macquoid and Edwards, *Dictionary*, vol. 2, figs. 5, 6, 8; Macquoid, *History of English Furniture*, vol. 1, figs. 213, 214; Gilbert, *Furniture at Temple Newsam House*, vol. 1, no. 151; and two English chests in the Society's collections (1931.231, 1971.66).

NOTES ON STRUCTURE AND CONDITION: The joined frame has a one-panel back. A medial brace is set in notches in the cornice rail and the upper rail of the back. The top is pinned to the medial brace and frame; the bottom is held with rose-headed nails. The front stiles are round-tenoned completely through the crisply turned feet. The rear stiles form the rear feet. The drawer dividers are tenoned and pinned to the stiles. The cornice and base are one-piece moldings. The pine drawer fronts are faced with flat strips and moldings of black walnut. Each drawer side is joined to the front with a large dovetail reinforced with one or two rose-headed nails; the back is nailed to the sides. Each bottom fits into a groove in the front and is nailed to the sides and back. The drawers are side-hung.

The chest is in superb condition, retaining almost all the original applied moldings. The feet, base, and cornice show little wear.

MATERIALS: *Black walnut* all finished surfaces; *Spanish cedar* medial brace beneath the top; *white pine* case bottom and drawer fronts and backs; *red*

oak drawer sides, drawer supports, base rail, and dividers; *tulipwood* case back, drawer bottoms, and one drawer back. Original brass hardware and iron locks.

PROVENANCE: The chest belonged to Mary Thacher, a prominent Massachusetts collector in the early twentieth century who bought much of her antique furniture in Boston, and descended to the donor.

ACCESSION: 1971.66   A gift of Guido R. Perera

12 / Chest of Drawers

1665–1685
Middlesex County, Massachusetts, possibly Cambridge
H. 36⅞ (93.7); W. 44⁵⁄₁₆ (112.6); D. 21½ (54.6)

Chests whose drawers are of equal height are rare, and the authors know of no other decorated with broad channel moldings like those on this example.[1] Originally this chest also featured a front cornice of angled dentils, a detail more often seen on cupboards (12a). The dentils were removed long ago, but traces of the glue that held them remain under the cornice molding, an eighteenth-century alteration. (The top rail with the cornice molding removed appears in 12b.)

Although no provenance or maker's inscription documents the chest's origin, its design and construction show strong similarities to a group of furniture, including several cupboards, attributed to Middlesex County.[2] One cupboard descended in the Stone family of Middlesex County and reportedly belonged to Gregory Stone, a resident of Cambridge from 1637 until his death in 1672.[3] A second cupboard in the group was purchased in Concord in 1898.[4]

Another, more elaborate cupboard (12a) shares with the Society's chest of drawers several design features: angled cornice dentils, drawers of equal size, and a base molding with angled ends applied to the front only. Further comparison of the Society's chest and the illustrated cupboard is impossible because the whereabouts of the cupboard is unknown. When it was illustrated by Nutting, it belonged to Dwight Blaney of Boston.[5]

The other Middlesex cupboards and the Society's chest share similarities in construction.[6] The drawer fronts are dovetailed to the sides, and the backs are nailed to the sides. The drawer bottoms are thick pine slabs, deeply chamfered on all sides. The case backs, similarly of thick chamfered pine, are nailed as backboards rather than inserted as panels. The feet on this chest are closely related to those on a chest with drawer

12

attributed to Middlesex County.[7] The base molding on that chest is also applied to the front only and is similarly angled at the ends.

One construction idiosyncrasy evident in the Society's chest is the incised numbering (12c) of each drawer (I, II, III, 4) on each drawer element to be dovetailed; that is, on the oak drawer fronts and sides. The pine drawer backs were merely nailed on. The incised numbers on the oak pieces allowed the joiner to identify the matched parts as he put together four drawers of equal size.

Chisel-numbering of joints in house construction was routine in the seventeenth century. Chisel-numbering of chairs in sets was commonplace in the eighteenth. But chisel-numbered drawers are rare.[8] The Middlesex cupboards available for examination and the chest with drawer in the group need no numbering; each has but one drawer. If the

Blaney cupboard can be located and if its three drawers are similarly numbered, these chisel marks would tie the cupboards and this chest of drawers to one shop with certainty.

1. Nutting illustrates only three chests of equal drawers in *Pilgrim Century*, rev. ed., nos. 93, 94, and 96.

2. Trent, "Joiners and Joinery," 126–33. Angled dentils are also featured on cupboards from Wethersfield, Conn., but the Society's chest of drawers is not constructed like the Connecticut pieces. *Connecticut Furniture* illustrates a cupboard with angled dentils as number 106.

3. Trent, "Joiners and Joinery," 127–30.

4. *Seymour Collection*, 42–43.

5. Number 210 in Nutting, *Pilgrim Century*, rev. ed.

6. In "Joiners and Joinery," Trent links the Gregory Stone cupboard at the Concord Antiquarian Society to the Blaney cupboard, to one at Colonial Williamsburg, and to one formerly at the New-York Historical Society and attributes them to John

Taylor of Cambridge. The authors examined the Stone cupboard.

7. Ibid., fig. 5.

8. An eighteenth-century Concord case (high chest no. 48) has drawers chisel-numbered I, II, III, 4. Forman brought to the authors' attention a joined chisel-marked chest, no. 56.10.3 at the Winterthur Museum, similarly numbered on the drawer fronts and sides, but marked IIII on drawer four.

NOTES ON STRUCTURE AND CONDITION: The frame is joined, but the back is two horizontal boards nailed to the case and the bottom is one board with wide beveled edges nailed to the case. Nails and wooden pins hold the top to the frame. Drawer dividers are set in mortises in the stiles and are secured with pins. The turned feet are round-tenoned into holes in the front stiles. The rear feet are

12a. Cupboard. Middlesex County, Massachusetts, 1655–1685. Illustrated in Nutting, *Pilgrim Century*, pl. 210. Photograph, Robert F. Trent. *The cupboard was in the Dwight Blaney Collection.*

12b

12c

extensions of the rear stiles. The drawers are side-hung.

The contour of the channel-molded façades of the drawer dividers matches that on the side rails and that at the center of the broad design on the front stiles and on the applied strips in the middle of the drawer fronts. The chest was painted black long ago, but was cleaned and refinished before 1949. The left front foot is a replacement, and the rear corners of the top are pieced.

MATERIALS: *Red oak; white pine* top, back, bottom, cornice molding, drawer backs, and drawer bottoms; *poplar* right front foot. Replaced brass hardware.

PROVENANCE: The chest was purchased from Israel Sack, Inc., New York.

ACCESSION: 1949.85   Museum purchase

13 / Chest of Drawers

1715–1735
New England
H. 35¹³⁄₁₆ (91); W. 40⅛ (101.9); D. 19⅝ (49.8)

This unique painted chest of drawers (plate 2) is from rural New England. Two factors hinder narrowing its attribution: its lack of a documented history and its uniqueness. The woods — white pine, maple, red oak, tupelo, and poplar (the latter used only for the turned front feet, 13a) — indicate New England. The presence of the seldom-used tupelo, which grows in low-lying swampy terrain throughout New England, helps only to exclude origin in the mountains.[1]

The workmanship — the nailed case and nailed drawers — indicates the hand of a carpenter. He was neither a joiner nor a cabinetmaker but was aware of high-style joinery and cabinetry, both vital crafts in the first years of the eighteenth century. He seems to have been inspired by a drawer configuration seen in joined pieces and by the flat surfaces seen in cabinetry.

The configuration of the drawers (large, small, small, large) is a pattern used on stylish joined chests of drawers made in the Boston area during the early eighteenth century (13b).[2] Their drawer fronts have applied moldings that create the illusion of panels. The painted façade of this chest echoes the applied drawer fronts. Joined chests with this configuration have fielded side panels enhanced with applied moldings, but the case sides on this chest are flat and suggest dovetailed cabinetry.

The paint also hints at the veneered façades of cabinetry. Early veneered cases with graduated drawers have drawer fronts similarly divided, but with the application of flat veneers instead of three-dimensional moldings.[3] The breadth of the painted bands on this chest suggests molding; the striped texture implies veneer.

The painted decoration on this piece is unique, although the use of different colors for drawers of different sizes is occasionally seen.[4] So much decoratively painted furniture

13

has lost its original finish that we cannot even guess at the popularity of this type of work. Similarly, nailed furniture was made in far greater numbers than surviving examples suggest. Such pieces proved more ephemeral than the more valued work of furniture craftsmen. Thus, the Society's collection is enriched by this work of an unknown carpenter who simulated fashionable furniture using nails and paint.

1. Emerson, *Report on Trees*, 2:353–57.

2. The drawer configuration can also be seen on chests at the Brooklyn Museum (*Antiques* 69 [April 1956]: 344); at the North Andover Historical Society (Kettell, *Pine Furniture*, no. 34); at the Winterthur Museum; at Colonial Williamsburg; two at the Metropolitan Museum; and three in Nutting, *Furniture Treasury*, vol. 1, nos. 224, 228, 229.

3. A veneered desk with a panel-like design is number 35 in Warren, *Bayou Bend*.

4. Two examples with large drawers on top and bottom painted in one fashion and the drawers between painted in another are those at the Brooklyn and Winterthur museums cited in note 2.

NOTES ON STRUCTURE AND CONDITION: T-shaped nails hold the top and bottom to the sides; each surface is a single board. The two backboards are

13a

13b. Chest of Drawers. Boston area, 1690–1710. Oak, maple, and pine; H. 36⅜ (92.4); W. 39¾ (101.0); D. 23⅜ (59.4). Mabel Brady Garvan Collection, Yale University Art Gallery.

rabbeted at the sides and nailed to the case with rose-headed nails. The drawer dividers, their edges cut to a single arch, fit into notches in the sides and are reinforced by T-shaped nails. A single-arched molding faces the edges of the case sides.

Each front foot is of two pieces of wood, a turned ball and a rod that pierces both the ball and the bottom of the case. The rear feet are rectangular blocks that pierce the bottom. Wooden pins set horizontally into the case bottom secure each foot. Each drawer back is rabbeted and nailed to the sides; the sides are nailed to the rabbeted front. The heads of the two rose-headed nails at each front joint are sunk into square gouges in the drawer sides. The drawer bottoms fit into grooves in the fronts and sides, and the drawers run on the bottom edges of the sides. The case sides and top are painted black. The worn painted decoration

was restored in 1976 by John Hill. The side base moldings are missing.

MATERIALS: *White pine; tupelo* drawer bottoms; *red oak* drawer supports and rear feet; *poplar* front feet; *maple* vertical strips nailed to case sides. Replaced brass hardware.

PROVENANCE: The antiques dealer who sold the chest to Florence Evans Bushee vaguely remembered buying it in Connecticut.

ACCESSION: 1976.234   A gift of the estate of Florence Evans Bushee

14 / Chest of Drawers

1755–1765
Charlestown (now part of Boston)
Attributed to the shop of Benjamin Frothingham
H. 30⅞ (78.4); W. 34⁹⁄₁₆ (87.8); D. 21¹⁄₁₆ (53.5)

No furniture has been more highly prized than the sophisticated blockfront furniture of Boston and Newport. Consequently, blockfronts tend to survive, and museum collections display so many that it is hard to believe that these were special objects, afforded only by the wealthy.

The prosperous and prominent Otis family of Boston owned this chest, an excellent example of a Boston blockfront chest. It belonged to Samuel Allyne Otis (1740–1814) and apparently is the "old bureau" listed in Otis's estate inventory.[1] Otis probably acquired the chest at about the time of his marriage to Elizabeth Gray in 1764. She was the daughter of the receiver-general of Massachusetts; he was the son of a judge and the younger brother of James Otis, an outspoken patriot, and Mercy Otis Warren, a writer. After Samuel's graduation from Harvard, he became a merchant, an occupation for which he had both the means and the social connections. The Otises were typical of the Bostonians who owned blockfront furniture.

The blocked façade occasionally appears in English furniture of the early eighteenth

14

century, particularly in desk interiors and on the drawer fronts of dressing glasses. Dressing glass no. 142, which shares a history with this set of drawers, is typical of the genre, although its shaped façade is not strictly a blocked one. Dressing glasses made in London and imported in considerable number may have provided a design source for the American blockfront. English cabinetmakers rarely expanded the blocked form to larger surfaces, but cabinetmakers in New England did.

Blocking became fashionable in fine Boston case furniture in the 1730s. The earliest documented example is a blockfront desk and bookcase made in 1738 by the Boston cabinetmaker Job Coit for a prosperous local stationer.[2] For the next half century, the blockfront remained stylish in Boston and spread along the New England coast to other urban centers.

Boston craftsmen developed two basic shapes for their blocking. Rounded façades, as on this chest, were generally reserved for small chests of drawers, kneehole bureau tables, and other diminutive articles. Flattened contours (see desk and bookcase no. 50) were more common and were used on both small and large cases.[3]

"Blockfront" is a modern term for a shaped façade that, in the eighteenth century, was called "swelled." Unfortunately, "swelled" does not distinguish among the several shaped façades — bombé, blocked, oxbow, and serpentine — all of which were wasteful of expensive primary wood and required considerably more labor.[4] The Charlestown cabinetmaker Thomas Wood, appraising his losses after a fire in 1775, listed "desks" at £43 but "swell front desks" at £60.[5]

This chest is one of a group that is outstanding even in the select company of blockfronts. For example, the dovetailing in this group is finer than that generally found in contemporary Boston cases. The group includes the Society's chest, an identical privately owned chest, a wider chest also privately owned, a chest with somewhat different feet in the Metropolitan Museum of Art, and a kneehole bureau table (14a) in the Museum of Fine Arts, Boston.

The kneehole bureau table belonged to the Amorys, another prosperous Boston family. Although of another form, it shares with this chest identical base moldings and brasses, the same support blocking, and the same foot, bracket, and drawer construction. Even identical plugs help affix the top to the case (see *Notes on Structure and Condition*). Such idiosyncrasies of construction suggest a single school of cabinetmakers (several shops working in the same manner), if not one shop or an individual craftsman.

Detailed examination of the chests in the group narrows the possibilities to a single shop or craftsman. One of the privately owned chests shares with the Society's, not only identical dovetailing and drawer and case construction, but the same design of the base molding, feet, and brackets and, in addition, the identical contour of the blocking.[6] The chest at the Metropolitan has somewhat different feet but also shares the identical blocked contour.[7] Identical blocking suggests the use of a single template, the work of one shop. But whose?

The chest identical to the Society's has two chalk inscriptions: "Wm Frothingham / Charlestown" on the underside of the bottom of the top drawer and "Joseph Hallowell" on the inside of the back. The Frothingham inscription has been known from its publication in *Antiques* in 1953, but, because the inscription has been tampered with ("alter" was added under the superscript *m*), it was erroneously attributed to a Walter Frothingham, although none of the Frothinghams of Charlestown was named Walter.[8]

The progenitor of the American Frothinghams was a William.[9] None of his namesakes is previously known to have been a cabinetmaker. The family did include Benjamin (1734–1809), a cabinetmaker who had a large shop in Charlestown.[10] The men who worked in his shop had a penchant for writing their names on the furniture being made. A privately owned desk with the signature "Benj. Frothingham" bears the scratched signatures of apprentices or shopworkers.[11] "Wm Frothingham" probably was one of Benjamin's cousins and an apprentice in his shop.[12]

Little is known of Joseph Hallowell. In 1751, a fifteen-year-old of that name became a ward of his uncle upon the death of his father.[13] Both uncle and father were shipwrights, laboring in another woodworking trade. Hallowell, not known to have had a shop of his own, apparently worked for Frothingham.

The privately owned chest that is wider than the Society's has different feet but identical dovetails, drawer construction, and blocking contour at the curves from convex to concave. It also has a paper label inside the top drawer: "Benjamin Frothingham / Charlestown N.E."[14]

With many workmen employed at one time or another in Frothingham's shop, it is best not to attribute cases to the master but rather to cite only the shop. The similarly constructed cases discussed here — the labeled chest, the signed chest, the Society's chest, the Metropolitan chest, and the kneehole bureau table — can all be attributed to the Charlestown shop of Benjamin Frothingham.

14a. Kneehole Bureau Table. Attributed to the shop of Benjamin Frothingham (1734–1809), Charlestown, Massachusetts, 1750–1775. Mahogany and white pine; H. 31 (78.7); W. 33⅞ (86.0); D. 18¼ (46.4). M. and M. Karolik Collection, Museum of Fine Arts, Boston.

1. Samuel Allyne Otis's 1814 inventory, old series, vol. 112, p. 320, Suffolk County (Mass.) Probate.

2. Evans, "Genealogy of a Bookcase Desk."

3. For an excellent article on blockfront furniture, its history, design, and construction, see Lovell, "Boston Blockfront Furniture."

4. Ibid., 79.

5. Accounts of losses from the burning of Charlestown, June 17, 1775, Thomas Wood Account, Boston Public Library.

6. Comstock, "Frothingham," figs. 13, 14. The chest is now in the collection of Jacob and Celia Richmond.

7. Metropolitan Museum of Art, chest 1971.180.41.

8. Comstock, "Frothingham."

9. Wyman, *Genealogies and Estates of Charlestown*, 1:381.

10. For Frothingham, see Jobe, "Desk by Benjamin Frothingham"; Randall, "Benjamin Frothingham"; Spalding, "Benjamin Frothingham"; and Swan, "Major Benjamin Frothingham."

11. Records of an examination of the desk by the authors are in the Society's files.

12. The signature is not that of William (1729–1801), who signed the 1784 administration of the will of William Frothingham, Jr., docket 8701, Middlesex County (Mass.) Probate.

13. The 1751 guardianship of Joseph Hallowell, old series, vol. 45, pp. 198–99, Suffolk County (Mass.) Probate.

14. Illustrated in Ingate, "History in Towns," 309. Owned by Mr. and Mrs. Stephens Croom.

NOTES ON STRUCTURE AND CONDITION: The grooves in the top to receive the sides are half-dovetail shaped. The top extends 3/8 inch beyond the back, and mahogany plugs fill the grooves at the back. Facing strips, glued to the front edges of the sides, and the drawer dividers are cut to form a beaded edge surrounding each drawer opening. The giant dovetail (detail 20a) often seen on Boston-area blockfronts is not present. The support blocks for the base molding are randomly spaced. The rear elements of the rear feet are of the same profile as those in detail 15b, a profile characteristic of Boston, and fit over the support blocks.

Each drawer bottom is nailed into the rabbeted edges of the front and sides. Originally each drawer ran on the rabbeted lower edges of the sides and on runners glued alongside them and finished at the back with a 45-degree-angle cut. Drawer supports are set into shallow grooves in the case sides. The bottom drawer slides on the case bottom.

The drawer runners, supports, and stops are replacements. The bottom of the feet were cut and mounted on casters. In 1976 the feet were restored to their original height, a new right rear foot was installed, and the left rear foot was reinforced.

MATERIALS: *Mahogany; white pine* secondary wood. Original brass hardware; original locks.

PROVENANCE: The chest descended to Mary, the second wife of Samuel Allyne Otis, and then to her daughters, Harriet (b. 1787) and Mary (1794–1869). The survivor, Mary, bequeathed it to her friend Mary Isabella Webb Mason, and it descended to the latter's daughter, Mina Mason Van Sinderen, who left it to the Society.

ACCESSION: 1933.1508   A gift of Mrs. Howard Van Sinderen; conserved through the generosity of Peter Lynch

15 / Chest of Drawers

1770
Boston
George Bright
H. 31 (78.7); W. 39 (99.1); D. 20 11/16 (52.5)

This chest is among the most historically important pieces of documented New England furniture. The chest and its extant bill of sale (15a) date this version of the blockfront, they add significantly to our knowledge of the work of Boston's premier cabinetmaker

15

of the Revolutionary War era, and they document an eighteenth-century term whose meaning has been only partly understood.[1] Much of the other furniture sold with the chest survives, illuminating the way of life of the well-to-do eighteenth-century Bostonian removed to newly settled territory.

In 1770, Jonathan Bowman (1735–1804) married Mary Emerson of Portsmouth, a widow, and bought new furniture for his house in the hinterlands of what is now Maine. Bowman, a graduate of Harvard, where he roomed for a while with his cousin John Hancock, was from Dorchester (now part of Boston). He was sent by his and John's uncle, the wealthy merchant Thomas Hancock, to Pownalborough, in newly incorporated Lincoln County, to watch over his uncle's business interests.[2] Thomas Hancock managed to have Bowman appointed collector of the excise, register of probate, register of deeds, clerk of the court of sessions and the court of common pleas, and justice of the peace for the new county.

Bowman moved to the new settlement, taking along his Boston way of life. His house was built of elements fabricated in Boston and was probably assembled by Boston craftsmen brought north for the task. Its furnishings also came from Boston.

George Bright (1726–1805) made Bowman's furniture. Bright, according to a contemporary, was "an extraordinary good Workman" and was "esteemed the neatest workman in town."[3] He was held in such regard that the Suffolk County Court turned to him to arbitrate cases between cabinetmakers, and he was accorded the honor of leading the Boston cabinetmakers in the Federal Procession of Mechanics and Artisans in 1788 and in the Washington procession in 1789.[4] He supplied stylish furniture for Boston's fashionable houses, including Thomas Hancock's.[5]

Bright signed the splendid desk and bookcase now at the Museum of Fine Arts, Boston, a piece that leaves no doubt about the opulent work of which he was capable.[6] The Society's chest, modest by comparison, is the only other case documented to him and the only one with bracket feet. Because it is in original condition, with all its construction details intact, the *Notes on Structure and Condition* and the illustration of the underside (15b) will help in attributing other case furniture to this highly skilled craftsman. (See also the interior without drawers, III-19.)

Bowman's rounded Boston blockfront differs in design from Otis's rounded Boston blockfront of an earlier date (chest no. 14): the blocking is flatter; the case is wider; and it stands on ogee bracket feet, called "swelled brackets" in the eighteenth century.[7] Thanks to the dated Bright-Bowman bill, these characteristics can now be recognized as Boston high style of 1770.

This blockfront chest of drawers is one of the "2 Mahogany Buroe Tables" in the 1770 bill. The term "bureau table" has been used by furniture historians to refer only to kneehole cases (such as 14a). Inventory references to "bureau tables" have been assumed to refer solely to that form.[8]

However, this chest is without doubt one of Bright's "Buroe Tables." It descended with the other objects in the bill — two of the "12 Mahogany Chairs with Leather Seats" (no. 113), two of the 12 "Ditto Stufft in Canvis" (no. 123), one of the "2 Dineing Tables 3 foot 9 ^{inch} Squair" (no. 63), and "A Pembroke Table" (no. 66). Most conclusively, a scrap of marbleized paper caught between a drawer front and drawer bottom, in the otherwise cleaned and bare drawer interiors, shows that they were once lined, as the next to last item on the bill suggests: "To Lineing the Buroe Tables Draws with Marble paper."

By 1805 the language had changed, and Jonathan Bowman's estate inventory lists two "bureaus" and no bureau tables. Illustrated English design books and American price lists of the era show a plethora of overlapping terms. "Bureau table," "dressing table," "bureau," "low case of drawers," and "low chest of drawers" denote, at times, chests of four case-wide drawers, although each term was also used for other forms. Fortunately, the Bright case and its bill prove that in Boston in 1770, this blockfront chest of drawers was a "Buroe Table."

1. The bill is in the collection of the Lincoln County (Me.) Cultural and Historical Association, Box 1, section 2, folder 4.

2. An excellent biography of Bowman is in Shipton, *Sibley's Harvard Graduates*, 13:545–50.

3. Randall, "George Bright," includes the quoted accolades in the 1787 correspondence from David Spear, Jr., of Boston to his fiancée (136, 139), first published in Haas, "Forgotten Courtship," 69, 70.

4. Bright and the Suffolk County Court is from Kaye, "Furniture Craftsmen," 273. The parade is from Randall, "George Bright," 140, 141.

5. Randall, "George Bright," 136.

6. *Boston Furniture*, fig. 124.

7. Weil, "Cabinetmaker's Price Book," 181, "Sweld Braget."

8. Goyne, "Bureau Table in America."

NOTES ON STRUCTURE AND CONDITION: The upper edges of the sides fit into dovetail grooves in the top. The top does not extend beyond the back. The drawer dividers are thin mahogany strips — no deeper than they need be — backed by 3½-inch-deep white pine boards. The facing strips and the drawer dividers are cut to form a beaded edge surrounding each drawer opening.

The front base molding is joined to the case with a giant dovetail. A series of small rectangular support blocks is glued beneath the bottom along the inside edges of the base molding. The glue blocks along the side base moldings are nailed in addition. The rear elements of the rear feet (15b) have a profile characteristic of Boston work and are cut to fit over the support blocks. Behind each rear foot is a vertical glue block, a common feature that seldom survives; those that do are not as neatly chamfered as this one. A carved fan, cut from a mahogany block, is glued to the center of the front base molding.

The drawers have thick but precise dovetails. The top of the drawer sides is cut with a small bead on the inside edge. Forged finishing nails hold each drawer bottom to the rabbeted edges of the front and sides. Runners, each a full-depth strip of white pine, are glued to the drawer bottoms just inside the lower edges of the drawer sides. Each runner is finished at the back with a 45-degree-angle cut (III-17), a feature many have previously attributed only to Benjamin Frothingham. Drawer supports are nailed to the case sides (III-19).

The chest, in excellent condition, was repaired and refinished in 1895 by August Bixby. The left front foot is pieced 2¾ inches at the bottom; the feet once had casters.

15a. Bill. George Bright to Jonathan Bowman. Lincoln County Cultural and Historical Association.

15b

MATERIALS: *Mahogany; white pine* secondary wood. Original brass hardware; original locks. The key escutcheons are 1976 replacements cut to match the original handles.

PROVENANCE: The chest was made for Jonathan Bowman, whose widow, Nancy Goodwin Bowman, inherited it and took it to her brother's house in 1809. It was inherited with the house by Mrs. Bowman's nephew and his wife, David and Lydia Goodwin; it was taken by the latter in 1895 to the California home of her daughter Mrs. Mary Goodwin Bixby, who inherited it in 1903 and left it to her children in 1909. The surviving child, the donor, returned it to New England.

ACCESSION: 1980.79   A gift of Florence L. Bixby

16 / Chest of Drawers

1745–1760
Portsmouth
H. 31⅜ (79.7); W. 38¼ (97.2); D. 22⅛ (56.2)

The Society's collection includes two exciting additions to the history of American blockfront furniture. Blockfront cases from Newport, Boston, and Connecticut have long been identified, but almost nothing has been written about blockfront furniture from the area of Portsmouth, New Hampshire.

This chest and the following one are two excellent Portsmouth blockfronts. Although this chest is massive and the next one is diminutive, although the top of this chest barely covers the case and the top of the other has a broad overhang, and although the two chests differ in several design details, both chests present an illuminating introduction to the rectilinear Portsmouth blockfront. Both feature flat blocking, the alternative to the rounded contours of chests no. 14 and 15, and they stand on broader feet than their Boston counterparts.

Of the two, this chest is the more splendid. It is of extremely dense, dark mahogany with a beautiful grain. A special feature is the slide, a mahogany frame enclosing a pine panel with remnants of its original green wool cover; it enlarges the table surface of the already large top (38 by 22 inches) to 38 by 35½ inches.

Not as elegantly detailed or crafted as the preceding Boston chest, this example attains an imposing eminence from its massive size and the design of its façade. The broad feet continue the blocked façade to the floor. The thumbnail-molded drawer fronts stand out from the case, emphasizing the horizontal and adding heft to an already large chest. This extraordinary feature occurs on only a few early cases, one a related Portsmouth-area chest.[1] Drawer fronts on Boston blockfronts, except for a very few Queen Anne examples, are flush with the façade of the case. This is true in Newport, too, in spite of a fashion there for furniture with thumbnail-edged drawers.

By legend this stately chest originally belonged to Sir William Pepperrell (1696–1759) of Kittery, Maine, the only New Englander to be made a baronet.[2] Pepperrell, a phenomenally successful merchant and the informal banker for much of southern Maine,

16

received his title for leading the New England forces against the French at Louisburg, Nova Scotia, in 1745. Sir William provided his daughter and son with large, well-furnished houses in Kittery and, through his will, ensured that each of his four grandsons would receive a house.[3] His baronetcy and house passed to his grandson William (1745–1816), so his widow, Mary (1704–1789), New England's only titled lady, built for herself yet another house in Kittery.

This chest was apparently acquired with a similarly constructed, similarly massive blockfront desk and bookcase, also in the Society's collection (I-35). Sir William, the hero of the siege of Louisburg, may have purchased them for one of the several houses he furnished. Most of the Pepperrell family furniture was confiscated after the Revolution; virtually all of it stayed in the Kittery area until this century. Lady Pepperrell apparently retained some furniture, and it was divided among her grandchildren. This chest and the related desk and bookcase may be those owned by her grandson Nathaniel until 1815.[4] During the nineteenth century, both cases reportedly were in the Gerrish house, Kittery, and, until acquired by the Society, remained in southern Maine.

Yet this chest that has always been in Maine was made in Portsmouth, New Hampshire, across the mouth of the Piscataqua from Kittery. A 1742 bill shows that Sir William patronized at least one cabinetmaker in Portsmouth, Joseph Buss, Jr.[5]

An eighteenth-century chalk inscription on the backboard of the chest reads: "To go in the Cabben." Although furniture was usually crated for shipping, one can imagine that this instruction told a vessel's crew — accustomed to placing cargo from Portsmouth to Kittery on deck — to stow the new, valuable, but uncrated chest in the cabin, where no salt water would mar its splendid wood.

Another possibility comes to mind when we read in an 1855 account of Sir William's baronial style of living: "his park stocked with deer, a retinue of servants, costly equipage, and a splendid barge with a black crew dressed in uniform."[6] Could the blockfront have been "in the Cabben" of Sir William's splendid barge?

1. The chest descended in the Pearson family of Exeter, N.H.; the King Hooper, Inc., Hyman Kaufman, and Herbert Lawton Collections, National Art Galleries, sale 22, December 1931, lot 470. It appears to the authors to be number 167 in Downs, *Queen Anne and Chippendale*. Thumbnail-molded drawer fronts can also be seen on two dressing tables at the Winterthur Museum (*Boston Furniture*, figs. 65 and 67; the latter was found in Saco, Me.); on two others illustrated in Sack, *Fine Points*, 193, and *Israel Sack Collection*, 3:738–39; and on two kneehole bureau tables, one illustrated as lot 497 in the Hooper, Kaufman, and Lawton catalogue mentioned above and one in *Boston Furniture*, fig. 18.

2. For an early biography of the baronet, see Parsons, *Sir William Pepperrell*.

3. William Pepperrell's will, vol. 10, folio 63, docket 14820, York County (Me.) Probate.

4. Nathaniel Sparhawk's inventory, docket 17573, York County (Me.) Probate.

5. According to a bill of 1742 (transcript in the Society's files), Buss sold Sir William two double chests of drawers, two tables, six chests, and a maple desk. Buss was listed as working in Portsmouth in 1752; Burroughs, "Furniture Widely Made in New Hampshire," 15.

6. Parsons, *Sir William Pepperrell*, 232.

NOTES ON STRUCTURE AND CONDITION: The construction of this chest varies noticeably from that of Boston blockfronts and other cases: (1) The thumbnail-cut edges of the drawer fronts are decidedly different from the Boston plain edge set into a beaded opening. They also contrast with thumbnail drawers made elsewhere in that the thumbnail edges are not lipped. (2) There is no giant dovetail to help hold the front base molding. Instead the molding, glued and nailed to the case, is additionally supported by two large T-shaped nails driven from beneath through the front base molding into the bottom. (3) The surviving original vertical block behind the left front foot is a two-part quarter-round support, not the common one-piece square support. (4) Unlike on most New England case furniture, the rear element of each rear foot is glued to the rabbeted edge of the side element. This precludes the need for the vertical block that Boston cabinetmakers placed behind each rear foot. (5) The back, two lap-jointed boards, is not only nailed into the rabbeted edges of the sides and the butt edges of the bottom, but it fits into a groove in the top. (6) The drawer dividers, 2-inch-deep mahogany backed by 10- to 12-inch white pine boards, are set into grooves in the case sides. The depth of the pine precludes the need for drawer supports.

The two-board sides are joined with rather small dovetails to the one-board bottom. The two-board top — both boards cut from the same plank — is cut with half-dovetail-shaped grooves to receive the sides. Facing strips cover the shouldered dovetail joints of the dividers and case sides. Drawer stops are nailed with two rose-headed nails each at the rear of the case sides. The base moldings are flush with the top surface of the bottom. Horizontal strips are glued beneath the bottom behind the base moldings, and at the back they extend beneath the backboard.

The bottom of each dovetailed drawer is set into grooves in the front and sides. The drawers run on their sides and long strips glued to the bottom along the sides. Two strips are glued to each drawer bottom along the drawer front. The front of the slide is outlined with a scratch bead. (The related desk and bookcase is identically constructed except that instead of thumbnail-edged drawer fronts, it has drawer fronts with an applied bead.)

The chest is in good condition, although it evinces much wear and some repair. The facing strips are replaced. Vertical blocks and one horizontal block for the rear feet and all the blocks for the right front foot are replaced; nails reinforce the front feet. The lower edges of the drawer sides are very worn; those on the lower two drawers have been replaced. One drawer stop is missing.

MATERIALS: Mahogany; white pine secondary wood. Replaced brass hardware; original steel locks.

PROVENANCE: The chest was purchased by the Society from the heirs of the family that bought the chest and the related desk and bookcase in the late nineteenth century from the Gerrish family of Kittery, in whose house it had been for many years.

ACCESSION: 1981.4   Museum purchase

17 / Chest of Drawers

1760–1780
Portsmouth
H. 30⅞ (78.4); W. 34¾ (88.3); D. 21¹¹⁄₁₆ (55.1)

Whereas the preceding Portsmouth chest is massive, this one is so diminutive that its top, almost the same size as that on chest no. 14, broadly overhangs the slender case. The chest has wide bracket feet and angular corners on shallow flat blocking. A close look along the edge of the top reveals a pronounced fillet, which does not appear on any of the preceding blockfronts. Originally the skirt had a small, half-round central drop similar in shape to that on chest no. 15.[1]

The designer of this chest was a devotee of the straight line. He was acquainted with Boston construction (compare *Notes on Structure and Condition* with those on chests no. 14 and 15) but did not slavishly copy Boston design. His name is unknown, but his home was in the Portsmouth area. This chest has been in Portsmouth throughout this century and was refinished in 1913 by a local painter.

A related blockfront chest descended in the Pearson family of Exeter, New Hampshire, and has similar massive feet, sharply cornered blocking, and the unusual feature of the fillet on the top edge of the top.[2] The Pearson chest differs from this chest in that, like the Pepperrell chest (no. 16), it has unlipped thumbnail-molded drawer fronts.

1. A similar blockfront, which descended in the Moulton family of Newburyport, Mass., retains a drop of about the same size and shape; *Antiques* 96 (September 1968): inside cover.

2. See chest no. 16, note 1.

NOTES ON STRUCTURE AND CONDITION: The dovetailed case has a top with grooves in the shape of half-dovetails to receive the sides. The shallow blocking projects only ⅜ inch. The facing strips, applied to the front edges of the case sides, and the drawer dividers are cut to form a beaded edge surrounding each drawer opening.

The bottom of the base molding is flush with the underside of the case. The front base molding is backed by a rail set inside the case and nailed to

17

the bottom with countersunk rose-headed nails. A giant dovetail, used in many Boston blockfront and oxbow cases (detail 20a), joins the front base molding to the rail and bottom. The rear element of each rear foot is diagonally cut, unlike the curved rear elements in most Boston work. Originally, there were vertical blocks behind as well as in front of each rear element.

The top of each drawer side is cut with a bead on the inside edge. The drawer bottoms fit into grooves in the fronts and are nailed to the rabbeted edges of the sides. The drawers run on the bottom edges of the drawer sides and on runners glued to the bottom along the sides. Drawer supports are nailed to the case sides with rose-headed nails.

The chest is inscribed on the bottom: "Repaired and refinished / By G. P. Fernald / Nov. 1913." The side element of the left rear foot is pieced 1¾ inches at the bottom. Modern screws bind the front feet

to the vertical blocks behind them, and wooden plugs cap the screw holes. The chest had casters at one time. The large dovetail joint at the base molding has been tightened with a wedge.

MATERIALS: *Mahogany; maple* rear elements of the rear feet; *white pine* other secondary wood. Original brass hardware except for the top and bottom escutcheons and the lower right handle. Original locks in the top and the next to the bottom drawers.

PROVENANCE: The chest, which came to the Society with the Governor John Langdon Mansion in Portsmouth, was listed in the donor's 1947 inventory.

ACCESSION: 1966.352   A bequest of Elizabeth Elwyn Langdon

18 / Chest of Drawers

1760–1780
Boston or Salem
H. 33³/₁₆ (84.3); W. 37³/₁₆ (94.5); D. 21⅛ (53.7)

This chest of drawers illustrates another costly swelled case shape, the bombé. Rarer than blockfronts, bombés were made only in coastal Massachusetts, specifically in Boston and Salem. The term "bombé" is a modern one. "Ogee" was occasionally used to describe the shape in eighteenth-century London.[1] What term was used by Americans is not known. Boston inventories rarely mention case shape. For example, the estate inventory of Martin Gay, who owned the bombé desk and bookcase that descended in his family, lists merely "a Mohogany Desk & Boock Case $30."[2]

By the 1720s London cabinetmakers were producing bombé furniture, and the shape

remained stylish in England into the 1760s.[3] In America, the bombé contour is seen as early as 1749 in the pine pulpit made for the Ipswich, Massachusetts, meetinghouse by Abraham Knowlton,[4] and bombé furniture remained stylish in eastern Massachusetts through the Revolution. Elias Hasket Derby, a merchant of Salem who ordered only the most fashionable goods, had a bombé chest-on-chest made for him by John Cogswell of Boston in 1782.[5]

Imported English bombé cases probably served as design sources for Massachusetts bombé furniture. A London bombé clothes press (I-16) belonged to Charles Apthorp (1698–1758), a wealthy Boston merchant.[6] Although the Apthorp press cannot be singled out as the prototype, early Boston bombé furniture relates closely to it. The desk and bookcase made in 1753 by Benjamin Frothingham for Dr. John Sprague (I-17) shares with the Apthorp piece the straight vertical line formed by the side edges of the drawer fronts.

Soon Boston cabinetmakers were making bombé cases in which the outer edges of the drawer fronts echoed the curved case sides, as they do here. Sometimes this was done with drawers whose sides conformed to the swelled contour. Other times the drawer fronts alone conformed to the swell while the drawer sides continued to form a straight vertical line, as in the Society's bombé where the case sides, bombé on the outer surfaces, are vertical on the interior (18a).

The most sophisticated bombé shape features a serpentine façade superimposed upon the bombé swell. Such an elaborate form, the culmination of the bombé shape in America, was a most ambitious case-shaping task for American cabinetmakers.[7] The Society's chest is far simpler than serpentine-façaded bombés. It is a standard, common version of a special, uncommon shape. It has standard bracket feet rather than claw-and-ball feet and no carving or veneer.[8]

This chest is one of several similar chests. One example is so similar that although the Society's chest is larger, clearly the two were made in the same shop.[9] Not only do they show the same construction techniques and the identical brasses, but the same molding planes and templates were used in making both pieces. Of the other related bombés, five have similarly indented corners on the tops, similarly shaped feet and center drops, and similarly positioned base rails and base moldings that leave the rails exposed.[10] At least one additional chest matches the others in most details but lacks the inverted corners on the top.[11]

The related group cannot be attributed more specifically than to Boston or Salem. Merchandise and craftsmen moved readily between the two towns in the era in which this chest was made. The similar chest without indented corners is reputedly from the Crowninshield family of Salem. However, the foot bracket design and case construction of the group do not correspond with features on documented Salem pieces, but instead relate to Boston furniture.[12]

The small chest made in the same shop as chest no. 18 was thought to be the clue to the origin of the group. It came from the Northey family of Salem and was reportedly marked "Boston" on the bottom board. Alas, it was really inscribed in chalk (as craftsmen were wont to do) "Bottom."

1. Vincent, "Bombé Furniture of Boston," 143.

2. Martin Gay's 1809 inventory, old series, vol. 107, p. 102, Suffolk County (Mass.) Probate. The desk and bookcase is figure 131 in Vincent, "Bombé Furniture."

3. A desk and bookcase made by Samuel Bennett in the 1720s; Macquoid and Edwards, *Dictionary*, vol. 1, fig. 30. In 1761, William Vile made a bombé secretary for Queen Charlotte; Vincent, "Bombé Furniture," fig. 109.

4. Benes and Zimmerman, *New England Meeting House*, 39–42.

5. The history and a color illustration of the Cogswell bombé now at the Museum of Fine Arts, Boston, appear in Vincent, "Bombé Furniture," 178, fig. 125.

6. See *Paul Revere's Boston*, 43, 44, for a brief biography and portrait of Apthorp and his inventory references to the press.

7. *Paul Revere's Boston*, no. 88, is a bombé with a serpentine façade originally owned by Ebenezer Storer of Boston, now in the Department of State, Washington, D.C.

8. A bombé chest of drawers at the Museum of Fine Arts, Boston (37.34), has veneer and carving; Vincent, "Bombé Furniture," fig. 128.

9. The privately owned chest was advertised by Charles W. Lyon in *Antiques* 79 (April 1961): 319, and sold in the Lansdell Christie Collection, Sotheby Parke Bernet, sale 3422, October 1972, lot 60.

10. One was owned by John Walton many years ago (DAPC Files, Winterthur Museum, 70.3778); another was advertised by Israel Sack, Inc. (*Antiques* 110 [August 1976]); still another was sold by Sack at Parke-Bernet in 1957, sale 1776, lot 91; the fourth was sold in the Garbisch Collection, Sotheby Parke Bernet, sale H2, May 1980, vol. 4, lot 1159; and the fifth was advertised by Ginsburg & Levy, *Antiques* 57 (February 1950): 101.

11. A chest privately owned in Michigan; *Americana, Midwest Collectors Choice*, 15 and no. 31. An apparently identical piece was once owned by Katrina Kipper, a Massachusetts antiques dealer; DAPC Files, Winterthur Museum, 66.2373.

12. Boston construction is covered in Vincent, "Bombé Furniture," 181–92. The documented Salem pieces — two chests of drawers, one at the Winterthur Museum (Vincent, "Bombé Furniture,"

fig. 136), another owned by the Osgood family of Salem and now at the Lee Mansion of the Marblehead Historical Society — have wide foot brackets. Similar brackets appear on a chest at Bayou Bend and a desk at the Museum of Fine Arts, Boston; Vincent, "Bombé Furniture," figs. 137 and 138. These Salem pieces have drawer sides that conform to the bombé.

NOTES ON STRUCTURE AND CONDITION: On this chest and the related examples, a front base rail and a straight vertical section below the curve of the case sides are prominently seen above the base molding. On many bombé cases, the straight sections are hidden by the base molding. The straight portion at the bottom of the sides allowed the use of a standard dovetail joint to bind the sides and bottom.

A full dust board is dovetailed into the case sides between the two middle drawers. Full dust boards are very unusual in New England furniture and may indicate a direct borrowing from an English prototype, since full dust boards are commonplace in English cases. Like other bombé furniture with drawer fronts conforming to the sides, no applied strips face the case sides.

18a

Full-length support strips are glued and nailed to the underside of the bottom along the front and side edges. The base molding is glued and nailed to the case and the strips. The central drop is glued to the front base molding and supported by a block glued to the support strip. The rear element of the rear foot is curved in common Boston fashion (detail 15b).

The drawers have small but not finely tapered dovetails. The drawer bottoms are set into grooves in the drawer fronts and sides.

The chest survives in good condition with one major change: about 2 inches of the feet had been cut off and the missing portions were restored. The side element of the left rear foot and its blocking are replacements. The chest was refinished in 1975.

MATERIALS: *Mahogany; white pine* secondary wood. Original brass hardware. Three original steel locks; the bottom drawer never had a lock.

PROVENANCE: Frances Elizabeth Everett Sawyer (d. 1915) of Newton, Mass., left the chest to her daughter Frances E. Sawyer Pratt, whose daughter Katherine Pratt Dewey gave it to the Society.

ACCESSION: 1970.51   A gift of Mrs. William R. Dewey, Jr.

19 / Chest of Drawers

1764–1780
Boston area
H. 30¼ (76.8); W. 34 (86.4); D. 21³⁄₁₆ (53.8)

Another "swelled" case shape used by New England cabinetmakers in the second half of the eighteenth century is the oxbow, or reverse serpentine, façade. Both are modern terms. The oxbow undulates out, in, and out; the serpentine curves in, out, and in.

The façade of this chest follows an oxbow curve, but the curve does not begin at the corners of the façade the way it does on most oxbow cases (see chest no. 20). Here the oxbow begins in from the side edges, leaving flat corner areas similar to those on blockfront cases.

The oxbow may have evolved from the blockfront, which it so closely resembles. The sharp vertical lines dissolve in favor of a flowing sculptural shape. On early oxbows such as chest no. 19, crisp vertical lines do remain near the corners to continue some of the blockfront's verticality. (Compare chests no. 15, 19, and 20.)

This handsome chest is a companion to chest-on-chest no. 27. Case pieces for bedchambers were often sold *en suite*; that is, a tall two-part case and a matching one-part case. This chest and its companion are what were termed in a 1772 Philadelphia price book "Drawers Chest on Chest / Table to Suit with Strait Braget."[1] "Table" indicated a chest of drawers of table height. "Strait Braget" meant straight bracket feet such as those on this chest.

Both the chest here and its companion are in superb condition; they were virtually unused in the nineteenth and twentieth centuries (see *Provenance*). Both pieces descended in the Barrett family of New Ipswich, New Hampshire, and apparently belonged originally to Charles Barrett, Sr. (1740–1808). Barrett was born in Concord, Massachusetts;

19

he married Rebecca Minot of that town and moved to New Ipswich, where he became a wealthy shopkeeper, entrepreneur, and land speculator. Barrett most likely bought this chest between 1764, the year of his marriage, and 1780, the year he built the New Ipswich house that was his home until his death.

This chest probably was made in the Boston area. Its foot brackets and central drop correspond quite closely to those on a desk and bookcase (no. 50) owned by William Foster of Boston prior to the Revolution. Similar central drops are seen on several Boston examples.[2] The top edges of the drawer sides on this chest are cut to form a double arch, seen also on the Foster desk and other cases from Boston. Originally the chest had narrow moldings glued along the sides beneath the top. Such cornice moldings were occasionally featured on chests of drawers made in eastern Massachusetts.[3]

None of the design components of the chest is unusual, yet only one piece (in addition to the companion chest-on-chest) is closely related to it. The other chest is known only from an advertisement, which does not mention any history.[4]

1. Weil, "Price Book," 181.

2. A desk owned by John Amory of Boston (Hipkiss, *Karolik Collection*, no. 26).

3. In *Boston Furniture*, figures 50 and 55 show a typical Boston chest with cornice moldings.

4. *Antiques* 102 (September 1972): 294.

NOTES ON STRUCTURE AND CONDITION: Facing strips on the case sides hide the dovetail joints of the shallow drawer dividers (less than 4 inches deep). The support blocks under the bottom are a series of butting rectangular blocks. Although its companion chest-on-chest has a giant dovetail binding the base molding to the bottom, this chest does not. The rear element of each rear foot has a straight diagonal edge instead of the curved edge usually seen in Boston work. The rear elements of the rear feet are not glued directly to the bottom, as in most Boston chests, but are glued to rectangular blocks that are glued to the bottom.

The drawers' dovetails are of average quality. The drawer fronts, sides, and backs are rather thick by late-eighteenth-century Boston standards. Each drawer bottom is nailed to the rabbeted lower edges of the front and sides. The drawers run on the lower edges of the sides and on applied runners glued to the bottom along the sides and finished at the back with a 45-degree-angle cut.

The chest survives in excellent condition except for the missing moldings along the sides beneath the top.

MATERIALS: *Mahogany; white pine* secondary wood. Original brass hardware. Original steel locks; the bottom drawer never had a lock.

PROVENANCE: The chest descended with Charles Barrett, Sr.'s house, known in recent years as the Bullard-Barr House. A series of single people — widows and unmarried women — resided in the house: Charles Sr.'s widow, Rebecca, until 1838; her widowed daughter-in-law, Martha Minot Barrett, until 1842; the latter's daughter Mary Ann Barrett Bullard Hersey until 1875; Mary Ann's daughter, Sarah Jane Bullard, until 1903; Sarah's cousin's stepdaughter Laura Maria Barr, who resided there until 1949 and was the donor's sister.

ACCESSION: 1958.80   A gift of Caroline Barr Wade

20 / Chest of Drawers

1770–1795
Boston area
H. 32½ (82.6); W. 38½ (97.8); D. 23⅛ (58.7)

This chest is of the more usual oxbow form — the curve begins at the corners. Oxbows of this type were far more prevalent than other "swelled" case furniture, and this example relates closely to many others. Three chests almost identical to this one have been sold at auction since the 1940s.[1] Neither the Society's chest nor any of the three counterparts have a family history or maker's inscription.

Nevertheless, all four pieces can be attributed to the Boston area because the Society's chest bears all the design and construction characteristics of furniture made in the Boston area between 1770 and 1795. The feet are very similar to those on a desk labeled by

20

Benjamin Frothingham of Charlestown.[2] The giant dovetail binding the base molding to the bottom (20a) appears on many Boston cases.[3]

The bottom drawer slides directly on the case bottom, a characteristic of Boston case furniture with the exception of bombés. The support arrangement for the feet (20b) is like that on the Bright chest (detail 15b) and the Frothingham shop product, chest no. 14. These three pieces as well as many others have the same curved outline of the rear element of the rear feet.

The corner-to-corner oxbow shape seems to have been made in Boston from about 1770 until 1810. Many oxbow chests and desks have original oval brass hardware of the type popular in the early nineteenth century, but this chest originally had large rococo hardware. None of its features speak of the new Federal design.

chest, was sold in the Mrs. J. Amory Haskell Collection (sale 570, part 2, May 1944, lot 567); it has bail handles with small circular back plates, but it is not known if they are original. A second, sold in sale 1669, April 1956, lot 431, is apparently a little wider. A third, sold in sale 2016, February 1961, lot 341, reputedly descended in the family of Francis Scott Key and is very similar to the Society's but has bail handles with small circular back plates; it is not known if they are original.

2. *Boston Furniture*, fig. 166.

3. Lovell, "Blockfront Furniture," 84–86.

NOTES ON STRUCTURE AND CONDITION: The grooves in the top are in the shape of a half-dovetail. Facing strips on the case sides hide the dovetail joints of the drawer dividers. The front base molding is dovetailed and glued to the bottom and the front support strip. Support blocks of random length are common in Boston cases; continuous strips such as these are unusual.

The drawers have finely cut dovetails. Each drawer bottom sits in grooves in the front and sides. The drawer supports are notched and fastened with short rose-headed nails.

The chest is in excellent condition.

MATERIALS: *Mahogany; white pine* secondary wood. Replaced brass hardware; locks replaced in the upper two drawers and removed in the lower two.

PROVENANCE: The chest came to the Society with the Nickels-Sortwell House in Wiscasset, Me., which was furnished by Alvin Sortwell with "suitable antiques" after 1899.

ACCESSION: 1958.202   A bequest of Frances A. Sortwell

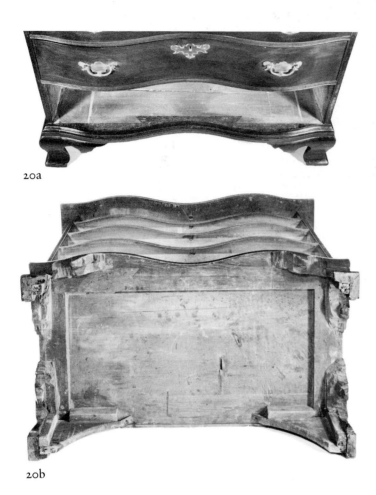

20a

20b

1. The three sold at Parke-Bernet. One, its measurements virtually matching those of the Society's

21 / Chest of Drawers

1760–1775
York, Maine
Attributed to Samuel Sewall
H. 30⅝ (77.8); W. 37½ (95.3); D. 21⅝ (54.9)

"A Serpentine Dressing Chest or Beaureau" was listed in the 1796 *Journeyman Cabinet and Chair Makers' New-York Book of Prices*.[1] This serpentine chest or bureau predates the New York price guide and, in its time, was probably called "swelled." It closely

21

resembles stylish Boston serpentine chests such as that owned by John Leach of Boston and now in the Museum of Fine Arts, Boston.[2] The bracket feet are related to those on chest no. 19, from the Boston area. But this is not a Boston case. Though Judge Jonathan Sayward, the richest man in York, bought his elegant English tea chest (no. 4) from a Boston importer, he prudently ordered large case furniture, such as this serpentine chest, from a local craftsman.

We can pinpoint the craftsman to York because of the history of this chest and the histories of related cases: Sayward's desk, his desk and bookcase, his high chest (no. 37), his dressing table (no. 33), a desk that descended in the Chaste family of York and is now at York's Old Gaol Museum, two desks still privately owned in York, and a chest of drawers acquired in York early in this century that is also at the Old Gaol. Either the York cabinetmaker was familiar with Boston case design or the judge, very familiar with Boston fashions since he represented York in the Massachusetts legislature, was explicit when placing his order.

Beneath the surface, however, the Sayward chest and the cited York pieces are entirely different from furniture made in Boston. Elements in Massachusetts cabinetry that are nailed together are here fastened with wooden pins. Even the top of chest no. 21 is fastened with wooden pins, whereas tops on Boston pieces were invisibly joined (III-14).

The long supporting blocks beneath the bottom (21a) are neatly chamfered along the edge and precisely mitered at the front corners. Most New England cabinetmakers did slapdash work wherever the workmanship did not show; here the support work looks like the product of a man used to finishing everything neatly. (Why he chalked *V* on many boards is a mystery.)

The York craftsman ignored or was ignorant of the standard way feet were made. This chest lacks the horizontal blocks invariably found flanking the vertical load-bearing blocks on coastal New England furniture. The rear feet have neither vertical nor horizontal blocks. Instead, extraordinarily thick rear elements carry the weight of the case. The well-crafted sturdy feet on this chest and the several cases made like it evince none of the weakness or breakage usually found on eighteenth-century case feet.

This group of York cases manifests a solidity and quality in construction rarely seen in New England. The use of wooden pins, which expand and contract with the wood, helps. Remarkably little splitting has occurred.

The artifactual evidence suggests a highly skilled woodworker. The judge's younger brother, Henry (1719–1748), was a York joiner. Henry died, however, before the judge renovated and furnished his house in the late 1750s and the 1760s. We know of two joiners who were working in York in those years, Caleb Preble (1728–1791) and Samuel Sewall (1724–1814), Henry Sayward's brother-in-law.

Preble worked as a joiner and cabinetmaker until his death, and the inventory of his estate includes all the tools of a well-equipped shop.[3] Sewall, a joiner, architect, and bridge builder, was working at the joinery trade by the late 1740s. He is credited with designing and building York's 1747 meetinghouse, although he was only twenty-three at the time.[4] The wooden drawbridge he built in York in 1757 won such renown that he was employed in 1786 as the architect and contractor for the first bridge to span the Charles River in Boston.[5]

The solid construction of this chest suggests the well-engineered work of a bridge builder. Indeed it is. In the 1760s, Sewall did joinery work on Sayward's house. Among the many references to him in Sayward's diary is one on November 10, 1761, when the judge "sold a province note to Saml Sewal the Joyer [joiner] and paid him out of it £45 old tener towards his work on my House."[6] Some of the interior moldings in Sayward's house match the distinctive cornice on his high chest (see entry 37); Sewall almost certainly installed the moldings and made the furniture.

21a

The deep base molding, also of an unusual contour, is wood-pinned to support strips, which are held to the case bottom by wooden pins. The vertical blocks behind each front foot are fastened to the base molding; on most New England furniture they are attached to the case bottom or to support blocks glued to the bottom. The large, thick rear elements of the rear feet are notched in the corners to fit over the side support strips and are pinned to the bottom. The side and rear elements of each rear foot are pinned together. The drawers have thick dovetails. A wide double arch is cut on the top edge of the drawer sides. The drawer bottoms rest in grooves in the fronts and sides and are wood-pinned to the backs.

With the exception of one replaced drawer stop, every original wood element survives intact. The chest, in superb structural condition, had a discolored finish and was refinished in 1978.

MATERIALS: *Mahogany; white pine* secondary wood. Original brass hardware. Original steel locks in three drawers; the lock for the bottom drawer is missing.

PROVENANCE: The chest has always been in Judge Sayward's house. It is probably the "Bearough" that he left to his widow, Elizabeth, from whom it passed to Mary Plummer Barrell (d. 1814), thence to the latter's husband — the judge's grandson — Jonathan Sayward Barrell, and descended as did tea chest no. 4.

ACCESSION: 1977.324   A gift of the heirs of Elizabeth Cheever Wheeler

1. Montgomery, *American Furniture*, 179, 488.

2. Randall, *American Furniture*, no. 29.

3. Caleb Preble's inventory, docket 15449, York County (Me.) Probate.

4. Banks, *History of York*, 2:108.

5. Ibid., 293, 294.

6. Jonathan Sayward Diary, 1760–99, American Antiquarian Society; it includes no mention of payments for furniture.

NOTES ON STRUCTURE AND CONDITION: The back is attached to the rabbeted edges of the case sides with wooden pins. Facing strips hide the joints of the drawer dividers to the case sides. The bead surrounding the drawers is a sharp-edged variant of the usual contour.

22 / Chest of Drawers

1775–1800
Salem, Massachusetts, area
H. 32⅞ (83.5); W. 38¾ (98.4); D. 20¹⁵/₁₆ (53.2)

A claw-and-ball foot was simply a "claw foot" in the 1755 inventory of William Empson, a Boston merchant ("1 round Claw Foot Mohog. Table").[1] Another term, "eagles foot," was used in the 1750 Boston inventory of Theodore Wheelwright: "7 Chairs Eagles Foot & Shell on the Knee."[2]

As on Wheelwright's chairs, both the claw foot and shell motifs are used on this attractive serpentine chest. The carved motifs, elements of English Early Georgian design,

22

remained fashionable in American Chippendale furniture. In comparison with other carvings, the claw feet of this chest are large and rather prominent and the shell stylized and plain.

Six other case pieces have similar shell drops, feet, knee brackets, and base moldings: three serpentine chests of drawers, one oxbow chest, and two oxbow desks (22a).[3] The desks and one chest have string inlay, a feature associated with furniture of the Federal period. All seven cases were apparently made in the last quarter of the eighteenth century in the same shop.

The design elements below the base molding are clues to the location of that shop. The knee brackets stretch out along the skirt like the brackets on documented Salem cases (I-28). The carvings on the central drops are reminiscent of the scallop shells on the Salem examples.

However, this chest and the six cases like it are distinguished from the documented

Salem pieces by shells that are simplified and less expertly carved, by brackets that are not as long as those on the Salem pieces, and, at least on this chest, by oversized claws. These distinctive characteristics suggest several possible origins: One, the pieces were made in Salem by a craftsman less skilled than the man or men who made the documented Salem cases. Urban craftsmen of various abilities worked near one another, copying designs from their competitors with various results. Two, the maker had worked in Salem but moved, carrying the Salem aesthetic with him. American craftsmen were very mobile; however, the high quality of the imported mahogany used on the Society's chest suggests an origin not far from the coast. Three, the cases were made in the vicinity of Salem but outside the town proper.

The traditional history of this chest and the documented history of the related desk (22a) do not clearly support one of these origins above another but tie the pieces to within a few miles of Salem. The Society's chest descended in the Dale family of Gloucester. Until 1811, the Dales lived in Danvers, next to Salem and called Salem

22a. Desk. Salem, Massachusetts, area, 1785–1800. Black walnut, maple inlay, and white pine; H. 43¼ (109.9); W. 43½ (110.5); D. 23 (58.4). Colorado Springs Fine Arts Center. Photograph, W. L. Bowers.

Village until 1752. Although in later years the Dales acquired some furniture from as far away as Connecticut (dressing table no. 34), this chest can now be assumed to have been owned by the Dales in Danvers because of the related desk.

The similarly designed desk has a signature that long remained undeciphered. A search through the names of people in the Salem-Danvers area yielded one name as a possible match for the scrawled inscription, that of David Fuller (d. 1821), a doctor in Middleton, the next town inland from Danvers. Probate records ended the search. Fuller owned a mahogany desk worth $12, and the signature on his will matched that on the desk.[4]

Fuller's Middleton home was close to the Danvers border. Either Fuller and the Dales patronized the same suburban craftsman or both men went to Salem, where Fuller owned real estate, and bought furniture in the same shop.

1. William Empson's 1755 inventory, old series, vol. 50, p. 399, Suffolk County (Mass.) Probate.

2. Theodore Wheelwright's 1750 inventory, old series, vol. 44, p. 381, Suffolk County (Mass.) Probate.

3. The serpentine chests are: (1) Philip Flayderman Collection, American Art Association, January 1930, lot 433; (2) Herbert Lawton Collection, Parke-Bernet, sale 158, January 1940, lot 186; and (3) *Antiques* 92 (October 1967): 417. The oxbow chest was advertised in *Antiques* 18 (July 1930): 2. One desk was advertised in *Antiques* 97 (May 1970): 643; the other was given to the Colorado Springs Fine Arts Center in 1939 by the Caldwell family.

4. Fuller's signature on his will (docket 10365, Essex County [Mass.] Probate) was compared with the signature on the desk by Elizabeth McCarthy, a handwriting expert, and found to be by the same hand. Fuller's inventory is also docket 10365.

NOTES ON STRUCTURE AND CONDITION: The boards of the back are vertical. The shallow drawer dividers are faced with very thin strips of mahogany. The facing strips on the case sides are thick ($1\frac{1}{16}$ inch). The joining of the front base molding to the bottom is most unusual. Three dovetails (instead of the one large dovetail common on Boston cases) tie the base molding to the front edge of the case bottom. The molding is flush with the undersurface of the bottom. The bottom drawer slides on blocks within the case and on drawer supports. The claw feet are tenoned into the bottom. Flanking the feet are knee brackets glued and nailed to the base moldings. Horizontal blocks glued behind the brackets give additional support. The shell-carved drop is a single piece of mahogany glued to the base molding without a support block. The drawers have finely cut dovetails. The drawer bottoms are set into grooves in the front and sides.

This chest has been taken apart, repaired, and refinished at least twice. The case bottom has a $\frac{1}{2}$-inch-wide shrinkage crack. One knee bracket support block has been replaced. New runners have been added beneath the drawer sides.

MATERIALS: Mahogany; white pine secondary wood. Original escutcheons, replaced handles; missing lock in top drawer, replaced locks in middle two drawers.

PROVENANCE: The chest descended in the Dale family of Massachusetts to Charles Dale Turnbull and to his daughter Lena Turnbull Gilbert, the donor. It apparently belonged to Ebenezer Dale (b. ca. 1781) of Danvers, who moved to Gloucester in 1811. The chest was in Dale's homestead until the family moved to Chicago, taking some of their furnishings. The chest returned to New England in 1963.

ACCESSION: 1963.350   A gift of Mrs. Huntly H. Gilbert

23 / Chest of Drawers

1790–1810
Medway, Massachusetts
Attributed to the shop of Luther Metcalf
H. 30⅞ (78.4); W. 40¼ (102.2); D. 21⅝ (54.9)

Furniture in the Chippendale style continued to be made after the Revolution. This serpentine chest of drawers is Chippendale cabinetry of a late date and features original oval brasses in the Federal style.

The case itself shows an approach toward the delicacy of Federal design. Chest no. 23 is wider than the chests of drawers described thus far, yet it has comparatively small and delicate feet. The simple base molding is light in appearance, as is the gentle curve of the serpentine. The bracket feet are an alternative form so seldom seen in New

23

England that they are significant in identifying related objects. Because only the recent history of the chest is known, related objects are important in discerning its origin.

Six very similar chests — four with oxbow façades but otherwise resembling the Society's chest — are known. Five have no histories, but the sixth, a chest of drawers with a cherry frame and mahogany drawer fronts and top, was made by Luther Metcalf, a cabinetmaker of Medway, Massachusetts.[1]

Metcalf, born in 1756, was apprenticed at the age of fourteen to the farmer and chairmaker Elisha Richardson (1743–1798) of West Wrentham (now Franklin), Massachusetts. Metcalf worked with Richardson until 1780, when he established a large two-story cabinet and chairmaker's shop on the top of Medway's Village Hill. There Metcalf, who lived to be eighty-two, employed and trained many men. One employee was apparently Ichabod Sanford, who in 1796 made a tall clockcase for Metcalf's own use.[2] Metcalf's brother Joseph (1765–1849) was an apprentice in the Medway manufactory. He then took his craft north to Winthrop, Maine, where in 1789 he established that village's first cabinetry shop.[3]

Luther remained on Medway's Village Hill, working in partnership with Cyrus Cleaveland of Providence, Rhode Island. Their 1801 advertisement in a Providence newspaper reads in part:

> as the Business is carried on upon a large scale by one of the Proprietors in the Country [Metcalf in Medway], where Furniture can be afforded much cheaper than in Town, (the work being chiefly done there, and transported here to be finished) it will be sold at such reduced Prices as cannot fail of giving Satisfaction.[4]

1. One is at the Lee Mansion, Marblehead Historical Society; another is at Wilton, Richmond, Va., and is apparently of cherry; a third, of cherry, was sold by Parke-Bernet, sale 629, January 1945, lot 81. The fourth and fifth were advertised in *Antiques* 54 (November 1949): 300; 80 (July 1961): 97. The sixth, the Metcalf chest, is figure 3 in Swan, "Some Men from Medway." This article is the source for most of the information on Metcalf and Richardson.

2. *Israel Sack Collection*, 1:87.

3. Swan, "Some Men from Medway."

4. Garrett, "Providence Cabinetmakers," 516.

NOTES ON STRUCTURE AND CONDITION: The case has facing strips on the sides. The base molding is backed by a series of blocks. The rear elements of the rear feet have a straight cut on the diagonal inner edge and are glued to rectangular blocks instead of directly to the bottom. A scratch bead outlines each drawer front. The drawers' dovetails are finely cut. The bottom of each drawer is nailed to the rabbeted edges of front and sides. The drawers run on the lower edges of the sides and on a series of small blocks glued to the bottom along the sides.

The chest retains all of its original elements except for one replaced drawer support. The chest was refinished in 1977.

MATERIALS: *Mahogany;* white pine secondary wood. Original brass hardware except for the escutcheon on the top drawer. Original steel locks in the upper three drawers; the bottom drawer never had a lock.

PROVENANCE: The chest was among the contents of the Dedham, Mass., home of Caroline Barr Wade (1865–1954).

ACCESSION: 1948.154   A gift of Caroline Barr Wade; conserved through the generosity of Henry Stokes

24 / Chest of Drawers

1803
Henniker, New Hampshire
H. 48⅛ (122.2); W. 38⁵⁄₁₆ (97.3); D. 18⁷⁄₁₆ (46.8)

This plain, almost styleless chest of five drawers is important because it is inscribed in chalk "L[evi] Colby/Heniker March 12ᵗʰ/1803" (24a). In a surprising reversal of the

24

usual importance of an inscription, "Colby" tells us little, "Heniker" a good deal more, and "1803" is interesting new evidence.

The "1803" proves the continuation of the Chippendale style into the nineteenth century and documents the early use of cut nails in American furniture. All the original fasteners in the chest are cut nails. Numerous nail-making machines were invented and patented in the 1780s and 1790s, and cut nail manufactories were soon established in the Northeast.[1]

Henniker, New Hampshire, is the only place of that name in the world. In 1803 it was the home of fifteen hundred people, enough to support a joiner–furniture maker. Samuel Dunlap, of the well-known family of furniture craftsmen (see entries 25 and 42), had worked there from 1779 to 1797.[2]

Of the Henniker Colbys, only "Levi" seems to fit the unreadable first name inscribed on the chest; there were two adult Levi Colbys in Henniker in 1803.[3] Neither was a cabinetmaker, so the inscription probably refers to the owner, very likely Levi Colby, Jr. (1781–1869), a farmer who married in about 1803 and was apt to be acquiring furniture at that time.[4]

Chippendale chests of five (or more) drawers were popular in inland New England, and many survive. This documented example of southern New Hampshire furniture may help attribute other pieces to the Henniker area. The unusual contour of the bracket feet is a notable feature. The chest also has feet of one piece with the base molding, drawer dividers of a single wood with unfinished back edges, the large, crudely cut dovetails common on many rural New England cases, and, of course, the cut nails.

1. "Nail Chronology as an Aid to Dating Old Buildings," by Lee H. Nelson, was written for a National Park Service Historic Structures Training Conference, July 1962; published as Technical Leaflet 15, *History News* 19, no. 2 (December 1963).

2. Dunlap's dates in Henniker come from the research of Charles S. Parsons; Parsons to the authors, September 25, 1977.

3. Cogswell, *Henniker*, 517, 519. The signature on the will of Levi Colby, Sr. (1757–1827), docket 378, Merrimack County (N.H.) Probate, is inconclusive. Colby bought four chairs from Dunlap on March 8, 1791; the entry in Dunlap's account book is quoted in Society correspondence; Parsons to the authors, September 25, 1977.

4. Cogswell, *Henniker*, 519. Colby's marriage date is unknown, but his first child was born in 1805.

NOTES ON STRUCTURE AND CONDITION: The sides join the top with mitered dovetails. Eight pine glue blocks help hold the top to the sides and upper front rail. The top backboard is nailed to the rabbeted edges of the top as well as to the sides. The dividers are dovetailed through the case sides, leaving the dovetails exposed on the case sides as well as on the front edges of the sides. The boards that form the base molding and feet are mitered at the corners and nailed to the lower edge of the case. The construction of the feet and base molding of one piece contrasts significantly with urban work.

The drawers have large, thick dovetails. Each drawer bottom fits into grooves in the front and sides. The bottom drawer slides on the base rail and supports.

The chest has several minor pieced repairs. Wire nails were added throughout the case. Only the left front foot has a complete set of original blocks.

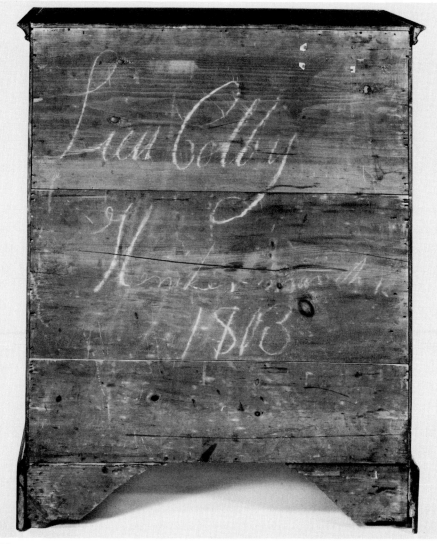

24a

The chest, which had been stripped, was restained in 1977 to match the evidence of original dark mahogany stain.

MATERIALS: *Maple; white pine* secondary wood. Original brass hardware; original lock in the top drawer.

PROVENANCE: The nineteenth-century history is unknown. The chest descended in the twentieth century from Mrs. John Howes Burton to the donor.

ACCESSION: 1966.608   A gift of Mrs. F. Gordon Brown

25 / Chest-on-Frame

1790–1805
Southern New Hampshire
Attributed to the Dunlap school
H. 58 (147.3); W. 40 1/16 (101.8); D. 19 5/8 (49.8)

This chest is an even more obvious example of the extended popularity of mid-eighteenth-century fashion than Levi Colby's Henniker chest (no. 24). The pad feet, cabriole legs, skirt of C and cyma curves, and the wide complicated cornice are characteristic of the Queen Anne style. Replacement rococo brasses reinforce the impression that this is a pre-Revolutionary chest.

However, this chest was made at about the same time as Colby's. The drawer fronts originally had oval Federal brasses; cut nails fasten the drawer bottoms to the drawer backs; and the drawer bottoms were cut to a feather edge by a molding plane, a technique seen in drawers of nineteenth-century manufacture.

In the eighteenth century, chests like nos. 24 and 25 were called "low cases of drawers" or "low chests of drawers" to distinguish them from high chests such as no. 41 and 42.[1] Low cases of drawers with five case-wide drawers were more common than those with six, to judge from surviving examples. The "Low Chest of Drawers," according to a Philadelphia price book, could be five or six tiers tall and have long and small drawers. The six-tier version was available "on A frame 18 Inch high With out drawers."[2] This chest has such a frame without drawers.

The frame, a separate piece upon which the case sits, is for this chest the principal clue to its origin. The skirt is very similar to that on a chest-on-chest-on-frame found in Bedford, New Hampshire, and attributed to Major John Dunlap.[3] In addition, the chest has the creased knees, the slender legs with a pronounced curve, the pointed knee brackets, and the deep and complex molded cornice that are regarded as Dunlap details (II-19).[4] The boldly coved disks beneath the turned feet (see also high chest no. 42) are another Dunlap characteristic.

The Dunlap cabinetmakers lived in southern New Hampshire. The brothers John and Samuel, their sons Robert, Archibald, John II, Whitfield, Samuel II, James, John (son of Samuel), and Daniel, in addition to John (son of Robert), Robert (son of John II), and Dan (father unknown), worked in various towns that were rapidly growing in the post-Revolutionary era — Salisbury, Henniker, Chester, Antrim, Goffstown, and Bedford (see pages 67–68).

Samuel made twenty-four low cases of drawers between 1789 and 1800 and only six in the next fifteen years. He sold them for almost two thirds the price of high chests such as no. 42, the latter running about £3:0:0, the low cases £1:19:0.[5]

This chest is an important addition to the known low cases by the Dunlap school. In

25

his fine study on the Dunlaps, Parsons illustrates several chests of five drawers on cabriole legs, a six-drawer chest on bracket feet, but no chest-on-frame.[6] Although numerous Dunlap chest-on-chests stand on frames, this chest-on-frame illustrates a rare form.[7]

1. Montgomery, *Federal Period*, 179.

2. Weil, "Price Book," 182.

3. Parsons, "Dunlap Cabinetmakers," 8 and fig. 50.

4. Charles S. Parsons to the authors, November 8, 1979.

5. Ibid., 31, 41.

6. *Dunlaps* illustrates eleven of the chest-on-chest-on-frame type (figs. 40–50), five five-drawer chests (figs. 57–61), and one six-drawer chest (fig. 63).

7. Ibid., figs. 40–50; a related chest on a plain-skirted frame was sold at auction, Andrew M. Williams Collection, Parke-Bernet, sale 955, April 1948, lot 128.

NOTES ON STRUCTURE AND CONDITION: The neatly dovetailed case rests on a joined frame. A coved molding is glued and nailed to the top of the front and side rails of the frame. Two braces, tenoned into the front rail and set into notches in the rear rail of the frame, help support the case. The drawer dividers are shallow; their shouldered-dovetail joints remain exposed on the front edges of the case sides. The drawer fronts have four thumbnail-molded edges, lipped on the sides and top. The drawers are precisely dovetailed. Drawer bottoms fit into grooves in the drawer fronts and sides. The bottom drawer runs on a front rail and drawer supports. The two-board cornice is applied above a one-piece bead molding.

The chest, now refinished to a honey color, was originally stained reddish brown. All the original elements survive except one drawer support.

MATERIALS: *Hard maple; soft maple* back rail of frame; *white pine* other secondary wood. Replaced brass hardware; original steel lock in the third from bottom drawer, locks for the upper two drawers are missing.

PROVENANCE: The chest is from the collection of Charles K. Davis.

ACCESSION: 1952.84   A gift of Charles K. Davis

26 / Chest-on-Chest

1765–1785
Newport area
H. 82⅞ (210.5), excluding finial 81⅝ (206.5); W. 40⅜ (102.6); D. 21⁹⁄₁₆ (54.8)

The chest-on-chest of the late eighteenth century continues a long tradition of stacking cases. By 1650, London joiners familiar with Dutch design were making two-part chests of drawers, usually with doors hiding the drawer fronts.[1] In the eighteenth century, two-part cases of dovetailed cabinetry replaced the joined chests of the earlier era, and the most stylish English form was the clothes press (I-16) with paneled doors in the upper section. New Englanders rarely made presses, preferring instead the chest-on-chest, or "double chest."[2]

In 1792, a plain chest-on-chest could be bought in Hartford, Connecticut, for £7, one with columns for £8:4:0, and one with "scrowl'd head" for £11.[3] This chest-on-chest has such a scrolled "head," or pediment, one completely defined by moldings. The

26

pediment, scrolled or pitched (desk and bookcase no. 51), was the finishing architectural touch in making the stacked piece a unified whole.

From its pediment to its feet, this chest-on-chest evokes comparisons with the furniture of Newport and of the area influenced by Newport design — all of Rhode Island, eastern Connecticut, and nearby Bristol County, Massachusetts. The design of the bracket feet and the use of bold moldings are characteristic of Newport (I-41). The very contours of the base, waist, and pediment moldings are virtually standard in Newport furniture, although an architrave molding is rarely seen. The shape of the pediment, the fluting of the plinths, and the use of a single finial are all seen in Newport pieces. A stylish chest-on-chest with corner quarter-columns, which belonged to the Clarke family of Jamestown (on the adjacent island across from Newport Harbor), has the same base, waist, and pediment moldings, the same feet, pediment shape, and fluted plinth as the Society's chest-on-chest.[4]

The Clarke chest-on-chest is of mahogany, the fashionable wood of the era; this one is of maple. Frequently found in furniture made outside the urban area, maple was also used in high-style centers. In 1787 Townsend Goddard, of the large and famous clan of Newport cabinetmakers, the Townsends and the Goddards, made a large bedstead with "Fluted Posts & Bases" of maple.[5] The 1792 inventory of John Cahoone, a Newport cabinetmaker, listed maple as well as mahogany boards.[6] Maple was stained to imitate finer wood; a privately owned chest-on-chest with a Newport history was made of maple, stained to resemble mahogany, and topped with a mahogany finial.[7]

While much has been written about Newport cabinetmakers of the second half of the eighteenth century, there is little information about the construction of their case furniture even though it was the most skillfully wrought in New England.[8] The authors have found in a brief comparative study that this chest shares many idiosyncrasies of construction with other Newport furniture. The bottom drawer runs on a front rail and drawer supports, not directly on the case bottom (26a). Beneath the case, the base molding is flush with the bottom (26b). The joints between the drawer dividers and the case sides remain exposed. The waist molding is applied to the upper case (outside Rhode Island, it is on the lower case).

A usual but little-known feature of Newport two-part cases is an opening in the top of the lower case (26a). On the Society's chest the opening is used to join the cases securely. When chest is upon chest, a cleat nailed beneath the upper case keys into the opening in the top of the lower case.

The dovetails on this chest, like those on chests of the Townsend-Goddard school, are exceedingly fine.[9] They are far more precise than those on another maple chest-on-chest, rich in Townsend-Goddard design details but with a history tying it to southeastern Connecticut.[10] The Connecticut chest-on-chest was inspired by Newport furniture; the Society's is Newport furniture. Although a well-made urban object, it is of plain design and inexpensive wood. Aptly, its finial is simple and devoid of carving.

26a

26b

1. Forman, "Joined Chest." For Boston two-part chests with and without doors, see *New England Begins*, vol. 3, nos. 481, 493.

2. A September 1736 bill to Nathaniel Holmes from Thomas Johnson is for a "Double Chest of Draws"; bills 1728–59, vol. 8, Bourn Papers, Baker Library, Harvard University.

3. The 1792 Hartford Cabinetmakers Table of Prices is quoted in Lyon, *Colonial Furniture*, 3rd ed., 268.

4. The Clarke family chest-on-chest is in the Newport Historical Society.

5. Swan, "John Goddard's Sons."

6. Garrett, "Newport Cabinetmakers."

7. The chest-on-chest came from the Buffum family of Newport and still has its original finial.

8. Lovell ("Boston Blockfront Furniture," 80–89) discusses the joinings of tops, drawer dividers, front base moldings, and drawer bottoms on Newport chests of drawers.

9. The dovetails on chest no. 26 are indistinguishable from those on a Newport desk and bookcase in the Museum of Fine Arts, Boston, number 19 in Hipkiss, *Karolik Collection*.

10. The chest-on-chest with a tradition of coming from New London County, Conn., is in the Mabel Brady Garvan Collection, Yale University Art Gallery, and was illustrated in Kirk, "Distinctive Character of Connecticut Furniture," fig. 1.

NOTES ON STRUCTURE AND CONDITION: The scrolled pediment has a conforming bonnet roof and full backboard. The one-piece cornice molding is fastened not only to the sides and pediment but also along the entire depth of the bonnet opening. The continuation of the molding from the front to the back of the bonnet opening is an unusual feature, seen occasionally in Newport and its environs but rarely elsewhere. The one-piece finial fits into a hole in the fluted plinth. Inside the upper case against the back, a horizontal slat, which is made like a drawer divider, braces the drawer supports for the two small drawers. The lip of the waist molding overlaps the lower case.

The lower case top is two narrow boards dovetailed to the sides but separated from each other by a 9½-inch gap. The bracket feet are glued and nailed to the base molding with one rose-headed nail in each element. The rear feet are constructed in an unusual manner that appears in some Newport furniture: the rear element of each rear foot fits into a groove in the thick side element. The drawer fronts, cut to a thumbnail on all four edges, are lipped at the top and sides. Each drawer bottom is chamfered to fit into grooves in the front and sides.

The chest was refinished in this century to a light honey color. Traces of the original mahogany-colored wash remain. The bottom of the left rear foot has a 3-inch pieced repair. Six support blocks for the feet are replacements.

MATERIALS: *Soft maple; white pine* secondary wood. Original brass hardware; original steel locks in all long drawers.

PROVENANCE: The piece came to the Society with a collection of furnishings acquired early in the twentieth century.

ACCESSION: 1949.215   A bequest of Elizabeth R. Vaughan

27 / Chest-on-Chest

1764–1780
Boston area
H. 83⅜ (210.8), excluding finial 77³⁄₁₆ (196.1); W. 43⁹⁄₁₆ (110.7); D. 21½ (54.6)

A chest-on-chest was frequently ordered with a matching table-high chest of drawers, often called a "bureau" or "table to suit." Chest of drawers no. 19 is the "table to suit" this chest-on-chest. The large piece cost about twice the price of its companion. For example, in the 1776 inventory of William Cazneau, a Boston merchant, a "chest upon chest" was evaluated at 120 shillings and a bureau listed on the next line at 60; one year earlier, Joseph Tyler of Boston had "1 Chest on Chest of Drawers £6 — 1 Bureau Table £3."[1]

This mahogany chest-on-chest with fashionable scrolled pediment and a swelled lower case is rather modest in height and design; the feet are not swelled, and it has no columns or other carvings. In addition to the Boston characteristics shared with its companion, the chest-on-chest has two distinctive features: the finials and the top edge of the oxbow.

The twisted flames on the finials are ordinary for New England; however, the central urn and the turned support beneath it (the side finials are missing their urns) are unusual. The finials have virtually the same turned elements (i.e., ring, spool, ring, vase, and up to the flame tip) as those on documented Boston cases, but these are coarser and of poorer proportions. The finials are original and may help pinpoint the origin of the chest if similar finials are found on a well-documented piece.

The modeling of the upper drawer of the lower case is noteworthy. The segmental arches at the top of the oxbow combine crisp edges on the two convex areas with a gradually dissolving arch in the concave center.

The Boston characteristics of this chest-on-chest make an interesting contrast to the Newport characteristics of the previous chest. Here, in typical Boston fashion, is a central drop on the skirt. The outline of the bracket feet is considerably more complicated than that of the very simple Newport feet. All the moldings on this chest appear thin when compared to bold Newport moldings.

Boston designs for bonnet-topped cases are not fully conceived in three dimensions, like the Newport ones. Here the molding terminates at the opening in the pediment; on chest-on-chest no. 26 the molding continues back to the rear of the opening. The walls supporting the bonnet on the Boston-area chest are straight, denying the curves of the pediment. Boston bonnets almost always carry three finials; in Newport, quite often one suffices. The plinth design on this chest is the usual Boston design, neither fluted like Newport plinths nor carved in any way.

Fashionable Boston cases have drawer fronts with plain edges and drawer openings surrounded by a beaded edge. Cases made elsewhere, including Newport, often use the popular thumbnail-edged drawer fronts and drawer openings with plain edges.

27

1. William Cazneau's inventory, old series, vol. 75, p. 383, and Joseph Tyler's inventory, old series, vol. 74, p. 283, Suffolk County (Mass.) Probate.

NOTES ON STRUCTURE AND CONDITION: At the top, the case sides are held by the pediment and the uppermost backboard, which are nailed to the edges of the case sides. A single thin pine board forms each half of the bonnet roof. The cornice is a one-piece molding. Facing strips cover the joints of the drawer dividers to the case sides. The one-piece waist molding is attached along the top edge of the lower case; the upper case fits behind it.

The base moldings are flush with the upper surface of the bottom. Beneath the lower case, a series of support blocks of various lengths are glued to the bottom along the base moldings. The front molding is joined to the bottom with a single long and shallow dovetail. This feature, a typical one on Boston oxbows and blockfronts, does not appear on the companion chest of drawers. The feet follow the same pattern as on the companion chest.

The drawer bottoms are nailed into the rabbeted edges of the fronts and sides. Applied runners are set against the sides and glued to the bottom. The back of each runner is cut on a 45-degree angle. The top edges of the drawer sides are cut with a double-arched bead. The two lower drawers of the upper case are of a lighter mahogany than the rest of the case. All the drawers are original; apparently, the lighter drawers were stained to match. The chest-on-chest was refinished early in this century; it evinces more wear than its mate.

MATERIALS: *Mahogany; white pine* secondary wood. Original brass hardware; original steel locks in the upper three drawers of each case.

PROVENANCE: The chest shares a provenance with its companion, chest of drawers no. 19.

ACCESSION: 1958.79   A gift of Caroline Barr Wade

28 / Chest-on-Chest

1785–1800
Southern Maine or eastern New Hampshire
H. 77⅞ (197.8); W. 39⁵⁄₁₆ (99.9); D. 20⁹⁄₁₆ (52.2)

Rural cabinetwork presents an imaginative array of flamboyant feet. An interesting contrast is seen between the feet on chest-on-chest no. 26, from Newport, and those on this one. Nothing could be more sedate than the simple Newport bracket foot that supports some of New England's most sophisticated and expensive furniture; it is hard to imagine feet less sedate than those on this chest.

Yet the bold, busy outline of the feet is only the most obvious and delightful of its many rural features. From flashy feet to cornice, each aspect of this chest bespeaks its rural origin. Tall, unpedimented cases are often found in rural areas. Feet and base moldings cut, as these are, from a single board are seen in provincial construction. The drawer backs are grooved to receive the drawer bottoms, a most unusual construction that eliminates the need for nails or wooden pins in assembling the drawers. Wooden pins, instead of nails, secure the waist and cornice moldings. The craftsman's choice to expend labor making pins rather than spend money buying nails points again to the upcountry origin. But where? In the late eighteenth century, most of New England was rural.

The primary wood of this chest, birch, commonly appears in furniture made north of

28

Boston. The chest has been in Wiscasset, Maine, in this century, but its previous history is unknown. The authors, presented with something of a mystery, submitted a query to the readers of *Maine Antique Digest*, enclosing a photograph. Responses came from Maine to Virginia; one yielded a virtual mate, purchased in Limerick, Maine. Apparently the two originated in or near southern Maine.

Trying to localize country furniture design is very difficult. Whereas urban furniture was made in large numbers by specialists in contact with others of their craft, country furniture was made by isolated craftsmen, often practicing several trades and producing few pieces. Finding two identical rural chests is a rare triumph.

NOTES ON STRUCTURE AND CONDITION: The joints of the shallow drawer dividers are left exposed on the front of the case sides. The cornice is a one-piece molding. The drawer supports for the upper tier that are mounted behind the partitions are tenoned through the backboard. The cove-shaped waist molding, attached to the top of the lower case, is of a novel contour. The upper case fits behind the waist molding. Instead of the usual miter joint at the corners of the feet, only the very edge of the joint is mitered; possibly the joint is a mitered dovetail. Each rear foot has a rear element set into a shallow groove in the side element and nailed to the bottom. Widely spaced small horizontal blocks, glued to the underside of the bottom, support the base molding.

The drawers have large, precisely cut dovetails, but the drawer backs are dovetailed to slide onto the sides rather than the usual fashion of drawer sides onto backs. Each drawer bottom, chamfered underneath at all four sides, fits into grooves in the front, sides and — here is the unusual feature — back. Usually there is no groove in back, and the bottom is merely nailed up to the flush bottom edge of the back. The bottom drawer of the chest rests on a front rail and drawer supports, not directly on the chest bottom.

The chest was originally stained red. Minor restorations include splines added to the sides of both cases to compensate for shrinkage and one replaced board on the upper back. Only one drawer support is original.

MATERIALS: *Birch* primary wood and drawer supports; *white pine* secondary wood. Replaced brass hardware; never had locks.

PROVENANCE: The chest came to the Society with the Nickels-Sortwell House, Wiscasset, Me., which was furnished by Alvin Sortwell, father of the donor, following his 1899 purchase of the house.

ACCESSION: 1958.201   A bequest of Frances A. Sortwell

29 / Dressing Table

1720–1735
Boston area
H. 33 (83.8); W. 33¾ (85.7); D. 21½ (54.6)

Dressing tables and high chests went by other names in the eighteenth century; for example, Captain William Warner of Boston owned in 1745 "1 case of Draws Steps & Table."[1] Warner's "case of Draws" was no doubt a high chest. The "Steps" were stepped shelves placed on a high chest to display china and glass, for Warner's inventory continues: "Glasware on the Case Draws." The "Table" was included in the same entry

29

because it was made to accompany the high chest. Sets seldom have remained together; this dressing table and its mate (29a) are an exceptional pair.

The smaller form has been known variously as "table," "chamber table," "dressing table," or by the modern "lowboy." "Dressing table" denotes function and appears occasionally in eighteenth-century inventories. It was generally listed with mirrors — either a dressing glass, which sat upon the table, or a looking glass, which hung above it. "Chamber table," a popular eighteenth-century term, denotes location. A typical one-line inventory entry reads: "1 Case Draws & Chamber Table 12:15/   1 Looking Glass £10."[2] High chests and their tables were chamber (i.e., bedroom) furniture.

In 1715 Thomas Platts of Boston had in his chamber "drawers Looking Glass and

Table."[3] Platts's "[case of] drawers" and "Table" would have been of the William and Mary style. Still popular in the early eighteenth century, the style was current when these furniture forms first appeared at the end of the seventeenth century. A sharp break with earlier design, the William and Mary style featured veneered surfaces on dovetailed cases supported by turned legs and feet.

In Boston, where this dressing table and its mate were probably made, cabinetmakers purchased turnings from specialists in the craft. In 1733, the turner John Underwood sold the Boston cabinetmaker Nathaniel Holmes "2 Sets of Pillers [legs] & Balls [feet] & Drops."[4] The "pillers" on this dressing table are a shape Underwood may well have been making in 1733, for early William and Mary turned legs are heavier. The thin pillars of the 1720s and 1730s were made in two styles: this type and the more expensive turnings that resembled trumpets with mutes in them.

The drawer configuration of this "Case Draws & Chamber Table" also indicates that the high chest and table are of late William and Mary fashion. Earlier, high-chest bases and dressing tables were made with a single drawer or one tier of drawers. The two-tiered façade, rare on a William and Mary dressing table, became common in the Queen Anne era.[5]

William and Mary high chests and dressing tables proved flimsy. Dovetailed cases on turned supports are inherently less stable than joinery. A joined dressing table has sides, a back, and a front skirt tenoned into stiles that are of one piece with the legs. In time, when the Queen Anne style prevailed in New England in the 1730s, cabinetmakers returned to joinery to make stable dressing tables and high-chest bases.[6]

This dressing table exemplifies fragile William and Mary construction. The sides are dovetailed to the back; glue holds the skirt in front. The legs are not tenoned directly into the case but into blocks glued to the case. Such reliance on glue joints produces a case that is vulnerable to breakage and makes stretchers essential. The high chest stands on six stretchered legs, a William and Mary stylistic consideration that helps lend stability to the taller, heavier cases.

The cross stretchers of the four-legged dressing tables usually have a finial round-tenoned through the intersection to fasten and decorate it. This dressing table never had a finial. The skirt retains its original drops and plates. Considering the fragility of William and Mary construction, the entire table is in very good condition except for a marred and patched top.

1. William Warner's inventory, old series, vol. 38, p. 523, Suffolk County (Mass.) Probate.

2. Edward Morberly's 1749 inventory, old series, vol. 42, p. 509, Suffolk County (Mass.) Probate.

3. Thomas Platts's inventory, old series, vol. 19, p. 48, Suffolk County (Mass.) Probate.

4. The February 6 bill, among bills 1728–59, vol. 8, Bourn Papers, Baker Library, Harvard University.

5. Israel Sack, Inc., advertised in *Antiques* in

October 1968 a related piece (one drawer over three) as "to our knowledge unique in a William and Mary dressing table." A high chest with a drawer configuration like that of dressing table no. 29 and its companion appear in Lockwood, *Colonial Furniture*, rev. ed., vol. 1, fig. 69.

29a. High Chest. H. 70⅛ (178.1); W. 40 (101.6); D. 21⁹⁄₁₆ (54.8). Private collection. *The mate to dressing table no. 29.*

6. In Rhode Island, cabinetmakers continued to make dressing tables and high-chest bases of dovetailed construction.

NOTES ON STRUCTURE AND CONDITION: The top skirt, stiles, and drawer fronts are veneered. The drawer openings are surrounded by a double-arched molding. The original bead still edges the front and side skirts. The partitions between the drawers taper and are tenoned through the backboard as in detail 30b. Forged nails hold the drawer bottom to the rabbeted lower edge of the drawer front and the flush edges of the drawer sides and back. Each drawer rests on a medial drawer support tenoned through the backboard and nailed into a notch in front.

Four forged nails fasten the lapped joint of the cross stretchers. The legs are round-tenoned through the stretchers and feet. The veneered top has a thumbnail edge on all four sides; otherwise it is of the pattern seen in detail 30a. It overhangs 1⅝ inches at the front and back, 2 inches on the right side, and 2⅜ inches on the left side. Originally the top was secured to the case sides by glued blocks. Now the blocks are screwed to the top and case sides.

The dressing table was refinished about eighty years ago. The case sides have split from skrinkage. The thumbnail edge of the top is pieced at the right front corner; much of the burled surface in the center of the top is replaced. The old drawer stops remain; some have been repositioned.

MATERIALS: Black walnut veneer on the top, drawer fronts, and case front; *black walnut* case sides; maple legs, stretchers, feet, and drops; *white pine* secondary wood. Original brass hardware; never had locks.

PROVENANCE: The table was purchased with the high chest for $24.75 in 1883 or 1884 in Scituate, Mass., at the auction of the property of a Miss Clapp by Laura P. Stone, later Mrs. Charles F. Batchelder, Sr., and descended to her daughter-in-law, the donor.

ACCESSION: 1980.379   A gift of Mrs. Charles F. Batchelder

30 / Dressing Table

1730–1740
Boston area
H. 30¾ (78.1); W. 34¹⁄₁₆ (86.5); D. 20⁷⁄₁₆ (51.9)

The top of this splendid walnut dressing table shows the mirroring achieved with four flitches of veneer (30a). The love of walnut veneer continued during the second quarter of the eighteenth century, and early Queen Anne cases such as this one are resplendent in figured veneer.

From top to skirt, the design of this dressing table resembles the preceding William and Mary example. The drawer supports and partitions of this dressing table (30b) follow the same pattern as those of the preceding one. But the cabriole legs are distinctly Queen Anne. William and Mary design introduced cyma curves such as those that outline the skirts on both dressing tables. In the Queen Anne style, the use of curves

30

became extravagant, and even the legs adopted the cyma shape. In the 1730s, turned William and Mary legs were superseded in American furniture by cabrioles, first called "horsebone" or "horse leg" and later "crooked."[1]

The Society's collection includes several fine cabriole dressing tables, five of which are included here. The first two are elegant examples of early Queen Anne style. This one not only has dressy veneers and "horse legs" but an extraordinary skirt that originally had two more drops.

Dressing tables with simpler skirts but related in proportion, line, and drawer configuration are recognized as typical of Boston. An example at the Museum of Fine Arts, Boston, has similar brasses and similarly constructed drawers, supports, and partitions.[2] Yet a complex skirt such as this is exceedingly rare, making this Queen Anne dressing table, otherwise a standard example of stylish design, a very important variation.

1. "Horsebone" comes from Samuel Grant, Account Book, October 14, 1729, p. 65, Massachusetts Historical Society; "horse legg" appears in James Jackson's 1735 inventory, old series, vol. 32, p. 335, Suffolk County (Mass.) Probate; "crooked" in another Grant Account Book, August 16 and November 13, 1739, June 25, 1740, pp. 110, 124, 159, American Antiquarian Society.

2. Randall, *American Furniture*, no. 45.

NOTES ON STRUCTURE AND CONDITION: The top, secured by four pins and reinforced by four thin glue blocks, overhangs the front by 1 1/4 inches, the sides by 2 1/2 inches, and the back by 1 inch. Original bead moldings surround the drawer openings and edge the skirt and sides, except for a missing portion beneath the right side. To make the legs, the cabinetmaker used stock made of two boards rather than one thick block, and the piecing is visible on the knees and feet. The drawer partitions are tenoned into the backboard.

The drawers have large, thick dovetails. The bottoms are nailed into the rabbeted lower edges of the fronts and the flush edges of the sides. The top edge of the drawer sides is cut to a double-arched bead. Each drawer runs on its bottom, resting on a narrow medial support that is tenoned into the back. Drawer stops, of scraps of walnut veneer, are glued and nailed to the backboard.

The table was rescued from a fire in 1945. Four of the six knee brackets and all the drops and plates are replacements. In 1977, because of lifting veneers, bleached surfaces, loose moldings, and a large chip in the left front foot, the table was repaired and refinished.

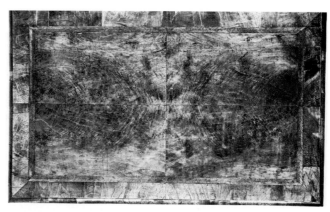

30a

30b

MATERIALS: Black walnut veneer on the top, drawer fronts, and case front; *black walnut* legs, drawer divider, and case sides; *white pine* secondary wood. Original brass hardware; never had locks.

PROVENANCE: The history of the table before 1942 is unknown. It came to the Society with a collection of furniture principally from the Portsmouth area.

ACCESSION: 1942.1228   A gift of Virginia L. Hodge and Katherine D. Parry

31 / Dressing Table

1735–1745
Boston or Essex County, Massachusetts
H. 31 (78.7); W. 32¼ (81.9); D. 20⅛ (51.1)

Typical of furniture design of the first half of the eighteenth century, this dressing table stresses flat decoration and features showy veneers (plate 5). Veneering — a technique that, with dovetailing, was the stock in trade of cabinetmakers — required particular tools. So in addition to the joiner's molding planes, chisels, and jointers, the cabinetmaker had veneers and a glue pot. William Howell's 1717 inventory includes "2 Glew Potts 4/[shillings] . . . 80ᵗᵇ of Lead [weights to press the veneer] £1 . . . Walnut Fenere £8:18:7 . . . 15ᵗᵇ of Glew 15/ . . ." as well as "Walnut tree at Mʳ. Edes 10/6."[1]

In 1717 Howell was making veneered furniture in the William and Mary style. In 1740, when the Queen Anne style was in fashion and about the time this dressing table was made, John Brocas of Boston also owned joiner's tools and "150 feet of black walnut . . . Sundry Verneers . . . 1 Glue pot."[2] The splendid burl of the wood on this dressing table, juxtaposed with a spectacular herringbone banding, makes clear and understandable the enduring enthusiasm for the decorative figure of wood.

As would be expected of veneered cabinetry, the drawers are dovetailed. The frame, however, is not. In most of New England, cabinetmakers used mortise-and-tenon joints to frame Queen Anne dressing tables and the lower cases of high chests; in Rhode Island, such pieces were dovetailed. Thus, the stiles of this piece (of one piece with the legs) are joined to the sides and skirt with mortise-and-tenon joints reinforced by wooden pins, which are hidden on the front by veneer.

Veneers could not be applied to the curved surfaces of the cabrioles, nor were costly veneers applied to case sides. At first glance, the burl on this dressing table seems to continue around the corners and down to the floor, but this effect is achieved on the sides and legs with that wonderful cheat, paint.

The daubed paint is the original finish. Save for one notable example, it may be unique. The exception, a high chest at the North Andover Historical Society (31a),

31

features different but equally spectacular veneers. The sides and legs of the high chest have been overpainted, but evidence of the earlier painting survives. Its skirt outline is the same as that on the dressing table. The drawer construction reveals that the two pieces were made by the same man.

1. William Howell's inventory, old series, vol. 26, pp. 33–35, Suffolk County (Mass.) Probate.

2. John Brocas's inventory, docket 7521, Suffolk County (Mass.) Probate.

NOTES ON STRUCTURE AND CONDITION: The top, pinned to the joined frame, overhangs 1 inch, but only at the front and sides. The rear feet point toward the front of the case. Applied strips of beaded channel molding surround the drawer openings. A beaded edge is nailed to the underside of the front skirt but was never present beneath the case sides. The drawer partitions are tenoned into the backboard. The lower edge of the partitions for the bottom tier of drawers is straight rather than tapered, like that on dressing table no. 30.

The drawer supports are glued and nailed to the partitions and case sides. The drawers are assembled with broad dovetails typical of early-eighteenth-century workmanship in urban Massachusetts. The bottom of each drawer is nailed into the rabbeted edges of the front and the flush edges of the sides. Runners are glued to the drawer bottoms at the sides.

The table survives in fine condition. The painted and veneered decoration is original. The knee brackets on the right side and the drops and plinths are replacements.

MATERIALS: Black walnut and ash veneer on the top; black walnut and maple veneer on the drawer fronts and case front; *soft maple* legs; white pine secondary wood. Original brass handle on the middle drawer; never had locks.

PROVENANCE: The table was apparently purchased at auction, "Important American Antiques from the King Hooper Mansion, Marblehead, Massachusetts, Part Two," American Art Association, sale 2112, November 1927, lot 177.

ACCESSION: 1949.192   A gift of Mary Thacher

31a. High Chest. Boston or Essex County, Massachusetts, 1735–1745. Black walnut, ash, maple, and white pine; H. 89⅜ (227.0); W. 37¼ (94.6); D. 21½ (54.6). North Andover Historical Society.

32 / Dressing Table

1740–1760
Salem-Danvers area, Massachusetts
H. 30 (76.2); W. 34⅞ (88.6); D. 22⅜ (56.8)

Dressing tables served two functions: as cases for drawers and as tables. They added some storage space to that provided by their tall companions, high chests, but the space was not secured by locks, standard equipment for most drawers. Evidently these compartments were not intended for valuables.

The main function of this furniture form was that of a table. Of the six examples here, this one, with its unusually wide top, most looks like a table. The top is given prominence by a striking veneered design, an extraordinary overhang, and a wide walnut molding of distinctive shape applied along all four edges.

This dressing table manifests several post-1740 features: the curve of the skirt (which precludes drops), the flat arch of the case sides, and the design of the brasses. A mid-eighteenth-century example, it illustrates the continued popularity of veneer.

The façade has a distinctive feature: veneered drawer fronts with thumbnail-molded edges. Thumbnail edges generally were used on drawer fronts of solid wood and over-lapped the drawer openings only at the tops and sides; here, the drawer fronts overlap the bottoms as well. Usually the thumbnail edge is an integral part of the drawer front, here it is applied.

This unusual feature appears also on a remarkably similar high chest with closely

32

related veneer.[1] The high chest, reportedly from Essex County, and this dressing table are apparently the work of the same man. Seven other cases — five high chests and two dressing tables — have the same skirt design, drawer pattern, and leg and knee conformation.[2] Of these, a veneered high chest and dressing table originally belonged to James and Mary (Orne) Dimon of Salem, and a solid mahogany high chest descended from Aaron Putnam of Danvers, adjacent to Salem in Essex County.[3] Apparently all nine cases were made in the Salem-Danvers area.

1. The high chest is number 13 in Clunie, Farnam, and Trent, *Furniture at the Essex Institute*. It and the dressing table have the same double-arched top edge on the drawer sides and backs.

2. Three of the high chests are veneered: (1) sold at auction with a matching dressing table (Sotheby Parke Bernet, sale 4116, April 1978, lot 1044); (2) sold at auction (Israel Sack Collection, American Art Association, sale 3787, November 1929, lot 138); (3) advertised by Elizabeth Stokes (*Antiques* 87 [March 1965]: 258). Two of the high chests are solid wood: (1) advertised by Nathan Liverant in the 1977 Essex Antiques Show catalogue, Essex, Conn.; (2) no. 72 in *Israel Sack Collection*, 1:21. The dressing tables are veneered: (1) cited above with its matching high chest; (2) number 410 in Nutting, *Furniture Treasury*, vol. 1. The skirt design on the Essex Institute high chest cited in note 1, the two solid wood chests, and the Stokes chest includes quarter-round curves near the knee brackets, a slight variation from the plainer style seen on the rest of the furniture in the group.

3. The Dimon high chest and dressing table were sold at auction in 1978, and the Putnam high chest appeared in *Israel Sack Collection* (see note 2).

NOTES ON STRUCTURE AND CONDITION: The top, secured to the joined case with glue blocks, overhangs the case by 3¾ inches on the sides, 1⁷⁄₁₆ inches on the front, and by 1⅞ inches on the back.

A beaded strip is nailed to the lower edge of the front skirt but never was present beneath the case sides. All but the left rear leg are pieced at the knees and the feet, a feature often seen on cabrioles made in New England.

The drawer partitions are tenoned into the backboard; their lower edges taper like that seen in detail 30b. The lower tier of drawers slides on medial drawer supports tenoned into the backboard and glued into notches in the front. The drawers have rather crude dovetails. The drawer bottoms fit into grooves in the fronts and sides.

The dressing table is in excellent condition. The only major repair is a 4-by-5-inch patch in the veneered top.

MATERIALS: Black walnut veneer on the top, drawer fronts, and case front; *soft maple* legs and case sides; *white pine* secondary wood. Original brass hardware; never had locks.

PROVENANCE: The dressing table, which came to the Society from the Dedham, Mass., house of the donor, may have descended with the house of Charles Barrett, Sr., and thus may share a provenance with chest of drawers no. 19.

ACCESSION: 1958.69   A gift of Caroline Barr Wade

33 / Dressing Table

1745–1760
York, Maine
Attributed to Samuel Sewall
H. 28¹¹⁄₁₆ (72.9); W. 35⅛ (89.2); D. 22⅝ (57.5)

This dressing table belonged to Judge Jonathan Sayward of York, whose household furnishings represented a range of fashion that encompassed this rural interpretation of

33

a dressing table and the elegant English tea chest (no. 4). The dressing table offers interesting comparisons with several objects in the catalogue. It is a provincial version of the form epitomized by dressing tables no. 30, 31, and 32; it was made by the joiner who made the Sayward serpentine chest (no. 21) and remains in its original household with its companion high chest (no. 37).

When compared with the three preceding dressing tables, this one presents obvious differences: the lack of veneer, the ungainly cabrioles, and the drawer configuration. Although it is a distinctly individual interpretation of the form, it was not designed in a vacuum. The awkward stance of the cabrioles and the forward-facing rear feet of this rural table are reminiscent of early urban Queen Anne examples. A single tier of three drawers — a shallow drawer flanked by deeper ones — was the popular configuration in William and Mary dressing tables; rural furniture often perpetuates earlier design.

The double arch in the center of the skirt is a timid echo of that on the more sophisticated dressing table no. 31. When compared to the bold skirt of table no. 32 — similarly, a skirt without drops — the outline of this skirt meanders. Both this table and the preceding one have the wide overhanging tops featured on many Boston examples of the William and Mary style and on some Queen Anne examples made outside the city. Dressing table no. 32 originated in or near Salem; this one was made in York.

The construction as well as the design of this dressing table would never be confused with urban work. The large wooden pins securing the top remain visible on the surface. Wooden pins are used instead of nails throughout the case; the only nails attach a bead to the lower edge of the front skirt.

The skirt bead is of sumac, a wood unknown in urban cabinetry.[1] For the rural furniture maker, however, many woods were available. Sumac, a very pliable wood, was a natural choice for the undulating skirt bead. In all, six woods are used, an extraordinary number for a small and simple piece.

The dressing table makes an interesting comparison with the high chest (no. 37) made by the same man for the same house. It has a similar skirt and brasses and the legs are alike, yet the dressing table clearly appears of secondary importance. Its drawer fronts have no showy veneers, but are solid walnut with thumbnail-molded edges; its skirt is not banded. Otherwise, every facet of construction is like that of its companion.

Construction similarities show that the high chest, the dressing table, and the serpentine chest (no. 21) of a somewhat later date were made for Sayward by the same man, probably Samuel Sewall of York (see entries 21 and 37). The serpentine chest is of rather sophisticated design; the high chest, because of its veneer, is spectacular; and the dressing table derives its charm from its lack of sophistication and its modest façade.

1. Except for this dressing table and the matching high chest, the authors know of no other furniture made with sumac. However, the wood caught the attention of Governor John Wentworth of New Hampshire. In 1774, he listed the colony's timber resources: pine; spruce; white, red, and black oak; beech; birch; acacia; cedar; and bass or poplar, adding, "Sumack which is indigenous here [yields] wood highly curious for Fine cabinet work"; Oedel, "Portsmouth," 931.

NOTES ON STRUCTURE AND CONDITION: The case front consists of two boards: the skirt and a rectangular board glued to it between the drawer partitions. The two-board top is thumbnail-edged on the front and sides and overhangs 2⅜ inches at the front, 2½ inches at the sides, and 1¾ inches at the back. Beaded moldings like that nailed to the skirt never edged the case sides. The ½-inch-deep drawer partitions are backed by drawer supports tenoned into the backboard. The drawers have large, thick dovetails. The top edges of the drawer sides are cut to a double-arched bead. Each drawer bottom fits in grooves in the drawer sides and front and is fastened to the back with three wooden pins.

The table survives in excellent condition with its original wax finish.

MATERIALS: *Black walnut* case sides, front, legs, top, partitions, and drawer fronts; *hard maple* case back; *sumac* skirt bead; *red oak* drawer sides and bottom of right drawer; *white pine* drawer backs, drawer supports, and middle drawer bottom; *elm* left drawer bottom. Original brass hardware; never had locks.

PROVENANCE: Always in Jonathan Sayward's house, the dressing table shares a provenance with tea chest no. 4.

ACCESSION: 1977.290   A gift of the heirs of Elizabeth Cheever Wheeler

34 / Dressing Table

1760–1785
Hartford-Wethersfield, Connecticut, area
H. 33⅜ (84.8); W. 34¹¹/₁₆ (88.1); D. 21 (53.3)

This handsome dressing table is beautifully designed and skillfully wrought. The fan and legs are well proportioned and crafted. The dovetails on the drawers are slender and evenly cut. Yet one aspect of the construction falls short of high fashion, for the wooden pins that hold the top to the frame remain visible on the top.

The drawer arrangement is a standard one on late Queen Anne and Chippendale dressing tables and high chests; the skirt design, however, is distinctive, and very closely

34

relates to skirts on two dressing tables and a high chest.[1] The high chest has a history of ownership in Wethersfield, Connecticut. One of the dressing tables descended in the Hubbard family of Glastonbury, across the Connecticut River from Wethersfield. In the late eighteenth century, some of the most stylish and well-crafted furniture in New England was being made in the Hartford-Wethersfield area (e.g., I-49–53).

Of the six Society dressing tables included here, this Connecticut example is by far the most neatly constructed. It is also the latest one. The two factors are connected, although it is certainly not a rule that the finer the construction, the later the piece.

1. The Wethersfield high chest and one dressing table are at Bayou Bend; Warren, *Bayou Bend*, nos. 69 and 65 respectively. The other dressing table was advertised in *Antiques* 60 (October 1951): 255, as the Hubbard lowboy. Although "Bloomfield, Conn" is written on the family history, Bloomfield was not incorporated until 1835, and Nathaniel and Norman Hubbard were of Glastonbury. All three towns are in Hartford County.

NOTES ON STRUCTURE AND CONDITION: The top, cut with a thumbnail bead along all four edges, overhangs the case by 1¾ inches at the sides and by 1½ inches at the front and back. The shallow drawer partitions are backed by drawer supports tenoned into the backboard. The drawer bottoms fit into grooves in the fronts and sides. The drawer fronts, cut to a thumbnail bead on all edges, are lipped at the top and sides on the small drawers but only at the sides on the top drawer. The dressing table retains almost all of its original structural elements, but it has been taken apart and refinished.

MATERIALS: *Cherry; white pine* secondary wood. Replaced brass hardware; never had locks.

PROVENANCE: The dressing table came to the Society without a known history.

ACCESSION: 1963.348   A gift of Mrs. Huntly H. Gilbert

35 / High Chest

1735–1745
Northeastern Massachusetts or coastal New Hampshire
H. 71⁷⁄₁₆ (181.5); W. 40⁹⁄₁₆ (103); D. 22 (55.9)

This Queen Anne walnut high chest is the first of eight distinctive, even idiosyncratic, high chests in this book. The group indicates the richness of regional differences in New England and illustrates a range of design variation within a single form.

Throughout the early eighteenth century, the high chest was called "case of drawers," "chest of drawers," or merely "drawers." Inventory references place "drawers" within bedchambers and often place glassware on the "drawers": "In the Great Chamber . . . a parcell Glass & China Ware on Chest of Drawers."[1] This chest presented a superb platform for the valuable display.

The entablature on the chest is unusually massive and complex, yet well articulated. The frieze, which masks the popular frieze drawer, is not the commonplace cushion

35

molding seen on high chest no. 37. Its multiple contours and those on the cornice form a many-tiered crown whose outline suggests movement.

The exaggerated cyma curve of the cabriole legs also connotes movement. Rarely is the lower part of the leg so curved. The cabinetmaker succeeded in capturing the elongated S shape, the essence of the new Queen Anne style. But when he tackled attaching the knee brackets, he devised an unusual and perhaps unique method (see *Notes on Structure and Condition*).

The high central arch in the skirt bespeaks late William and Mary and early Queen Anne design. The skirt is somewhat akin to that of the early Queen Anne dressing table (no. 31). The drawer configuration of the bottom tier conforms in typical fashion to the skirt design. What is most unusual, however, is the presence of three drawers in the tier directly above, a rare pattern in New England that appears only on a few late William and Mary and early Queen Anne examples.[2] The massive waist molding harks back to William and Mary design, which featured waist moldings on both the upper and lower cases. The drawer construction follows techniques common on William and Mary cases.

This early Queen Anne high chest has no history, and the dearth of related objects makes pinpointing its origin difficult. However, the exaggeration of detail, the retention of William and Mary features, and especially the construction and woods mark it as an ambitious and early product, probably made in a coastal community north of Boston.

1. Samuel Greenwood's 1742 inventory, old series, vol. 36, p. 69, Suffolk County (Mass.) Probate.

2. Two examples are figures 70 and 100 in Lockwood, *Colonial Furniture,* rev. ed., vol. 1.

NOTES ON STRUCTURE AND CONDITION: The construction of the upper case is unusual. Mitered dovetails tie the sides to the top. The case has two full walnut-on-pine dust boards, one beneath the frieze drawer and one beneath the upper tier of three drawers. The dust boards are not only set in grooves in the case sides but are additionally secured by wooden pins, which pass through the case sides into the dust boards. The shallow drawer dividers of pine faced with walnut are similarly secured with wooden pins. The entablature, four pieces of molding, is unusually heavy and complex. The top of the two-board-thick cornice is flush with the top of the case.

The top of the lower section is four boards running front to back and nailed into the frame. The upper case does not rest on this top but on the wide slats that form the lower waist molding. The vertical partitions between the drawers of the lower case fit into 45-degree-angle notches in the skirt, a neat and unusual feature. The drawers in the lower case rest on medial supports tenoned into the back-

board and nailed into notches in the front. A narrow bead is nailed to the underside of the skirt at the front and sides. Drops originally flanked the central arch of the skirt.

The knee brackets are attached in an unusual manner; each is shaped like an L to fit behind as well as under the skirt and is glued. The legs are made of stock two boards thick, and the piecing is visible on the knees and feet.

The drawer dovetails are of good quality. Each drawer bottom is nailed into the rabbeted edge of the front and the flush edges of the sides, a manner common in New England drawer construction of the early eighteenth century. Each drawer front is thumbnail-molded and lipped on all four edges.

The chest has suffered from hard use and poor repairs. The waist molding is pieced, and the thumbnail edges on the drawer fronts have been worn, chipped, and patched in numerous places. The drawer front of the bottom drawer in the upper section has a replaced lower edge. The drawer dividers in the upper case were removed and poorly reinstalled. All but two of the knee brackets have been replaced. The beaded molding below the frieze drawer is replaced, as are the tips of the feet.

MATERIALS: *Black walnut; white pine* secondary

wood. Replaced brass hardware; the original hardware also had cotter-pin fasteners; all locks are missing.

PROVENANCE: The high chest has no known history before the middle of the twentieth century, when it

entered the collection of Florence Evans Bushee of Newbury.

ACCESSION: 1976.189   A gift of the estate of Florence Evans Bushee

36 / High Chest

1733–1745
Boston
Decoration attributed to Robert Davis or Stephen Whiting
H. 84⅞ (215.6), excluding finial 82⅛ (208.6); W. 42½ (108); D. 23¼ (59.1)

Whereas the structural elements on the preceding high chest are ebullient and eccentric, on this urban chest they are restrained and standard. The legs appear sturdy and static; the outline of the skirt is subdued; the lower center shell drawer quietly echoes the highly arched skirt of high chest no. 35, and the moldings have standard, simple contours. This case, made at about the same time and in the same style as the preceding high chest, is spectacular in an entirely different way.

"Jappanning a Piddement Chest & Table Tortoiseshell & Gold" presented flamboyant surfaces that generate excitement even today, when the vibrant color has darkened and dulled (plates 3 and 4).[1] Japanning imitates oriental lacquerwork; "Chinese" figures and buildings are dwarfed by exotic plants and fantastic beasts, all in raised gold arrayed across a painted ground, in this case of vermilion and black (see *Notes on Japanning*).

In 1723, Giles Dyer of Boston had in a fashionable chamber "A Chest of Drawers, one Table, one Dressing Glass, one Looking D°, one pr Bellows, all Jappaned."[2] Dyer's japanned ware may have been either imported or made in Boston.

In the first half of the eighteenth century, japanned objects were imported from England in great number. In addition, a dozen Boston japanners were busily putting occidental furniture forms in oriental attire.[3] The most prolific seem to have been Robert Davis, Thomas Johnston, and William Randle, three craftsmen born and trained in England.[4]

Surviving Boston japanned furniture includes a dressing glass, five clock cases, three dressing tables, seven William and Mary high chests, and seventeen Queen Anne high chests (nine with pedimented tops).[5] The Society's chest is one of the best documented and preserved.

It was originally owned by Josiah Quincy (1710–1784), a wealthy merchant of Boston and Braintree, and, to judge by its construction, probably was acquired shortly after his marriage in 1733. Quincy's estate inventory listed "1 Japan Chest Draws 36/ 1 Table D° 12/."[6] According to his great-granddaughter Eliza Susan Quincy, the chest was first

36.

in Quincy's home on Marlborough Street in Boston.[7] Quincy, who lived in a series of houses, moved the chest in 1770 to an elegant two-story house in Braintree, which is now the Society's Quincy House.

The good condition of the chest is surprising because it was moved often (see *Provenance*) and twice was removed from burning houses. The finial is a nineteenth-century replacement, and the flanking finials and plinths and the drops have been lost, but the japanning is well preserved. The decoration on the sides, darkened by the discoloration of the varnish, is nevertheless intact. The case front has lost some decoration but survives in better condition than most japanned pieces. To consolidate the flaking surface, the japanned finish was restored in 1978 by John Hill (36a and 36b, before and after views of an extensively damaged area).[8]

The designs on the Quincy chest invite comparison with three other pedimented chests: a privately owned high chest, one at Colonial Williamsburg, and one at the Winterthur Museum, signed by the Boston cabinetmaker John Pimm. The four chests all have a parade of similar figures such as the doglike creature (here, on the top right drawer) and the paired birds (the top long drawer), and they share a similar spacing of disconnected motifs, a distinctive diaper design (surrounding the shells), a triangular cluster of three leaves (lower left drawer), and apparently the same brasses. The shells on the Society's chest and on the privately owned case are very similar, somewhat like those on the Colonial Williamsburg example, but distinctly different from the carved shells on the Pimm.[9]

The japanned designs on these four pedimented chests are closely related to those on three with flat tops: one at the Baltimore Museum of Art, another at the Shelburne Museum, and one sold at auction.[10]

The high chest at the Baltimore Museum of Art has the signature of the japanner Robert Davis (d. 1739) and bears the initials "WR."[11] (Davis's father-in-law was the japanner William Randle, but to judge from a William and Mary high chest that Randle signed, his style differed from that of his son-in-law.)[12] Stephen Whiting was Davis's apprentice and probably adopted his decorative style.[13] The seven distinctively japanned high chests are the work either of Davis or, if made after 1739, of Whiting.

1. The quotation is from the accounts of Nathaniel Holmes, a Boston cabinetmaker. William Randle charged Holmes for the work finished on August 21, 1733, and billed on February 11, 1734; bills 1728–59, vol. 8, Bourn Papers, Baker Library, Harvard University.

2. Giles Dyer's inventory, new series, vol. 11, p. 346, Suffolk County (Mass.) Probate.

3. Boston's japanners in the eighteenth century were Robert Davis, John Gore, Abigail Hiller, Robert Hughes, Thomas Johnston, David Mason, Nehemiah Partridge, Roger Pendleton, William Randle, Joshua Roberts, John Waghorne, and Stephen Whiting.

4. Additional information on Davis can be found in Rhoades and Jobe, "Recent Discoveries"; on Randle, see Randall, "William Randall"; and on Johnston, see Hitchings, "Thomas Johnston." For general works on japanning, see Fales, "Boston Japanned Furniture" and *American Painted Furniture*, 58–69; Downs, "American Japanned Furniture"; Brazer, "Early Boston Japanners"; Ran-

36a

36b

dall, *American Furniture*, 66–68; and Hill, "History and Technique of Japanning."

5. The locations of the japanned furniture are listed in the Society's files.

6. Quincy's 1784 inventory, docket 18158, Suffolk County (Mass.) Probate.

7. Eliza Susan Quincy, "Memorandums relative to pictures, China & furniture," 1879, 31, photostat copy, unpublished manuscript (location of original unknown), Joseph Downs Manuscript Collection, Winterthur Museum.

8. A complete conservation report on the procedure followed by Hill is on file at the Society.

9. Another similar shell is on a legless pedimented high chest with the same brasses but with a more integrated design. It is owned by the Museum of Fine Arts, Boston.

10. Rhoades and Jobe, "Recent Discoveries," pl. 1 and fig. 2; Christie's, New York, May 5, 1979, lot 388.

11. Rhoades and Jobe, "Recent Discoveries," fig. 1 and 1083.

12. Randall, "William Randall," fig. 1; compare with Rhoades and Jobe, "Recent Discoveries," pl. 1.

13. Rhoades and Jobe, "Recent Discoveries," 1090, n. 11.

NOTES ON STRUCTURE AND CONDITION: The case displays many features of Boston construction of the 1730s, including: (1) two-part waist molding; (2) beaded channel molding surrounding the drawer openings; (3) ogee curves in the central arch in the skirt; (4) large crude dovetails for the drawers; (5) thin drawer sides; (6) drawer bottoms nailed into the rabbeted edge of the fronts and flush edges of the sides; and (7) engraved brasses similar to those on the pre-1739 Davis high chest.

The nailed upper case — the case bottom is rabbeted and nailed, not dovetailed, to the lower edges of the case sides — is unusual and may indicate early construction. The sides are held by the pediment and the thick uppermost backboard, which are nailed to the edges of the case sides. The uppermost backboard is grooved on its lower edge and slips over the chamfered edge of the board below. The three lower backboards of the upper case are thin and are set into grooves in the case sides, an unusual construction method.

The cornice is a two-piece molding. The waist moldings are made in a manner common to William and Mary high chests: the upper waist molding is attached to the upper case; pine slats faced with maple form the lower waist molding. Three front-to-back boards form the top of the joined lower case.

The cabrioles are thick, crudely shaped, and of red oak, an unusual wood for cabriole legs. The rear feet point toward the front. The top edges of the drawer sides are ½ inch below the top edge of the drawer front. Runners, beveled at the back, are applied to the bottom along the sides. The bottom drawer of the upper case rests directly on the case bottom. Most of the drawer backs are chipped, and in 1846 the interiors of the drawers were painted green over an old paper used to line the drawers.

NOTES ON JAPANNING: All decorated surfaces were covered with two layers of vermilion and then streaked with lampblack, creating a tortoiseshell effect. The design was laid out, and raised figures were created with gesso and coated with gold. Fine details were painted on the flat tortoiseshell surface with gold and on the raised gold with lampblack. Several layers of spirit varnish simulate lacquer.

Changes in humidity cause japan work to shrink, expand, crack, and flake. This chest, although in relatively good condition, has sustained losses. In

1978, John Hill conserved the chest according to the method he used on the Pimm high chest at Winterthur (Hill, "History and Technique of Japanning").

MATERIALS: *Red maple* cornice, waist moldings, beaded channel moldings, and drawer fronts except on the shell drawers; *red oak* legs; *white pine* shell-drawer fronts and secondary wood. Original brass hardware except for one plate and two bales. Steel locks, originally in all the long drawers and the upper tier in the lower case, survive only on the two uppermost long drawers.

PROVENANCE: The high chest descended in the family of Colonel Josiah Quincy. In 1784, the colonel's widow took it to Marlborough, Mass.; her daughter Mrs. Packard took it to Lancaster, Mass.; and it was purchased in 1846 from the latter's daughter, Ann Carter, by the colonel's great-granddaughter Eliza Susan (1798–1884) and her siblings to be returned to the Quincy homestead. Although the house did not stay in the family, the chest did and descended to Josiah Phillips Quincy (1829–1910), to Josiah Quincy (1859–1919), to his widow, and to the donor.

ACCESSION: 1972.51   A gift of Edmund Quincy; conservation funded in part by the Massachusetts Council on the Arts and Humanities

37 / High Chest

1745–1760
York, Maine
Attributed to Samuel Sewall
H. 74¼ (188.6); W. 40⁷⁄₁₆ (102.7); D. 21¾ (55.2)

The splendid play of walnut veneers makes this high chest (plate 6) another spectacular example of the form. The peculiarities of its construction made it the key to discovering the identity of the joiner who made Sayward's case furniture. And what a surprising discovery! It was as if John Roebling had designed and made furniture before designing and building the Brooklyn Bridge.

Veneer makes this high chest more striking than its plain companion, dressing table no. 33. Veneer was rarely used by rural craftsmen, yet for this piece, the craftsman cut wood of splendid figure. Similar veneers appear on high chests made by others, but seldom are veneers used as imaginatively as on the Society's chest, where the wood figure on the upper drawers flows from one tier to another.[1]

In a curious fashion the veneer modestly decorates only the drawer fronts, not the skirt or the front of the stiles on the lower case. Paint, which continued the veneer pattern on dressing table no. 31, was never applied to this case. One detail, however, adds to the striking appearance. On the skirt, a herringbone band of sumac is inlaid in the solid walnut.

This high chest is closely related to Judge Sayward's other furniture and additional case pieces from York.[2] Wooden pins affix moldings, drawer bottoms, and even drawer stops. Only the beading beneath the skirt is fastened with nails. The lower case is made just like the companion dressing table (no. 33). The cornice molding (37a) is backed

37

with the same unusual type of chamfered strips as that which holds the base moldings on Sayward's chest (detail 21a) and other cases in his house.

In one way this high chest differs from the other Sayward furniture: it has an entablature. The cornice, which extends above the top of the case in an unusual fashion, was the first clue in the search for the identity of the joiner. The uppermost piece of molding (A) is chamfered in back like an architectural cornice molding. The cornice moldings in Sayward's house were the next clue. Although most of them are from the early eighteenth century, those in Sayward's sitting room, the southeast parlor, had an added two-piece cove-and-bead molding. The two pieces proved identical in contour to the uppermost molding of the high chest cornice (A) and the bead architrave (D). The wall moldings and furniture moldings were evidently made with the same molding planes.

The last clue came from Sayward's diaries: Samuel Sewall did joinery work in Sayward's house in 1761 and 1767.[3] He apparently updated the southeast parlor, using the molding planes he had used in making the high chest. Sewall, the house joiner, surveyor, and — according to local history — architect, evidently was also a furniture maker.[4] In Sayward's diary, he eventually appears as a bridge engineer and bridge contractor:

> 20 June 1786
> Great Bridge built over Charles River to Boston was finished the 17th of this month. S[d] day was Cellebrated in an extraordinary manner, it is really a Great and Grand Bridge. Major Sam[ll] Sewall of this town and Capt John Stone of this town was the undertakers and Engineers.[5]

The furniture Sewall solidly constructed is what might be expected from a builder of wooden bridges. The veneered façade of this chest shows that the bridge engineer also had a good eye for decoration. The high chest is the high-water mark of Sewall's cabinetwork.

1. Similar veneers appear on one high chest illustrated in *Israel Sack Collection,* 1:101, and another owned by Mrs. Charles Hallam Keep of New York City and York Harbor, Me., illustrated as figure 554 in Girl Scouts Loan Exhibition.

2. Entry 21 lists the related pieces.
3. Sayward Diary, November 10, 1761, and August 7, 1767, American Antiquarian Society.
4. Banks, *History of York,* 2:108.
5. Sayward Diary, American Antiquarian Society.

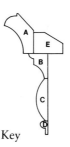

Key

37a

NOTES ON STRUCTURE AND CONDITION: The upper case is capped with an entablature (see the key to 37a): a two-piece cornice (A and B), a cushion frieze (C) that conceals a drawer, and a one-piece architrave (D). All the moldings except the upper section of the cornice are fastened to the case with wooden pins. The upper section (A) projects above the top of the case and is pinned to strips (E) pinned to the top. These strips are identical in design to the supports for the base molding on Sayward's chest of drawers (detail 21a) and on two desks in Sayward's house. This unusual feature as well as the drawer construction helps tie the cases to a single shop.

Applied walnut moldings surround the drawer openings. The top two drawers run on medial supports. The other drawers in the upper case run on drawer supports set into grooves in the sides and fastened with wooden pins. The lower case is constructed like the Sayward dressing table (no. 33), even having the same two-board skirt construction. The drawer construction throughout follows that in the dressing table.

The skirt was laid out with a compass, as evidenced by surviving pivot points. The upper case rests on a front waist rail and on two front-to-back slats. Originally, the bottom of the upper case had two pins that fitted into holes in the waist rail of the lower case and prevented the upper case from sliding. The case never had knee brackets. The rear feet point toward the front of the case.

The high chest survives in excellent condition, still preserving its original wax finish. The two uppermost drawers originally locked with wooden spring latches mounted to the underside of the drawer bottoms; both latches are missing.

MATERIALS: Black walnut veneer on the drawer fronts; *black walnut* case sides, skirt, front legs, applied moldings, and entablature; *birch* rear legs; *sumac* skirt bead and skirt inlay; *elm* drawer dividers, drawer sides, backs, and some fronts and bottoms; *white pine* upper case top and bottom, case back, drawer partitions, supports, stops, most drawer fronts, and some drawer bottoms.

Original brass hardware; steel locks originally present in all the drawers of the upper section except the two narrow drawers; all but one remain; the lower section never had locks.

PROVENANCE: Always in Jonathan Sayward's house, the high chest — called an "11 draw chest" in the 1884 inventory of Mary Barrell's estate — shares a provenance with tea chest no. 4.

ACCESSION: 1977.326   A gift of the heirs of Elizabeth Cheever Wheeler

38 / High Chest

1755–1775
Concord, Massachusetts
Attributed to Joseph Hosmer
H. 67⅞ (172.4); W. 42⅜ (107.6); D. 21¼ (54)

This sturdy high chest made by a Concord house joiner is not as handsome as the York bridge builder's product (no. 37). The Concord chest manifests in every aspect of its design the solidity expected from a house joiner. Unlike the prevailing rococo fashion for movement and delicacy, it features sober, modest, even rigid characteristics: (1) square feet; (2) stiff legs with squarish knees; (3) a skirt, which is boxy in spite of repeated ogee arches; (4) an angular fanlike shell; (5) a chamfer instead of a thumbnail curve around the drawer fronts; and (6) a cushion molding as both the capital and base of each pilaster.

The peculiarities of design are matched by peculiarities of construction. Especially odd are stiles in the corners of the upper case (38a) and nails passing through the drawer sides to secure the bottoms (see *Notes on Structure and Condition*). Also unusual are the chisel-numbered drawers and the unplaned mill-sawn boards used as case backs.

Although the accomplished joiner who made this high chest and its pedimented relation (38b) worked only twenty miles inland from Boston, he developed his own peculiar construction solutions, quite distinct from those practiced in the urban center.[1]

The Concord joiner, to judge by surviving examples, had a substantial, albeit local, furniture trade. The pedimented high chest (38b) at the Concord Antiquarian Society belonged to Ebenezer Stow of Concord, who married in 1775. A chest-on-chest in the same collection and clearly by the same hand belonged to Hugh Cargill, who immigrated to Concord in 1774 and died there in 1799. A related blockfront high chest now at the Winterthur Museum was reportedly made for Phoebe Bliss of Concord in 1769, when she married William Emerson, the town minister.[2] A privately owned high chest with similarities to the Bliss and Stow cases descended in the Wheeler family of Concord.[3]

The Bliss chest was attributed many years ago to a Concord joiner, Joseph Hosmer (1736–1812). Based upon that attribution, the other cases have been called "Hosmer."[4] An oxbow desk and an oxbow chest of drawers that descended in Hosmer's family have also been attributed to him.[5] However, the cabinetry of the Hosmer family oxbows is typical of eastern Massachusetts, far different from the idiosyncratic Concord cases, and not by the man who constructed this chest and the related furniture.

In 1982, a chest-on-chest from the Tarbell family of Acton, adjacent to Concord, was brought to the authors' attention. It is inscribed "Made by Joseph Hosmer / Concord Mass / 1782." We have not been able to see the chest, and it is impossible to determine from the owner's photographs if it is made like the idiosyncratic Concord cases. The Tarbell chest has a scroll pediment, but it has neither the applied keystone nor the brass plate seen on the Stow chest (38b). It has no flanking pilasters; the bracket feet are not similar to those on the Cargill chest-on-chest. Most notably, its drawer fronts are thumbnail-molded, not chamfered.

Yet the static carving of the shell drawer is somewhat akin to that on the Stow high chest. The backboards are reputed to be very rough (mill-sawn?) and at least one drawer is chisel-numbered.[6] And the photograph of the inscription revealed that the Tarbell chest-on-chest shares an odd similarity with the Cargill case; both have very similar compass-made pinwheel doodling on the hidden top boards of their lower cases.

There now seems a good possibility that this flat-top high chest and its pedimented relations were made by Joseph Hosmer, farmer, joiner, furniture maker, eloquent speaker for the patriot cause, and participant in the events at the old North Bridge.

---

1. Kaye, "Concord Case Furniture."

2. Downs, *Queen Anne and Chippendale*, no. 189.

3. Figure 7 in Scott and Kettell, "Joseph Hosmer," 359.

4. Ibid., 358, 359.

5. Ibid.

6. Telephone interview with the owner in May 1982.

NOTES ON STRUCTURE AND CONDITION: Four stiles in the upper case, braces at the top of the lower case, and tenoned knee brackets are some of the

38a

38b. High Chest. Concord, Massachusetts, 1760–
1780. Maple, white pine, and yellow pine; H. 84¼
(214.0); W. 40 (101.6); D. 18⅛ (46.0). Concord
Antiquarian Museum. Photograph, J. David Bohl.

features that illustrate the general overbuilding of
the chest.

The dovetails joining the upper case are reinforced with rose-headed nails. The two horizontal
backboards of the upper case have wide chamfered
edges and pronounced vertical mill-sawn marks on
their back surfaces. The rear stiles are tenoned into
the bottom of the upper case and are held by nails
that pass through the top. The front stiles are tenoned into the waist and cornice rails, which are
tenoned into the case sides. A 1-inch gap separates
the front stiles from the case sides and is covered
with pilasters with off-center fluting. Each drawer
divider, notched to fit around the front stiles, fits

into slots in the case sides. The cove cornice is
nailed to the front and sides of the case. The
thumbnail cap for the cornice is nailed down into
the cornice molding and the upper edge of the case
sides.

The joined lower case has a medial and two
diagonal braces tenoned into the front waist rail
and fastened into notches in the back. The drawers

in the lower tier slide on medial supports tenoned into the front skirt and set into notches in a rail nailed to the back. No part of the feet is turned; the bottom edges of the feet are chamfered. Each knee bracket is tenoned into the leg and nailed to the skirt, an eccentric joining.

The drawer dovetails are thick and coarse. The bottom of each drawer is nailed into the rabbeted edge of the front and the flush edge of the back. The drawer sides overlap the bottom and are nailed into its side edges, a very unusual technique. The drawers are numbered with chisel marks: I, II, III, and 4 (the last in Arabic; see also the Middlesex chest of drawers, no. 12). Each wide drawer runs on its bottom and the lower edge of its sides. The edges of each drawer front are cut with a chamfer, instead of the more common thumbnail bead, and are lipped on all four sides.

The chest has had little damage and few repairs. One drop and both plates are replacements. The top right corner and lower edge of the shell drawer front are pieced. The chest was refinished early in this century.

MATERIALS: *Cherry; hard maple* legs; *red oak* rear stiles and back of the upper case; *white pine* back of the lower case, drawer supports and top and bottom of the upper case; *yellow pine* (probably pitch pine) medial drawer supports and drawer guides in the lower case. Replaced brass hardware; never had locks.

PROVENANCE: The high chest came to the Society with a house in Weston (which abuts Concord), whose collection was assembled locally in the late nineteenth and early twentieth centuries.

ACCESSION: 1973.328   Bequest of Ellen M. and Alice E. Jones; conserved through the generosity of Anne Farnam

39 / High Chest

1755–1780
Newbury, Massachusetts, area
H. 73³⁄₁₆ (185.9); W. 38⁵⁄₈ (98.1); D. 20½ (52.1)

This plain high chest is far more typical of New England cabinetry than the preceding examples. It uses the standard design vocabulary of New England Queen Anne and Chippendale high chests: (1) the five-tier upper case; (2) the four-drawer lower case; (3) the flat-headed arched skirt; and (4) one carved shell drawer (standard in flat-topped chests; pedimented chests often have a second shell in the upper case). The construction of this chest evinces better than average workmanship and epitomizes the unpretentious work of a skilled craftsman.

The cabinetmaker worked in or near Newbury. This chest apparently came from a family in neighboring Byfield and was in Newburyport in the second half of the nineteenth century.[1] An almost identical chest, owned by the Historical Society of Old Newbury, is reported to be from Newbury.[2] It shares with the Society's chest several distinctive features: the same intricate top edge on the drawer sides, a full dust board between the second and third drawers from the top, and two-board-thick sides in the lower case (see *Notes on Structure and Condition*). Such similarities indicate the work of one man.

The legs and feet of the two chests closely resemble those on a flat-top high chest made and inscribed by Joshua Morss and Moses Bayley in Newbury in 1748 and 1749.[3]

39

The Morss-Bayley chest, however, features the older skirt style (with a high arch in the center) and earlier brasses. The conformation of the legs and feet is indicative more of the area than of a particular shop. In and near Newbury in the late eighteenth century, cabinetmakers were making fine furniture, equal in the quality of its construction to that produced in Salem and generally better than that from the Boston area. This chest is a good example of their work.

1. "Newburyport five cent savings Bank" (a bank founded in 1854) is written in nineteenth-century script on a paper label on the case back.

2. The authors are indebted to Susan Mackiewicz for bringing the Old Newbury high chest to their attention.

3. The Morss-Bayley high chest is in *Israel Sack Collection*, 6:1590–91.

NOTES ON STRUCTURE AND CONDITION: The full dust board is pine faced with maple; the shallow dividers are solid maple. The lower case has no top. The upper case rests on the waist rail and on the sides of the lower case, which, unlike those in most such pieces, are two boards thick: the outer board is of maple, the inner of pine. The one-piece waist molding is nailed to the lower case. The shallow drawer partitions are backed by drawer supports tenoned into the backboard. All of the dovetail joints are precisely cut. The drawer bottoms fit into grooves in the front and sides. The thumbnail-molded drawer fronts are lipped on the sides and top.

The chest has had a few repairs. A thin strip was added to the rear edge of the right side. Two knee brackets and the drops and plates beneath the skirt are replacements. The chest was stripped before it was given to the Society; it was refinished in 1977 to match traces of its original reddish-brown stain.

MATERIALS: *Soft maple;* white pine secondary wood. Replaced brass hardware; three original locks and one modern replacement; the top two drawers and the bottom tier of three small drawers never had locks.

PROVENANCE: The chest is reported to have been purchased from a Byfield family by Florence Evans Bushee.

ACCESSION: 1976.256   A gift of the estate of Florence Evans Bushee

40 / High Chest

1760–1780
Boston area
H. 82¹⁵⁄₁₆ (210.7); W. 40¹⁵⁄₁₆ (104); D. 22³⁄₁₆ (56.4)

A mahogany high chest could be ordered with a flat or pedimented top and with turned-pad or claw-and-ball feet. In 1757 a customer in Providence paid dearly for the dressier top and carved feet, the "Crown and Claws":

> Mehgny high Case of Drawers @ £100.
> Do with Crown and Claws @ £150.[1]

The "Crown" for this claw-footed high chest originally included three finials but never a full bonnet. The pediment is only a façade. Most "Crowns" have bonnets behind the

40

pediments; this sham is backed by braces resembling the rear bracket feet of Boston chests and desks (compare 40a with the rear feet in detail 15b).

This chest is typical of furniture made after 1760 in the Boston area and therefore offers an interesting contrast to high chest no. 36, a japanned example of early Queen Anne work. In construction, the drawer sides of this mahogany chest are rabbeted to receive the drawer bottoms; on the earlier piece they remain flush. The lower case here has no top; the japanned one has.

Differences in design are numerous. Knees with sharp corners replaced the rounded knees of the earlier fashion. Stylish claw-and-ball feet, often with raked side claws like those on this chest, gained in popularity, although inexpensive turned feet remained a commonly used option. These subtle changes lessened the rounded quality dominant in early Queen Anne furniture.

The japanned chest features a broad waist molding attached to both the upper and lower cases; this chest has the slender single waist molding of later fashion. Here a single bead flanks the drawer openings in contrast to the beaded channel on the japanned case. The earlier case has an ornate shell and distinctive center arch; the later case features a stylized fanlike shell and a simplified skirt outline (the drops are missing). Large rococo brasses, fashionable by 1760, superseded the smaller engraved brasses that served the japanned piece.

1. "Table of Prices for Joiners' Work," quoted in Lyon, *Colonial Furniture,* 3rd ed., 266.

NOTES ON STRUCTURE AND CONDITION: The pediment molding is one piece. Mahogany on white pine drawer dividers are dovetailed into the upper case sides; the joints are covered by mahogany strips. The dovetails binding the drawer dividers to the stiles are left exposed on the joined lower case. The upper case rests on the waist rail and on rails glued and nailed to the sides of the lower case. The shallow drawer partitions in both the upper and lower cases are backed by drawer supports tenoned into the backboard.

The drawers have somewhat thick but precise dovetails and a double-bead cut on the top edge of the sides. The drawer bottoms are nailed into the rabbeted edges of the fronts and sides, and full-length runners are glued to the bottoms along the sides and cut at the back at a 45-degree angle.

The piece was refinished in this century. Both rear legs have split and have been reglued. Shrinkage cracks have appeared in the case sides.

MATERIALS: *Mahogany; white pine* secondary wood. Six handles and one escutcheon were reproduced to match the remaining originals; the long drawers of the upper case have original steel locks; the other drawers never had locks.

PROVENANCE: The high chest shares a provenance with chest of drawers no. 22.

ACCESSION: 1963.349   A gift of Mrs. Huntly H. Gilbert

40a

41 / High Chest

1765–1785
Lower Housatonic River valley, Connecticut
H. 87⅝ (222.6), excluding finial, 84½ (214.6); W. 43⅞ (111.4); D. 22⅝ (57.5)

The massive, architectural upper case of this high chest contrasts with the lighter case of its counterpart from the Boston area (no. 40). The high chests remind one of front doorways; this chest resembles those in the Connecticut and Housatonic River valleys (41a), while the preceding chest recalls the more delicate doorways of coastal Massachusetts (41b).

The people within a given area — as small as a town or as large as a river valley — enjoyed their own distinctive design, and they expected certain motifs and proportions in their furniture and architecture. Occasionally a house joiner and a furniture maker were one man, but the unity of design within a region resulted more from customer taste than from craftsman talent.

The decorative details on this chest — pediment rosettes of this design, squat ovoid "flame" finials, rosette capitals, snakeskin notched knees (41c), and a deep, central shell carving — are variations seen in the lower Housatonic River valley. Housatonic Valley cases with more than one shell usually have shells of more than one design. This piece might too if the top shell drawer had been carved by the maker. It was not; the top central drawer was originally ornamented only by a small rococo brass. (Small rococo brasses were original to all the drawers.) The case was embellished with a second shell early in this century.

Whether with one shell drawer or two, this high chest presents a handsome and imposing design in richly dark, dense mahogany. An almost identical high chest stands on claw-and-ball feet.[1] The two majestic chests were skillfully made by the same hand. Another high chest with similar finials and fan carving seems to suggest a craftsman and town; it has a Stratford history and is believed to have been made by Eli Lewis for his niece Helen Lewis when she married Thaddeus Birdsey in 1784.[2] The splendid mahogany of the Society's chest would bespeak a coastal (Stratford) origin, but the presence of eight different woods and the unusual construction (see *Notes on Structure and Condition*) suggest otherwise. We cannot attribute this high chest to Lewis or to any particular craftsman, although there has been no lack of attribution in the past.

One was to Elijah Booth. This chest was owned in Woodbury, purchased by Samuel Griswold at about the turn of this century for $65 from a Mr. Swan, an undertaker accustomed to picking up estate antiques in exchange for his services.[3] Swan received the chest from the estate of Stiles Russell of Woodbury, whose brother had inscribed "John Russell / Woodbury Ct." on the backboard.[4] Southbury, part of Woodbury until 1787, was the home of the cabinetmaker Elijah Booth; in 1957, Ethel Hall Bjerkoe attributed the Society's chest to him.[5]

Much furniture from the Stratford-Newtown-Southbury-Woodbury area has been routinely attributed to Elijah Booth, although all are clearly not by the same man. Elijah (1745–1823) survived his brother Ebenezer (1743–1789) and Ebenezer's son Joel (1769–1794), both Newtown cabinetmakers.[6] Elijah's longevity may have garnered for him the credit of making all the furniture produced by the Booth family or by an even larger group of local craftsmen.[7] The trade of Booth's father, Ebenezer (1718–1803), of Newtown, is unknown, but whoever trained the brothers must have used the motifs that eventually were attributed to Elijah.

A high chest (41d) in the collections of the Connecticut Historical Society added a second problem of attribution. It was made for Hannah Grant of Newtown, who took the new chest from the Housatonic Valley up the Connecticut River when she married Stephen Mix Mitchell of Wethersfield in 1769.[8] Through a compounding of errors, both it and the Russell family chest were erroneously linked and attributed.[9]

Both were thought to be by the same hand, but they are not. High chest no. 41 was assumed to be signed by Brewster Dayton of Stratford; it is not. On that doubly faulty basis, Hannah Grant Mitchell's piece was attributed to Dayton. A high chest that Dayton

41a. Doorway of the Elijah Williams House. Deerfield, Massachusetts, ca. 1760. Photograph, Philip Zea.

41b. Doorway of the Chipman-Conant House. Beverly, Massachusetts; house built ca. 1715, doorway added 1750–1770. Photograph, Essex Institute.

actually signed has a different design.[10] Neither the Society's chest nor Hannah Grant Mitchell's can be attributed to Dayton.

Hannah's high chest illustrates even more Housatonic Valley features: pediment pinwheels instead of pediment rosettes, a vine design (bordering the snakeskin carving on the knees), a basketwork carving (flanking the pediment drawer), and scrollwork pilasters, each pierced and backed by a reversible slat — painted green on one side, finished wood on the other. Hannah could change the color of the scrollwork to suit her fancy or decor.

An almost endless vocabulary of decorative motifs was used in central and western Connecticut. This plethora of carvings contrasts sharply with the select and routinely repeated motifs current in Boston or Newport. Whatever else may have been dull about living in western Connecticut, looking at its furniture (or doorways) was not.

1. The privately owned high chest was called to the authors' attention by Edward S. Cooke.

2. The information on the Eli Lewis case is from Cooke, "Furniture in Stratford," 46, fig. 25. A high chest with identical finials, a large rosette on the carved drawer of the upper case, canted corners, and Spanish-footed cabrioles was lot 1075, Sotheby Parke Bernet, sale 4180, November 1978.

3. Bjerkoe, "The Booth Family."

4. "Stiles" has a long history as a given name in Mr. Russell's mother's family (the Curtises). There is no evidence that Stiles Russell was related to the Stiles family of neighboring Southbury, as was claimed by Bjerkoe, ibid., 10.

5. Ibid.

6. Ibid., 8–11; see also Cooke, *Fiddlebacks and Crooked-backs*, 27–33, 99–105.

7. Other craftsmen in the area are discussed in Cooke, *Fiddlebacks and Crooked-backs*, 86–97 and especially 31.

8. Kirk, *Connecticut Furniture*, no. 90.

9. "Connecticut Cabinetmakers, Part 1," 119.

10. Winterthur Museum (68.772); an almost identical one was advertised in *Antiques* 98 (July 1970): 27.

41C

NOTES ON STRUCTURE AND CONDITION: The chest is overbuilt. The most obvious example is a 1-by-1½-inch horizontal brace that originally tied the sides of the upper case together. To accommodate the brace, which was set into notches in the back edges of the case sides, the back of the uppermost case-wide drawer has a stepped rear surface. A full dust board is used above this drawer; dust boards also separate the small drawers flanking the shell. The dividers for the long drawers in the upper case are birch boards (about 5 inches deep) faced with mahogany strips (⅛ inch deep). The bottom drawer in the upper case slides on a narrow waist rail and drawer supports. The pediment molding is one piece. Each pilaster is glued to a thick pine stile backed with glue blocks. The waist molding has two parts: one applied to the upper case, the other to the lower. The upper case rests on the rabbeted back edge of the lower waist molding and on an oak slat nailed to the top edge of the backboard in

41d. High Chest. Newtown, Connecticut, area, ca. 1769. Cherry, pine, bass, and oak; H. 84½ (214.6); W. 42½ (108.0); D. 20½ (52.1). Connecticut Historical Society.

the lower case. The drawer partitions in both cases are shallow and backed by drawer supports that are tenoned into the backboard. The elements of the drawers are thick; the dovetails are closely spaced. The drawer bottoms fit into grooves in the fronts and sides and pinned to the backs. The thumbnail-molded edge of the drawer fronts is lipped at the top and sides.

The chest is in good condition. The horizontal brace for the upper case has been missing for many years. Splits in the left rear leg were repaired with wooden pins. The drawer supports in the lower case and the right waist molding on the upper case are replaced.

MATERIALS: *Mahogany; red oak* two lowest backboards of the upper case; *hard maple* lower case backboard; *soft maple* uppermost backboard; *birch* drawer dividers and waist rail of the lower case; *white cedar* drawer bottoms, *tulipwood* waist rail of the upper case and glue block behind the center plinth; *white pine* other secondary wood. Replaced brass hardware. The long drawers of the upper case are missing locks; the other drawers never had locks.

PROVENANCE: The early history of the chest is unknown. It descended from John Russell (b. ca. 1845) of Woodbury to his brother Stiles, from whose estate it was acquired by Mr. Swan of Woodbury. It was sold at about the turn of this century to Samuel Griswold, the husband of the donor.

ACCESSION: 1952.166   A bequest of Ruth Lee Griswold

42 / High Chest

1780–1800
Southern New Hampshire
Attributed to the Dunlap school
H. 77⅜ (196.5); W. 40⁵/₁₆ (102.4); D. 19⁹/₁₆ (49.7)

This high chest has much in common with the preceding one although it is very different in appearance. Both represent fine craftsmanship and rural regional motifs. Both are easily attributed to a locale. This one can be ascribed, even more specifically, to a school of rural cabinetmakers — the Dunlap school (see page 67 and II-19).

Chest-on-frame no. 25, also the Dunlaps' work, relates to this chest in several aspects. Most obvious is the similar central skirt. The simple cove waist moldings and the sharply creased knees are also similar. Both cases have complex cornices and unusual disks beneath flat-top feet.

The Dunlaps produced many case pieces similar to this chest — upper cases of five or more tiers of drawers on lower cases of three, or in one case four, tiers.[1] Each tier is not necessarily a drawer. This chest has a two-drawer lower case: a shallow top drawer above a very deep drawer that simulates two drawers. What appears to be three small drawers in the upper case is actually one wide drawer. The Dunlaps exhibited a penchant for masking large drawers with drawer fronts simulating more than one.

The carved fan here, called a spoonhandle shell in *The Dunlaps & Their Furniture*, is said to be characteristic of Dunlap work. Two look-alikes of this chest have shells of nine and eleven rays; the Society's has thirteen.[2] An eleven-ray spoonhandle shell is on the chest-on-chest-on-frame signed "John Dunlap / 1784."[3]

Here, the shell varies from the typical spoonhandle shell (compare with II-19). This carving looks like one shell superimposed upon another, while on other shells the flat portions between the rays continue into the center. This variant is unique in published photographs of Dunlap pieces.[4]

The Society's maple chest left the shop with a coat of mahogany stain and oval brasses typical of the 1780–1800 era. The Dunlaps used maple and sometimes birch or cherry in lieu of mahogany. Major John Dunlap had a recipe "To stain wood to Resemble Mehogany":

> Take 2 pounds Logwood Chipd fine put it in a Clean Brass kettle add 1 Gallon of water Boil this 4 hours then take out your chips — evaporate to 1 quart — strain and Brush your maple 3 times over let it dry between each brushing — Then take 1 oz. of Curkmy root — 1 oz of Dragons Blood — 1 oz of logwood all made fine put it in a quart Bottle add to this 1 pint of Spirits of wine let it steep 24 hours — turn it of Clear — brush it once over after the Logwood is brushed — and so Done.[5]

We cannot attribute the Society's high chest to either John or his younger brother Samuel, who worked for him from 1773 to 1779. It possibly was made by Joel Joslyn (b. 1776), Samuel's apprentice between 1793 and 1797.[6] A high chest signed by Joslyn in the collections of the New Hampshire Historical Society resembles this chest in more than appearance. The drawer bottoms of both are rabbeted (instead of chamfered or feather-edged [page 170]) to enable them to fit into grooves in the drawer fronts and sides.[7]

The many southern New Hampshire case pieces in the Dunlap style are clearly the work of several men. Whether this chest is by Joslyn or some other craftsman, it is an interesting addition to the existing literature on the fine cabinetwork produced by the Dunlaps and their apprentices in the last decades of the eighteenth century in southern New Hampshire, a region growing rapidly in a new economic climate but remaining tied to the old colonial fashions.

1. *Dunlaps* illustrates twenty-four high chests with a five- (or more) tier upper case on a three- or four-tier joined base: figures 3, 4, 5, 7, 8, 10, 11, 12, 13, 14, 15, 21, 22, 25, 26, 29, 30, 31, 33, 34, 35, 36, 37, and 38.

2. Figures 36 and 37, ibid., most resemble the Society's piece. The latter chest was made by Joel Joslyn and is now in the collections of the New Hampshire Historical Society.

3. Ibid., fig. 44.

4. A privately owned high chest, known only from a photograph, has a shell almost identical to that on chest no. 42. The piece differs only at the uppermost drawer, which does not simulate three drawers.

5. *Dunlaps,* 57.

6. Donna-Belle Garvin, "Two High Chests."

7. Ibid., 183. In a letter to the authors, March 23, 1981, Charles S. Parsons cites nine high chests with the rabbeted drawer bottoms as well as the three low chests of drawers referred to by Garvin.

NOTES ON STRUCTURE AND CONDITION: The dovetails binding the upper case are closely spaced. The shouldered dovetails of the shallow (2¾ inches) maple drawer dividers and cornice rail pass through the case sides and are left exposed. The top of the one-piece cornice is flush with the case top; the one-piece waist molding is attached to the top edge of the lower case. The upper case rests on the front rail of the joined lower case, on the rear stiles, and on the back. The thumbnail-molded edge on the drawer fronts is lipped at the sides and front. Wooden pins, not nails, fasten the bottoms to the backs. The drawers run on both the bottoms and the lower edges of the sides. The bottom drawer of the upper case rests on supports and a waist rail.

The chest was restained mahogany in this century and has had several minor repairs. The right foot is patched; splines fill shrinkage cracks in the sides of the lower case, and the lipped edges of several drawer fronts have been patched.

MATERIALS: *Soft maple; white pine* secondary wood. Brass hardware replaced; never had locks.

PROVENANCE: The high chest came to the Society with the contents of the Barrett House of New Ipswich, N.H., and may have belonged to Charles Barrett, Sr. If it was the "High Case of Drawers" in Barrett's 1808 estate inventory, it descended as did chest of drawers no. 19.

ACCESSION: 1948.147   A gift of Caroline Barr Wade

43 / Desk-on-Frame

1735–1760
Newbury, Massachusetts, area
H. 40¾ (103.5); W. 33⅝ (85.4); D. 20 (50.8)

In the seventeenth century, boxes with slanted lids served as desks. To elevate them to a usable height, the boxes were either placed upon other furniture or made with a separate frame.[1] The frames had sturdy turned and stretchered legs, which evolved in the early eighteenth century to slender turned supports and, with the advent of the Queen Anne style, to legs of cabriole design. Few cabriole examples were made in New England. Most desks of this era were the familiar one-piece type sometimes called "bureau desk" (desk no. 45).[2]

A desk like this one was probably called a "desk on a frame" or a "writing desk and frame."[3] Of the few examples of the form, two are closely related to the Society's.[4] Their exteriors, including the drops and moldings, are identical in design except that in the center of the skirt, where this frame has a cut-out arch, the other two have carved shells

43

with pinwheel centers. Their interiors have the same pigeonhole partitions and general arrangement as the Society's desk (43a), although its interior is by far the most elaborate.

The three desks were made in the same shop, probably in Newbury or a nearby community. The feet have central ridges characteristic of turned pad feet made in Essex County, Massachusetts.[5] The drops on the Society's desk and the flat pinwheels on the two desks with carved skirts are sometimes seen on furniture from the Newbury area.[6]

The centrally arched skirt here and the shell-carved skirts of the related examples resemble those on high chests and dressing tables.[7] The sculptural character of a frame with cabrioles and a skirt lends itself to graceful decoration. The interior, decorated with a recessed arch, simple pilasters, and a busy valance, nevertheless speaks principally of function. When the lid is down, the writing surface, small drawers, and pigeonholes denote business. Many eighteenth-century businesses were conducted from the home, and desks served as offices. Inventories reveal that fine desks were kept in one of the principal rooms and, after beds, were usually the most valuable piece of furniture in the house.

Probably more than any other household furnishing, desks vary in form, size, shape, and quality, reflecting the diversity of their owners' businesses and wealth. Although the history of the Society's desk-on-frame is unknown, something of its past can be imagined from the desk itself. This is apparently a residential office. A desk-on-frame for a warehouse or shop would be of pine and closer in design to that of the standing desk (no. 44). The owner selected a modest desk; he did not buy a walnut or mahogany one or order the more costly shell-carved skirt. He picked a traditional form, the desk-on-frame, instead of the more sophisticated "bureau desk." Nevertheless, he graced his house with a handsome desk: the cabrioles are graceful; the pigeonhole arches neatly echo the skirt center; and the fine workmanship includes details such as a hidden drawer and mitered dovetails to make the joints on the top of the desk invisible.

43a

1. An example of a desk box kept upon other furniture is a "writing desk on Chest of Drawers"; James Orr's 1752 inventory, old series, vol. 46, p. 59, Suffolk County (Mass.) Probate.

2. David Craigie had "A bureau Desk"; 1721 inventory, old series, vol. 22, p. 166, Suffolk County (Mass.) Probate.

3. A desk "on a Frame" belonged to Samuel Wentworth of Boston (1736 inventory, old series, vol. 32, p. 479); and "1 writing desk & fram" belonged to William Taylor of Boston (1760 inventory, old series, vol. 56, p. 164), both in Suffolk County (Mass.) Probate.

4. One was collected by Dwight Blaney of Boston and is number 196 in Comstock, *American Furniture*. The other is the *best* in Sack, *Fine Points*, 142.

5. Fales, *Historic Deerfield*, fig. 429.

6. Similar drops appear on the Newbury high chest cited in entry 39, in the collection of the Historical Society of Old Newbury. Similar pinwheels appear on a Newburyport clock; Montgomery, *The Federal Period*, no. 168. Furniture from the Portsmouth area also displays related features; see, for example, the pinwheels on the Kittery, Me., clock (no. 55).

7. A related high chest, acquired in the twentieth century in York, Me., was apparently made by the craftsman who built the desks; Andrew M. Williams Collection, Parke-Bernet, sale 955, April 1948, lot 343.

NOTES ON STRUCTURE AND CONDITION: The two-board back of the upper case fits into grooves in the top and sides and is nailed at the bottom. The desk board, set into grooves in the case sides, is held at the front corners with shouldered dovetails that pass through the sides. A secret drawer is behind the wide center drawer. Turned pilasters are applied to the fronts of the document drawers. The lid supports, of solid maple, are chamfered on their front edges.

The lower case is joined. The waist molding is glued and nailed to the top of the lower case. The upper case rests on the waist rail and on the stiles of the lower case. The exterior drawer partitions are tenoned into the waist rail, rabbeted to rest on the top edge of the front skirt, and glued to the back of the front skirt.

All the drawers have thick dovetails. The top edges of the drawer sides are chamfered. The thumbnail-molded edge on the drawer fronts overlaps the case on the sides and top. The bottom of each exterior drawer is set into grooves in the drawer front and sides and is held to the back with wooden pins. The drawer supports in the lower case rest in slanted notches in the front skirt, are rabbeted to fit behind the partitions or the front stiles, and are tenoned into the back of the case. The plates and drops are original.

The desk survives in good condition with most original elements. The major repair has been to the finish. The desk, once painted bright yellow, was stripped before it entered the Society's collection and has been restained, matching traces of its original reddish-brown stain. The original brasses were secured with cotter pins.

MATERIALS: *Hard* and *soft maple; butternut* interior drawer fronts, dividers, partitions, pigeonhole arches, and some drawer sides; white pine other secondary wood. Brass hardware replaced. The drawers never had locks; the lid has the original lock.

PROVENANCE: In the late nineteenth century, the desk was in eastern New England, for the drawers are lined with newspapers: the Concord, N.H., *Independent Statesman* of 1873 and the *Boston News* of the same era. The desk belonged to G. N. Strong (address unknown) before being purchased early in this century by the donor's family.

ACCESSION: 1975.44   A gift of Stephen Greene

44 / Standing Desk

1785–1795
Portsmouth area
H. 54¼ (137.8); W. 40½ (102.9); D. 28⅛ (71.4)

Daniel Marrett of Lexington, Massachusetts, married Mary Muzzy on July 24, 1796. He was ordained as the Congregational minister of Standish, in what is now Maine, on

44

September 21 and established his home there by October 13. On November 16, he purchased for 12 shillings a standing desk on which to write his sermons. The desk had belonged to an honored guest at Marrett's ordination, the Reverend Mr. John Tompson, the Congregational minister of Berwick.

This is Daniel Marrett's desk. Whereas some furniture in the Society's collection, like the preceding desk-on-frame, permit us only to surmise an object's background, others, like Marrett's desk, come with a rich and documented history. Marrett wrote his name and the date and cost of his purchase on the pine lid, which was already inscribed "Reverend Tompson / Berwick 1795."

At Marrett's death in 1836, the "old standing desk" was worth $1.[1] Marrett owned a newer $5 desk and bookcase, but, according to a family history, he wrote his sermons on this one.[2] And when he wrote them, he stood. The writing surface on this desk is the closed lid. On most desks of the era, one wrote on the inner surface of an opened horizontal lid — an irony because desk lids were originally slanted to enable the writer to have comfortable posture and good penmanship.

The standing desk, often made of pine, was especially common in warehouses, schools, and shops. Some had turned legs, others, chamfered straight legs, like those on Marrett's pine desk.[3] The writing surfaces were usually upholstered in green cloth and outlined with brass nails.[4] On October 31, 1732, Samuel Grant, a Boston upholsterer, billed Hannah Willard for:

1 ^{yd} green Shalloon	0:7:6
5½ ^{yd} Green bind^g	0:2:9
Tax 3^d Brass nails 1½ $^{[lb]}$ 3/5	0:3:8
covering a Small Desk	0:3:0[5]

Shalloon was a woolen cloth, as were serge and ratteen, other common desk covers.

Marrett's desk was upholstered on the lid and top in a green woolen; the uncovered wood was painted blue. The original paint and almost all the brass nails survive, and though the upholstery was lost, fragments of the original green cover and binding remained beneath the nails.

When the Society received Marrett's house and its contents, the desk was in the attic; the feet were cut off just above the stretchers, and a crude, unpainted bookshelf stood on the top. The added bookshelf dated from after Marrett's lifetime; the shortening of the legs probably did too. The Society reupholstered the desk and restored it to the height that was standard for such desks (see *Notes on Structure and Condition*).

The gentle curve on the front of the gallery, the well-molded edges of the waist strip, and the good porportions of the case make this an attractive example of a utilitarian form. The original paint, tacks, and fragments of upholstery and its unusually fine history make it an uncommon example of what was once a ubiquitous type.

1. Marrett's 1836 inventory, vol. 34, p. 249, Cumberland County (Me.) Probate.

2. In the Society's files is a Marrett family history, written in 1889, which includes excerpts from Marrett's diary.

3. Standing desks on turned legs are at Colonial Williamsburg (Greenlaw, *New England Furniture at Williamsburg*, no. 94) and at the Old Gaol Museum; examples with straight legs are at the Beverly Historical Society and the Essex Institute, and one that belonged to the Reverend Mr. Samuel Ripley of Concord, Mass. (Sotheby Parke Bernet, sale 4180, November 1978, lot 966).

4. Prown, *Copley*, vol. 1, figs. 132, 201.

5. Grant Account Book, Massachusetts Historical Society, p. 178.

NOTES ON STRUCTURE AND CONDITION: The dovetailed upper case has a typical cleat-edged lid hinged at the back. No partitions, drawers, or tills are inside. The gallery is nailed to the sides and back. The upper case rests on the stiles, sides, and back of the joined frame. A waist strip nailed at each side holds the desk and frame together. The dovetailed drawer has a bottom set into grooves in the front and sides. Handles and escutcheons were never present.

When the legs were cut, small portions of the stretcher mortises survived, proving their original placement. Repairs were made using closely related desks at the Beverly Historical Society and the Essex Institute as prototypes. The back of the gallery is a replacement; the right waist strip is patched. The new wood was painted to match the old.

MATERIALS: White pine. Original locks and hinges.

PROVENANCE: The desk remained in Daniel Marrett's house and descended with it to the donor.

ACCESSION: 1959.324   A bequest of Frances S. Marrett

45 / Desk

1750–1770
Southern New England or possibly New York
H. 42¼ (107.3); W. 40¼ (102.2); D. 20¾ (52.7)

This desk, although made of maple and only stained mahogany, is of sophisticated design. The interior (45a) features handsomely turned pilasters, serpentine drawer fronts, and a molded shelf beneath the drawers. The carved claw-and-ball feet are fashionable supports. Miters hide the dovetails on the top and make neat joints on the lid. And in the eighteenth century the very form of this desk, the case with four wide exterior drawers, was far more desirable than the desk box or desk-on-frame.

This popular form, often called "fall front" or "slant lid" today, was designated in estate inventories as "bureau desk," "desk of four drawers," "scrutore," or just "desk."[1] The descriptive "bureau desk" and "desk of four drawers" were early terms. "Scrutore," especially popular before 1770, was reserved in New England for elegant pieces: "Escrutore with glass Doors 9:10:8," "2 Scrutores one of them with a Book Case £17."[2]

The popularity of the bureau desk may have resulted from the great increase in personal possessions in the eighteenth century. The exterior drawers added significantly to the desk's storage capacity. Bulky articles could be kept in the large locked drawers, small valuables behind the locked lid.

The large drawers generally contained fabric:

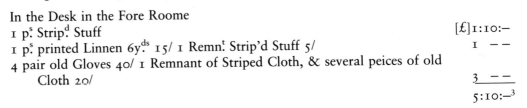

In the Desk in the Fore Roome
1 pˢ Stripᵈ Stuff   [£]1:10:–
1 pˢ printed Linnen 6yᵈˢ 15/ 1 Remnᵗ Strip'd Stuff 5/   1 – –
4 pair old Gloves 40/ 1 Remnant of Striped Cloth, & several peices of old
    Cloth 20/   3 – –
                                                                    5:10:–[3]

45

In the days before bank vaults, small interior drawers contained an enormous portion of one's personal property:

In the Scrutore — Viz.^r —

Paper Money (old Tenar[)]	1339:14:8
Sterl.^g money £4:15:6 at 900 [per] Cent is old Tenor	47:15
7½ ounces of Silver money Forreign Coin &c at 58/ [per] oz.	41: 5
1 Girdle Buckle w.th 26 Briliant Cristials	5
1 p.^r 3 Drop Christial Ear Rings	3
1 Oriental Saphire Ring	40

45a

1 Red Single Stone Ring	5
1 Seven Stone Chrystial Ring	4
1 Chrystial Heart Hook	2
1 p.^r Stone Buttons Cypher set in Gold	8
1 Mourning Ring with 2 Brilliant Diamond Sparks	12
1 Single Stone Beryl Ring	10
1 Correl Necklace	1:10
1 p.^r Men's Shoe Buckles, 1 p.^r K[n]ee Buckles	
1 p.^r Women's Shoe Buckles Black'd w.^t 2 oz. 12 dw.^t w.th Steel Flukes & Tongs @ 65/	8: 8
1 Snuff Box	4
1 Gold Locket Enameld, 1 p.^r Gold Sleeve Buttons, part of a Gold Necklace & a Mouth piece for a Mask w.^t 18 dw.^{ts} @£40 [per] oz	36
1 Wilk Shell Snuff Box	2:10
1 Gold Seal	10
1 Silver Seal for a Counting House	1: 5
1 Ivory Pencil Book	4
1 old Pocket Case	: 2[4]

The storage place for such valuables was itself likely to be valuable. Even unembellished desks were costly; they required a lot of wood and workmanship. Of the two, wood was of far greater value. In Providence in 1757, "A Desk with two teer of Draws one Square Draw" cost £39.[5] Since a "Mehogny" desk on the same list is £90 and a "walnot" one is £75, the £39 one is probably maple. The listed price was for the basic model.[6]

Optional additions for a desk like this one included dividing the "Square Draw" or "prospect" into three sections (pilaster drawers and a central door with drawers behind), carving a concave-blocked door, turning the pilasters, cutting the swelled fronts of the small drawers, carving the front feet, and, most expensive, supplying the brasses.

Old numerals inscribed within this desk on an interior drawer may be the price of the desk:

$$[\pounds]4:\ 7:9$$
$$\underline{12}$$
$$4:19:9$$
$$\underline{13:3}$$
$$5:13:0$$

The figures represent new devalued money ($\pounds4$: 7:9 = $\pounds43$:17:6 in old tenor).[7] The added 12 shillings probably were for cabinetmaking extras, the 13 shillings 3 pence for brasses.

The inscribed prices are consistent with the values of lawful money in Massachusetts after 1750 and in Connecticut after 1756.[8] Yet the desk was donated by members of the Chace family of Providence and apparently was always owned in that area. A similar desk has a Providence history.[9] Rhode Island currency remained inflated old tenor until 1763, so the desk, if made before 1763, probably was made elsewhere.

Thus the attribution must remain broad. The desk clearly was not made north of Providence. The configuration of the exterior drawers — three graduated drawers below a short drawer — is seen generally in southern New England. The construction of the dust boards — large rectangular panels set into grooves in the drawer dividers and drawer supports — is an English technique more typical of New York than New England.[10] The squarish claws and the use of different feet in the rear appear on Rhode Island, Connecticut, and New York furniture. The extensive use of tulipwood is also characteristic of southern New England and New York.

1. For "A bureau Desk," see desk no. 43, n. 2. James Boyer had "a Walnut Scrutore with Drawers" (1741 inventory, old series, vol. 35, pp. 400–401), and a "Desk of four Draws" belonged to John Dupee (1743 inventory, old series, vol. 36, p. 499), both Suffolk County (Mass.) Probate.

2. The two scrutores belonged to Henry Marshall of Boston (1732 inventory, old series, vol. 31, p. 243) and the glass-doored one to William Foye (1760 inventory, old series, vol. 56, p. 73), both Suffolk County (Mass.) Probate.

3. Anthony Stoddard's 1748 inventory, old series, vol. 41, p. 169, Suffolk County (Mass.) Probate.

4. George Rogers's 1748 inventory, old series, vol. 41, p. 464, Suffolk County (Mass.) Probate.

5. "Table of Prices for Joiners' Work," quoted in Lyon, *Colonial Furniture*, 3rd ed., 266.

6. These prices are in inflated Rhode Island currency; McCusker, *Money and Exchange*, 135.

7. Ibid., 120, 133.

8. Ibid., 135.

9. The desk of Ebenezer Knight Dexter (1773–1824) of Providence, in the collections of the Rhode Island School of Design, is at the Hunter House, a property of the Preservation Society of Newport County.

10. The technique was used on a New York chest-on-chest; Randall, *American Furniture*, no. 38.

NOTES ON STRUCTURE AND CONDITION: The desk board, drawer dividers, and drawer supports are set into grooves in the case sides. The lower two dividers have thick facing strips. The bottom drawer runs on the base rail and drawer supports. The lower edge of the one-piece base molding is flush with the underside of the bottom. The rear elements of the rear feet are glued to the bottom. Because the bottom of the case extends under the back, no additional vertical blocks are needed behind the rear feet. In the desk interior, a shelf with a molded edge is nailed to the desk board. The shelf is grooved to receive the primary partitions.

The exterior drawers are joined with large, precisely shaped dovetails. The top edges of the drawer sides and back are rounded. The bottom of each drawer is nailed to the rabbeted lower edges of the drawer front and sides. The drawer fronts have thumbnail-molded edges that overlap the case at the top and sides.

In the eighteenth or early nineteenth century, the desk board broke at the hinges, and three hinges were used to replace the original two. During the late nineteenth century, the desk was given a bookcase, the desk interior was sponge-painted, the exterior wood was grained, and massive Victorian hardware was substituted for the old brasses. By 1975 the added bookcase was gone (a bit of molding remained), the left four interior drawers were lost, and the graining had deteriorated beyond restoration. Even the Victorian drop handles were broken. In 1977 the graining and hardware were removed, the piece was restained, using traces of the original color as a guide, and handles approximating the design of the original hardware were mounted. Cabinetry repairs at that time included making interior drawers to duplicate the extant ones and replacing the side knee bracket of the left front foot and most of the side element of the right rear foot.

MATERIALS: *Soft maple; beech* side element of original right rear foot; white pine backboard and support blocks for feet; *tulipwood* other secondary wood. Replaced brass hardware and iron hinges and locks.

PROVENANCE: The desk apparently belonged to the Chace family of Providence in the nineteenth and twentieth centuries.

ACCESSION: 1975.185   A gift of Lydia G., Frances L., and Alice B. Chace

46 / Desk

1780–1803
Boston, Charlestown, or Salem
Carving possibly by John Austin
H. 44 (111.8); W. 44⅜ (112.7); D. 24 (61.0)

Four exterior drawers are standard on slant-lid desks made in the Boston area. The three-drawer form is so rare that only four examples are known to the authors: this oxbow (plate 7), a blockfront, a serpentine front, and an oxbow without blocking on the top drawer.[1] The four desks are very different from one another, but they share one attribute, a tall base.

In Newport, where three-drawer desks and chests were relatively common, the drawers are larger than those in four-drawer cases and the feet are of standard height. The three-drawer desks from Boston are fitted with drawers comparable in size to the lowest three in four-drawer cases and so require a tall base. The prominent, almost foot-high cabrioles invite decoration. Carved masks adorn the knees of the related blockfront. The base on the serpentine desk features cabrioles almost identical to these in form and carving. The crisp and fluid leafage delineated on this desk (46a) creates an illusion of depth by means of overlapping foliage.

This appears to be the latest of the four Boston desks. Veneer, used here on the top of the desk and on the writing surface of the desk board, is characteristic of the Federal style. (The veneer on the top neatly hides the dovetails joining the top to the sides of the case.) The use of inlay, here a handsome rope pattern flanking the central door, was

46

also popular in Federal period work. The simple base molding is typical of late Chippendale design, and the pattern of the interior (46b), with the drawers above the pigeonholes, became standard after the Revolution.

The undulating valance applied to the long drawers on the desk interior is a rare finishing touch. The pierced and carved central drop is most extraordinary. But if much of the desk's design is unusual, in other respects it is well within the mainstream of Boston Chippendale construction (see *Notes on Structure and Condition*) and design. The oxbow was almost the standard "swelled front" for desks made in eastern Massachusetts. This swelled façade features a crisp outline of blocking at the top of the oxbow, a shaping often seen in the Boston area (chest-on-chest no. 27).[2] The splendid swirling figure of the wood typifies the quality of lumber that Boston cabinetmakers chose for their best furniture.

Of the four Boston three-drawer desks, this is the only one with a provenance. It bears a scratched inscription on the back, "Thomas Austin/August 10, 1803," and until the early twentieth century it was in the Frost family house in Cambridge, the house into which Thomas Austin (1762–1816), a Boston merchant, moved soon after he married Martha Frost in 1807.

According to the family members who inherited the house and desk, the desk was made in Charlestown in 1787 by two brothers, relatives of the family and believed to be named Frost. However, the 1803 inscription suggests that Austin's desk entered the Frost-Austin house with the 1807 marriage. If the desk was made by relatives, they probably were Austins, not Frosts.

No Charlestown Frosts are known to have been making furniture in this era; however, Austins were. John Austin (b. 1722) was a carver still working at his trade in 1786. His sons John Jr. and Richard were chairmakers. Josiah Austin (1746–1825), a cabinetmaker, was probably John's nephew, although by some accounts he was a son.[3] All worked in Charlestown, but John Sr. moved to Boston in 1770 and Josiah moved to Salem between 1782 and 1803.[4] One son of carver John Austin who did not work in the furniture trades was Thomas, the man who inscribed the desk in 1803.[5] It seems probable that if Thomas wanted an elaborately carved desk, he would have gone to his father, for John did carve six mahogany chairs that Thomas owned.[6]

We do not know the cabinetmakers with whom John Austin worked; his nephew (or son) Josiah is but one possibility. Carvers worked for many cabinetmakers. Further research (the desk came to the Society as this manuscript was being prepared for publication) may prove what is now only a possibility: that these carved feet, brackets, and drop are the work of John Austin.

46a

1. The blockfront is privately owned; the serpentine example is in *Israel Sack Collection*, 4:952; the oxbow desk without blocking on the top drawer was advertised by two different dealers, first in 1955, *Antiques* 68:175, and then in 1965, *Antiques* 87:550.

2. See also two labeled desks by Benjamin Frothingham; *Boston Furniture*, 237–39.

3. Swan cites Josiah as John's son, "Furniture-makers of Charlestown," 206; Wyman, *Genealogies*, 39, lists him as a nephew.

4. Wyman, *Genealogies*, 39. For John's working dates, see *Boston Furniture*, 271.

5. Wyman, *Genealogies*, 39.

6. Susan S. Austin's 1885 inventory, docket 19178, 1st series, Middlesex County (Mass.) Probate.

NOTES ON STRUCTURE AND CONDITION: The bottom drawer runs directly on the case bottom, which has the typical Boston "giant" dovetail binding the

46b

base molding to the pine bottom. The feet are tenoned through the bottom and braced with support blocks. The back and inside edges of the rear feet are uncarved, a common practice. A bead cut on the case surrounds all the exterior drawer openings. The drawer construction is typical of Chippendale work from the Boston area. The dovetails are rather coarse, and the top edge of the drawer sides is not decoratively cut. The drawer bottoms are nailed into the rabbeted edges of the front and sides, and runners were originally glued to the bottom along the rabbeted edge of the sides.

The desk received many pieced repairs and was refinished about a century ago. A section of the thumbnail molded edge along the top of the lid is replaced. The lid supports have been altered. Two knee brackets are replaced. Many support blocks behind the side base moldings have been replaced, and the feet have been reglued. Because the finish had bleached badly, the desk was refinished in 1983.

MATERIALS: *Mahogany;* mahogany facings on *cherry* lid supports; *white pine* other secondary wood. Original brass hardware on the bottom drawer and on the left and center of the middle drawer; original steel locks in the lower two drawers and brass lock in the lid.

PROVENANCE: The desk descended from Thomas Austin's widow to their daugher Susan, who apparently bequeathed the desk with her half of the family house to her cousin Martha Frost Kuhn. It subsequently passed to her daughter Martha A. K. Clarke, to her son Charles, and to his daughter, the donor.

ACCESSION: 1982.7   A bequest of Eleanor Clarke Bowser

47 / Desk

1780–1800
Newburyport, Massachusetts
H. desk only 43 (109.2), with bookcase 94⅞ (241); W. 44 (111.8); D. 22⅝ (57.5)

The oxbow façade was an especially popular design for desks. Although Chippendale oxbow desks were made throughout New England, this one acquired a distinctive appearance while it belonged to its original owner, Richard Bartlet, a merchant in Newburyport. Bartlet (1763–1832), who may have acquired the desk at about the time of his marriage in 1783, had a bookcase made for it in about 1810 in the current fashion. Thus originated — in a manner by no means unique — Bartlet's hybrid, a Chippendale desk and Federal bookcase (47a). At Bartlet's death the desk and bookcase was worth $20, its value to the appraiser undiminished by being what is called today "a married piece."[1]

47

The fine documentation of these well-constructed cases makes Bartlet's desk and its bookcase valuable guides to the identification of related Newburyport furniture.

1. Bartlet's inventory, docket 1950, Essex County (Mass.) Probate.

NOTES ON STRUCTURE AND CONDITION: The 1-inch-thick mahogany top of the dovetailed desk is slightly thicker than most desk tops. The back, three lap-jointed boards, runs vertically. The desk board is mahogany and pine. The shallow drawer dividers and the lid supports are solid mahogany.

47a

The front edge of each case side is covered with a thick, ½-inch facing strip. A base rail is glued and nailed within the case to the case bottom. A supporting strip of pine is glued and nailed to the underside of the bottom. A giant dovetail joins the front base molding to the case bottom and the supporting strip beneath. The carved shell is nailed and glued to the base molding, and a support block is glued behind.

The shallow, 1½-inch step of the desk interior and the primary partitions are thick elements cut with a beaded channel molding on their front edges. The pigeonhole arches are supported by three blocks each. Both the interior and exterior drawers have above-average dovetailing. The bottom of each exterior drawer sits in grooves in the front and sides. The top edge of each drawer side is cut with a bead on the inner edge. The bottom drawer slides on the base rail and supports. A bead cut on the case surrounds all the exterior drawer openings. Four stops, two on each side, are glued to the case sides at the back for each drawer except the top one. Stops for the top drawer are glued to the underside of the desk board.

The only major repair to the desk has been to the feet. Long ago the lower 1½ inches of the feet were cut off, perhaps to fit the desk and its tall bookcase into a low-ceilinged room. In 1978 the missing portions of the feet were replaced.

MATERIALS: *Mahogany; white pine* secondary wood. Original brass hardware and hinges. Original steel locks in the two middle drawers and brass lock in the lid; the bottom drawer never had a lock.

PROVENANCE: The desk descended from Richard Bartlet of Newburyport to his daughter Abigail Bartlett Shaw (1805–1877), to her son Edward Payson Shaw, and to his daughter Annie Bartlett Shaw Andrew.

ACCESSION: 1940.799a   A museum purchase from Mrs. George C. (Annie Bartlett Shaw) Andrew

48 / Desk

1780–1810
Coastal Essex County, Massachusetts
H. 44¹⁄₁₆ (111.9); W. 45 (114.3); D. 22½ (57.2)

The oxbow desk remained in fashion well past the Revolutionary War era.[1] This desk and others like it originally had Federal brasses, and their interiors (48a) often were decorated with inlay instead of carving.[2]

The most distinguishing design features of the desk are at the base: the handsome

48

grasping claws, the knee brackets, and especially the graceful, shell-carved central drop (48b). Similar drops appear on numerous oxbow desks and chests.[3] Although stylish, this furniture is of native woods, maple or birch, as well as of imported mahogany or walnut.[4]

Maple and birch desks, as attractive as their more expensive counterparts, sold at prices many could afford. This birch desk belonged to Richard Lakeman (1749–1841) of Ipswich, a fisherman, ship master, captain, and trader who also owned shares in several schooners at different times in his long life.[5] In 1781, Lakeman's privateer *Diana* was licensed by the new national government to catch and loot vessels of hostile nations.[6]

Lakeman's desk and its numerous relations are the work of several different craftsmen. Two mahogany desks closely related in appearance to this desk can be documented to cabinetmakers in Salem: one to Elijah Sanderson, the other to William King.[7] Another example, remarkably similar to Lakeman's in design but not in construction, was originally owned in Gloucester.[8] Salem, Gloucester, and Ipswich, Lakeman's home, are ports about a dozen miles apart in easternmost Essex County. The Sanderson and King cases suggest that Salem was the likely source for the designs on Lakeman's desk. But related furniture was also produced in Newburyport, at the other end of the Essex County coast. Joseph Short (1771–1819), a Newburyport cabinetmaker, regularly sold birch furniture to Abel Keyes, a painter, who presumably stained the pieces a mahogany color and resold them. Accounts between Short and Keyes for 1808 list:

1 burch light stand	$ 2.50
1 3½ feet burch table	5.00
1 do. do	5.00
1 swell'd burch desk	20.00[9]

The design of this desk was a popular one, but the construction is so distinctive (see *Notes on Structure and Condition*) that a related and documented case may someday pinpoint its origin.

48a

1. Several cases related to this one are clearly post-Revolutionary. Dated oxbow desks include two desks and bookcases with central drops of a related shell form to that on this desk, both dated 1799 and marked "Gilmanton" (N.H.) and an oxbow with a dissimilar shell dated 1794, all illustrated by Young, "Five Secretaries." Two oxbow chests with similar feet and the same drop have original Federal brass bail handles (*Israel Sack Collection*, 2:447, 512). Federal brasses are also on two oxbow desks with the same drop, one *ex col.* Katrina Kipper (DAPC Files, Winterthur Museum, 66.773), another advertised in *Antiques* 96 (September 1969): 310. Of two chests at the Sargent-

Murray-Gilman-Hough House in Gloucester, one has Federal brasses, the other string inlay on the exterior drawers.

2. A desk labeled by Frothingham in the Currier Gallery of Art features stringing and an inlaid fan on the interior (*Boston Furniture*, fig. 167).

3. Similar pieces, not cited in note 1, include the Pierce family desk at the New Hampshire Historical Society; the Davis family desk at the Cape Ann Historical Association; a desk at the Winterthur Museum (G.52.254); a desk at the Baltimore Museum of Art (42.85); a desk advertised in *Antiques* 96 (December 1969): 851; a chest owned by the family of Governor Badger of New Hampshire (1834–36), *Antiques* 65 (January 1954): 57; two chests in *Israel Sack Collection*, 1:9 and 3:753; two chests in *Antiques* 91 (May 1967): 546 and 73 (March 1958): 230; a chest in Sack, *Fine Points*, 99; and three chests sold at auction — Hyman Kaufman Collection, Part 1, American Art Association, sale 4100, April 1934, lot 459; Hyman Kaufman Collection, Part 2, American Art Association, sale 4193, October 1935, lot 111; William Doyle Galleries, November 15, 1978, lot 627.

4. For example, the chests illustrated in *Antiques* 91 (May 1967): 546 and *Israel Sack Collection*, 2:447, both cited above, are also of birch; the Winterthur and Kipper desks cited above are of maple; *Israel Sack Collection*, 3:753, is of walnut; and *Israel Sack Collection*, 2:512, is of mahogany.

5. An 1803 bill of sale in the Ipswich Historical Society is for the schooner *Betsey*, a one-deck, two-masted vessel without a galley or head owned by Lakeman and Joseph Lord, a merchant.

6. Waters, *Ipswich*, 2:352–53.

7. A desk at the New England Historic Genealogical Society which descended in the family of the cabinetmaker Elijah Sanderson (*Antiques* 113 [May 1978]: 1082), and a chest labeled William King (*Antiques* 12 [September 1927]: 200–203).

8. The very similar desk is in the Cape Ann Historical Association and descended in the seafaring Davis family; a related chest at the Sargent-Murray-Gilman-Hough House descended from David and Mary Plumer of Gloucester.

9. Short, Account Book, 1804–8, Essex Institute.

NOTES ON STRUCTURE AND CONDITION: The dovetailed birch case has a bottom of pine faced with birch. The shallow drawer dividers are entirely of birch; the lid supports are pine faced with birch. The front edges of the case sides are covered with thin facing strips.

The base molding is nailed beneath the bottom of the case. The birch front edge of the bottom is visible above the base molding. Thus, the desk looks like a case with an applied base rail behind the base molding, such as desk no. 45. Long support strips are glued to the bottom behind the base molding. The claw-and-ball feet are secured in an unusual manner: the feet have dovetail-shaped tenons that key into the base molding. Knee brackets and their support blocks surround the dovetail and help anchor the feet.

A bead, cut on the case, surrounds all the drawer openings. The bottom of each drawer is set into grooves in the front and sides. Small supporting blocks are glued beneath the drawer bottom in the front corners, an unusual feature. Equally distinctive are a central batten and the drawer stops. The vertical batten, set at the back of the case, is tenoned into the desk board and case bottom to support the desk board. Stops are nailed to the top of the drawer dividers, a method common in English furniture but rare on New England examples.

The desk survives in good condition. Because of severe sun bleaching, the desk was restained a mahogany color and given a shellac finish.

MATERIALS: *Birch; white pine* secondary wood. Replaced hardware, hinges, and locks.

PROVENANCE: Richard Lakeman's house and furniture, including the desk, passed to his son Ebenezer (d. 1838), his grandson Ebenezer (d. 1885), to the latter's widow, Susan, and then to their surviving child, Sarah E. (d. 1937), who left the house and desk to Arthur W. Johnson.

ACCESSION: 1948.705   A bequest of Arthur W. Johnson

48b

Color Plates

1. Chest of Drawers No. 11.

2. Chest of Drawers No. 13.

3. High Chest No. 36.

4. Japanned Decoration on the Lower Right Drawer of High Chest No. 36. *The brass handle has been removed to show the original color.*

5. Dressing Table No. 31.

6. High Chest No. 37.

7. Desk No. 46.

8. Side Chair No. 99.

9. Settee No. 107.

10. Side Chair No. 114.

11. Side Chair No. 118.

12. Looking Glass No. 147.

49 / Desk

1785–1805
Boston area
H. 42⅞ (108.9); W. 42¾ (108.6); D. 21³⁄₁₆ (53.8)

Between 1730 and 1760, desks with flat façades often had undulating interiors (detail 45a). The middle of the century brought the popularity of undulating exteriors (desks no. 46, 47, and 48). The flat exterior, nevertheless, remained the less expensive option. Both shaped and straight-front desks continued to be made into the era of Federal design, but increasingly they had simpler, flatter, and starker interiors.

49

This is a desk of the post-Revolutionary era. The flat façade of the interior (49a) closely resembles that of two labeled desks, one by Benjamin Frothingham and another by Archelaus Flint and Samuel S. Noyes, all of Charlestown.[1] Charlestown and Boston, flanking the mouth of the Charles River, functioned in the furniture trades as one market.

The Frothingham desk was made in about 1800, the Flint-Noyes desk between 1803 and 1813. The interiors of all three desks have pigeonholes beneath the drawers, straight-fronted pigeonhole partitions, the same pigeonhole-arch design, and the same drawer configuration above the pigeonholes. The Frothingham desk features an inlaid shell in the center of the interior. The Flint-Noyes desk, like the Society's, has no inlay or carving.

The Frothingham desk, an oxbow, has the familiar applied bead surrounding the drawer openings, as on desks no. 46, 47, and 48. The Flint-Noyes desk has a later feature: an applied bead on the drawer fronts, not on the case. On the Society's desk, a scratch bead on the drawer fronts emulates such an applied bead. Beading, actual or scratched, on drawer fronts (not on the case proper) is a hallmark of the Federal style in Massachusetts.

The Society's desk is of dense mahogany with finely cut dovetails and far better than average craftsmanship. (See III-15, a detail of a front foot of this desk.) A notable detail that exemplifies the quality of the workmanship is the top edge of the facing strip. Facing strips are usually flat; some have corbels to conform to the lower edge of the lid; few have corbels so gracefully designed or so neatly executed.

The desk, which descended in the Brown family of Watertown, Massachusetts, apparently belonged to Adam Brown (1763–1827), whose estate included a mahogany desk worth $6.[2] Watertown, just to the west along the Charles, had close ties with Boston and Charlestown, and the similarity of the Brown desk to the two from Charlestown suggests Brown may have purchased his desk there.

49a

1. The Frothingham desk is owned by the Currier Gallery of Art, and is figure 167 in *Boston Furniture*; the Flint-Noyes desk is privately owned.

2. Brown's 1828 inventory, docket 2945, Middlesex County (Mass.) Probate.

NOTES ON STRUCTURE AND CONDITION: The back, of three horizontal boards nailed to the rabbeted edges of the sides and top, overlaps the bottom in typical eastern Massachusetts fashion. The drawer dividers are of 4¼-inch-deep pine with ³⁄₁₆-inch mahogany facings. The one-piece cove-shaped base molding extends a bit above the bottom of the case and ½ inch below it. A thin base rail is glued and nailed behind the base molding within the case. Below the bottom, the base molding is supported by a series of narrow rectangular blocks. The design of the feet and their support blocks (III-15) are typical of furniture from eastern Massachusetts, but the vertical corner blocks for the front feet are made of mahogany rather than the usual pine. The rear element of each rear foot has an ogee outline and is notched to fit over the support blocks behind the base molding.

The pigeonhole arch behind the door in the desk interior is a drawer front. Each of the other pigeonhole arches is supported by three glue blocks.

The bottom of each exterior drawer is nailed into the rabbeted edges of the front and sides. Runners are glued and nailed to the bottoms along the sides and cut at the back on a 45-degree angle. Stops for the top drawer are glued to the underside of the desk board; stops for the other drawers are glued to the case sides.

The desk is in excellent condition. All original elements survive except the stop for the left lid support and a block for the right rear foot.

MATERIALS: *Mahogany;* mahogany vertical blocks for the front feet, mahogany facings on *cherry* lid supports; *white pine* other secondary wood. Original brass hardware except one interior button, lid escutcheon, and bail posts for the lowest drawer. Original locks; replaced lid hinges.

PROVENANCE: The desk descended in the Brown family of Watertown, apparently from Adam to his widow Abigail, to their son Francis (b. 1796), to his son Francis Jonathan (b. 1820), whose daughter Marietta Frances Josselyn left it to her daughter, the donor.

ACCESSION: 1966.509   A gift of Miss Mabel Josselyn

50 / Desk and Bookcase

1765–1775
Boston
H. 95½ (242.6); W. 49 (124.5); D. 27½ (69.9)

During the British occupation of Boston at the beginning of the Revolution, William Foster (1745–1821), a prominent merchant and ardent patriot, fled to a farm in neighboring Brighton. Before departing, he put his name on several items he left behind. He signed his desk and bookcase in chalk in seven places on the backs of drawers (50a) and the backboards of the case. When he returned after the evacuation of the king's troops, he discovered that the officers had confiscated his desk for their own use at the Province House. Challenged to prove that the desk was his, Foster pointed to the inscriptions and was permitted to reclaim his prize possession.[1] Today Foster's signature makes his desk and bookcase important to the study of Boston furniture.[2]

Two hundred years of use have altered the appearance of what Susan Foster Batchelder referred to as "the old mahogany secretary which formerly belonged to our grandfather, William Foster."[3] A photograph taken in about 1890 (50b) suggests that the carved borders on the bookcase doors, and possibly the pilasters, were originally gilded. In the 1950s a Boston cabinetmaker thoroughly refinished the piece, making it impossible to find any trace of the gilding. During the nineteenth century, the finials and the central door of the desk interior (50c) were removed, and the feet altered noticeably. The desk originally stood on ogee bracket feet, but someone cut the feet just below the mitered knees and added large hairy-paw feet holding flattened balls (50d, the left rear foot).

The plan of the Foster desk is firmly rooted in English tradition. By the 1720s, London cabinetmakers had introduced the chief characteristics of the design — a slant-lid desk surmounted by a bookcase with mirrored doors and a scrolled pediment — and such architectural details as pilasters and dentiled moldings.[4] They continued to produce this form for at least thirty years, gradually grafting onto the case carved rococo details, ogee bracket feet, and serpentine surrounds for the mirrors.[5]

While inspired by the London formula, the Foster desk displays certain trademarks of Boston design. The most obvious is the blocked façade of the lower case. In addition, the interior is an early example of a pattern that became very popular in the Boston area later in the eighteenth century (compare details 49a and 50c). The bookcase interior is typical in its row of pigeonholes, series of shelves, and row of small drawers.

The Foster desk relates closely in proportion and overall design to many desks and bookcases.[6] It may have been constructed in the same shop as a blockfront example owned by David Stockwell in 1978 (50e) and a bombé that originally belonged to Josiah Quincy, Jr. (photograph 117a).[7] Both blockfronts have similar desk interiors and upper case details, including identical bands of wavelike carving along the upper edges of their pediment moldings. The bombé and Foster's desk share some carved details, many decorative contours, and the layout of the bookcase interior.

In addition to its design, the Foster desk exhibits three notable characteristics of Boston cabinetwork: the "giant" dovetail (see III-19), the scanty use of secondary woods, and an indifference to construction details. Although this desk and bookcase is massive, the use of secondary wood is extremely economical: the drawer dividers are shallow, the drawer supports thin, and the original blocking for the feet insubstantial, considering the immense weight they carry. Although the design is elaborate, the drawers are coarse, with large, slightly uneven dovetails.

Boston construction like this is rough, especially compared with the precision of the best Newport cabinetwork. The techniques of Boston craftsmen do not indicate a lack of experience or skill, as is sometimes the case with rural artisans. Instead, they apparently reflect a tradition of producing a large quantity of furniture quickly and inexpensively.

50a

50b. Photograph of Desk and Bookcase No. 50 in situ. Cambridge, Massachusetts, ca. 1875. Photographic Archives, Society for the Preservation of New England Antiquities.

1. The story was recorded in 1890 by Foster's granddaughter and is pasted on one of the pilaster drawers.

2. The desk and bookcase is treated in detail in Jobe, "New Discoveries."

3. The will of Susan Foster Batchelder, recorded October 25, 1890; private collection.

4. A desk and bookcase made by Samuel Bennett of London during the mid-1720s illustrates all of these features; Hayward, *English Desks*, no. 11.

5. Hinckley, *Directory*, figs. 212–14, and Macquoid and Edwards, *English Furniture*, 1:145, figs. 48, 49.

6. See the blockfront desk and bookcase from the Alsop family in the collection of the Detroit Institute of Arts (*Antiques* 76 [December 1959]: inside cover) and two bombé desks and bookcases, one made by George Bright, in the Museum of Fine Arts, Boston, and one that descended in the Gay family (*Boston Furniture*, figs. 124, 131).

7. The desk is now privately owned.

NOTES ON STRUCTURE AND CONDITION: The desk and bookcase divides into three sections: bonnet, bookcase, and desk. The bonnet detaches just above the architrave. Although the desk is dovetailed and the bottom of the bookcase is dovetailed to the rabbeted edge of the sides, the top of the bookcase is set into grooves in the sides. The frame of the bonnet consists of the sides, the pediment glued and nailed to the front edge of the sides, and the back glued and nailed to the rabbeted rear edge of the sides. Horizontal blocks are glued at the corners of the bonnet, and a roof of thin pine boards is nailed to the top of each scroll of the bonnet. The plinths and plates for all but the center plinth are original.

The sides and waist rail of the bookcase, and not the bottom, rest on the desk. The sides and architrave project above the top of the bookcase. Small blocks are glued beneath the bottom and above the top of the bookcase. The rails of the mirrored doors are tenoned through the stiles; the joints are tightened with wedges.

The cleated ends of the desk lid are fastened to it with tongue-and-groove joints. The thumbnail-molded edges of the lid form a lip only on the sides. The shouldered dovetails binding the drawer dividers to the case are left exposed on the front edge of the case sides. The bottom drawer runs directly on the case bottom. The front base molding is secured to the bottom with a squarish "giant" dovetail. The knee brackets and much of their support blocking are original.

In the desk interior, the pigeonhole valance in the prospect is a drawer front. Each document drawer is nailed together. The other interior drawers are dovetailed, and the bottom of each is glued to the rabbeted lower edges of the front, sides, and back. In contrast, the bottoms of the interior drawers of the bookcase section are set in grooves in the fronts and sides. A beaded edge surrounds each opening for an exterior drawer. The top edge of the exterior drawer sides is cut with a double arch. Each drawer bottom is nailed into the rabbeted lower edges of the front and sides. The

50c

50d

runners are glued along the lower edge of the sides to the bottom of each drawer.

MATERIALS: *Mahogany; white pine* secondary wood. Original brass hardware, drawer locks, and door and lid hinges.

PROVENANCE: The desk and bookcase descended in the family of William Foster to his son Charles Chauncy Foster (1785–1875), to Charles's daughter Susan Foster Batchelder (1823–1900), to her son Charles F., to his son Charles F. Jr., and to his wife, the donor.

ACCESSION: 1976.167   A gift of Mrs. Charles F. Batchelder

50e. Desk and Bookcase. Boston, 1760–1780. Mahogany and white pine; H. 96¼ (244.5); W. 49 (124.5); D. 25½ (64.8). Collection of David Stockwell. Photograph, Helga Studio; courtesy, Bernard & S. Dean Levy, Inc., New York.

51 / Desk and Bookcase

1770–1790
Boston
H. 98⅛ (249.2), excluding finial 94¼ (239.4); W. 47¼ (120); D. 24⅜ (61.9)

In contrast to the curved lines of the preceding example, with its scrolled pediment, serpentine paneled doors, and blockfront drawers, this Boston desk and bookcase presents a surprisingly rectilinear aspect. The pitched pediment, dentiled cornice, rectangular

door panes, and straight-fronted drawers create a design that — except for the legs, drop, and finial — is entirely of straight lines. The rectilinear fashion was more prevalent in England than in New England, and at first glance this case with its lid closed looks English (see Charles Apthorp's imported clothes press, I-16).

Yet each component of the design manifests Boston taste. The claw feet, knee brackets, central drop, and the pattern of the interior (51a) are all typical of Boston.[1] The removable fall-front prospect door (usually the door in a central prospect is hinged on one side) appears far more often on Boston cases than on desks made elsewhere.[2] The pilasters flanking the prospect and the shell carvings typify those that decorate many Boston desks, including some documented to Benjamin Frothingham.[3] The blocking beneath the pigeonholes matches fine Boston examples (I-24a), and the coved drawer fronts serving as pigeonhole valances correspond with those on a bombé desk and bookcase by the Boston cabinetmaker George Bright.[4]

Other details, however, set this object apart. The cabriole legs are unusually tall for a four-drawer case. The egg-and-dart molding at the cornice and base — also on the Bright bombé, but only at its base — seldom ornaments Boston furniture. On this example, the pattern dissolves into leaves at the corners (51b). A carved bird finial (51c) adorns two other Boston bookcases, both at the Museum of Fine Arts, Boston: the Bright bombé cited above and a blockfront desk and bookcase from the Low and Cutler families of Boston (I-24).[5]

Two of the three birds are almost identical, and the cases on which they stand are from the same shop. The carvings on the interior drawers and the very construction of the drawers show that the Low-Cutler blockfront and the Society's desk and bookcase are by the same unknown cabinetmaker. In producing the blockfront, he stayed within the mainstream of elegant cabinetry; in making the Society's example, he strove for a different design.

This case is extraordinarily architectural. The pitched pediment and dentil moldings are reminiscent of architectural elements. The egg-and-dart molding, while unusual on Boston furniture, was popular for fine interior woodwork. The bookcase doors reinforce the architectural feeling. With the candle slides placed behind the bookcase doors, we are presented with an unobstructed view of doors whose rectangular panes of clear glass recall sash windows. Doors with solid wooden panels were common, and mirrored doors were made for the finest cases, but doors of clear glass were rare. When clear glass was used, it generally was not set in a rectangular pattern but in a latticework of muntins (see III-6).[6]

Although a case with a flat façade was less expensive than a bombé or blockfront, and small panes of clear glass are cheaper than large mirrors, cost seems not to have been a factor here. The design is so well developed, its elements so well coordinated, that one is led to believe that the patron wanted a particularly architectural design, which his cabinetmaker achieved with distinction.

51a

1. For comparable feet, knees, and central drop, see Randall, *American Furniture,* nos. 58, 64, the latter by George Bright (see brackets in fig. 64d). For examples with similar interiors, see *Boston Furniture,* figs. 131, 160, 168, and Fales, *Historic Deerfield,* fig. 475.

2. For example, see a desk in Randall, *American Furniture,* fig. 58a, and a desk and bookcase in the Philip Flayderman Collection, American Art Association, January 2–4, 1930, lot 455.

3. *Boston Furniture,* figs. 160, 168 (Frothingham examples), and 131, among others.

4. Examples with the blocking: *Boston Furniture,* figs. 131, 133, and Randall, *American Furniture,* no. 58 (see fig. 58a). For coved drawer fronts, see Randall, *American Furniture,* fig. 64c.

5. The detail of the eagle on the Bright bombé is figure 64b in Randall, *American Furniture,* and the detail of the bird on the blockfront, 63a.

6. Among the few New England examples with rectangular panes is one illustrated in *Antiques* 74 (October 1958): 276.

NOTES ON STRUCTURE AND CONDITION: Both the upper and lower cases are dovetailed. Facing strips cover the dovetail joints of the drawer dividers to the case sides. A series of blocks of random lengths are glued below the desk bottom to support the base molding. The tall claw feet are tenoned through the bottom. Small blocks add support for the knee brackets, which are glued and nailed to the base molding (the detail of a claw foot and its supports [III-16] is of this desk). On the lid, the cleats are mitered to the main board at the outside corners. A desk shelf is mounted on the 9⅞-inch-deep solid mahogany desk board and extends to the back of the case. The major partitions for the desk interior are set into the shelf and the top of

the desk. Behind the prospect door are two drawers and a pigeonhole. The pigeonhole valance drawers run on narrow strips; the other interior drawers run on solid dividers or the shelf.

A beaded edge surrounds the exterior drawer openings. The bottom of each large drawer is set in a groove in the front and sides (a detail of the rear corner of one large drawer is III-18). A series of blocks, glued to the bottom, line the lower edge of the drawer sides. The drawer sides are rounded at the top edge; the drawer backs have a narrow chamfer. The bottom of each interior drawer is glued to the rabbeted edge of the front and sides.

The rails of the bookcase doors are tenoned through the stiles. The doors are outlined with a scratch bead. All but one of the glass panes are original. Old tack holes behind the doors show that curtains were used. The design of the bookcase interior is a simplified version of a common eastern Massachusetts pattern. At the bottom is a tier of three drawers constructed like those in the desk interior, a central compartment with an adjustable shelf is flanked by tall, narrow openings for ledgers, and at the top there was originally a row of four large pigeonholes (one pigeonhole partition is missing). The pediment is supported much like that on high chest no. 40 (detail 40a). A wooden plate is nailed to the plinth. A metal pin in the ball upon which the bird stands fits into a hole in the plate and plinth. The bird was apparently never gilded.

In 1982, the desk and bookcase was cleaned and refinished, a new prospect door was made, and green silk curtains were installed. The tail of the bird is missing. The bookcase shelves have been rearranged.

MATERIALS: *Mahogany; cherry* candle slides; *white pine* other secondary wood. Original carrying han-

51b

51c

dles on case sides; replaced brass handles and escutcheons. Original locks and lid and door hinges.

PROVENANCE: The desk and bookcase reportedly belonged to the historian William Hickling Prescott (1796–1859) of Boston and was given by him to Charles Inches (1808–1888) or to his son Charles

Edward Inches (1841–1911). It descended to the latter's widow, Louise, to their son Henderson, to the donor.

ACCESSION: 1982.1   A gift of Elizabeth Inches Chamberlin in memory of her father, Henderson Inches (1885–1947)

52 / Desk and Bookcase

1775–1800
Newburyport, Massachusetts, or possibly coastal New Hampshire
H. 94⅞ (241), excluding finials 91⅛ (231.5); W. 43⅜ (110.2); D. 25³⁄₁₆ (64)

A desk and bookcase was a valuable furnishing, highly esteemed by its owner and prominently displayed in his house. The Boston merchant John Salmon's "1 Mahogany Desk & Book Case with glass doors [£] 13..6..8" stood "in the front South room," a prime location in cold New England.[1] While desk and bookcase no. 52 is less spectacular than Salmon's or the preceding two examples, within its original setting it was probably as prepossessing.

This example, although it is neither glazed nor blocked, shares much with the Foster desk and bookcase (no. 50): a scrolled pediment, serpentine door panels, fluted pilasters, a shaped drop at the center of the base, and ogee bracket feet (which Foster's desk originally had). Its interior (52a) is more ambitious, featuring a stepped arrangement

52a

that was used by Massachusetts cabinetmakers on their most expensive products (I-24a). The three sections of the lower tier are typical, for the center (here without a drawer) is wider than each flanking drawer. The pattern of the upper tier is characteristic, although pinwheels take the place of stylish shells.

Several features, however, distinguish the desk and bookcase from Boston work. The front edges of the lid supports are beveled (also seen on desk no. 43, attributed to the Newbury area) and the turnings of the document drawer pilasters are of a distinctive pattern (comparable to the pillars on clock no. 55, from Kittery). Fluted plinths and diagonal supports for the bonnet roof are not seen on Boston furniture, but both details are present on two desks and bookcases with histories of ownership in New Hampshire.[2]

And the carved pinwheels, popular in Essex County, Massachusetts, and neighboring New Hampshire, are another clue to the origin of this object. The pinwheels that are most similar can be documented to Salem and Newburyport by: (1) a desk and bookcase signed by the cabinetmaker Jacob Sanderson of Salem; (2) one by the cabinetmaker Abraham Watson of Salem; (3) desk no. 47, which belonged to Richard Bartlet of Newburyport; and (4) a Bannister family desk and bookcase (I-32). The last example has always been owned in Newburyport and is attributed to Abner Toppan, a Newburyport cabinetmaker, on the basis of a 1795 bill (now missing).[3] It more closely resembles this one than do others in the group and helps tie the Society's example to the Newburyport area.

1. John Salmon's 1754 inventory, old series, vol. 4, p. 489, Suffolk County (Mass.) Probate.

2. One desk and bookcase is at the Moffatt-Ladd House; Giffen, "Moffat-Ladd House, Part 2," fig. 13. The other was owned by the Bartlett family of Kingston, N.H.; Fales, *Historic Deerfield*, no. 474.

3. The desk and bookcase made by Jacob Sanderson was illustrated on the inside cover of *Antiques* 72 (December 1957). For the desk and bookcase made by Abraham Watson, see Fales, *Essex County Furniture*, no. 44. Swan, "Newburyport Furnituremakers," includes Toppan's desk and bookcase (fig. 6), a Toppan chest-on-chest (fig. 7), and mentions the bill for them, 224. Spalding, "Abner Toppan," has more on Toppan.

NOTES ON STRUCTURE AND CONDITION: The desk back is three lap-jointed vertical boards. The shallow drawer dividers and lid supports are entirely of cherry. Facing strips cover the front edge of the case sides. A bead, cut on the case, surrounds all the drawer openings. The bottom edge of the base molding is flush with the underside of the bottom. The bottom drawer runs on drawer supports and on a base rail, backing the base molding. The exterior drawers have rather thick dovetails. Each drawer bottom is set into grooves in the front and sides. Inside the desk, there may never have been a central drawer in the lower tier. The pilaster drawers are nailed; all the other interior drawers are dovetailed. The bottom of each dovetailed drawer is pinned into the rabbeted edges of the front, sides, and back.

The bookcase top is behind the architrave and is set into grooves in the case sides. The bonnet is formed by the pediment (glued and nailed to the case sides), a horizontal backboard (nailed to the rabbeted edge of the case sides and the rear edge of the top), and the case sides. The cornice and architrave are each a one-piece molding. A support block glued behind the central portion of the pediment helps support the middle finial. Below the pediment, the bookcase back has three lap-jointed vertical boards. The waist molding is glued and nailed to the lower case. The bottoms of the drawers in the bookcase interior are made in the same manner as those in the desk interior but are fastened by iron nails driven in through the sides and back.

The desk and bookcase was repaired in 1977.

The feet had been cut down by 2 inches, the finish was bleached by the sun, and the finials had been lost. Because of the similarities with the Bannister family desk and bookcase (I-32), and especially because both have the same contour on the bracket feet, the Bannister desk served as a model when the bottom 2 inches of the feet on the Society's desk were replaced and new finials were made.

MATERIALS: *Cherry; mahogany* pigeonhole arches; *white pine* secondary wood. All brasses replaced except the escutcheon on the right door; original locks in the lid and two of the pinwheel-carved drawers.

PROVENANCE: Nothing is known of the history of the desk and bookcase before 1942, when it came to the Society with a collection of furniture principally from the Portsmouth area. A house fire in 1945 occasioned $20 worth of repair.

ACCESSION: 1942.1200   A gift of Virginia L. Hodge and Katherine D. Parry; conserved through the generosity of an anonymous donor

53 / Desk and Bookcase

1790–1800
Newport area
H. 83¾ (212.7); W. 44⅞ (114); D. 22¾ (57.8)

This desk and bookcase is not only more modest than the preceding three examples, but it follows an entirely different design tradition, that of the Newport cabinetmakers (I-41). Thus, it exhibits the very fine construction and careful attention to detail for which their cabinetry is known (note the spectacular wood selected for the door panels).

Although the design is understated, its several parts conform to the aesthetics of Rhode Island. The simple shape of the bracket feet and the austere arrangement within the bookcase are both in the Rhode Island tradition.[1] The types of partitions in the desk interior and the organization of its several compartments are typical (compare 53a with I-41a). The serpentine shaping of only the top of the paneled doors is commensurate with Rhode Island design on both flat and blockfront bookcases.[2] The applied bead that finishes the bottom edge of the base molding, faintly reminiscent of the applied gadroon on New York furniture, is a fine touch used on many Rhode Island cases.

This desk and bookcase, made with cut nails, dates from the last decade of the eighteenth century. The quality of the cabinetry and the appearance of the desk with the lid closed differ little from work of the 1750s.[3] Only the simplicity of the desk interior suggests a difference. Here, as in desk no. 49 from Boston, one sees the continued popularity of the Chippendale style into the Federal era.

1. Simple bookcase interiors appear in Hipkiss, *Karolik Collection,* supplementary illustration 19, and Nutting, *Furniture Treasury,* vol. 1, no. 63.

2. For a blockfront example, see I-41; for an example with a flat façade, see *Israel Sack Collection,* 5:1369.

3. A dated example, the desk made by Jonathan Swett in Newport in 1753, is figure 8 in Carpenter, "Newport Furniture and Silver."

NOTES ON STRUCTURE AND CONDITION: Both cases are dovetailed. Their backboards are attached with cut nails. The lid supports are of mahogany faced with a darker mahogany. A base rail behind the

53a

front base molding is tenoned to the case sides and backed with glue blocks. All drawer supports including those for the bottom drawer are nailed to the case sides. The construction of the base molding and feet follows standard Rhode Island practice. A thin strip with a beaded front edge is nailed to the underside of the front base molding between the feet. The beaded strips along the sides are missing.

The drawer dovetailing is fine but not on a par with the best Newport furniture. The bottom of each drawer is set into grooves in the front and sides and nailed to the back with cut nails. The thumbnail-molded edge on the drawer fronts is lipped at the top and sides. A cornice rail of pine faced with mahogany is set into grooves in the case sides at the lower edge of the cornice. The cornice is a complex four-part molding glued and nailed to the case.

The desk and bookcase is in excellent condition, with only minor damage and restoration: e.g., patches on two drawer fronts and one foot and a crack in the lid.

MATERIALS: *Mahogany; birch* top and bottom of lower case; *white pine* other secondary wood. Replaced brass hardware; original door hinges, replaced lid hinges. Original lock in lid, replaced locks in all exterior drawers.

PROVENANCE: The desk was among the "suitable antiques" with which Alvin Sortwell furnished the house in Wiscasset, Me., he bought in 1899. It descended with the house to his daughter, the donor.

ACCESSION: 1958.223   A bequest of Frances A. Sortwell

54 / Tall Clock

1770–1777
Portsmouth area
H. 92 (233.7); W. 21 (53.3); D. 10¼ (26)

> The room into which we were ushered was furnished with furniture made a hundred years ago . . . a tall eight-day clock stood, like a sentinel, in one corner.[1]

The clock described in this 1869 newspaper account still stands where Jonathan Sayward had it installed, secured to the wall with nailed boards, and further held by the ceiling, which has settled on top of it.

Clocks were the first mechanical devices introduced into American homes. Enclosed in wooden cases, they became important house furniture. Their engineering and classical proportions manifested the thinking of the Enlightenment and appealed to men whose advancement in business required knowing the correct time. The valuable brass clockworks demanded prominent display and were housed in tall cases of the most fashionable cabinetry the customer could afford.

In 1884, Sayward's "Ancient Hall Clock" continued to be the most valuable piece of furniture in the house.[2] The sitting room, the room used more often than the elegant parlor, was the obvious choice for so costly and useful an object.

The low ceilings in Sayward's sitting room could not accommodate the central finial, an integral part of the design of such clocks. Nevertheless, a central finial was delivered with the clock and, although it has not been on the case for two hundred years, it has remained in the room.

The mahogany case was probably made in the Piscataqua area by a cabinetmaker familiar with current London taste. The arched hood and the carved fretwork panels became fashionable in London in the 1770s. By 1777, Sayward owned his clock, for he wrote in his diary that May 12: "I heard the Clock every Hour Last night. Little or no Sleep."[3]

The stepped base of the clockcase is also English in form. The imported brass face (54a) enhances the English appearance of the clock, although the chasing at the center of the dial may be by a later American hand. The eight-day clock movement is apparently of American manufacture.[4]

54

54a

54b. Tall Clock. Works by Thomas Hughes (1734–1785). London, 1770–1780. Mahogany, oak, and *spruce;* H. 103¼ (262.3); W. 21 (53.3); D. 10¼ (26.0). Society for the Preservation of New England Antiquities.

The Sayward clock closely relates in appearance to an English tall clock (54b) with a long, though undocumented, history of ownership in nearby Exeter, New Hampshire. The English clockworks by "Thomas Hughes / London" (working 1755–1783) and English case of mahogany, oak, and spruce were supposedly given by Governor John Wentworth to Reverend John Odlin and descended through the Pearson and Perry families.[5]

Comparing the clocks suggests that an imported tall clock similar to that made by Thomas Hughes was the prototype for the American tall clock purchased by Jonathan Sayward. The characteristics of the Hughes and Sayward clocks document the cultural ties in taste and technology between Great Britain and its colonies in New England.

1. *Historical Magazine*, 6, 2nd ser. (August 1869): 101; reprinted from the *Salem Gazette*, "A Visit to Cape Nedrick."

2. In the Society's files is a copy of Mary Barrell's 1884 inventory. Original at York County (Me.) Probate.

3. This note was written after learning of the death of an old friend, Brigadier General Jotham Moulton; Sayward Diary, American Antiquarian Society.

4. Herschel Burt of Exeter, N.H., cited the mounting of the bell post within the movement and the placement of the posts at the corners of the front and back plates as possible characteristics of American manufacture.

5. A ca. 1900 label inside the case gives the local tradition of ownership.

NOTES ON STRUCTURE AND CONDITION: The arched hood is of nailed and glued construction. The dome consists of three convex boards, a flat top, and a backboard. On either side of the dome, a thin pine board forms each roof of the bonnet and is nailed into place. The plinths are tenoned through the top of the hood. The arch of the hood door is composed of two lapped boards. An applied strip forms a threshold below the hood door and frees the door from scratching the molding beneath. A single backboard behind the bonnet conforms to the contour of the bonnet up to the molding below the dome.

The unsigned clock face has parts probably cast in England and assembled in this country. The dial is most unusual because the Arabic minute ring is as broad as the Roman hour ring. The brass finials are original but somewhat shortened.

The case is of thick boards; however, the pine backboard is thin, only ½ inch thick. Two flanking pine strips widen the backboard behind the hood, a common eighteenth-century practice. The case door, of one piece of wood 1 inch thick, has no wooden cleats; the thickness has deterred warping. The rails on the front of the waist are tenoned, but not pinned, to the stiles. The sides of the waist sit on the upper molding of the base section and are nailed to the rabbeted front edges of the stiles. Support blocks for these joints are within the waist. The base is similarly constructed; glue blocks reinforce the corners of the base.

The saddle board, to which the works are affixed, is a replacement. The upper edges of the case sides have been recut. The case bottom and the glue blocks in the base at the back are missing. The carved fretwork panels of the hood are lined with yellow silk. A series of inscriptions by people who cleaned the clock is on the inside of the door.

MATERIALS: Mahogany; birch saddle board; mahogany glue blocks; *white pine* other secondary wood. Original escutcheons, hinges, and locks.

PROVENANCE: The clock shares a provenance with tea chest no. 4.

ACCESSION: 1977.255   A gift of the heirs of Elizabeth Cheever Wheeler

55 / Tall Clock

1778–1781
Kittery, Maine
Works by Thomas Jakson (Jackson)
H. 88 (223.5), excluding finial 87⅝ (222.6); W. 23 (58.4); D. 12¹⁵/₁₆ (32.9)

This tall clock, signed "Thoˢ Jakson" (55a), further illustrates the relationship between English and American furniture. The brass eight-day movement behind the costly dial and cast rococo ornament was apparently made in America by a craftsman from England, Thomas Jackson (ca. 1733–1806).[1] Jackson had settled in Portsmouth by 1774 and may have been the "Workman from London" hired by Nathaniel Sheaff Griffith, a local clockmaker.[2] Between 1778 and 1781, "Mr. Thomas Jackson Clockmaker of Kittery" appears in accounts kept by Edward Sargent, a Portsmouth merchant.[3] Of the twelve

55

55a

known tall clocks with Jackson's name, two place the clockmaker in Portsmouth, and two — including the Society's clock — are inscribed "Kittery."[4] After the Revolution, Jackson moved to Preston, Connecticut, near Norwich, where he resided until his death. Eight Jackson clocks marked "Preston" survive; one of them reads: "Thos Jackson In Preston From London."[5]

Whereas Jackson retained his London credentials, his clockworks were housed in cases with only a passing resemblance to London fashion. This clock relies for most of its decorative impact upon the shallow carved pinwheels popular on coastal furniture from southern Maine to northeastern Massachusetts. The scrolled pediment and bracket feet bespeak the case's late-eighteenth-century origin, but the squat proportions and short base draw on earlier design.[6] The superimposition of the bracket feet on a solid base adds to the awkwardness of the proportions. The side windows on the hood and especially the full rear columns contribute to a topheavy design. Clearly, this cherry case is far from high style.

The complex construction of the case (see *Notes on Structure and Condition*) indicates that it is the work of a craftsman unfamiliar with conventional clockcase construction, let alone with London fashion. Nevertheless, he cleverly worked out a viable, practical, albeit eccentric, method for the problem of encasing a clock.

1. Parsons, *New Hampshire Clocks*, 321.

2. *New Hampshire Gazette and Historical Chronicle* (Portsmouth), April 29, 1774, 4.

3. Edward Sargent, Account Book, 1771–1802, New Hampshire Historical Society, 4.

4. Eleven are cited by Jobe, "New Discoveries," 47. The twelfth was owned in Kittery in 1956, *Manchester* (N.H.) *Union Leader*, May 26, 1956, 1.

5. Chase, "Old Clocks," 100.

6. For a desk with squat proportions and a pinwheel at the center of its base, see *Antiques* 100 (August 1971): 155.

NOTES ON STRUCTURE AND CONDITION: The distinctive cabinetwork is exemplified by the stiles of the waist section, which extend to the floor. They are mortised and tenoned to the rails above and below the door. The stiles are also rabbeted and nailed to the sides, which are rabbeted to receive the back. The sides bear no weight and terminate within the base 5 inches above the floor. Wooden strips are nailed to each side of the top of the backboard to accommodate the width of the hood. The waist door is of one board, thumbnail molded and lipped on all four edges. The case never had a bottom.

The hood is of heavy construction. The rear columns are full, free-standing columns. A top is behind the pediment and is dovetailed to the sides of the hood. Two thin pine boards, forming the bonnet roof, are nailed to the pediment and a backboard. The glass in the door and in the windows on each side of the hood is original. The finial is a nineteenth-century replacement. The case was originally stained reddish-brown. A series of inscriptions by the men who cleaned the clock is on the inside of the door.

MATERIALS: *Cherry;* cherry glue blocks in the hood; *white pine* other secondary wood. Replaced escutcheons, hinges, and locks.

PROVENANCE: Purchased in the twentieth century from a Newburyport, Mass., antiques dealer by the Newbury dealer who sold it to Florence Evans Bushee.

ACCESSION: 1976.243   A gift of the estate of Florence Evans Bushee

Tables

56 / Table

1730–1770
Probably Connecticut
H. 27⅛ (68.9); W. 37¼ (94.6); D. 26⁵⁄₁₆ (66.8)

Unlike high chests, desks, or tall clocks, tables were used in any room of the house, sometimes in every room. In 1773 Benjamin Curtis, a feltmaker of Roxbury, Massachusetts, had:

> *. . . in the lower Room*
>   . . . 1 Mohog.^y Table 1:12/
>   . . . a tea Table 13/4^d 1 small d.^o 13/4^d
> *. . . in the front Chamber*
>   . . . Cham.^r Table 18/8^d
> *. . . in the back Chamber*
>   . . . a Table 8^d
> *. . . in the Kitchen*
>   . . . 2 Tables 7/4^d
>   a small Table 2/ . . . .[1]

Only Curtis's shop and garret were without some sort of table.

To inventory takers and furniture makers, tables went by many names, denoting their many shapes (round, oval, square), sizes (large, small, 3-foot, 4-foot), purposes (dining, tea, card, backgammon), woods (oak, pine, maple), and even their construction (one-leaf, turned top). No table, however, went by the name most often used today for the table shown here: "tavern table."

"Thre tables, eleven Chairs" were in the "Bar Room" of Nathaniel Ames, a physician in Dedham, Massachusetts.[2] (More than one occupation was standard in 1764, but combining those of tavern keeper and physician evokes images of Ames curing with drink what his library of "Physick" could not.) In 1692, Samuel Ruggles, an "Inholder" of Roxbury, Massachusetts, had:

> *In the Parlour*
>   . . . a Table . . .
> *In the Little New Room; . . .*
>   a Square Table . . .
> *In the old Kitchen; . . .*
>   a Table . . .
> *In New House below;*
>   a table . . .
> *In the Chamber [having the best bed], . . .*
>   2 tables . . . ;

Ruggles's tavern also was without a "tavern table."[3]

Undoubtedly some tables like this one, especially those without drawers, were in taverns; most, however, furnished residences. Many household inventory citations of "square" tables probably refer to this form. "Square," frequently used in the early eighteenth century when few if any tables were made with square tops, referred not to the shape of the top but to the shape of the "squared" corners.

The simply constructed tables — four legs joined to rails and stretchers, with a top pinned on and a drawer inserted — were popular for over a century with only minor stylistic changes. Thick turned legs were fashionable in the seventeenth century; thinner legs, turned or Marlborough, were commonplace in the next. The tops of most tables measured about 3 feet wide, though much larger versions were occasionally made. James

Rundlet, a Portsmouth merchant, acquired a 6-foot table of painted pine (56a) for the kitchen of the house he built in 1806.

Hundreds of New England examples of this utilitarian form survive. This table is distinctive in two ways. The turnings, though of a typical pattern, are particularly bold and well executed. The woods, instead of the usual maple and pine, are tulipwood and sassafras.

The recent history of the table suggests a Connecticut origin. Tulipwood (known in the eighteenth century as whitewood) and sassafras are native to Connecticut and were used there in the construction of such furniture as small "square" tables. For example, the inventory of Stephen Douglas (1719–1748) of New London, Connecticut, included turning tools and "400 feet of maple, 500 feet of whitewood timber, 2 table frames."[4]

56a. Table. Portsmouth, 1790–1810. White pine; H. 27⅝ (70.2); W. 58⅞ (149.5); D. 29 (73.7). Society for the Preservation of New England Antiquities. *The front stretcher is missing.*

1. Cummings, *Inventories,* 253–55.
2. Ibid., 210–11.
3. Ibid., 66–69.
4. "Connecticut Cabinetmakers, Part 1," 121.

NOTES ON STRUCTURE AND CONDITION: The two-board top is pinned to the joined frame and never had cleated edges. A quarter-round bead is cut on the edges of the stretchers and on the lower edge of the front rail. The thumbnail-molded edge on the drawer front overlaps the frame only at the sides. The drawer elements are thick, the dovetails broad. The bottom fits into grooves in the front and sides; the drawer originally ran on its sides but now has added runners.

The table is in good condition except for warpage to the top and wear to the feet and stretchers. The original red paint, although worn, survives on the frame.

MATERIALS: *Sassafras* legs and stretchers; *tulipwood* all other wood. Replaced wooden drawer knob.

PROVENANCE: The table came to the Society with a collection gathered largely in Connecticut in the early twentieth century.

ACCESSION: 1952.178   A bequest of Ruth Lee Griswold

57 / Table

1750–1770
New England
H. 26¾ (67.9); W. 31⅝ (80.3); D. 23⅛ (58.7)

This table is a dressy version of the ubiquitous, utilitarian, turned-leg, one-drawer table. The attractively turned legs and feet bring to mind pad-footed cabrioles. The drawer

57

has brass hardware, an expensive addition rarely seen on this form. This is clearly not a kitchen table but a bedchamber or parlor piece that served as a dressing, tea, or work table.

Single-drawer tables with splayed legs without stretchers are far less frequently seen than tables with stretchered vertical legs.[1] The two known tables with related turnings have no drawers.[2] Neither they nor the Society's table has a history to help indicate a more specific origin.

1. Number 126 in Greenlaw, *New England Furniture,* is another of this unusual type.

2. One at the Golden Ball Tavern, a historic house museum in Weston, Mass., was acquired locally; the other was advertised in *Antiques* 116 (December 1979): 1255.

NOTES ON STRUCTURE AND CONDITION: The drawer, including its sides and back, conforms to the splay of the legs. The two-board top is pinned to the joined frame. The thumbnail-molded edge on the drawer front is lipped only at the sides. Each drawer side has a double-arched top edge. The elements of the drawer are thick and joined with rather broad dovetails. The bottom is set into grooves in the front and sides.

Although the drawer front has split and several pins in the top have been replaced, the table is in very good condition. It retains its original red paint.

MATERIALS: *Hard maple; white pine* secondary wood. Original brass hardware; missing the lock.

PROVENANCE: The table came from the collection assembled by Chauncy C. Nash early in the twentieth century, principally of objects from coastal Massachusetts south of Boston, and descended to the donors.

ACCESSION: 1971.380 A gift of Mr. and Mrs. Stephen H. Nash in memory of Chauncy C. Nash

58 / Drop-Leaf Table

1715–1740
Boston area
H. 29¼ (74.3); W. 54½ (138.4); D. open 64⅝ (164.1), closed 21⅞ (55.6)

In the principal room of his house, John Welland, a Boston distiller, had "1 Eighth Day Clock with Walnut Case £30, a Large Looking Glass £16 . . . a Cane Couch[,] Squab & pillow £5.10/ . . . 1 Elbow & 6 small Cane Chairs at 30/" and three tables:

an oval Holland Table	30/
one Square Tea Table	10
1 la. [large] Walnut Oval Table	£5. [1]

Welland's large walnut oval table probably looked much like this one. In early-eighteenth-century Boston, drop-leaf tables with large oval tops and turned frames apparently were so common that the best table in just about every house fit the same description. Many tables with mirrored baluster turnings like those on this example survive, suggesting by their number that this turning was fashionable in Boston, then the most thriving and populous port in New England.[2]

The tables follow a pattern, but there are variations. The tops measure from 3 to 5½ feet. The largest tables occasionally have four swing legs.[3] A very few have Spanish feet.[4] Some have no feet on the pivot posts (see the next table). A few are maple or mahogany; the majority are black walnut.

The tables were the products of Boston chairmakers, whose busy shops produced chairs (such as 91a) and tables in volume for the home market and for export. These craftsmen, skilled at turning and joining, were not necessarily proficient at dovetailing. Many chairmakers' tables, like this one, have nailed — not dovetailed — drawers.[5]

Turned-leg, oval, drop-leaf tables were based on English models of the late seventeenth century. Fashionable in America by 1700, they remained stylish through the first four decades of the eighteenth. Today they are known as "gateleg" tables.

The drop-leaf table had many uses. To judge from inventory references, dining was probably primary. But it was also used for writing and other work. No other type of table could be indicated by this 1776 reference: "maple writing Table, turn'd Frame 2 Flaps 0:13:4."[6] When the table was in use, no matter what its function, the top was usually covered with a cloth. When it was not in use, the flaps or leaves were dropped and the table kept against the wall (58a). Such versatile tables were ideally suited to colonial living in rooms that, although sometimes cramped, served many purposes.

58a. "Mr. Foote in the Character of Major Sturgeon in The Mayor of Garratt." Published by John Boydell, engraved by T. G. Haid, London, 1765. Mezzotint engraving after a painting by John Zoffany; H. 16⅝ (42.2); W. 20 (50.8). Colonial Williamsburg Foundation. Photograph, Hans E. Lorenz.

1. Welland's 1737 inventory, old series, vol. 33, pp. 386–87, Suffolk County (Mass.) Probate.

2. Eighteen related tables are listed in the Society's files.

3. Nutting, *Pilgrim Century*, rev. ed., no. 716.

4. Ibid., no. 722.

5. The table advertised by Israel Sack, Inc., in *Antiques* 117 (February 1980): inside cover, has a nailed drawer, a history in the Boston area, and except for size is identical to the Society's.

6. Account of losses from the burning of Charlestown, June 17, 1775, Thad Mason Account, Boston Public Library.

NOTES ON STRUCTURE AND CONDITION: The feet are extensions of the legs except for the bases of the pivot legs, which are separate units tenoned into the stationary stretchers. The mutual edges of the top and the leaves are tongue-and-groove. The top is pinned to the joined frame. The drawer is nailed: the sides to the rabbeted edges of the front, the back to the rear edges of the sides, and the bottom to the rabbeted edges of the front and the flat edges of the sides and back. The drawer slides on a medial support.

The table was once taken apart and the surface refinished. The top and leaves are slightly warped; two braces are screwed to the underside of each leaf, and added screws hold the top to the frame. The drawer has been renailed.

MATERIALS: *Black walnut; white pine* secondary wood. Replaced hinges; never had a lock.

PROVENANCE: The table, part of an exceptional furniture collection assembled by Mary Thacher in the early twentieth century in Massachusetts, descended from Miss Thacher to the donor.

ACCESSION: 1971.65   A gift of Guido R. Perera

59 / Drop-Leaf Table

1730–1750
Probably York, Maine
H. 27⅛ (68.9); W. 47¾ (121.3); D. open 51⁹⁄₁₆ (131), closed 17⅛ (43.5)

Turnings, whether for chairs or tables, varied from area to area in the seventeenth and eighteenth centuries. The urn-and-baluster turnings on this drop-leaf differ notably from the mirrored baluster turnings on the previous example. Urn-and-baluster turnings, popular in England, are unusual in America except in New York.[1] The thin turnings on this table, however, are unlike English and New York examples.

More than turnings differentiate the previous table, made in Boston, from this one, made in York. This table is of birch not walnut, with pivot posts instead of full-height pivot legs, no rail above the drawer front, and a dovetailed, not a nailed, drawer.

The table descended with the Sayward family's house in York and may have belonged to Judge Jonathan Sayward's father, from whom the judge bought the house in 1735. A very similar example has been in the Old Gaol Museum in York since 1900. The presence of two tables with such distinctive turnings in one town suggests that they were made locally. Two turners worked in York in the early eighteenth century: John Donnell (1660–ca. 1744), whose father, Thomas (d. 1699), was also a turner, and John Sedgly, who was working from about 1715 to 1745.[2]

59

1. A walnut drop-leaf table with urn-and-baluster turnings with a New York history is illustrated by Morse, *Furniture*, rev. ed., 247–48.

2. The Donnells are listed in George Ernst, "Donnell Genealogy," an unpublished manuscript at the York library; Sedgly appears in an unpublished list compiled by Edwin A. Churchill, "Furniture Makers and Joiners of Early Maine," in the Society's files.

NOTES ON STRUCTURE AND CONDITION: Four pins hold the one-board top to the legs. Stops for the swing legs are glued and pinned to the underside of the leaves. The drawer bottom is set into a groove in the front and nailed into rabbets in the sides. The drawer slides on a medial support to which a drawer stop is glued and pinned.

The table, in very good condition, nevertheless shows general wear throughout: the top is refinished, and there are some splits in the top and leaves. The frame was painted or stained red and later black.

MATERIALS: *Birch; white pine* secondary wood. Replaced hinges.

PROVENANCE: The table descended with Jonathan Sayward's house. It may have belonged briefly to his apprentice and grandson-in-law Richard Keating and was returned to the house by Keating's widow. It belonged to the judge's great-granddaughters Elizabeth and Mary Barrell and then descended as did tea chest no. 4.

ACCESSION: 1977.266   A gift of the heirs of Elizabeth Cheever Wheeler

60 / Drop-Leaf Table

1740–1770
Newbury, Massachusetts
H. 27⅝ (70.2); W. 50¼ (127.6); D. open 48¼ (122.6), closed 17³⁄₁₆ (43.7)

In the 1730s the cabriole drop-leaf table supplanted its turned-leg counterpart. The stretcherless cabriole version was similarly placed within the house and similarly used. But it could not be similarly constructed. The absence of stretchers dictated by the new style precluded the use of a pivot post between stretcher and rail.

To redesign support for the leaves, craftsmen adopted an entirely new technique of construction. Only two legs, at diagonal corners, were made stationary. The other two were placed at the ends of swing rails, which in turn were hinged to the frame. With two of the four legs movable, the frame was far more fragile than one with four stationary legs. Whereas drop-leaf tables with turned legs were made with drawers, the less stable frames with two stationary cabrioles were not.

60

In the early years of the preference for cabrioles, round and oval tops remained fashionable. However, the contours of the edges of the top and leaves changed. An ovolo-molded outer edge replaced the flat or slightly rounded edge of earlier tables. The hinged edge was cut to a rule joint, replacing the tongue-and-groove in popularity. In 1757 a customer could get either joint: "Maple rule Joynt tables @ £6 Pr foot; old fashen Joynts @ £5.10."[1]

The tops of turned-leg tables were secured with wooden pins driven through the tops into the frames. For cabriole drop-leaf tables, craftsmen introduced invisible fastenings for the tops: screws set through the frame into the top or blocks glued to the frame and top. Wooden pins continued to be used on some less expensive cabriole tables of birch and maple, including this maple example.

The table descended in the Coffin family of Newbury and bears an old chalk inscription, "EC." Edmund Coffin (1764–1825) was twenty-one and still unmarried when he took possession of the north part of his father's house, the other two portions going to his widowed mother and older brother.[2] The table was probably made locally and purchased by Edmund's father, Joshua (1732–1774).

1. "Table of Prices for Joiners' Work," quoted in Lyon, *Colonial Furniture*, 3rd ed., 265.
2. Spring, "The Coffin House," 16–18.

NOTES ON STRUCTURE AND CONDITION: Thick skirts, each cut with a narrow ogee arch, are glued to the end rails. The top and leaves are each a single board. Six wooden pins secure the top. The condition of the table is excellent. The original brown stain or paint, worn on the top, remains on the frame.

MATERIALS: *Hard maple; cherry* side rails. Original hinges and screws.

PROVENANCE: The table descended to Edmund Coffin's widow, Lucy, to their unmarried daughter Lucy (1811–1893), and to the latter's niece Margaret Colman Merriam, the donor.

ACCESSION: 1963.128   A gift of Mrs. Arthur Merriam

61 / Drop-Leaf Table

1745–1775
Portsmouth area, possibly Berwick, Maine
H. 27¾ (70.5); W. 47¹³⁄₁₆ (121.4); D. open 46¾ (118.7), closed 16½ (41.9)

The maker of this table developed an unusual, possibly unique, solution to the problem of joining the table top to the base invisibly. Other craftsmen secured tops to cabriole bases using a series of glue blocks or screws or both. On this table and on three others known to the authors, a single large block in each corner is glued to the top and wood-pinned to the frame (61a).[1]

61

The overall design of the table is not unusual. The shape of the cabrioles, far less rigid than those on tables no. 60 and 62, is often seen. Sharply creased knees are frequently found on Chippendale furniture, especially on pieces from Essex County, Massachusetts. However, the design of the pad feet — a complete ring-turning above the disk — is distinctive. A walnut table with a marble top at the Winterthur Museum has similar feet, is stamped "I Hill," and probably belonged to either Isaac Hill (ca. 1724–1806 or 1807) of Kittery or John Hill (1703–1772) of neighboring Berwick, Maine.[2] John purchased some furniture from Timothy Davis (d. 1772), a joiner born in Portsmouth who was John's neighbor in Berwick after 1729.[3]

The Society's table is inscribed under the top "Sheply Ricker's Table / So Berwick / Me." One Shipley Ricker was a Berwick selectman in 1868–1869; a namesake lived into the twentieth century. The Ricker family did not collect antiques; instead, in the twentieth century, they sold the furniture they inherited with the Ricker homestead in South Berwick.

61a

"Queen Anne and Chippendale Furniture," pt. 1, 900–901, 903. In Portsmouth there was a fashion for stamping furniture with the owner's name: see Kaye, "Marked Portsmouth Furniture." For Isaac Hill, see Stackpole, *Old Kittery*, 517, 519; for John Hill, see Hummel, "Queen Anne and Chippendale Furniture," pt. 1.

3. Hummel, "Queen Anne and Chippendale Furniture," pt. 1, 903.

NOTES ON STRUCTURE AND CONDITION: There is no applied skirt. The top and leaves are each of a single board. The feet once had casters. The table, in excellent structural condition, was refinished in 1976.

MATERIALS: Mahogany; *birch* hinge rails; *white pine* other secondary wood. Original hinges and screws.

PROVENANCE: The table came from the Ricker family of South Berwick; possibly it was sold early in this century by Jennie De Rochemont Ricker and was eventually purchased by Florence Evans Bushee.

ACCESSION: 1976.233   A gift of the estate of Florence Evans Bushee

1. An almost identical walnut table was sold by Sotheby Parke Bernet, sale 4478Y, November 1980, lot 1322; a smaller but otherwise identical version is privately owned; a related example with claw-and-ball feet is at the New Hampshire Historical Society (1940.14.1).

2. The table (Downs, *Queen Anne and Chippendale*, no. 353) is discussed further in Hummel,

62 / Drop-Leaf Table

1755–1770
York, Maine
Attributed to Samuel Sewall
H. 28¼ (71.8); W. 47⅝ (121); D. open 48¹³⁄₁₆ (124), closed 17⅛ (43.5)

Judge Jonathan Sayward's house contained many tables. An 1884 inventory lists:

> Pine table
> 1 – 3 draw Table [$] 2.50 [dressing table no. 33]
> 1 Narrow table . . .
> 1 Mahog. Parlor table 5.00 [tea table no. 68, seen in photograph 62a]
> 1 Centre table $5. [the tilt-top table in 62a]
> 1 sq table (Mahog) 5.00 [table no. 62, also in 62a]
> 1 Mahog Card Table 2.00 [no. 69]
> 2 Tables 1.50
> 2 Tables 6.00
> 2 Tables 1.25
> Mahog. Entry Table 2.00
> 1 Centre Table 2.50 [probably no. 59]
> 1 2 leaf Table 3.00 [a Marlborough-leg drop-leaf][1]

This drop-leaf cabriole table was the "1 sq table (Mahog)."

62

All but two of Sayward's tables remain in the house; seven have leaves and five of them were made in one shop. Their swing hinge rails and swing legs are joined in an unusual manner (see *Notes on Structure and Condition* and 62b). Most are marked with chalk "V"s (like that beneath chest no. 21; see detail 21a). These tables, like chest no. 21, are the work of Samuel Sewall of York.

Two of the tables stand on angular cabriole legs resembling those of Sewall's dressing table (no. 33). But the shape of the legs on this table is quite different. Sewall's early work, like his dressing table, is of a naive cabriole style we can call "Sewall's Queen Anne period." His later work, "Sewall's Chippendale period," is more sophisticated and is exemplified by chest no. 21, card table no. 69, this drop-leaf table, and a related one at the Moffatt-Ladd House in Portsmouth, which has an oval top and claw-and-ball feet.

During both periods, Sewall's cabinetry for Sayward, a lumber merchant, is distinguished by superb, often highly figured woods. The walnut veneer on his high chest (plate 6) is spectacular. On this table, the swirling crotch mahogany top and leaves are stunning. No other table top in the Society's collection displays such dramatic figure.

While the legs on this table resemble those on the Coffin table (no. 60), a comparison of the two points up the superb design of this applied skirt and the importance of skirt design to the beauty of a table. The wood and skirt make this an exceptionally handsome Chippendale drop-leaf. The legs are well designed (especially when compared with the "horsebones" of Sewall's Queen Anne period),[2] but lack the graceful, flowing lines of the cabrioles seen on the next two tables.

1. Mary Barrell's inventory: manuscript copy in the Society's files, original at York County (Me.) Probate.

2. "Horsebones" is among the early terms for cabriole legs; see entry 30.

NOTES ON STRUCTURE AND CONDITION: The frame is constructed in an unusual manner, which sets this and other Sewall drop-leaf tables apart. The swing hinge rail is thinner than the top of the leg. When the swing leg is closed, the swing hinge rail is not parallel to the side rail (compare 62b with detail 63a). The top is set slightly askew to compensate for the rails not being parallel. See *Notes on Structure and Condition* for table no. 64 and detail 64b for a better solution.

The top and leaves are each of one board. The condition of the table is excellent except for minor

62a. Photograph of Table No. 62 in situ. York, Maine, ca. 1875. Photographic Archives, Society for the Preservation of New England Antiquities.

62b

woodworm damage. All original elements, including seventeen blocks glued to the top and frame, survive.

MATERIALS: *Mahogany; birch* hinge rails; white pine other secondary wood. Original hinges and screws.

PROVENANCE: The table shares a provenance with tea chest no. 4.

ACCESSION: 1977.257　　A gift of the heirs of Elizabeth Cheever Wheeler

63 / Drop-Leaf Table

1770
Boston
George Bright
H. 28¾ (73); W. 45 (114.3); D. open 44¹³⁄₁₆ (113.8), closed 16¼ (41.3)

Here is one of the "2 Dineing Tables 3 foot 9 ^{inch} Squair aᵗ 48/ ——[£]4:16:0" for which George Bright billed Jonathan Bowman in 1770 (bill 15a).

By purchasing two drop-leaf tables, Bowman could enjoy the greater versatility afforded by their square tops. Not only could they be used individually, like the oval or round tops that they superseded in the late Chippendale era, but they could be placed against one another to form a much larger table. Most square tops were made with flat outer edges, which, unlike the ovolo edges fashionable on oval and round table tops, butt neatly.

Only one of Bowman's tables survives. It and its bill are valuable furniture documents. They date the design, place it in Boston, indicate what 48 shillings could buy, and reveal the drop-leaf design and construction of George Bright (63a). Other tables may now be attributed to that time, town, and craftsman.[1]

The design of the feet, seen on many pieces of furniture made in the Boston area, is especially interesting, for it proves a theory of Randall's.[2] He pointed out that "chairs with this foot have often been dated before 1760 and are generally thought to be earlier than claw-and-ball examples. They are, in fact, of the same period." Both were cut from stock of the same size and represent the two common options available to the customer.

This table (like the Bowman chest of drawers, no. 15) reinforces our impression of Bright as a capable craftsman who could transform fine woods — in this case, dense figured mahogany — into handsome shapes. The subtle curve of the legs flows gracefully into simple, bold knee brackets and on to the peak of an ogee arch. The table is the epitome of fine furniture from eastern Massachusetts.

63

1. For example, a table in the Society's collection (1933.6042) and another illustrated in *Maine Antique Digest*, April 1983, 37-C.

2. Randall, *American Furniture*, 192, no. 154.

NOTES ON STRUCTURE AND CONDITION: Knee brackets are glued to the legs and end rails. The top and leaves are each a single board. The top is secured to the frame with a series of horizontal glue blocks. An additional vertical block is set behind each dovetail joint in the frame.

The table is in excellent condition. All but one of the original supporting blocks survive.

MATERIALS: *Mahogany; birch* hinge rails; *white pine* other secondary wood. Original hinges, three of which are marked "RF" (see *Materials* under the Pembroke table, no. 66), and original screws.

PROVENANCE: The table shares a provenance with chest of drawers no. 15.

ACCESSION: 1980.78   A gift of Florence L. Bixby

63a

64 / Drop-Leaf Table

1760–1775
Coastal Essex County, Massachusetts, probably Newburyport
H. 27 5/16 (69.4); W. 48 1/8 (122.2); D. open 48 13/16 (124), closed 18 5/8 (47.3)

On this attractive "Four foot Mehogany Table w. Claw feet," shaped end rails gracefully arch the span between the cabrioles without either the applied skirts or applied knee brackets seen on the preceding two tables.[1] Handsome cabrioles, slender claw feet, and richly figured woods make it the most elegant of the Society's many drop-leaf tables. Table frames with similar end rails and knees were occasionally made with round tops,[2] and a few related frames have pad feet, the less expensive alternative.[3]

The Society's table is as skillfully made as it is designed (see *Notes on Structure and Condition* and 64a). Although more sophisticated than table no. 60, this example shares a history with it. Both descended in the Coffin family of Newbury, Massachusetts, and may have originally belonged to Joshua (1732–1774), a prosperous tanner. He appar-

64

ently obtained the tables from different craftsmen, for this example seems to be the work of a more adept individual.

Of the few similar tables with clear histories, the most closely related one reportedly was owned by Offin Boardman of Newburyport.[4] A shipbuilding center, Newburyport separated from its parent, Newbury, in 1764 and burgeoned over the next few decades as newly wealthy merchants built large and splendid mansions, the furnishing of which provided work for many cabinetmakers. Their products were stylish and well crafted. The table's documented provenance and high quality of workmanship make it easy to believe that this drop-leaf was made near the mouth of the Merrimack.

1. A contemporary table was so described in John Baker's 1780 inventory, old series, vol. 79, p. 427, Suffolk County (Mass.) Probate.

2. For a related round-top table, see Randall, *American Furniture*, no. 87.

3. *Israel Sack Collection*, 2:561.

4. Francis P. Garvan Collection, American Art Association, sale 3878, January 1931, lot 275.

NOTES ON STRUCTURE AND CONDITION: The method of construction permits the use of thin hinge rails. Two blocks are set between each thin hinge rail and side rail. The outer surfaces of the leg and the swing hinge rail are thus flush, yet when the table is closed, the inner surface of each leg fits against the side rail, and the hinge rails remain parallel to the top. The technique is an efficient solution to a common problem confronted by New England craftsmen.

The top and leaves are of a single board. Four screws secure the frame to the top. Two support blocks are present: a vertical glue block behind each dovetail joint, binding the end and side rails.

The table is in excellent condition; damage and repairs are minor.

MATERIALS: *Mahogany; hard maple* hinge rails;

white pine other secondary wood. Original hinges and screws.

PROVENANCE: The table descended in the family of Joshua Coffin, probably to his widow, Sarah, to their son Edmund (1764–1825), to the latter's widow, Lucy, to their daughter Lucy (1811–1893), and to her niece, the donor.

ACCESSION: 1963.110   A gift of Mrs. Arthur Merriam

64a

65 / Drop-Leaf Table

1785–1805
Coastal Massachusetts, probably south of Boston
H. 27½ (69.9); W. 47 (119.4); D. open 46⅛ (117.2), closed 15 (38.1)

Mr. & Mrs. John B. Barstow lived and prospered in the town of Hanover, south of Boston, on the North River. John (1764–1854) was a shipbuilder, farmer, and politician;

65

Betsey (1760–1851) was the daughter of a wealthy blacksmith who, with John's father, owned the shipyard.[1] They married in 1788, set up housekeeping at Broad Oak Farm in 1792, and expanded the house in 1797. Any of these events may have occasioned their purchase of this table, a drop-leaf typical of the 1788–1797 era, when straight, unturned, Marlborough legs were the height of fashion.

The squared skirt, the simple scribed outline on the bottom edge of the end rails, as well as the molded Marlborough legs bespeak the new rectilinear style that descended directly, albeit modestly, from English designs of Chinese inspiration (see 66a). Although a square-top table, it was never intended to serve as one of a pair. The outer edges of the top, unlike those on the preceding square tables, are molded to an ogee.

1. Barry, *Historical Sketch*, 162, 163, 227.

NOTES ON STRUCTURE AND CONDITION: The side rails do not extend as low as the hinge rails or end rails. The hinge rails are as thick as the legs. The bottom of the legs are edged with a thick chamfer. The top and leaves are of one board each. Six screws secure the frame to the top; no support blocks are present.

The table is in excellent condition, though some elements are warped.

MATERIALS: Mahogany; *beech* hinge rails; *white pine* side rails. Replaced hinges and screws.

PROVENANCE: John B. Barstow left his furniture to be distributed among his six children by having them draw lots. The table remained at Broad Oak Farm, where John's daughter Salome Barstow Torrey (1801–1878) continued to live and which her sons Benjamin (1837–1905) and Herbert (1841–1905) inherited. The donor bought the farmhouse and its contents from Benjamin.

ACCESSION: 1928.1307   A gift of L. Vernon Briggs

66 / Pembroke Table

1770
Boston
George Bright
H. 28 (71.1); W. 30³⁄₁₆ (76.7); D. open 38⅞ (98.7), closed 22 (55.9)

This handsome table, the epitome of the rectilinear Chippendale design seen in the preceding drop-leaf table, is the "Pembroke Table" George Bright sold to Jonathan Bowman for £2:0:0 in 1770. The table and its bill (15a) show that the Pembroke form was made in Boston as early as 1770, that the term "Pembroke" already denoted the form, and that the Boston Pembroke was designed and constructed like English examples of the period.

The Pembroke form — two leaves, four fixed legs, and swing rails but not swing legs — became popular at the end of the eighteenth century. Few Pembroke tables from America's colonial era survive, and this one may be unique in its documentation to pre-Revolutionary New England.

The 1770 reference to "Pembroke" is noteworthy. Thomas Chippendale, in the 1754 edition of his *Director,* calls the form "Breakfast" table (66a), a term he retained in the 1762 edition and in a 1765 bill for a table with "a Drawer and a Shelf underneath."[1] "Breakfast" table was current in Boston as well. A 1772 Philadelphia price book uses "Pembroke" and "breakfast" interchangeably.[2]

George Bright probably used an imported English table as a prototype for this one, for it resembles contemporaneous English tables in design and construction. As in many English examples, screws reinforce the tenons holding the shelf to the legs (66b).

Bowman probably placed the Pembroke in one of his parlors. Eighteenth-century parlors not only served as sitting rooms but were equipped as well for enjoying large meals or light repasts.

> In the Parlour . . .
> 1 Walnut Dining Table   :12:–
> 1 Meohogany Breakfast D°   : 4:–[3]

66

Bowman, like his English contemporaries, would have breakfasted at his table (as Chippendale's term suggests) but also would have used it for reading and writing (as do Dr. and Mrs. John Brewster of Hampton, Connecticut, 66c).

1. Bill, Chippendale to Sir Lawrence Dundas, November 6, 1765, cited by Gilbert, *Thomas Chippendale,* 1:160.

2. Weil, "Price Book," 186.

3. Mrs. Elizabeth Trefry's 1770 inventory, old series, vol. 69, p. 77, Suffolk County (Mass.) Probate.

NOTES ON STRUCTURE AND CONDITION. The shelf consists of two lapped boards held where they lap with two original round-headed screws. The wooden brace beneath the center of the lapped shelf is a later addition. The top and leaves are each one board. A series of small horizontal glue blocks secure the top to the frame. Each leaf is supported by two swing rails hinged to the side rails. The dovetailed drawer slides on a drawer support nailed to each side rail. Drawer stops are nailed to the side rails at the back corners of the frame. The

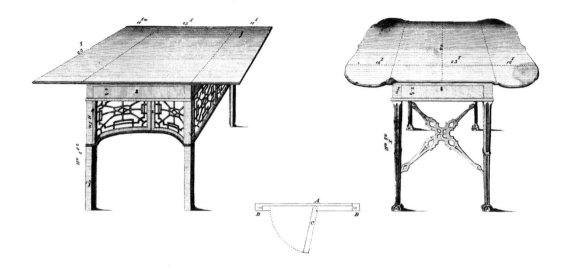

66a. Design for a Table. Chippendale, *The Director*, 1st ed., 1754, pl. 53. Society for the Preservation of New England Antiquities Library.

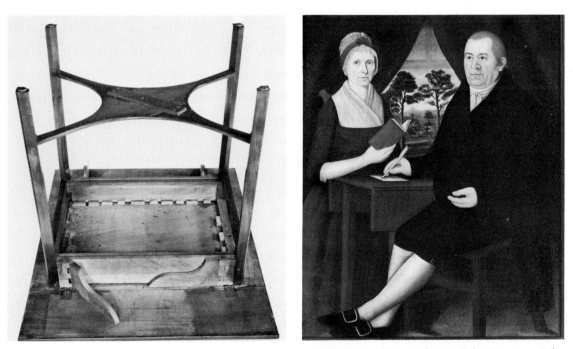

66b

66c. Portrait of Dr. and Mrs. John Brewster. John Brewster, Jr. (1766–1854), probably Hampton, Connecticut, 1790–1800. Oil on canvas; H. 49⅝ (126.0); W. 40½ (102.9). Old Sturbridge Village.

drawer bottom is nailed to the rabbeted edges of the front and sides and has no applied runners.

The table, in excellent condition, retains all but three of its original glue blocks.

MATERIALS: *Mahogany; birch* side and swing rails; *white pine* other secondary wood. Original brass escutcheon, steel lock, and iron hinges and screws. All hinges are marked "RF"; one hinge is also marked "FILDUS."

PROVENANCE: The table shares a provenance with chest of drawers no. 15.

ACCESSION: 1980.77   A gift of Florence L. Bixby

67 / Tea Table

1755–1765
Boston
H. 26⁷⁄₁₆ (67.2); W. 29¹⁄₈ (74); D. 20³⁄₄ (52.7)

The accouterments of tea drinking required a keeping place, which, to judge from eighteenth-century inventories, was the top of a "china," or "tea," table.

> In the Eastermost Lower Room, or Parlour
> a Jappand Tea Table wth 9 Cups & Saucers 1 Tea Pott &
> Stand 1 Slop Dish & Plate 1 Saucer 1 Milk Pott & 1
> Sugar Pott & 1 Boat all of China   [£]6:10:–.[1]

Some tables were japanned; a few had stone or tile tops; most were of varnished wood. Those with rectangular tops had four fixed legs, but most tea tables were round and stood on pillar-and-tripod bases (tables no. 72–74). To protect the china, rectangular tops had molded edges (like this one) or galleries (I-36), and some round tables had dished tops (table no. 74).

This tea table, which descended in the Barrett family of New Ipswich, New Hampshire, probably belonged to Charles and Rebecca Barrett and was purchased at about the time of their marriage in Concord, Massachusetts, in 1764. They needed a tea table to set up a proper household and apparently bought theirs in Boston, the port city that set the style for Concord. Sarah Bradly and John Fulton, Bostonians who married two years earlier, owned an almost identical table, with the added detail of a slide in each end rail.[2]

The Barrett and Fulton tea tables were based on Chinese and English forebears, for tea equipage followed the same route as tea, from the Orient to England to England's colonies. Oriental trays with lipped edges and indented corners were, no doubt, the source for the traylike tops of this table and its English cousins (I-18).[3] The Chinese influence on the design of rectangular tea tables in Boston is most apparent on examples with straight skirts (I-19).

Boston tea tables, while based on Chinese and English furniture, would never be mistaken for foreign products. The Barrett tea table epitomizes the Boston cabriole style in the shape of the feet, the stance of the legs, and the scallop of the skirt.[4] Many

67

comparable tables were made, for the style was popular from about 1740 until the Revolution. Few, however, are the equal of this handsome example.

1. The 1735 inventory of a Boston merchant, Arthur Savage, old series, vol. 32, p. 204, Suffolk County (Mass.) Probate.

2. *Thirtieth Report of the Record Commissioners*, 347, gives the date for the marriage of the owners of the table, number P3757 in *Israel Sack Collection*, 4:975.

3. See an English-owned tray that was made in Java, *Furniture History*, fig. 89.

4. A large marble-top side table at the Lee Mansion, Marblehead Historical Society, with an oral history of coming from Boston, has a skirt of the same pattern.

NOTES ON STRUCTURE AND CONDITION: Mortise-and-tenon joints bind the rails to the legs. A scal-loped skirt is glued to each rail and a thin bead is glued and nailed just above the skirt. The rabbeted edges of the top are rounded to a bead and extend beyond the rails. The indented corners of the molding applied to the top are separate pieces.

The frame originally had a vertical glue block in each corner and a medial brace nailed into slots in the long rails. Three blocks have been replaced, and the brace has been augmented by flanking supports nailed into the rails. One leg was repaired at the knee. By 1976 the table had become badly bleached and was refinished.

MATERIALS: *Mahogany; hard maple* medial brace; white pine corner blocks.

PROVENANCE: The table apparently descended with the furnishings of Charles Barrett, Sr., to his widow, Rebecca; in 1838 to her daughter-in-law Martha Minot Barrett; and in 1842 to one of the latter's children. Objects that went to Mary Ann Barrett passed to her daughter Sarah Jane Bullard, to Laura Barr, and to the donor; objects that went to George or Charles Barrett passed to George R. Barrett and then to the donor.

ACCESSION: 1948.150   A gift of Caroline Barr Wade; conserved through the generosity of Dr. David C. Marshall

68 / Tea Table

1755–1770
Coastal New England from Boston to York, probably Boston
H. 27 (68.6); W. 28¹⁵/₁₆ (73.5); D. 21³/₁₆ (53.8)

Subtle differences distinguish this handsome tea table from the preceding one: the rail — not an applied molding — forms the skirt, the skirt differs slightly in outline, a molding is applied beneath the top, and the legs are broader. Tea tables with shaped rails are more unusual than those with applied skirts. Only three related tables are known, neither with any documentation.[1] Although this table has two hundred years of documented history, the specific place of manufacture remains uncertain.

68

This was Jonathan Sayward's best tea table and was photographed in the parlor of his house in York, Maine, during the 1870s (see photograph 62a). Apparently it had stood in that room since the judge purchased it. Sayward acquired his furniture in two distinct periods. The walnut furniture, probably bought in the 1740s, included a tea table that was used in the sitting room in the nineteenth century.[2] Later, between about 1755 and 1767, when he was renovating his house, Sayward added mahogany furniture in the Chippendale style, much of which apparently furnished the best parlor. This tea table was an important part of those acquisitions and may have been purchased in 1759, the year Sayward bought his tea chest (no. 4).

Most likely the tea table was made in Boston, which Sayward frequently visited and where he bought his tea chest and easy chair (no. 101). Knee brackets of the same shape as those on the tea table were used by the Boston cabinetmaker George Bright on a drop-leaf table (no. 63).

A possible origin along the coast north of Boston, however, cannot be ruled out. In his diary, Sayward notes many visits to Newbury, Portsmouth, and Cape Ann. He had financial and personal ties with Portsmouth through the Portsmouth merchant Nathaniel Barrell, who married Sayward's only child. And then, most of Sayward's furniture — cases, tables, and chairs — were made in York.

1. A table in Cheek, "Rare Gift to Stratford Hall"; a table in the Herbert Lawton Collection, American Art Association, sale 4314, April 1937, lot 209; and a table advertised in *Antiques* 72 (November 1957): 384.

2. The 1901 appraisal of the estate of George Octavius Barrell in the Society's files indicates that a black walnut tea table in the sitting room left the house at that time as partial payment to the appraiser. Lot 1008, Sotheby Parke Bernet, sale 4478Y, November 1980, may well be that table; it is now in a private collection.

NOTES ON STRUCTURE AND CONDITION: Mortise-and-tenon joints, each joint secured with a single pin, bind the rails to the legs. Knee brackets are glued to the rails. The rabbeted edges of the two-board top are rounded to a bead and extend beyond the rails. A narrow cove molding is nailed to the rails just below the top. A wide molded lip is nailed to the top; the indented corners are separate pieces. Paired vertical blocks are glued at each corner of the frame.

The table is in good condition with few signs of wear except for the top of one leg, which was broken and patched with maple strips above and behind the knee.

MATERIALS: *Mahogany; white pine* corner blocks.

PROVENANCE: This tea table apparently shares a provenance with tea chest no. 4.

ACCESSION: 1977.208   A gift of the heirs of Elizabeth Cheever Wheeler

69 / Card Table

1760–1775
York, Maine
Attributed to Samuel Sewall
H. 29¾ (75.6); W. 33 (83.8); D. open 33¹¹⁄₁₆ (85.6), closed 16⅞ (42.9)

The preceding tea table and this card table were acquired by Jonathan Sayward in an era when card playing and tea drinking were fashionable domestic pastimes. The passion

69

for card playing, like the fashion for tea drinking, required a special table. Card table tops were often made with optional features reflecting their function: dished corners to hold candlesticks (to illumine the playing cards), scooped receptacles for gaming counters, and recessed center surfaces covered with fabric (I-25). These features were popular on cabriole card tables; they rarely appear on ones with Marlborough legs and are not present on Sayward's.

Like virtually all New England card tables, Sayward's has a folding top and swing leg. Card tables, like most furniture, were kept against the wall when not in use, as shown by contemporary housekeeping advice:

> One of the most useful directions [to a new servant] is that of putting away chairs, tables, and anything that goes next to the wall, with the hand behind it. For want of this trifling attention, great pieces are frequently knocked out of the stucco and [furnishings] leave a mark on the wall.[1]

Card playing and tea drinking were parlor or sitting room activities. Sayward had two tea tables, one in the parlor and one in the sitting room; his one card table was kept in the entry hall between the two rooms.[2] His diary, full of business matters and brief on social activities, does not mention card playing, although it probably formed part of his many "entertainments" and "agreeable visits" with family, friends, and traveling notables.

At about the same time Sayward purchased this card table, he bought a large drop-leaf table with Marlborough legs. Both tables are of the same "plum pudding" mahogany (some of which was also used on his chest, no. 21), both have molded legs of similar contour (very different from the common molded contour seen on table no. 65), and both were made with the same unusual arrangement of hinge and side rails as characterizes the cabriole drop-leaf tables in Sayward's house (see *Notes on Structure and Condition* for table no. 62 and detail 62b). All are undoubtedly by the same maker, Samuel Sewall.

1. Susanna Whatman, *Housekeeping Book,* a mid-eighteenth-century publication, as quoted by Harrison, *People and Furniture,* 86–87.

2. Eighteenth-century records do not cite location, but nineteenth-century inventories of the house make this clear.

NOTES ON STRUCTURE AND CONDITION: The table is constructed like a drop-leaf table; the leaf is supported by a swing leg. The drawer dovetails are thick. The drawer bottom is set into grooves in the front and sides and fastened to the back with wooden pins. The thumbnail-molded edges of the drawer front form a lip at the sides and top. The one-board top is fastened to the frame by means of two front-to-back braces, tenoned into the frame, and screwed to the top. No glue blocks are used. The one-board leaf is hinged to the top with rule hinges.

Virtually all the original elements of the table survive in good condition.

MATERIALS: *Mahogany; basswood* drawer supports and braces for top; *soft maple* swing rail; *white pine* other secondary wood. Original brass handle; replaced hinges.

PROVENANCE: The card table shares a provenance with tea chest no. 4.

ACCESSION: 1977.241   A gift of the heirs of Elizabeth Cheever Wheeler

70 / Card Table

1780–1800
Newport
H. 29⁷⁄₁₆ (74.8); W. 36¹¹⁄₁₆ (93.2); D. open 30¼ (76.8), closed 15⅛ (38.4)

This beautiful interpretation of a common form, as superbly made as it is designed, originated in Newport. The motifs — stop fluting, rope carving, fretwork brackets, and gouged notches — were repeatedly used by Newport craftsmen on their finest furniture. The workmanship — the skillful cut of the carvings, the fine dovetails binding the left and rear rails, and the neatly made glue blocks — is consistent with the best Newport cabinetwork.

70

The design, harmonizing straight and curved lines, epitomizes the restraint and delicacy characteristic of New England furniture. While some of the lightness bespeaks the late-eighteenth-century neoclassical style, the primary influence is the New England penchant for the modest and diminutive. (Philadelphia and New York tables of the era are decidedly heavier.) The straight legs and fretwork brackets are in the Chinese Chippendale style, yet no Chippendale plate or English table served as a prototype. The handsome design was apparently developed by Newport craftsmen.

Card tables made in the surrounding area echoed the Newport pattern. A related table with tapering legs, not the equal to this one in its construction, has a Providence history.[1] Even among Newport tables, variations in the general design occur: some examples have molded legs, different knee brackets, or straight skirts. And the construction of the tables occasionally varies.[2]

This table is virtually identical to five others, two of which are a pair (card tables were often sold in pairs).[3] Although none has a specific Rhode Island provenance, the Society's has a close geographic association with Newport in the nineteenth century; it was then on Nantucket.

Myron S. Dudley (1837–1905), a Congregational minister, lived in Otego, New York; Peachum, Vermont; Cromwell, Connecticut; and in North Wilbraham, Massachusetts; finally settling on Nantucket. He apparently acquired the table while living on the island, where he became noted for his antiquarian interests. Among the antique furniture in his Nantucket house (70a) was this card table, which, in late-nineteenth-century fashion, was set catercorner with its leaf raised and its top serving as a display shelf.

70a. Photograph of Card Table No. 70 in situ. Nantucket, Massachusetts, 1880–1900. Photographic Archives, Society for the Preservation of New England Antiquities.

1. *Israel Sack Collection*, 6:1456.

2. For example, the tables made by the noted Newport craftsman John Townsend differ noticeably in construction with this example. See *Notes on Structure and Condition* and Moses, "Authenticating John Townsend's Later Tables."

3. The pair, formerly in the Taradash Collection, is Carpenter, *Arts and Crafts of Newport*, fig. 67. The three other tables are: one in *Antiques* 105 (May 1974): 948; one at the Winterthur Museum

(M53.93.2); and number 657 in the Girl Scouts Loan Exhibition catalogue.

NOTES ON STRUCTURE AND CONDITION: The front and side rails are shaped on both the façade and lower edge. Rope carving edges the skirt and a rope-carved bead is glued to the legs. Original knee brackets, embellishing the front legs only, are held in place with two small forged finishing nails each. The bottom edges of each leg are slightly chamfered. The table is constructed like a drop-leaf table; the leaf is supported by a swing leg. A thin block is set between the rear rail and the fixed hinge rail. Nails pass through the rear rail, block, and fixed hinge rail. A vertical quarter-round block is glued behind the dovetail joint holding the left side and the rear rail. A feature seen on some Newport work — cross braces dovetailed into the rails — does not appear on this table. Thirteen horizontal glue blocks secure the top to the frame. The top and leaf, each of one board, have rule hinges.

The condition of the table is superb.

MATERIALS: *Mahogany; Spanish cedar* swing rail; *white pine* other secondary wood. Replaced hinges.

PROVENANCE: Mary Marrett Dudley, the widow of the Reverend Mr. Myron Dudley, took the card table to the Marrett House, Standish, Me., and it descended with the house to the donor.

ACCESSION: 1959.327   A gift of Frances S. Marrett

71 / Toilet Table

1790–1810
Portsmouth
H. 31½ (80); W. 36⅖₁₆ (92.2); D. 21³⁄₁₆ (53.8)

Toilet tables were cloth-covered dressing tables. Designed to be draped in "Silk, Sattins, Velvet or Tissue,"[1] they were of simple form and soft woods (this one is of spruce and

71

pine). The portrait of the elegant Anna Wendell Cuyler of Schenectady, New York (71a), illustrates the luxuriousness of the cloth covers used on toilet tables. The major element in the design of this table, the ogee-curved top, would have been clearly visible beneath a draped cloth. However, the table has no tack holes; if it ever had a cloth covering, the cover was not permanently attached.

By the Federal era, every woman mindful of her social standing had a toilet table in her chamber. Large houses had more than one but only in the principal chambers. A "Toilette with Covering [$] 4.00" and "Toilette, with Covering & Cushion [$] 6.00" were in the northwest and southwest chambers of Jonathan Hamilton's large house on the bank of the Piscataqua in 1802.[2]

Hamilton's fellow merchant and contemporary, James Rundlet (1772–1852) of nearby Portsmouth, owned this toilet table and a similar one with a serpentine top. Rundlet bought some of the furnishings for his house at the estate sale of Samuel Ham (d. 1813), one of Portsmouth's wealthiest citizens, and the toilet tables may have been the two among Ham's effects: "1 painted Toilet Table $3" in the "Upper Chamber Nº 5 (Front)" and another "painted Toilet Table" in the "Upper Chamber Nº 6 (Front)."[3]

Apparently some toilet tables were not permanently covered with a cloth. The several layers of paint on Rundlet's table — white, brown, blue, gray, and white — suggest that this may have always been a "painted Toilet Table." The woodwork suggests the same thing. The legs are finished with a beaded outer corner, the rails even more decoratively edged.

71a. Portrait of Anna Wendell Cuyler. Probably Schenectady, New York, 1765–1775. Oil on canvas; H. 26 (66.0); W. 20⅜ (51.8). Albany Institute of History and Art.

1. The *Oxford English Dictionary*, citing a 1696 use of "toilet."

2. Inventory of Jonathan Hamilton of Berwick, docket 8215, York County (Me.) Probate.

3. Ham's 1813 inventory, docket 8702, Rockingham County (N.H.) Probate. Rundlet owned Ham's painted window cornices.

NOTES ON STRUCTURE AND CONDITION: Four wooden pins through the top hold it to the rails.

MATERIALS: *Spruce* legs; *white pine* rails and top.

PROVENANCE: The toilet table descended with the house from James Rundlet to his children Caroline (1797–1880) and Edward (1805–1874). Caroline left her share to her sister Louisa Rundlet May (1817–1895); Edward, to Louisa's son James Rundlet May (1841–1918). James received his mother's share and left the whole to his wife, Mary Ann Morison May (1844–1936), who left it to her son, the donor.

ACCESSION: 1971.928   A gift of Ralph May

72 / Tilt-Top Table

1755–1785
Boston or coastal Essex County, Massachusetts
H. 28 (71.1); W. 32⅛ (81.6); D. 31½ (80)

"Tilt-top" is a modern term for a table with many earlier names. In England such tables were called "pillar and claw" or "claw tables" — whether or not the feet had claws — or "snap tables" because of the sound of the hinged top latching into the horizontal position.[1] Eighteenth-century American cabinetmakers usually called them "tea tables," and when the top was circular, inventory appraisers often added "round."[2]

At home in almost any room of the house, round tilt-top tea tables were far more popular than their rectangular stationary-top counterparts, such as table no. 67. Both types were sometimes in the same room. The tilt-top table could be retired against the

72

wall after tea, whereas the stationary-top table served as a china table, a place where the tea service remained when not in use.

Tilt-top tables served other purposes as well, but whatever their function, they were likely to be covered with a cloth, as these English prints (72a and 72b) illustrate. The claws and pillars, generally visible beneath the cloths, were places for embellishment.

The legs on this table are plain and the knees are not decoratively carved, but the lower edges of the pillar and knees are attractively scalloped. The feet have no claws; instead they are the pointed "snake feet" popular along the north shore of Massachusetts. As in many New England tilt-top tables, the pillar design provides most of the aesthetic appeal. The urn, tapering shaft, and ring are a simplified design based on English prototypes with spiral-reeded urns (72b). The latter embellishment is seen on some elaborate New England examples.[3]

In its simpler form, this was the most popular pillar design for tilt-top tables from Boston to Newburyport. The pattern is seen in John Singleton Copley's 1757–1759 portrait of the Boston merchant John Erving, Jr.; in Copley's 1764–1765 portrait of Mrs. Samuel Waldo of Boston; on a mahogany table in the Society's collection with a long Newburyport history; and on an example that descended in the family of President John Adams of Braintree, just south of Boston.[4] Table no. 72 belonged to Sarah Sutton Russell (b. 1775) of Ipswich, Massachusetts.

Tables of this design were made of maple or birch as well as of mahogany. Sarah Russell's birch table is a good example of a popular design rendered in a native wood.

72a. "December." Published by Carington Bowles, engraved by R. Dighton, London, ca. 1780. Mezzotint engraving; H. 14 (35.6); W. 10½ (26.7). Colonial Williamsburg Foundation.

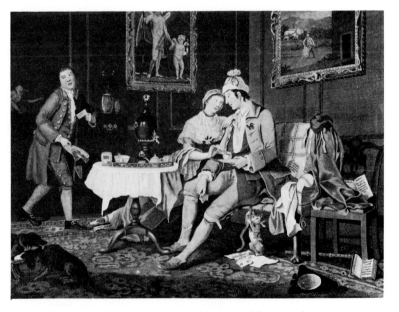

72b. "The Honey-Moon." Engraved by J. Goldar, London, ca. 1765. Colored engraving after a painting by John Collett; H. 14¾ (37.5); W. 18 (45.7). Colonial Williamsburg Foundation.

1. For "pillar and claw," see *Cabinet-Makers' London Book*, 266; and for the latter two terms, see Gloag, *Georgian Grace*, 191.

2. Weil, "Price Book," 187.

3. Fales, *Historic Deerfield*, 152, figs. 318–20.

4. The portraits are figures 80 and 161 in Prown, *Copley*, vol. 1. The table in the Society's collection (1934.573) is from the Bartlett-Atkinson House in Newburyport, Mass., and the Adams table is at the Adams National Historic Site.

NOTES ON STRUCTURE AND CONDITION: The upper end of the turned pillar forms a square tenon with rounded edges. Two oak wedges tighten the joint. An iron brace is nailed beneath the pillar and legs.

The three-board top has two cleats of the same shape as those on stand no. 76 (III–20).

The cleats are original but have been repositioned. Originally stained red, the table has been refinished.

MATERIALS: *Birch; cherry* cleats; *oak* wedges in the pillar tenon. Replaced cleat screws and latch.

PROVENANCE: The table descended from Sarah Sutton Russell to her daughter Susan Lord Russell Lakeman, then to her daughter Sarah (ca. 1850–1937), who left it to the donor.

ACCESSION: 1948.703   A bequest of Arthur W. Johnson

73 / Tilt-Top Table

1760–1790
Rhode Island
H. 28⅝ (72.7); W. 32⅞ (83.5); D. 32⅝ (82.9)

The design of this Rhode Island table makes an interesting comparison with that of the preceding tilt-top from coastal Massachusetts. Their differences reflect regional style variations. The rounded feet, blunt when compared to those on the Massachusetts table, are characteristic of Rhode Island design. On more expensive tables, such feet are carved into claws (see table no. 74). On the Rhode Island table, the undersides of the pillar and knees are not scalloped. The tops of the knees, however, are stepped in a stylish fashion unusual on American tables, although often seen on English examples (see 72b).

The most notable difference is in the pillar. The urn, supporting the shaft on the preceding table, is not incorporated into this design. Rhode Island cabinetmakers offered pillars with urns or without.[1] A few elegant Newport tables with pillars of the same design as this example have stop-fluted shafts.[2]

In construction, too, the table manifests its Rhode Island origin. Similar stepped cleats (73a) are used on a table that belonged to John Brown of Providence.[3] One construction feature is so unusual, it may eventually pinpoint the craftsman who made this table. A wooden brace beneath the top rests against the pillar, holding the top upright and perpendicular to the floor. The brace stabilizes the heavy vertical top and relieves the strain on the block, which on tilt-tops is vulnerable to breaking.

1. For a Rhode Island example with urn, see number 92 in *John Brown House Loan Exhibition*.

2. An example is in the collections of the Newport Historical Society.

73

3. The table is on loan to the Rhode Island Historical Society; see *Israel Sack Collection,* 5:1143.

NOTES ON STRUCTURE AND CONDITION: The turned pillar terminates in a square tenon. Three wedges set in a triangular pattern tighten the joint. An iron brace is screwed beneath the pillar and legs. The pads beneath the feet, once fitted with casters, show little wear. The top is constructed of three boards.

The table is in excellent condition with all of its original elements.

MATERIALS: Mahogany; *maple* block; *birch* cleats; white pine brace. Seven of the original twelve cleat screws remain. Original brass latch.

PROVENANCE: The table came from the 1797 General Ichabod Goodwin House in South Berwick, Me., and is believed to have been in that house for several generations.

ACCESSION: 1966.216   Museum purchase

73a

74 / Tilt-Top Table

1760–1790
Newport
Attributed to John Goddard
H. 28 (71.1); W. 30⅞ (78.4); D. 31¼ (79.4)

Here is a "claw table" (see entry 72) with claw feet. Its pillar is especially columnar, a quality that is enhanced with stop-fluting on some examples. A bead at the top edge of the cabriole legs echoes the turnings of the pillar, unifying pillar and claws.

Every aspect of this "pillar and claw," from its dished top to its carved toes, illustrates the superb craftsmanship and clean lines of Newport furniture. The contoured cleats (74a) are typical of the Rhode Island cabinetmaker's attention to detail. Even the unseen detail of a Y-shaped iron brace (74b) beneath the pillar and legs is meticulously cut and neatly fastened with both screws and rose-headed nails.

74

The claws, confined within the same contours as the blunt snake feet on the preceding table, are distinct to the Newport area and decidedly different from the three toes seen elsewhere (see table 75b). These five-toed claws are seen on the best Newport tilt-top tables, including a group with quadruple pillars.[1] One, at the Museum of Fine Arts, Boston (74c), has feet so like those on this table that both are surely the work of the same craftsman. The history of the museum's table states that it was made by John Goddard and given to his daughter Catherine, Mrs. Perry Weaver, in whose family it descended.[2] Another table with similar feet survives with its original bill from Goddard.[3]

Typically, tables with these carved claws also have dished tops; both features added to the cost. The dished tops function like the molded tops of tea tables no. 67 and 68, creating a secure traylike surface for the tea equipage.

The high point of the stylish elegance of this table is the subtle indentation on the side of each leg that lightens the mass, enhancing the grace of the cabriole. This most unusual feature is a modest version of the shaping on some French and English cabrioles.

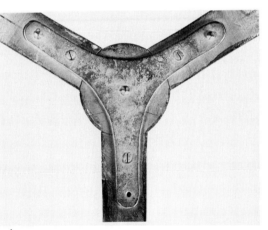

74b

74a

1. See *Antiques* 11 (May 1927): 364, 365.
2. Hipkiss, *Karolik Collection*, 110.
3. Carpenter, *Arts and Crafts of Newport*, fig. 79.

NOTES ON STRUCTURE AND CONDITION: This table shows what can happen without a brace such as that on the preceding table (detail 73a), for the block cracked severely at the pintle end. One foot is chipped at the toe. The one-board top is surprisingly free of warpage.

MATERIALS: *Mahogany*, including the cleats and the wedges that are driven through the pillar tenon; *maple* plate. Four of the original nine cleat screws

74c. Tilt-Top Table. Attributed to John Goddard (1724–1785), Newport, 1750–1780. Mahogany; H. 27½ (69.9); w. 31⅝ (80.3). M. and M. Karolik Collection, Museum of Fine Arts, Boston.

remain. Original brass latch. The metal strip to receive the latch is a replacement.

PROVENANCE: No history came with the table. The donor's family had ties with Newport.

ACCESSION: 1941.1701   A gift of Emma Franklin Estabrook

75 / Tilt-Top Table

1775–1800
Boston or coastal Essex County, Massachusetts
H. 28⁷⁄₁₆ (72.2); w. 46¾ (118.7); D. 46¾ (118.7)

Serpentine-edged "square" tops were second in popularity only to round tops on New England tilt-top tables. This two-board top is so large that the table probably lent itself to many purposes: working, writing, and card playing as well as tea, breakfast, or even dinner for four.

The pillar illustrates the standard design of coastal Massachusetts. The scalloping beneath the pillar (75a), a common pattern, smartly echoes the serpentine of the top. The angular, upright appearance of the cabrioles is typical of tripod design of the late eighteenth century.

Sharp creases running the length of the legs are an unusual feature occasionally seen in coastal New England north of Boston and found on the English globe stands that were owned in Boston (no. 77).[1] Here the crisp line leads the eye over the broad foot whose central crease and flanking knobs emulate the three claws seen on more expensive tables (such as 75b, which also features carved knees and an ogee molded edge along the top).

75

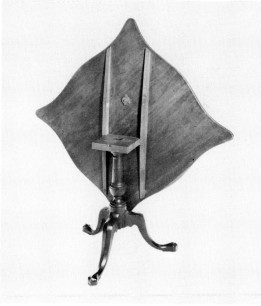

75a

75b. Tilt-Top Table. Boston or coastal Essex County, Massachusetts, 1775–1800. Mahogany; H. 26¾ (67.9); W. 32 (81.3). Photograph, courtesy, Israel Sack, Inc., New York.

1. Montgomery, *American Furniture*, no. 203, shows a pole screen with this feature.

NOTES ON STRUCTURE AND CONDITION: The tenon of the pillar is held tight by flanking wedges. The two-board top is warped. No triangular brace was originally fastened beneath the pillar and legs, but one has been added.

The table shows little wear except for one broken leg that has been glued together and reinforced by a brass brace. The block and cleats have their original reddish-brown stain.

MATERIALS: Mahogany; *birch* block and cleats. Three of the original eight cleat screws remain. Original brass latch.

PROVENANCE: The table has no known history.

ACCESSION: 1977.76   A gift of Mrs. Henry Lyman

76 / Tilt-Top Stand

1775–1800
Boston or coastal Essex County, Massachusetts
H. 28⅛ (71.4); W. 24¼ (61.6); D. 24¼ (61.6)

Echoing in smaller form the top of the preceding table and closely related to it in pillar, cleat, and leg design, this tilt-top stand has different proportions because its shaft is attenuated to keep the top at table height (III-20 is the rear view of this stand).

The term "stand" appears in early-eighteenth-century inventories but is mentioned more frequently in the last thirty years of the century. Philadelphia cabinetmakers referred to the form as a "folding stand," available with snake or claw feet, with smooth or leaf-carved knees, with a plain or fluted pillar, and with a plain or rotating top (the latter, rare in New England, required a box commonly known today as a birdcage):

folding Stands
Stand 22 Inches [presumably the diameter of the top] with A

box plain top & feet	1:15:0
Ditto plain top & Claw foot	2: 2:6
Ditto with leaves on the knees	2:10:0
Ditto fixed [top does not turn] 18 Inches	1: 4:0
Ad for fluting the piller 5 S[hillings] & to Jurneyman	[0: 2:6][1]

Easily moved, the stand served many functions. Although commonly called a candlestand today, it was used for writing and reading as well as an auxiliary surface for tea drinking.

Serpentine-top stands were very popular. Most have ogee-molded edges; this one does not. A stand at the Museum of Fine Arts, Boston, has a molded edge but is otherwise very similar to the Society's; it was made by Jonathan Gavet of Salem in 1784.[2] The Society's stand was made at about the same time, possibly in the same town.

This stand has never had an iron brace to reinforce the joints of the legs to the pillar

76

(detail 74b), and the preceding table was fitted with a brace only in recent years. The brace, called a "triangle" on a 1793 London price list, was commonly used but was, nevertheless, an optional feature:

A triangle on a pillar-and-claw table	0:0:2
Letting in a triangle plate, the sides not exceeding four inches long	0:0:4
Each inch in length when triangles, extra	0:0:1[3]

1. Weil, "Price Book," 187.
2. Randall, *American Furniture*, no. 106.
3. *Cabinet-Makers' London Book of Prices*, 266.

NOTES ON STRUCTURE AND CONDITION: Two wedges tighten the tenon of the pillar. One leg has been broken, the original elements reglued, and a spline added. The stand was refinished in 1976.

MATERIALS: Mahogany; *birch* cleats and block. Original cleat screws and brass latch.

PROVENANCE: The table has no known history.

ACCESSION: 1954.51   A bequest of Harriet L. Jewett Croy

77 / Terrestrial and Celestial Globes and Stands

1793
London
Globes by Dudley Adams
H. 22⅝ (57.5); W. 17⅛ (43.5)

These globes belonged to the founder of the Lowell Institute in Boston, America's first university without walls. John Lowell, Jr. (1799–1836), was a scholar and world traveler. He may have inherited his globes from his father, the wealthy industrialist Francis Cabot Lowell (1775–1817), who had profited much from travel. In England, the elder Lowell had learned how to design the machinery with which he revolutionized cloth production in America. The events of his son's life make it fitting and poignant that his globes survive. John Jr.'s favorite reading was of travel; while still an undergraduate at Harvard, he was thoroughly versed in geography. He traveled far and frequently, and after the tragic deaths of his young wife and their two children, he went for a protracted journey around the world that was never completed, for he died in Bombay of dysentery and exposure.[1]

77

77a. Portrait of the Morse Family. Samuel F. B. Morse (1791–1872), Charlestown, Massachusetts, 1811. Watercolor on paper; H. 12 (30.5); W. 15 (38.1). Smithsonian Institution.

77b

John Jr. left behind an extensive library. His will established the institute, designating his cousin and brother-in-law, John Amory Lowell, the trustee and giving him half the silver, half the furniture, and two hundred volumes of his choice from the library.[2] The globes were probably in the library when John Amory selected his share of the books.

In the enlightened eighteenth century, globes were not merely for colleges and classrooms; they were in the houses of those who could afford them, esteemed appropriate furniture for almost any room. A cultured Englishman might have a pair of globes in the morning room beside his bookshelves, in the stairhall flanking the archway, or near the telescope in the library.[3]

In his study, George Washington had a single terrestrial globe, ordered in 1789 from George Adams of London.[4] The globe of Jedidiah Morse, the famed geographer, takes center stage in the family portrait of 1811 (77a), standing on what appears to be a library table in his house in Charlestown, Massachusetts. In neighboring Cambridge, Francis Dana had, in a little middle chamber, "1 pair of Adams globes 18″ diameter [$] 40."[5]

Lowell's globes, dated 1793, are signed D. Adams (77b), denoting Dudley Adams (working 1791–1825), who like his father George (1704–1773) before him was the Royal Optician and an instrument maker. Dudley and his brother George (1750–1795) worked in London; the stands for their globes were constructed by London furniture craftsmen. Of the several Adams globes in America, most were made by Dudley.[6] This pair, so wonderfully documented, prove the longevity (to the end of the eighteenth century) of the tripod stand design commonly designated Queen Anne. They also show the presence in America of English tripods with ridges along the tops of the legs and scalloped edges beneath the pillars and knees, characteristics popular on tilt-top tables made in coastal Massachusetts (such as table no. 75).

1. Weeks, *The Lowells*, 15.

2. John Lowell, Jr.'s will, docket 31365, Suffolk County (Mass.) Probate.

3. Cornforth, *English Interiors*, figs. 56, 64, 111, 147, 148.

4. Fede, *Washington Furniture*, 43.

5. Dana's 1811 inventory, docket 5841, Middlesex County (Mass.) Probate.

6. Yonge, *Early Globes*, 1, 2.

NOTES ON STRUCTURE AND CONDITION: Each stand is of typical tripod construction with an iron brace screwed to the underside of the pillar and knees. The curved wooden supports for the zodiac ring are secured to the pillar with shouldered dovetails. The brass meridian circle rests in a brass track screwed to the pillar. Each globe is missing its compass, originally fastened beneath the pillar by three supports joined to the legs (77a).

The celestial globe stand was repaired in 1976 for a severely cracked pillar and two loose legs; the third leg had been broken earlier and reglued.

MATERIALS: *Alder* stand; paper on gesso globes. Original brass hardware.

PROVENANCE: The globes of John Lowell, Jr., descended from John Amory Lowell (1798–1881) to his daughter Ellen (Ella) (1837–1894), to her husband, Arthur T. Lyman (d. 1915), to their son Ronald T. (1879–1962), and finally to the latter's daughter Charlotte, the donor.

ACCESSION: 1966.495   A gift of Mrs. Benjamin S. Clark; conserved through the generosity of Edgar M. Bingham, Jr.

Seating Furniture

78 / Armchair

1670–1690
Coastal Massachusetts or New Hampshire
H. 38½ (97.8); W. at rockers 25½ (64.8); SEAT D. 14½ (36.8); SEAT H. 16¾ (42.5)

By 1683 Daniel Fisher, a well-to-do gentleman of Dedham, Massachusetts, had furnished his four-room house with what was then a considerable amount of seating:

> *In the Parlor . . .*
> Forme [bench], and three joined stooles . . .
> a joined chaire.
> 3.great turned chaires and five small chaires

Fisher had not one seat in the hall, no seats in one chamber, but in the other chamber:

> 4.small chaires.[1]

In its variety, Fisher's seating furniture was typical of a late-seventeenth-century house. Forms, joined stools, and joined chairs (such as the Ipswich example 1a) were joiners' products. The turner made simple stools, slat-back chairs (78a), and his specialty, the great turned chair. A surprisingly large number of New England great turned chairs survive; most are in poor condition or with major restorations. The Society's chair was converted to a rocker, a common fate, and is missing the tops of its finials and the ball-turned handholds above the front posts (compare with 78b).

Extant seventeenth-century turned chairs from New England have much in common. They are four-legged chairs whose stiles are straight-line continuations of the rear legs. Almost all are armchairs, and the arms are usually turned. The front and side stretchers are paired, but the rear stretchers are single. The uppermost back rail is more elaborately turned than the other back rails or the stretchers. One or two tiers of vertical spindles adorn the back. A few, more ornate examples have spindles beneath the arms, and some have spindles beneath the seats and stretchers as well. Squat baluster turnings often decorate the posts. The rear posts are finished with turned finials; the front posts terminate above the arm in ball or mushroom-like handholds.

The Society's example presents an interesting variation of the usual pattern. The arms are not turned but are slats of a shape often found on slat-back chairs (78a). The uppermost back rail is entirely of ball turnings.[2] On most chairs with two tiers of

78

spindles in the back, the spindles are of equal height; here they are not. The attenuated upper tier is an attractive variation that complements the attenuation of the baluster turnings on the stiles. (Note that the baluster turnings nearest the seat are squat, those above the arms are stretched, and those on the front posts are in between in size and in placement above the seat.)

Such differences may reflect the variant design vocabulary of a particular area and, if more were known about chairs of this type, might pinpoint the origin of this chair. In years past, an adoration of things Pilgrim led to attributions of most seventeenth-century turned chairs to Plymouth.

Actually, turned chairs were made throughout New England; the greatest number of surviving examples probably originated in or near Boston. This chair reportedly descended in the family of Leonard Weeks (d. 1717), who came to Portsmouth from England in 1656 and settled in what is now Greenland, New Hampshire. But corroborative facts and comparative examples are lacking, so these handsome turnings, clearly the work of an able craftsman, cannot yet be attributed to a particular locale.

Turners continued to produce spindle-back chairs well into the eighteenth century. Numerous late examples survive; many are side chairs, whose turnings are not at all comparable to the robust work epitomized here.

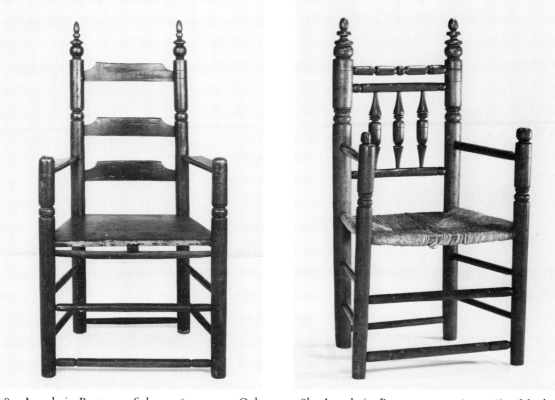

78a. Armchair. Boston or Salem, 1650–1700. Oak and pine; H. 48 (121.9); W. 24 (61.0); SEAT D. 16 (40.6); SEAT H. 17½ (44.5). Essex Institute. *The chair originally belonged to Mary Hollingsworth English of Salem and was later acquired by the Reverend Mr. William Bentley (1759–1819).*

1. Cummings, *Inventories*, 46.
2. Similar turnings appear on a split spindle applied to a Salem dressing cabinet dated 1679 in the Metropolitan Museum (10.125.168) and on the top rail of a Winterthur Museum side chair, number 186 in the *Harvard Tercentenary Exhibition.* Somewhat related crests are in *Israel Sack Collec-*

78b. Armchair. Boston area, 1650–1685. Maple; H. 44 (111.8); W. 16¼ (41.3); D. 23¼ (59.1); SEAT H. 17¼ (43.8). Wallace E. Nutting Collection, Wadsworth Atheneum. Photograph, E. Irving Blomstrann.

tion, 2:524, no. 1243, and Nutting, *Pilgrim Century,* rev. ed., nos. 322, 330.

NOTES ON STRUCTURE AND CONDITION: The round mortise-and-tenon joints are not pinned. The posts are scribed at all joints. In the late eighteenth or early nineteenth century, rockers were added, and the bottom of the feet were shortened slightly and notched to receive them. Probably at the same time, the chair was fitted with upholstery, the handholds and the tops of the finials were cut off, and where it was not covered by fabric, the chair was painted green. Coats of black and brown paint are under the green.

The left arm is an old replacement. The upper center spindle is a recent replacement. A large chip in the left rear foot has been patched. The old rush seat is not original.

MATERIALS: *Poplar* posts; *birch* rockers; *ash* all other work.

PROVENANCE: The chair was owned by Daniel Weeks of Sandwich, N.H., a direct descendant of Leonard Weeks, when it was acquired by the donor in 1950.

ACCESSION: 1961.104   A gift of Mrs. Bertram K. Little

79 / Armchair

1720–1750
Eastern Massachusetts
H. 43 (109.2); W. 24⅞ (63.2); SEAT D. 15⅞ (40.3); SEAT H. 15⅛ (38.4)

Slat-backs were turners' chairs. They were inexpensive and more numerous than any other chair during the late seventeenth and eighteenth centuries. They varied from heavy turned chairs in the seventeenth century (chair 78a) through higher-back models like this chair in the early eighteenth century to thin versions in later years (chair 80a).

Contemporary accounts often identify slat-back chairs by the number of slats. In 1732, Samuel Ridgway, Sr. (1700–1773), a Boston chairmaker, sold Samuel Smith "4 Chairs 3 Backs," meaning four chairs with three slats each.[1] Forty years later Ridgway was still producing slat-backs. His estate included a shop containing "27 3 Back," "23 4 Back Chairs," "2 4 Back Great Chairs," "& 2 Child[re]ns Chairs."[2] This is a "4 Back Great Chair."

Slat-backs were made in large numbers in shops such as Ridgway's, and this chair epitomizes the product. The legs and stiles have soft contoured ball turnings, the finials are a popular type, the stretchers feature a row of ball turnings at the center, and the back is composed of bowed slats with arched tops and flat bases. The slats are graduated in height, with the tallest at the top.

Many similar chairs survive, a large number with eastern Massachusetts histories.[3] Related examples with sausage turnings on the stretchers are also numerous,[4] and similar legs can be found on banister-back chairs as well.[5] The same craftsmen produced slat-backs and banister-backs.

Although of standard design, the armchair here has two unusual features. The ball turnings on the front stretchers are repeated on the side stretchers, and the handholds are pierced.

79

1. Grant Account Book, September 28, 1732, p. 173, Massachusetts Historical Society. Lyon, *Colonial Furniture*, 3rd ed., 164, introduced the interpretation of "backs" as "slats."

2. Samuel Ridgway, Sr.'s 1773 inventory, docket 15505, Suffolk County (Mass.) Probate.

3. Similar chairs are one from the Babbidge family of Salem at the Essex Institute; one from the South Church, Andover, at the Andover Historical Society; two from the Mann family of Scituate at the Scituate Historical Society; one from the Andrew family of Windham, Me., and Hingham, Mass., at the Old Ordinary, Hingham; one owned by Lucy Fairbanks Adams (b. 1789) of Dedham and Franklin, Mass., and now at the Fairbanks House, Dedham; and one having a local history since before 1800 at the Duxbury Rural and Historical Society.

4. A few examples are: Kane, *American Seating Furniture*, no. 9; *Israel Sack Collection*, 6:1572, no. P4652; and Fairbanks, "American Antiques in the Collection of Mr. and Mrs. Charles L. Bybee, Part 1," 836.

5. For example, Kane, *American Seating Furniture*, nos. 46, 47; Trent, *Hearts & Crowns*, nos. 28, 29, 30.

NOTES ON STRUCTURE AND CONDITION: All elements except the slats are joined with round mortises and tenons. Most joints are held tight with wedges. The rush seat is modern. The chair has several layers of paint; the outermost is oak graining outlined with yellow (ca. 1850). By the time of the graining, the chair had lost its feet and rear stretcher. In 1981 these elements were replaced.

MATERIALS: *Poplar* posts; ash stretchers, seat rails, and slats; oak arms.

PROVENANCE: The early history of the chair is unknown; it has been in Woodstock, Conn., since the middle of the nineteenth century.

ACCESSION: 1970.420   Museum purchase

80 / High Chair

1775–1820
Danvers-Lynnfield, Massachusetts, area
H. 36¹³⁄₁₆ (93.5); W. 14⁹⁄₁₆ (37); SEAT D. 11⁵⁄₁₆ (28.7); SEAT H. 22 (55.9)

80

Here the simple slat-back assumes most pleasing proportions. The arch of the slats enhances the upward thrust of the slender vertical chair, whose legs exhibit little of the customary splay helpful for stabilizing high chairs. The stylized urn-and-ball finials (compare with those on chair no. 85) also emphasize lift.

The finials are apparently the distinctive hallmark of a turner or chairmaker in the Danvers area. Two chairs — a full-size chair (80a) and a high chair identical to this one — were owned by Danvers families.[1] The Society's chair came from neighboring Lynnfield, where it evidently served generations of youngsters in the Perkins family.

1. Both chairs are in the collections of the Danvers Historical Society.

NOTES ON STRUCTURE AND CONDITION: Round mortises and tenons are used throughout except for the slats. A single pin secures each joint of the upper slat. The rush seat is modern. Otherwise the chair is in excellent condition with all of its original elements.

MATERIALS: Maple; *white oak* seat rails, arms, and all stretchers except a maple one at the lower right.

PROVENANCE: The high chair descended in the Perkins family within the John Hiram Perkins House in Lynnfield.

ACCESSION: 1918.545   A gift of Mrs. John Winslow Perkins; conserved through the generosity of Richard Candee

80a. Side Chair. Danvers-Lynnfield, Massachusetts, area, 1775–1820. Maple; H. 39 (99.1); W. 18 (45.7); SEAT D. 12⅞ (32.7); SEAT H. 16¼ (41.3). Danvers Historical Society. Photograph, J. David Bohl.

81 / Couch

1680–1690
London
H. 37⅛ (94.3); W. 20⅝ (52.4); SEAT D. 60⅜ (153.4); SEAT H. 15⅞ (40.3)

The Reverend Mr. Thomas Smith (1703–1795), the first minister of Falmouth, now Portland, Maine, died while resting upon this couch. When it belonged to the Falmouth worthy, the couch was already old, apparently a hand-me-down from either Smith's forebears, Boston merchants, or from his Boston in-laws. The couch probably was in Boston for much of its first century.

In the late seventeenth and early eighteenth centuries, couches were part of the fur-

81

nishings of best rooms in wealthy households. The best room of the Bostonian Nicholas Paige, inventoried in 1718, had probably remained the same since the prosperous merchant had furnished his house in the best fashion about forty years before.

The Furniture in the best Room

1 Large Looking Glass	7:–:–
1 Doz: Chairs being old and broken	3:–:–
2 Tables an old Couch and 2 Carpets	4:–:–
1 Clock	8:–:–
1 pr. old Doggs & 1 pr. brass Andirons	1:–:–.[1]

The furnishings throughout Paige's two-story house were old, his "2 Negroes . . . old," and his "Coach and harness . . . old and decay'd."[2] But his inventory gives a fine picture of a merchant's house of the last quarter of the seventeenth century. Six chambers have beds; the parlor and the best room do not. Instead, the best room has a couch. The room is easily visualized: a suite of twelve chairs lining the walls; two carpet-covered tables; a clock, a prestigious possession; a large, valuable looking glass; and, matching the dozen chairs no doubt, the couch, then a grand and new form.

The word "couch" designated either of two forms.[3] One, a form today called a daybed, was designed for reclining or sitting; its caned areas were appointed with a long cushion and a pillow.[4] The other form looked like a very wide armchair with hinged rests above the arms; it was upholstered in turkeywork, wool, or leather (81a, a couch that is missing its hinged rests).[5]

During the seventeenth century both forms were made; by the early eighteenth the upholstered armchair was no longer fashionable. Thomas Fitch, a Boston upholsterer, wrote in 1707:

> Leather couches [the armchair type] are as much out of wear as steeple crown'd hats; cane couches [the daybed type] or others we make like them wth a quilted pad are cheaper, more fash[ionable], easie & usefull.[6]

Fitch not only notes the decline in popularity of one type of couch in favor of the other but also hints at the widespread importation of cane furniture. The "others we make like them" substituted for the cane couches he did not make. Cane seating was almost exclusively imported from London (see entry 83). London chairmakers changed the

81a. Couch. Boston, 1697–1700. Oak and maple; H. 46¼ (117.5); W. 59⅝ (151.4); SEAT D. 20¼ (51.4); SEAT H. 15¾ (40.0). Essex Institute. *The couch was probably made for Margaret (Rogers) and John Leverett of Cambridge shortly after their marriage in 1697. The turkeywork upholstery is original.*

design of caneware over the years, and by the second decade of the eighteenth century, an early cane couch like this example looked old.

Many cane imports of the 1680s featured a carved crest on a spiral-turned frame, an incised diaper design on the unturned and uncarved elements, and a squat back with a wide splat divided into two caned areas.[7] Later, taller backs with single caned areas became the fashion, spiral turnings faded in popularity, and incised detail gave way to carved and then molded decoration (see chairs no. 82–84 and no. 90).

The cane couch shown here is most unusual, even among the small extant group of English cane imports with spiral turnings. Couches generally rest on eight legs; this has but six.[8] When carved figures are featured on the crest, usually two cupids support a crown; here the figure is a winged angel much like those carved on gravestones in England and New England.

1. Cummings, *Inventories,* 97.

2. Ibid., 98, 99.

3. Thornton, *Seventeenth-Century Interior Decoration,* 210–17.

4. Symonds ("English Cane Chairs, Part 2," 87) suggests that the form was used for reclining. That it was used for sitting is shown in Thornton, *Seventeenth-Century Interior Decoration,* figs. 205, 206.

5. Thornton, *Seventeenth-Century Interior Decoration,* 172–74.

6. Thomas Fitch, Letterbook, April 22, 1707, American Antiquarian Society.

7. Symonds, "English Cane Chairs, Part 1," fig. 4.

8. A six-legged spiral-turned couch was owned by the Revolutionary general John Sullivan; Reed Family Collection, American Art Association, sale 3849, May 1930, lot 383.

NOTES ON STRUCTURE AND CONDITION: The couch is joined with rectangular mortise-and-tenon joints except as noted. The medial legs are round-tenoned into the side rails. The stiles are canted extensions of the rear legs, and the back, now bolted in position, originally pivoted on the round tenon joints of the splat rail to the stiles. Chains, originally attached to the tenons of the crest rail and to open mortises in the stiles, allowed the back to fall to a more recumbent position.

The cane is replaced and the wood refinished. Three unexplained holes are in the central splat stile, and oak strips have been attached to the head and foot seat rails.

MATERIALS: Beech; added oak strips.

PROVENANCE: The couch descended in the family of the Reverend Mr. Smith to the donor.

ACCESSION: 1971.345   A bequest of Helen Webb Wicker

82 / Side Chair

1695–1715
London
H. 51 (129.5); W. 18½ (47); SEAT D. 15⅞ (40.3); SEAT H. 19 (48.3)

A Duzen of good black Walnut Chairs, fine Cane, with a Couch. A Duzen of Cane Chairs of a different figure, and a great Chair, for a Chamber; all black Walnut.[1]

In 1720, Samuel Sewall ordered these furnishings from his agent in London for his betrothed daughter Judith. Not everyone bought a set of cane chairs directly from

London; many patronized local merchants who offered and advertised sets of "Cain Chairs and Couches" and sundry other English goods.[2]

Importing furniture was risky business. A vessel bringing London goods to Thomas Fitch, a Boston upholsterer, was plundered by pirates. When the cargo arrived in Boston in 1725 Fitch noted:

> They took out Case N.º 10 and kept the two best [looking] Glasses, and they broke open Case Nº 4 and Nº 6 qt. [quantity] 2 doz. of the best Chairs w.ch they abus'd but I found very near all the parts of the whole of them.[3]

More than pirates plagued Fitch's imports. He received narrower chairs than he had ordered and "part of them not Walnutt but only Cuver'd over"; that is, stained or

painted to resemble walnut.[4] When not of walnut, English cane chairs were of beech. Chairs no. 82, 83, and 84 are "not Walnutt but only Cuver'd over" beech.

The cane seats on most such chairs were furnished with cushions. The aforementioned newspaper advertisement for "Cain Chairs and Couches" included "a Silk Bed and Cushions."[5] Sewall's order for Judith included bed hangings and "also of the same Camlet and Triming, as may be enough to make Cushions for the Chamber Chairs."[6]

The custom of using cushions influenced the design of cane chairs. The chair back is not decorated just above the seat because the space was hidden by a cushion. Trimmings on the cushion — a hanging fringe or corner tassels — made the uppermost portion of the front legs unimportant.[7] Thus English chairs have simple turnings directly beneath the seat, with expensive and elaborate carvings reserved for the area that was highly visible. (It is interesting that some American turners made the turned portion beneath the seat the most decorative feature of the front legs. See chair no. 85.)

Thousands of London cane chairs in the William and Mary style were imported into America; many of them survive. Early writers on New England furniture discussed the role of cane chairs in American interiors, but recent studies tend to overlook the subject. In 1977, Fales lauded Lyon for presenting information on cane chairs in 1891: "The caned-back chairs . . . although made in England, were American in their use and consequently colonial."[8] Indeed, imported objects should be regarded as part of America's heritage. This chair, like the preceding couch and chairs no. 83, 84, and 90, was made in London but owned in New England.

The popular design of this chair is related in appearance to a number of other cane chairs, several with colonial histories.[9] Two, from very similar sets, are believed to have belonged to Sir William Pepperrell (see entry 16).[10] Two sets of cane seating in one house were not uncommon. Sewall ordered a dozen plus a couch (apparently for the parlor) and, for the chamber, a dozen "of a different figure."

This example is from the same set as one of the Pepperrell chairs. While cane chairs were in vogue when Pepperrell married in 1723, the carved decoration on these chairs bespeaks an earlier date. The newly wed couple moved into a wing that Pepperrell's father, William (d. 1734), had added to his Kittery house; this chair and the related ones may have been part of the senior Pepperrell's furniture inherited by his son along with the house.

Compared with most other cane chairs (for example, chairs no. 83 and 84), this one is notable for its elaborate details, its bold and well-executed carvings, and its consistency of design. The scroll feet are large and handsome. The carved crest rail, splat, and front stretcher repeat the same motif, a consistency worth noting because cane chairs were made in large London shops by many hands, turning out products often inconsistent in design.

1. [Sewall,] *Letter-Book of Samuel Sewall,* 2:106.

2. *Boston News-Letter,* May 9–16, 1715, quoted in Dow, *Arts and Crafts,* 107.

3. Letter from Fitch to his London factor, Silas Hooper, September 23, 1725; Thomas Fitch, Letterbook, Massachusetts Historical Society.

4. Fitch, Letterbook, vol. 3, October 6, 1725, Massachusetts Historical Society.

5. Dow, *Arts and Crafts,* 107.

6. [Sewall,] *Letter-Book of Samuel Sewall,* 2:105.

7. Fowler and Cornforth, *English Decoration,* 168.

8. Introduction to Lyon, *Colonial Furniture* (1977), xv.

9. Chairs with histories are Nutting, *Pilgrim Century,* rev. ed., no. 451; two in Singleton, *Furniture of Our Forefathers,* 2:333, and Blackburn, *Cherry Hill,* no. 32.

10. The two in Singleton; see note 9.

NOTES ON STRUCTURE AND CONDITION: All elements are joined with rectangular mortises and tenons except the front legs, which are round-tenoned into the seat rail. Many joints are now repinned. The seat frame is new, all the cane replaced. The right stile was broken and reglued.

MATERIALS: *Beech.*

PROVENANCE: The chair belonged to Mrs. Woodbury (Elizabeth Elwyn) Langdon of Portsmouth at the end of the nineteenth century and came to the Society with her collection.

ACCESSION: 1966.287   A bequest of Elizabeth Elwyn Langdon

83 / Side Chair

1695–1715
London
H. 48⅛ (122.2); W. 17¾ (45.1); SEAT D. 14¹¹⁄₁₆ (37.3); SEAT H. 18¹¹⁄₁₆ (47.5)

This chair, removed from the Greenland, New Hampshire, Congregational church in the 1840s, apparently had been left to the meetinghouse in the eighteenth century, when it was common practice to will objects to one's church. The chair is of a popular pattern made for export in London around the beginning of the eighteenth century. Signs of its Old World manufacture are evident in the cane, the wood, the maker's marks, and the design of the rear posts.

The production of English cane seating of the William and Mary style was almost exclusively limited to London shops.[1] The Englishmen in America were like Englishmen everywhere: if they wanted cane chairs, they sought to import products from London.

This example is of beech, a wood seldom used in New England furniture but common in English wares. Painter-stainers finished the beech chairs, most of which left the shop looking like costly walnut or black japan.[2]

The initials IC stamped on the legs of this chair are believed to be the mark of a workman, not the shop owner.[3] English craftsmen commonly placed their initials on chairs, a practice rarely followed in America. Among the numerous chairs in America of this popular pattern is an imported armchair stamped IH.[4]

83

Another English feature is the presence of turnings on the rear posts both above and below the seat. The stiles of cane chairs of this period are canted backward, making necessary the use of offset chucks to lathe-turn the rear posts. London turners put the posts on the lathe twice: once (with the foot end in an offset chuck) to turn the stiles and a second time (with the finial end in another offset chuck) to turn the legs. American turners generally followed a practice used by the English on less expensive chairs: they placed the work on the lathe only once. On the great majority of canted-back chairs made in New England, the stiles alone are turned.

The carved design on this chair lacks unity, an almost commonplace trait of London cane chairs made for export. The carvings on the crest, splat, and front stretcher vary because several individuals worked on them. Not only were turned elements produced by one craftsman and carved ones by another, but on some chairs even the carved components appear to be the work of more than one man. London chairmakers might better be called chair assemblers.

It is easy to see how the Boston upholsterer Thomas Fitch, after his chairs suffered damage at the hands of the pirates (see entry 82), was able to reorder parts — "Inclos'd are patterns of the figures & of ye Exact dimensions wch are wanting" — and to replace the parts and reassemble the chairs.[5]

Fitch could easily assemble his imported chairs, but he could not produce them as cheaply as did the London chairmakers. The fact that chairs could be acquired from London cheaply inhibited their production in America and resulted in the great importation of caned chairs.

1. Symonds, "English Cane Chairs, Part 1," 11; "Part 2," 91.

2. Symonds, "Turkey Work, Beech and Japanned Chairs," 225.

3. Gilbert, *Furniture at Temple Newsam*, vol. 1, no. 61.

4. The armchair is at Gore Place, Waltham, Mass.

5. Fitch, Letterbook, October 6, 1725, Massachusetts Historical Society.

NOTES ON STRUCTURE AND CONDITION: All elements are joined with rectangular mortises and tenons except the front legs, which are round-tenoned into the seat frame. Before 1920, the chair was taken apart and reglued, the broken right finial was reattached, and the chair was recaned and restained.

MATERIALS: *Beech.*

PROVENANCE: The chair was given by the Community Congregational Church of Greenland, N.H., to Elizabeth Rogers, an aunt of the donor.

ACCESSION: 1920.243   A gift of Martha Codman

84 / Side Chair

1700–1720
London
H. 46⅜ (117.8); W. 17⁹⁄₁₆ (44.6); SEAT D. 14⁵⁄₁₆ (36.4); SEAT H. 18¾ (47.6)

Few imported cane chairs are as simply designed as this one. The stile turnings are simple columns, popular especially after 1700. The rear legs are unturned, a common characteristic of American, provincial English, and inexpensive London chairs. Turned (instead of carved) feet, undecorated splats, and unturned side and rear stretchers were ever-present cheaper alternatives.

The double-ball front feet, which in proportion mimic carved feet (see the preceding

84

chair), must have been more common than the number of surviving examples suggest. This chair is part of a set of which three survive; the feet of the other two were cut long ago to a single ball. The set had been in use for a century when it belonged to Samuel Batchelder (1784–1879) of Cambridge, Massachusetts, in whose house one of the cut-down chairs was photographed in the nineteenth century (84a).

This chair and the two others from the same set are numbered (chair no. 84 is VI) and have maker's marks (the IA mark, unclear on this chair, is clear on another). An identical chair that sold at auction in 1981 is stamped ID on the crest rail.[1]

1. Sotheby Parke Bernet, sale 4592Y, May 1981, lot 454. The seat rails, originally caned, appear to be beech. The chair is English.

NOTES ON STRUCTURE AND CONDITION: All elements are joined with rectangular mortises and tenons except the front legs, which are round-tenoned into the seat frame. Most of the joints are now secured with pins. The front and side seat rails are replaced. The chair has been painted black. The seat and back have been recaned.

MATERIALS: *Beech; birch* replaced front and side seat rails.

PROVENANCE: The side chair descended from Samuel Batchelder to his son Francis L., then to the latter's son Charles F. Sr., who left it to his wife.

ACCESSION: 1955.79   A gift of Mrs. Charles F. Batchelder, Sr.

84a. Photograph of Matching Side Chair in situ. Cambridge, Massachusetts, ca. 1875. Photographic Archives, Society for the Preservation of New England Antiquities. *The chair was upholstered in the mid-nineteenth century.*

85 / Side Chair

1710–1735
Boston-Salem area
H. 48¾ (123.8); W. 18¹⁵⁄₁₆ (48.1); SEAT D. 13¾ (34.9); SEAT H. 17⅞ (45.4)

This New England chair displays features common on contemporary London cane chairs: a carved crest, columnar stiles (see the preceding chair), spool-urn-ball-and-knob finials, the arrangement of stretchers (see chairs no. 82 and 83), and the overall proportions of William and Mary design. The proportions were so vital that even when rural New England turners sacrificed carved crests and columnar stiles, they retained verticality on their William and Mary chairs.

Other, less stylish features of this chair are often found on English provincial furniture as well as on American examples. Wooden banisters substitute for the cane splat. The rear posts are turned above but not below the seat. The front stretchers are turned instead of carved, and the seats are of indigenous fiber in lieu of imported cane.

In the eighteenth century, such chairs were not called "William and Mary" or "banister-back" chairs. Inventory references generally designated them by the seat material: "6 Leather bottom Chairs," "6 Rush Bottom Chairs and 1 small Ditto," "7 Flagg Bottom Chairs," "½ doz . . . & a great chair Cane back & flagg bottoms," "Bass Bottom'd chair," "7 blk frame Straw bottom Chairs."[1] Rush, flag, and straw refer to

85

local plant fibers. The chairs with the cane backs and flag bottoms suggest redone seats on imported cane chairs. "Bass," or "Bast," referred to hemp and apparently signified a cord seat.

Today these chairs are commonly designated not by their seats but by their "banister" backs. Molded banisters, such as those shown here, are unusual; the typical ones are turned-and-split banisters that echo the contours of the turned stiles (see 93a). A large group of chairs resembling this one feature turned-and-split banisters and plainer turnings; all but one lack the medial stretcher.[2]

The turnings of the legs and stretchers on this chair are extraordinary. On English cane chairs (see chair no. 82), the part of the front legs just beneath the seat was superficially decorated because it was often hidden by the fringe or tassels of a seat cushion. In New England, this turned portion received far more attention. The maker of this chair reserved his most intricate turnings for the area just below the seat. Evidently a cushion was expected to have neither fringe nor tassel to obscure the tops of these front legs.

The stretchers here are most unusual for an American chair. They follow the English arrangement of placing a medial stretcher between the side stretchers to form an H pattern. The front stretcher has a spool turning where many have a central ring. The side stretchers are especially notable because they are turned at the middle of the stretcher (85a). There the stretcher must remain broad for the mortise and is usually left as an unturned block. On this chair it is gracefully rounded.

A very small group of chairs share these beautiful turnings and this arrangement of stretchers (85b).[3] The features are so distinctive that they indicate a group from one shop. To judge from the design and craftsmanship, it was the shop of a highly skilled turner; to judge from the histories of the chairs — one from Lynn, one from Salem, and the Society's, purchased "from some old farmhouse" by a Bostonian[4] — he worked in the Boston-Salem area.

85a

1. As cited in inventories: "Leather" from Nyott Doubt, 1764, vol. 63, p. 393; "Rush Bottom" from Arthur Savage, 1735, vol. 32, p. 204; "Flagg Bottom" from Samuel Ridgway, 1779, vol. 78, p. 245; the "great chair," whose seat apparently had been replaced, from Sampson Mason, 1738, vol. 19, pp. 19–20; "Bass Bottom'd" from Samuel Wethered, 1759, vol. 54, p. 447; "black frame" from John Brown, 1785, vol. 84, p. 216; all from old series, Suffolk County (Mass.) Probate.

2. For examples, see Kane, *American Seating Furniture*, nos. 35–37; Randall, *American Furniture*, no. 125; Fales, *Historic Deerfield*, figs. 32, 33.

3. This group includes several almost identical chairs: another Codman family chair at the Players Club, New York; a privately owned chair that descended in the Gardner family of Salem; one that descended in the Collins family of Lynn, Mass., and owned by the Lynn Historical Society; and a

85b. Armchair. Boston-Salem area, 1710–1735. Maple; H. 50½ (128.3); W. 24¾ (62.9); SEAT D. 15½ (39.4); SEAT H. 16 (40.6). Bayou Bend Collection, Museum of Fine Arts, Houston. Photograph, Edward A. Bourdon.

pair of chairs advertised in *Antiques* 110 (July 1976): 63. Five somewhat related chairs are: one in the possession of Mrs. James Ticknor Fields of Boston in the nineteenth century; one illustrated in *Israel Sack Collection*, 5:1300; armchair 86b; another in the collections of the Currier Gallery, *Decorative Arts of New Hampshire*, no. 3; a side chair photographed *in situ*, *Antiques* 66 (November 1954), 379; and armchair 85b.

4. From the correspondence of Ogden Codman, Jr., October 21, 1933, in the Society's files.

NOTES ON STRUCTURE AND CONDITION: The splat rail consists of two strips — one plain and one molded in the same pattern as the banisters — glued together. The chair was upholstered in about 1870 and has been cleaned, repainted black, and rerushed, probably early in this century. Pins now secure many joints. Iron L-shaped braces reinforce the joints of the side seat rails to the rear posts. The right rear leg has a 5-by-1-by-1-inch pieced repair at the base.

MATERIALS: *Poplar* posts; *ash* seat rails and stretchers; *maple* banisters, crest, and splat rail.

PROVENANCE: Collected by Sarah Ogden Codman (1800–1844), the chair descended to her son Ogden Codman, Sr. (1839–1904), then to his daughter, the donor.

ACCESSION: 1969.635   A gift of Dorothy S. F. M. Codman

86 / Side Chair

1715–1740
Boston-Salem area
H. 48¼ (122.6); W. 19⅞ (50.5); SEAT D. 14⅝ (37.1); SEAT H. 17¾ (45.1)

Rarely does a New England chair of William and Mary design feature a crest resting upon the stiles instead of fitting between them. Arched crests, with earlike ends and a central crown, became popular on English cane chairs at the start of the eighteenth century. Examples were imported into America (the English armchair 86a was owned in New York) and became design sources for Pennsylvania chairs. But the arched crest was almost ignored in New England.[1]

The grooves outlining the crest and splat rail on this chair echo the molded surfaces that, in about 1715, superseded carvings on the crests and splat rails of English chairs. Molded crests and stiles became the fashion in New England (see chair no. 91), but banister-back chairs with molded crests or with the incised crests that imitate them are few.

The handsome carved feet capture exactly the proportions on English prototypes. Looking like robust tassels, they are reminiscent of the volutes popular on many earlier William and Mary chairs (see chair no. 83) and are generally called Spanish feet.

From the broad base created by the bold carved feet, the design of the chair carries the viewer's eyes upward. The front legs thrust up to conical points near the seat. The stiles continue the upward movement, and they also terminate in conical points, upon which sits the only element that visually holds the chair down — the distinctive arched crest.

86

The turner who made this chair also made an identical chair now at the Winterthur Museum and the closely related armchair (86b).[2] He used the same woods — poplar, ash, and maple — in a similar manner as the turner who made the preceding chair and armchair 85b.

1. For an English example originally owned in New England, see number 34 in Kane, *American Seating Furniture*.

2. The side chair at the Winterthur Museum is number 55.731.

NOTES ON STRUCTURE AND CONDITION: The rear legs are chamfered at the base on their inner edges, and the exposed corners of the front seat rail have a broad chamfer. The seat has been rerushed in recent years. The chair has been cleaned and refinished. Many joints have added pins. The left stile is cracked.

MATERIALS: *Poplar* posts and banisters; ash seat rails, splat rail, and stretchers; maple crest and splat rail.

PROVENANCE: The chair was purchased by Florence Evans Bushee in the twentieth century.

ACCESSION: 1976.236   A gift of the estate of Florence Evans Bushee

86a. Armchair. London, 1700–1725. Beech; H. 49 (124.5); W. 23 (58.4); SEAT D. 14¾ (37.5); SEAT H. 19 (48.3). Albany Institute of History and Art. *The chair, branded "SS," belonged to Stephanus Schuyler (1732–1798) of Albany.*

86b. Armchair. Boston-Salem area, 1715–1740. H. 50¼ (127.6); D. 20 (50.8); SEAT H. 16½ (41.9). Private collection. Photograph, courtesy, Archives of American Art and the Henry Francis du Pont Winterthur Museum.

87 / Side Chair

1730–1780
Connecticut River valley
H. 43⅝ (110.8); W. 19½ (49.5); SEAT D. 13 (33); SEAT H. 16⅞ (42.9)

This chair and the armchair following are examples of the common type of banister-back chair, with banisters that are split spindles, not molded slats. Chairmakers made banisters by splitting the wood to be turned, gluing it together with a thin softwood slat

87

between, turning the work, and resplitting it. The flat, or split, surface faced the front of the chair except on a few Connecticut and western Massachusetts examples.[1]

On English prototypes the banisters are flanked by the same type of carved splat-stiles as held the cane on contemporary London chairs.[2] On American chairs, banisters are not flanked by carved members but instead are set evenly across the width of the chair back or clustered toward the center, emulating a splat.

The work of turners, such chairs were made in both urban and rural America in great numbers and over a long period of time. A regional study of baluster, or banister, turnings on eighteenth-century New England stairways would help pinpoint designs of banister-back chairs, for the turner who supplied the house joiner with stair balusters also produced the local chairs.

Variations in banister-back chairs are endless. They came with carved crests, much like that on chair no. 85, or uncarved crests suggestive of carved ones in an imaginative variety of silhouettes (see II-1, III-23, and chair no. 88). All have turned front stretchers. The front stretcher on this chair is of the most popular pattern; it remained in use through the eighteenth century, appearing on rural Queen Anne and Chippendale chairs. The front legs are typical turner's work, appearing often on eighteenth-century ladder-back chairs (see chair no. 79). The uncarved crest is similar to that on some chairs from the Connecticut River valley.[3] The boldly turned, well-articulated stiles are of a common pattern but handsomer than most. The finials are neatly delineated and distinctive.

1. Kane, *American Seating Furniture,* no. 41; Fales, *Historic Deerfield,* figs. 41, 43.
2. Fales, *Historic Deerfield,* fig. 30.
3. Ibid., fig. 42.

NOTES ON STRUCTURE AND CONDITION: The posts are marked with scribe lines at all joints. The top of each front leg is decorated with scribed circles. The chair has a modern rush seat. The upper right stretcher is a replacement. Coats of black and red paint are beneath the present coat of brown.

MATERIALS: *Soft maple* posts and all but the second banister from the left; *ash* seat rails, stretchers, crest, and splat rail; beech banister second from left.

PROVENANCE: Mrs. John (Jane Curtis) Parker of Boston sold this chair to the donor.

ACCESSION: 1946.1006   A gift of William Sumner Appleton

88 / Armchair

1730–1770
Probably Portsmouth area
H. 30⅝ (77.8); W. 19⅞ (50.5); SEAT D. 13¼ (33.7); SEAT H. 15 (38.1)

This diminutive chair stands merely 15 inches high at the seat. In the eighteenth century an "arm chair Col'd Black" or "Elbow chair" — as an armchair was often called — may have been designated a "child's chair" if it was as small as this one. It probably matched a set of full-sized "strait back" chairs with "scollopt Top," to which it was merely "1 small Ditto."[1]

The Society's example is more attractive than the usual scalloped-top elbow chair. The arm supports and stiles have a handsome relationship in pattern and proportion. The splat rail is more decoratively contoured than most. The feet, although mere extensions of the front legs, are pleasing because they are set off by the rings above them. The design of the turned front stretchers is atypical; usually a thin central ring is flanked by bulbous turnings. An interesting prototype for this variant stretcher pattern can be seen in the medial and rear stretchers of chair no. 83.

88

This distinctive armchair, though it has no known history, can be attributed to New Hampshire; related finials, similarly shaped arms, and drooping handholds appear on chairs from the Portsmouth area (III-21).[2]

1. As cited in inventories: "arm chair Col'd Black" from Deacon Samuel Meriam of Concord, 1764, vol. 46, p. 66, Middlesex County (Mass.) Probate; "Elbow chair" from Edward Vail of Boston, 1749, vol. 43, p. 156; "child's chair" from Thomas Tilestone of Boston, 1794, vol. 93, p. 181; "strait back" from William Palfrey of Boston, 1766, vol. 65, p. 248; "scollopt Top" from Mrs.

Elizabeth Luckis of Boston, 1760, vol. 65, p. 59; "1 small Ditto" from Arthur Savage of Boston, 1735, vol. 32, p. 204; all but Meriam from old series, Suffolk County (Mass.) Probate.

2. The authors are indebted to Patricia Kane for pointing out that the arm and handhold designs are found on number 47 in Kane, *American Seating Furniture*, and on an armchair at the New Hamp-

shire Historical Society (no. 1966.30.14). Similar finials can be seen on number 4, *Decorative Arts of New Hampshire*.

NOTES ON STRUCTURE AND CONDITION: The front posts are round-tenoned into the arms and held with one wooden pin each; the arms are tenoned into the stiles and pinned. The old splint seat may be original. A ¾-by-5-inch strip has chipped away from the lower edge of the crest rail. The chair retains four coats of paint, black, red, gold, and black.

MATERIALS: Maple; *ash* stretchers and side and rear seat rails.

PROVENANCE: The chair is from the collection that Chauncy C. Nash assembled in the early twentieth century; it descended to the donors.

ACCESSION: 1971.377   A gift of Mr. and Mrs. Stephen H. Nash in memory of Chauncy C. Nash

89 / Side Chair

1775–1800
Southern Connecticut or possibly Long Island, New York
H. 42 (106.7); W. 19¾ (50.2); SEAT D. 13½ (34.3); SEAT H. 16¾ (42.5)

This crest rail, the antithesis of the high crests on the preceding chairs, sags as if loosely suspended between the stiles. The design, popular with turners in southern New England and Long Island, emulates the concave center of Queen Anne yoke crests, such as that on one from western Connecticut (III-22). Turners made chairs with this crest with either the baluster-shaped splat common on Queen Anne chairs or with molded banisters (89a) but not, it would seem from surviving examples, with turned banisters.[1]

The turnings are the most important elements in the design. The skillfully wrought squat baluster forms on the front legs of chair no. 89 are some of the finest on turners' chairs. The mirroring of the turnings on the stile above and below the columns is an unusual refinement. In unseen craftsmanship the chair excels as well; for example, the backs of the molded slats are neatly chamfered. Unfortunately, this example has replaced front stretchers, a considerable loss because the original pair were surely decoratively turned.

Of the many chairs to survive with dipped crests and molded banisters, the authors know of only one closely related example, a painted armchair with the same precise turnings, illustrated in a photograph of an elderly man taken near the turn of the century. The photograph, owned by the New Haven Colony Historical Society, appears in the best work on the turned chairs of the New Haven Colony area, Robert F. Trent, *Hearts & Crowns*.[2]

In the late nineteenth century, chair no. 89 belonged to Myron Dudley, a minister and antiquarian, but because his peripatetic career encompassed a number of ministries (see entry 70), it is impossible to say when and where he acquired it.

89

1. Trent, *Hearts & Crowns,* nos. 35, 43–45, 57, 58, illustrating baluster-shaped splat chairs, and nos. 36, 47–50, 55, 56, 59, illustrating molded banister-back chairs.

2. Ibid., 90.

NOTES ON STRUCTURE AND CONDITION: The joints of the crest and splat rails to the stiles are held by one pin each. The old rush seat is not original. The feet have been cut, the right front foot chipped, the left front foot pieced. Black paint covers an earlier coat of red paint.

MATERIALS: *Soft maple.*

PROVENANCE: The chair was apparently brought to the Marrett House in Standish, Me., by Mary Marrett Dudley, the widow of the Reverend Mr. Myron Dudley (1837–1905), and descended with the house to the donor.

ACCESSION: 1959.311   A bequest of Frances S. Marrett

89a

89a. Side Chair. Rhode Island, 1760–1800. Maple; H. 39 (99.1); W. 19⅛ (48.6); SEAT D. 13 (33.0); SEAT H. 16 (40.6). Society for the Preservation of New England Antiquities.

90 / Side Chair

1725–1735
London
H. 44¼ (112.4); W. 20¾ (52.7); SEAT D. 15⅛ (38.4); SEAT H. 18 (45.7)

When Englishmen went to China to trade, they brought home objects and ideas: tea and the fashion for tea drinking, china cups and the desire for tea equipage, choice woodenware and visions of exotic furniture design.

The "crooked" — that is, posture-conforming — shape of the back of this chair, the straight-sided splat, and the very idea of a splat are Chinese design features that were incorporated into English and American furniture. The cabriole leg and cyma-curved skirt, also of Chinese origin, probably were more directly derived from the French. London chairmakers wedded Chinese and French characteristics to produce the chairs we call "Queen Anne."

The new style reached America in the late 1720s in sets of cane chairs made in London. This chair and its two mates were part of a set of at least six, to judge from the inked numerals on the stretchers and skirts. These beech chairs, stained a walnut color, come from the same tradition of English manufacturing and American importing as cane chairs no. 82, 83, and 84.

Far fewer cabriole cane chairs were imported to America than cane chairs of the earlier sort, for soon after the introduction of the cabriole style, cane passed out of fashion. In the 1740s, the mass production of caneware virtually ceased in London, and the colonies' great importation of London chairs ended.[1] American chairmakers, never able to compete in the production of cane chairs, now took over the market for fashionable chairs, satisfying the colonists' desires for formal seating with colonial products.

This cabriole cane chair and its mates, American in their ownership, are important in the history of New England furniture because they illustrate the kind of imported

90

examples that introduced Americans to the new style. They presage the curved back, solid splat, shaped skirt, and cabriole legs of the new fashion while keeping the verticality of the old style, a combination that characterized the Queen Anne style in New England.

Chairs like this example were not copied exactly by American chairmakers. A small number of similar chairs were made with canted backs and cabrioles that are square in cross section (90a).[2] But the individual features seen on this London chair introduced New Englanders to all the design elements they would choose for their Queen Anne style.

The new curved back was to dominate chair design for years to come. Splats became standard for Queen Anne and later for Chippendale chairs. However, except for leather-backed chairs like the next one, straight-sided splats seldom appear on American chairs.[3] The shape of the crest was popular, but only for a short time, on canted-back and crooked-back chairs (see chair 91b). Shaped skirts and cabriole legs became the rule on Queen Anne chairs, yet exact copies of this early skirt and leg pattern are not known.[4]

The stretcher pattern, however, became more than common; it was ubiquitous in New England. The side stretcher design on this London chair — quickly dropped from London products — remained the standard on Massachusetts and Rhode Island chairs until the Revolutionary era (see detail 95a and chair no. 109).

This chair and its mates were acquired in the 1830s by Samuel Batchelder, a Boston industrialist, apparently when he purchased the Cutts house in Saco, Maine. The first Cutts to settle in Saco, then Pepperrellboro, was Thomas (1736–1821), who moved from Kittery, where he had been a clerk to Sir William Pepperrell (see entry 16).[5] Cutts made his fortune in Pepperrellboro and built his house on an island, part of which he purchased from Sir William.

Cutts was too young to have acquired these chairs when they were new. The original owner is unknown, but it is conceivable that Cutts bought them from his mentor. Certainly, the chairs are of a sort that might have belonged to such a wealthy man. Although this chair was a stock item in London, in America it was what every imported item was expected to be, an elegant example of "ye New fashion."[6]

1. Symonds, "English Cane Chairs, Part 2," 91.

2. Examples are a Boston chair advertised in *Antiques* 110 (December 1976): 1229, and a Connecticut chair in *Antiques* 96 (October 1969): 526.

3. A few distinctive Rhode Island chairs with straight-sided splats are known; see Kirk, *American Chairs*, nos. 154, 155.

4. The chairs cited in note 2 have related but not identical skirt and leg patterns to those of this chair. Similar examples that lack the turnings above the knees and whose cabrioles are square in cross sec-

tion are two canted-back armchairs at the Winterthur Museum (54.503 and 54.505) and an armchair at the Longfellow National Historical Site. Examples of canted-back chairs having the related skirt pattern and turned legs are found in the collection of the American Antiquarian Society, and a pair in Nutting, *Pilgrim Century*, rev. ed., nos. 455, 456.

5. Howard, *Genealogy of the Cutts Family*, 524–25.

6. "Pepperrell Manuscripts," *New England His-*

torical and Genealogical Register 19 (1865): 146, where Pepperrell asks for "a dos^n of hansome Chairs of ye New fashion" from his London factor. The chairs Pepperrell would have received in 1738 were presumably of a newer fashion than this chair.

NOTES ON STRUCTURE AND CONDITION: The front skirt is tenoned into the block ends of the front legs. Only the rear stretchers are round-tenoned; elsewhere rectangular mortises and tenons are used. The side seat rails are tenoned to the front seat rail. The rear seat rail is tenoned to the side seat rails and not, as is common practice, to the rear legs. Tack holes and old photographs show that the seat was upholstered for many years. The beaded edges on the front and side seat rails are replacements. The front skirt has new tenons and is backed with an added oak block. The right side knee bracket is missing. Iron L-shaped braces reinforce the rear legs and the seat frame. The chair is now stained dark brown. An old ink inscription "N°2" is on the left stretcher. (The other two chairs are "N°5" and "N°6.")

MATERIALS: *Beech.*

PROVENANCE: Apparently purchased with the Cutts house by Samuel Batchelder (1784–1879), the side chair descended to his son Francis L.; to the latter's son Charles F. Sr.; and then to Charles F. Jr. and his wife, the donor.

ACCESSION: 1976.168.2   A gift of Mrs. Charles F. Batchelder

90a. Side Chair. Boston, 1725–1740. Maple; H. 43 (109.1); W. 19 (48.2); D. 15 (38.0). Private collection. Photograph, courtesy, Bernard and S. Dean Levy, Inc., New York.

91 / Side Chair

1724–1750
Boston
H. 40^{13}/₁₆ (103.7); W. 18^7/₁₆ (46.8); SEAT D. 15^3/₈ (39.1); SEAT H. 17^1/₁₆ (43.3)

While cane chairs were being made in and exported from London, chairmakers in other English towns were producing related chairs with sturdy but less fashionable leather upholstery.[1] New England's counterpart to the provincial leather chair was exported in great number from the port of Boston; it is known today as the "Boston chair."

Four distinct types are identifiable:[2] (1) those with a flat plain crest between taller turned stiles (91a), the only type with canted backs; (2) those with an elegant undulating

91

crest and usually Spanish feet (91b); (3) those like this chair, with a round crest indented at the shoulder, usually standing on turned feet; (4) those with a rather traditional Queen Anne yoke crest (91c).

Relatively few of the first and earliest type survive. On some (91a), the turnings relate to Boston banister-back chairs; on others, the turnings suggest they were made in New York.[3] The fourth type comprises a small group of chairs, probably from Rhode Island.[4]

Many examples of the second and third types survive. Both types were produced by the same Boston chairmakers, although the third type (chair no. 91) apparently was popular later and longer than the elegantly crested variety. Following a simple design formula, Boston chairs were produced in volume and exhibit the casual craftsmanship to be expected from such production. Often the left and right legs are not identical (see III-31). Turned front legs, far cheaper to produce than carved cabrioles, were made with carved Spanish feet, usually formed with additional pieces of wood glued at the toes (chairs 91b and 91c are missing the additional pieces), or with baluster-turned feet, usually decorated with a central scribed ring.

These chair frames, made to be upholstered, follow in the upholstered chair tradition of the low-backed seats made in the second half of the seventeenth century (I-5). The old form, first modified with the verticality inspired by William and Mary design, was further modernized when it was given the crooked or curved backs of the Queen Anne fashion.

Leather — cheaper in the eighteenth century than cane or fabric — was an inexpensive material consistent with mass production. Yet the upholstered chairs cost more to produce than slat-backs or banister-backs. Samuel Grant of Boston sold slat-backs with three slats at 6 or 7 shillings each and leather chairs at 26 shillings each.[5]

91a. Side Chair. Boston, 1715–1735. *Maple and red oak;* H. 47 (119.4); W. 17¼ (43.8); SEAT D. 14⁹⁄₁₆ (37.0); SEAT H. 19³⁄₁₆ (48.7). Mabel Brady Garvan Collection, Yale University Art Gallery.

91b. Side Chair. Boston, 1724–1735. Maple and oak; H. 44⅝ (113.3); W. 18¾ (47.6); SEAT D. 15 (38.1); SEAT H. 18½ (47.0). Private collection, Milwaukee, Wisconsin. Photograph, P. Richard Eells. *The chair retains its original black leather upholstery.*

91c. Side Chair. Newport, 1730–1755. Maple; H. 41¼ (106.0); W. 19 (48.3); SEAT D. 14⅜ (36.5); SEAT H. 17½ (44.5). Newport Historical Society. *The chair probably belonged to William Ellery (1727–1820) of Newport. The black leather upholstery is original.*

Brass nails embellished the leather upholstery. Generally double rows of tacks outlined the splat and decorated the front seat rail but single rows decorated the side seat rails. This chair has been reupholstered following the pattern of holes left by the original tacking.

The production of great numbers of Boston chairs required successful mass export sales. The chairs sold so well in American ports that they offered strong competition to local chairmakers. A Philadelphia upholsterer had to fight for his share of his city's chair sales by making "Maple Chairs as cheap as from Boston."[6]

Part of the success of these chairs should probably be credited to the comfort afforded by their backs — curved to a body-conforming shape, high enough to support shoulders, and upholstered for pliant support. Boston chairs introduced a more comfortable form of seating than most urban Americans had previously enjoyed.

Chairs like this one were made for a quarter of a century, from at least 1724, when the Boston upholsterer Thomas Fitch first mentioned leather crooked-back chairs, until about 1750.[7] This period, the most prosperous in colonial Boston's history, was nurtured by impressive mercantile successes in the 1720s and 1730s.[8] Boston shipping carried all manner of merchandise to ports along the Atlantic coast and to the West Indies. Leather chairs made in Boston and the neighboring communities were part of these profitable cargoes. In the third quarter of the eighteenth century, Philadelphia supplanted Boston as the center of economic prosperity, and Philadelphia chairs — light, inexpensive Windsor chairs — supplanted the Boston leather chairs as the common export chair of America.

1. Symonds, "English Cane Chairs, Part 2," 91, nos. 21, 22.

2. Three forms are carefully analyzed by Randall, "Boston Chairs."

3. Forman attributed some of the group to New York, including the chair Randall suggests might be "Piscataqua."

4. See advertisement, *Antiques* 112 (July 1977): 60; a walnut example in the collection of Stanley Stone; *John Brown House Loan Exhibition*, no. 1; and Greenlaw, *New England Furniture*, no. 86.

5. Grant Account Book, September 15 and 28, 1732, pp. 170, 173, Massachusetts Historical Society.

6. Randall, "Boston Chairs," 13, quoting the *Pennsylvania Gazette*, June 14, 1744.

7. Fitch Account Book, account with Adam Powell, March 1724, p. 273, Massachusetts Historical Society.

8. Jobe, "Boston Furniture Industry, 1720–1740," 4, 5.

NOTES ON STRUCTURE AND CONDITION: Rectangular tenons are used except for the front stretcher. Originally the joints were not pinned. The seat rails have been reglued, and some wooden pins have been added. The rear seat rail has been inverted. The lower $1\frac{1}{2}$ inches of the feet have been replaced. The chair was refinished early in this century.

MATERIALS: *Soft maple.*

PROVENANCE: This chair was purchased with nine similar chairs from the Luke Vincent Lockwood Collection, Parke-Bernet, sale 1521, May 1954, lot 335; the set was in Lockwood's possession when illustrated by him in *Colonial Furniture*, rev. ed., vol. 2, fig. 485.

ACCESSION: 1954.32   Museum purchase

92 / Side Chair

1730–1770
Coastal New England, probably Connecticut
H. 41¼ (104.8); W. 20¹⁄₁₆ (51); SEAT D. 15½ (39.4); SEAT H. 18¾ (47.6)

The round-shouldered yoke crest that became standard on Queen Anne chairs made in New England first appeared on chairs with molded stiles. The crest, carved to carry the molded contours inward, draws attention to the splat. Here, the splat has a simple baluster shape often used by New England craftsmen.

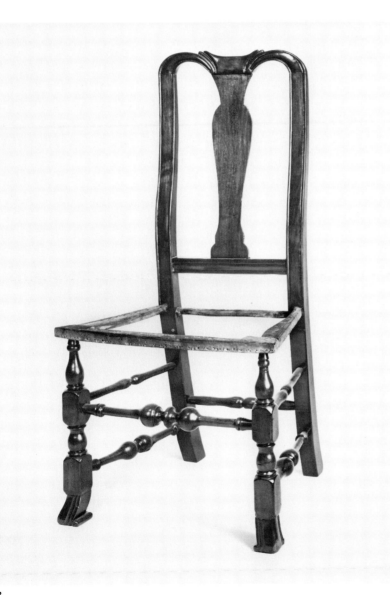

92

92a

92b

92a (far left). Armchair. Boston area, 1730–1740. Maple and white pine; H. 45 (114.3); W. 24½ (62.2); D. 24½ (62.2); SEAT H. 16 (40.6). Mr. and Mrs. Stanley Stone, Milwaukee, Wisconsin.

92b (left). Side Chair. Boston, 1730–1750. Maple; H. 41 (104.1); W. 18⅝ (47.3); SEAT D. 15³⁄₁₆ (38.6); SEAT H. 17¾ (45.1). Historic Cherry Hill. *The chair, branded "RS," originally belonged to Robert Sanders (1705–1765) of Scotia, New York.*

The most stylish examples with this back design feature square cabriole legs (92a), an early form of cabriole. The cabriole chairs are rare and date from about 1730; chairs like this one, with turned legs and Spanish feet, are common and were made over a far longer period.

Chairs of the turned-leg variety have been called "transitional" or "country" chairs; they are neither. The design is not a transition between styles but a combination of them. The turned base contains the earliest elements of the design; the molded façade of the stiles is of somewhat later origin; the curve of the back is a still later characteristic; the carved modeling of the crest and, last, the baluster-shaped splat are the most advanced features. The combination seen on this chair was popular for too long to be called "transitional" (see II-18, a chair probably made in 1775).

Nor are such chairs "country." The design elements — the block and baluster turnings on the front legs, the front stretchers, and the molded stiles — are so similar to those on urban leather chairs (92b) that it is apparent that baluster-splat chairs, both leather and rush-seated, were produced by the same urban chairmakers.[1] In seacoast towns without upholsterers, only the rush-seated version could be made, and it was, in great number.

Many surviving chairs closely resemble the Society's. An early theory divided the group on the basis of characteristics, such as the robustness or flatness of the crest rail and the flair or verticality of the feet.[2] The flatter crest and more vertical feet were ascribed to Connecticut, the better carved examples to Massachusetts. The theory ignored Rhode Island, although the crest rail, in stretched form, is on Rhode Island leather chairs (chair 91c). Surely the form was manufactured there as well.

This chair may be a Connecticut example. An identical chair and a related one are from Lyme, at the mouth of the Connecticut River.[3] The Society's chair apparently belonged to Myron Dudley, a Congregational minister (see entry 70) who owned furniture from Connecticut and Rhode Island.

This example is most handsome. The stretchers are robustly turned, as are the legs just beneath the seat. The crest rail is well carved. The chair is boldly and gracefully wrought, particularly at the splat. The original seat was rush. In the nineteenth century, wooden strips were added to enlarge the seat and curve its front rail (92c), an attempt at the appearance of a compass seat (III-24). The chair was then upholstered.

1. For examples, see Greenlaw, *New England Furniture*, no. 41; *Israel Sack Collection*, 3:743. John Singleton Copley portrayed the Boston merchant John Amory standing next to a chair with a baluster splat like that on this chair; see Prown, *Copley*, vol. 1, no. 220.

2. Keyes, "Study in Differences," 6–7.

3. The identical chair is number 14; a related roundabout chair, number 15 in Myers and Mayhew, *New London County Furniture*, 22. Number 75 in Kane, *American Seating Furniture*, is a closely related chair acquired by a Hartford collector in the nineteenth century. A related set of four chairs descended in a Wethersfield family and are now at the Webb-Deane-Stevens Museum.

NOTES ON STRUCTURE AND CONDITION: The Spanish feet are of one piece. A bleached and discolored finish was removed in 1977, and mahogany stain, matching surviving traces of the original finish, was applied. Pins have been added at the crest and stiles.

92c

MATERIALS: *Soft maple.*

PROVENANCE: The chair was brought to the Marrett House in Standish, Me., by Mary Marrett Dudley, the widow of Myron Dudley (1837–1905), and descended with the house to the donor.

ACCESSION: 1959.426   A bequest of Frances S. Marrett

93 / Side Chair

1730–1770
Eastern Massachusetts
H. 40⅞ (103.8); W. 18⁵⁄₁₆ (46.5); SEAT D. 13¹⁄₁₆ (33.2); SEAT H. 16⅞ (42.9)

The design of this chair back is most common on examples like chair no. 92, whose turned legs begin beneath the seat rail and terminate in carved Spanish feet. This chair is a rare variant whose turned legs extend above the seat rail and end in turned feet. Similar legs are often seen on banister-back chairs (93a). The top surface of the front legs of both chairs is decoratively scribed with circles, a finishing touch seen on slat-back chairs.

Chair no. 93 was one of several designs being made simultaneously in one shop. The chairmaker turned his standard front leg and front and side stretchers for use in several products: banister-back chairs with plain crests (93a); others with carved crests (93b), and baluster-splat chairs like no. 93. No mate to this chair is known, suggesting limited production of the last type. To judge from their turnings (compare with chair no. 105), the three chairs pictured here originated in eastern Massachusetts. The Society's chair is from a collection acquired principally along the coast south of Boston.

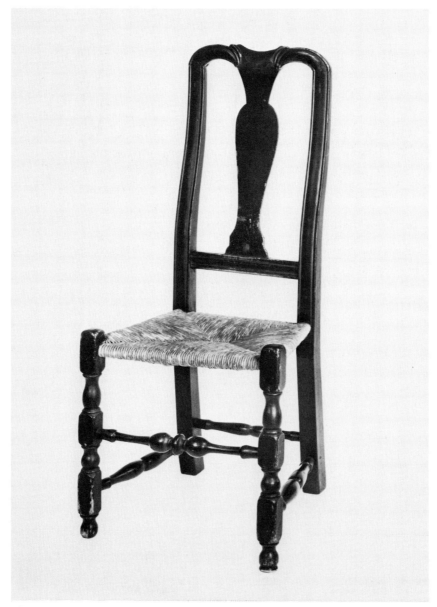

93

NOTES ON STRUCTURE AND CONDITION: The seat is modern rush. The chair, in fine condition, was painted black many years ago. The disk below the left front foot is nearly worn away.

MATERIALS: Maple; *poplar* front legs; *ash* seat rails.

PROVENANCE: The chair was acquired by Chauncy C. Nash in the early twentieth century and descended to the donors.

ACCESSION: 1971.375   A gift of Mr. and Mrs. Stephen H. Nash in memory of Chauncy C. Nash

93a. Side Chair. Coastal New England, probably Massachusetts, 1725–1750. Maple; H. 45 (114.3); SEAT D. 13 (33.0); SEAT H. 17¼ (43.8). Frank and Barbara Pollack Collections.

93b. Side Chair. Coastal New England, probably Massachusetts, 1725–1750. Maple; H. 45½ (115.6). Photograph, courtesy, Israel Sack, Inc., New York.

94 / Side Chair

1735–1760
Boston area
H. 41¾ (106); W. 21⅞ (55.6); SEAT D. 16½ (41.9); SEAT H. 18¹/₁₆ (45.9)

The standard New England Queen Anne chair features: a yoke crest, flat-façaded stiles, a baluster-shaped splat, a cavetto splat shoe capped by a quarter round, a loose seat, a

94

scalloped front seat rail, scooped side seat rails, cabriole front legs with ogee brackets, turned front feet on disks, chamfered back legs, block-and-turned side stretchers, and swelled medial and rear stretchers.

This formula, which became a New England classic, was adopted in Boston in about 1730. In 1732, the painter John Smibert depicted Mrs. Andrew Oliver in a chair similar to this one, and in the same year Samuel Grant, a Boston upholsterer, billed clients for "6 Leath Chairs maple frames hosbone round feet and Cus[hio]n Seats" and "8 Leathr Chairs horsebone feet and banist[er] backs."[1] Horsebone is today called cabriole, round feet are turned feet, cushion seats are loose seats, and banister backs are the baluster-shaped splat-backs.

The style was inspired by English models, yet Boston craftsmen did not duplicate English chairs.[2] They combined the graceful curved outlines inherent in the style with the strong vertical thrust of the older fashion, a verticality rarely seen in English counterparts of the second quarter of the eighteenth century. The Boston version of the design, which spread to other towns in Massachusetts, is closely related to Rhode Island examples (see the next chair). In Boston, there were few modifications of the pattern. Stretchers varied slightly. Claw feet such as those on chair no. 99 and rounded seats, called "compass" seats in the eighteenth century, were more expensive options. An example with a compass-shaped loose seat is among the numerous surviving chairs documented to the Boston area by their histories.[3] The over-the-rail upholstered seat of compass shape was the most expensive version (III-24), and in 1757 Thomas Marshall of Boston had John Singleton Copley paint his portrait sitting in just such a handsome chair.[4] The basic design remained the mainstay of stylish chair production in Boston for at least thirty years.

1. Jobe, "Boston Furniture Industry, 1720–1740," 42, 43.

2. For English examples, see Macquoid, *History of English Furniture*, vol. 2, fig. 181, and Hinckley, *Directory of Furniture*, fig. 30.

3. Documented chairs similar to this one include the John Leach chair at the Museum of Fine Arts, Boston, Randall, *American Furniture*, no. 139; the James Blake chair, Roland V. Vaughn Collection, American Art Association, sale 3926, November 1931, lot 98; the Samuel Pickering Gardner chairs, six of which are mentioned (two illustrated) in Fales, *Historic Deerfield*, 42–43, and a seventh illustrated on the inside cover of *Antiques* 118 (September 1980); the Jane Brown chairs, Fales, *Historic Deerfield*, 44–45; the Thomas Dering chair, Failey, *Long Island*, 65; the Shuttleworth family chair at the Dedham Historical Society; the Holyoke family chair, *Boston Furniture*, fig. 34, which has a compass-shaped loose seat.

4. The Marshall portrait, in the collection of the Daughters of the American Revolution Museum in Washington, D.C., is figure 52 in Prown, *Copley*, vol. 1.

NOTES ON STRUCTURE AND CONDITION: The rear legs are chamfered on all edges between the seat rails and stretchers and on the front edges below the stretchers. The back of the stiles is chamfered. The edges of the splat are slightly beveled. No corner blocks were ever present.

The replaced loose seat is upholstered in a modern reproduction worsted. The chair is in excellent condition.

MATERIALS: *Black walnut.*

PROVENANCE: The chair came to the Society with a house in Weston, Mass., whose collection was assembled locally in the late nineteenth and early twentieth centuries.

ACCESSION: 1973.324   A bequest of Ellen M. and Alice E. Jones

95 / Side Chair

1735–1760
Newport area
H. 42¹⁄₁₆ (106.8); W. 21¾ (55.2); SEAT D. 16⁹⁄₁₆ (42.1); SEAT H. 17⅝ (44.8)

Subtle differences in pattern distinguish this painted maple chair from the preceding walnut chair, and the barely discernible variations reveal the locale of the craftsmen.

95

The preceding chair was made in Boston, this one in or near Newport. A walnut, but otherwise identical, chair is in the collections of the Newport Historical Society and belonged to the Bull family of Newport.

Craftsmen in both cities made chairs of walnut, the preferred wood in the second quarter of the eighteenth century, or of maple. They either stained the maple to simulate the more elegant walnut or painted it black in the ebonizing tradition of English beech chairs.[1]

While the same design formula was used for Queen Anne chairs in both Newport and Boston, many Newport products have the more slender and deeply notched splat evident here. Newport stretchers, too, are thinner. The central swell on the medial and rear stretchers is more compact. The side stretcher shafts exhibit more flare, and the ring on each shaft is more pronounced (95a).[2] The rear feet lack chamfers.

This chair and its three mates in the Society's collection were part of a set of at least thirteen owned by Silas Casey (1734–1814), a merchant of East Greenwich, Rhode Island. The set may have been new when acquired by Casey (who married in 1759) or was possibly inherited from his father.

Silas Casey patronized furniture craftsmen in Warwick, North Kingston, and Newport, dealing in Newport with the cabinetmaker Edmund Townsend and the chairmaker John Proud. In 1773, Proud billed Casey for six chairs, which obviously is not for this much larger set.[3] Yet Proud may have made this chair if, as was often the case, the Casey family continued to deal with one chairmaker's shop for many years.

Casey's 1773 bill from John Proud of Newport provides a new and early working date for the chairmaker.[4] John Proud (1714–1794) was the brother of Joseph (1711–1769) and William (1720–1779), all chairmakers.[5] William and his sons worked in Providence, Joseph in Newport, and John in Newport and later East Greenwich. The Proud chairmakers were all trained in America; their father, John (d. 1757), a Yorkshire clockmaker, had come to America in 1713, when Joseph was only two years old.[6]

1. Figure 19 in Carpenter, *Arts and Crafts of Newport*, is a walnut example. The ebonizing tradition is discussed by Symonds, "Turkey Work, Beech and Japanned Chairs," 225.

2. The stretcher design appears on the documented walnut chair from the Bull family at the Newport Historical Society and on documented chairs of different patterns, such as the Bull family chair, figure 6 in Carpenter, *Arts and Crafts of Newport*, and figure 18, another Newport chair.

3. The bill, in the Society's collection of Casey family papers, is for six chairs costing £30.

4. The years 1776 and 1777 are cited by Ott, "Recent Discoveries," 22.

5. Arnold, *Vital Record*, 70.

6. Ibid. "Newport Records," compiled by Henry E. Turner, 181, Section 6, 4–5, Newport Historical Society. Scotti, "Rhode Island Cabinetmakers," 572, cites Joseph as born in Yorkshire and living in Newport by 1737.

NOTES ON STRUCTURE AND CONDITION: The back of the stiles is chamfered; the edges of the splat are beveled. No corner blocks were ever present. The chair is in excellent condition. The set has been repainted black and has new loose seats covered in modern green leather. The original seat frames also survive.

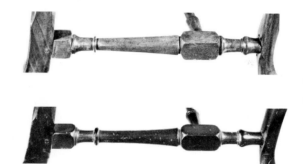

95a. Top: Side Stretcher of Chair No. 94. Boston, 1735–1760. Bottom: Side Stretcher of Chair No. 95. Newport, 1735–1760.

MATERIALS: *Maple.*

PROVENANCE: The chair descended in the family of Silas Casey to his son Wanton, to his grandson Silas, to his son Thomas, to Thomas's son Edward, and then to a niece by marriage, Phoebe McKearnan.

ACCESSION: 1973.27   Museum purchase

96 / Side Chair

1755–1765
Portsmouth, New Hampshire, or York, Maine
H. 39 (99.1); W. 22¼ (56.5); SEAT D. 16⅜ (41.6); SEAT H. 16⅝ (42.2)

While clearly based on the standard New England formula for Queen Anne chairs, this chair is distinctive, for it is shorter than the preceding two examples (39 inches as opposed to 42 inches on the Boston and Rhode Island chairs). Its squat appearance is reinforced by the stiles, which appear broad because the chamfers behind them are so slight. The proportions are a function of time and place.

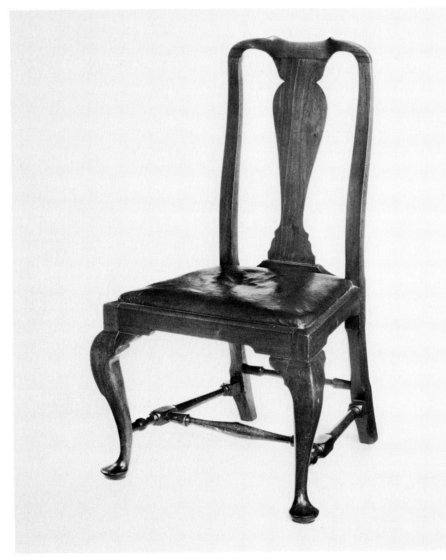

96

This is a later chair than the two preceding Queen Anne chairs. The pattern of the side stretchers differs from that on the others and is more often seen on Chippendale chairs (such as chair no. 108). Chippendale chairs also tend to be more angular than the Queen Anne, yet this Queen Anne chair excels in angularity, featuring sharp creases on the knees, sharp corners on the seat, and, instead of scalloping on the front seat rail, the flat arch (usually reserved for those Queen Anne chairs whose seats are rounded, such as chair no. 98).

While the distinctive design speaks at least in part of the era, it indicates place as well. Precisely what place would be hard to tell were it not for a fine provenance. The chair is part of a set of six, one of three sets acquired by Jonathan Sayward of York, Maine.[1] The other sets are Chippendale chairs (no. 112 and 118). Identical patterns appearing in at least two of the sets—at the ridged knees, knee brackets, seat rails, and stretchers— indicate that the three sets are from one shop.

Although based on Boston designs, the chairs are not from a Boston shop. Ridged knees are common on Salem chairs, but details such as the beveled top edge of the seat rails, the exaggerated knuckles on the claw feet of chair no. 118, and the angularity of this chair discourage attribution to Salem as well as Boston. The chairs may have been made in Portsmouth, where Sayward's son-in-law was a major merchant, or possibly in York. Perhaps the indefatigable joiner-architect-bridgebuilder of York, Samuel Sewall, who made Sayward's case furniture (see chest no. 21) and tables, also made his chairs.

Sayward probably sent the loose seats to Boston to be upholstered. His easy chair (no. 101), bought in 1759, was upholstered by Samuel Grant of Boston, and in 1787 Sayward had Boston's Ziphion Thayer upholster six chair seats in leather. Apparently they were the loose seat frames from chair no. 96 and its mates, then a generation old and in need of upholstering.

Sayward's three sets of chairs by one hand afford an opportunity to study different products coming from one shop within a short period of time. The next three chairs offer the same splendid opportunity.

1. Five originals are extant; a reproduction completes the set.

NOTES ON STRUCTURE AND CONDITION: The seat rails are of thicker wood than that used on chairs no. 94 and 95. No corner blocks were ever present. Modern leather covers the original loose seat. The chair is in excellent condition. Rarely does a chair show so little wear. The turned disks beneath the round feet are completely intact; even the original holes for securing the front legs on the lathe are clearly visible.

MATERIALS: *Black walnut; beech* front and rear loose seat rails; *soft maple* side loose seat rails.

PROVENANCE: The chair shares a provenance with tea chest no. 4.

ACCESSION: 1977.243.1   A gift of the heirs of Elizabeth Cheever Wheeler

97 / Side Chair

1750–1765
Newport
Possibly the shop of John Goddard
H. 41 (104.1); W. 22 (55.9); SEAT D. 16⁹⁄₁₆ (42.1); SEAT H. 17½ (44.5)

Chairs no. 97, 98, and 99 — from extant sets of six, four, and two chairs respectively — make an exciting contribution to the history of American furniture. The three sets, which share a common history, are demonstrably the work of one shop. Were it not for the shared provenance, only the origin of the set including chair no. 98 would have been easy to ascertain.

This chair resembles the Boston version of the standard Queen Anne chair (no. 94). The splat and side stretchers are closer in appearance to those on the Boston chair than

97

to those on Rhode Island chair no. 95. The medial stretcher repeats the pattern of that on the Boston chair, lacking the rings on the Rhode Island one. The rear legs are turned, as they sometimes are on both Boston and Newport examples.

Rounded stiles, seen on many English Georgian chairs and on some elegant Philadelphia chairs, are unusual in New England, where, with some exceptions, they are generally confined to Newport chairs of the very best type.[1] Chair no. 97 is not of the finest type. Of maple, originally stained reddish brown, it is not of expensive walnut or mahogany. It has no carved decoration; the contour of the splat is plain. Chairs just like it are unknown.[2] Were it not for chair no. 98, the authors could barely ascribe this chair to Rhode Island, let alone to Newport or to a particular shop.

But details of construction and tool marks make clear that the three sets — represented by chairs no. 97, 98, and 99 — are by one hand and possibly from about the same time. Were the chairs isolated from one another, the authors would have considered chair no. 97 the oldest, dating from about 1735, and chairs no. 98 and 99 later, midcentury chairs. Grouped together, they give evidence of the long-term availability of chairs of this design.

The three sets were probably ordered at one time for three different rooms in one house. They furnished the house of Charles Barrett, Sr., in New Ipswich, New Hampshire, and through the years moved between his house and the adjacent house of his son. One house was given gentle use by a succession of single women, the other used principally as a summer residence. Barrett's chairs remain in remarkably fine condition.

While chair no. 95 illustrates one tradition of Newport chair production, Barrett's three sets illustrate another. The picture they present of mid-eighteenth-century chair design is one of an enthusiasm for curves. Although square and angular forms were prominent on Newport case furniture and tables, round shapes — the glory of the Queen Anne style — continued as high fashion for Newport chairs.[3] Round shoulders (the yoke crest), rounded stiles, rounded rear legs, compass seats (on chairs no. 98 and 99), and rounded knees are all curves identified with Newport.

---

1. Exceptions are: a chair attributed to the Gaines family of Portsmouth, Randall, *American Furniture*, no. 132; and a set of chairs with a history in the Boston area closely related to this chair, Christie's, New York, sale 5028, December 1980, lot 622.

2. The closest known chairs are: one with a splat like that on chair no. 92, *Antiques* 67 (March 1955): 190, and the Boston set cited in note 1.

3. A 1762 Newport table (I-39) displays the angularity.

NOTES ON STRUCTURE AND CONDITION: The rails of the loose seat frame are thick (1⅛ inches), and the front rail is numbered by large chisel marks;

both characteristics are found on chairs no. 98 and 99 (see III-29). No corner blocks were ever present.

Sometime before 1948, the chair was stripped and refinished. Otherwise it is in excellent condition. All elements are original including the loose seat; the leather upholstery is modern.

MATERIALS: *Soft maple.*

PROVENANCE: The chair apparently descended in the family of Charles Barrett, Sr., to the donor. See chest no. 19.

ACCESSION: 1948.148f   A gift of Caroline Barr Wade

98 / Side Chair

1750–1765
Newport
Possibly the shop of John Goddard
H. 40^{15}/$_{16}$ (104); W. 22^{3}/$_{16}$ (56.4); SEAT D. 17^{1}/$_{16}$ (43.3); SEAT H. 16^{7}/$_{16}$ (41.8)

Stately in form and fluid in line, this chair is the consummate achievement of the Queen Anne style in New England. The elegant design successfully combines an aristocratic vertical posture with the gentility of the curved line. The curve is most prominent on the compass seat.

98

Often called a "balloon" seat today, the seat with rounded front corners was a "compass" seat to the men who scribed the lines of seat frames and rails with a compass. Graceful and ample seats, they were a part of many high-style chairs in England and America and occasionally are found on far less fashionable examples (such as chair no. 125). Their front seat rails are generally cut with simple flat arches.

Compared with the preceding chair, this example is a bit more vertical (the seat is lower, the back taller) and more rounded, although the rear legs are not turned. The splat presents a more elegant curve than that on the preceding chair, and the center crest features a shell that is a cluster of undulating lines.

This beautiful chair was one of a set of six; four are extant, two with their original leather upholstery. The set is the clue to the origin of chairs no. 97 and 99 because the three sets share a provenance and marks of manufacture (see *Notes on Structure and Condition*). Several chairs are very similar to the Society's set, although the form was by no means ordinary.[1] One related set belonged to Moses Brown, a wealthy Providence merchant, who apparently bought his furniture from John Goddard of Newport.[2]

Goddard's correspondence with Brown speaks of his need to "keep my Boys Imploy'd'," indicating that at least in 1763, several workmen were in Goddard's shop.[3] The chairs in the Moses Brown set exhibit variations in the executions of the shell carvings and stretchers, to be expected when more than one hand was at work in the shop. The Society's set is so finely crafted that it seems to have benefited from more of the master's hand, with less help from his "Boys."

1. Similar chairs are one in the Historical Society of York County (Pa.) and others in Greenlaw, *New England Furniture*, no. 51; *Israel Sack Collection*, 3:745, Nutting, *Furniture Treasury*, vol. 2, no. 2130; *American Queen Anne Furniture*, 25, and a set that belonged to Moses Brown, now on loan to the Rhode Island Historical Society (Carpenter, *Arts and Crafts of Newport*, fig. 11).

2. Letters discussing a furniture order including chairs are dated October 10 and 12, 1763, the former from Brown, the latter from Goddard; Moses Brown Papers, Rhode Island Historical Society.

3. Goddard's letter of October 12; see note 2.

NOTES ON STRUCTURE AND CONDITION: The shell is carved on the crest, not applied. Chisels and gouges as well as a rabbet plane were used to cut the seat rails to receive the loose seat. The similarity of the gouge marks on the rails of chairs no. 98 and 99 attest to the work of one man. The loose seat is thick and marked with a chisel like those on chairs no. 97 and 99 (see III-29). No corner blocks were ever present. The loose seat retains its original upholstery (i.e., webbing, linen, marsh grass and curled hair stuffing, linen, and leather).

The condition is excellent; the only damage is a crack in the crest and wear to the leather. The feet retain disks ⅜ inch thick.

MATERIALS: *Black walnut; soft maple* loose seat frame.

PROVENANCE: The chair apparently shares a provenance with chair no. 97 and descended as did chest of drawers no. 19.

ACCESSION: 1948.153a   A gift of Caroline Barr Wade

99 / Side Chair

1750–1765
Newport
Possibly the shop of John Goddard
H. 38¹⁵⁄₁₆ (98.9); W. 22 (55.9); SEAT D. 17 (43.2); SEAT H. 16⁵⁄₁₆ (41.4)

This chair (plate 8) — one of a pair, from a set of at least eight — was made in the same shop, in the same manner, and with the same tools as the two preceding examples and evidently at the same time, although this type of chair remained popular in Newport until at least 1775. Had not all three sets come to the Society together, a common origin

99

would not have been suspected, and although chairs such as this one are always said to be from Newport (and often attributed to a name such as John Goddard), the authors would not have easily attributed this one even to Rhode Island.[1] Numerous chairs like it were owned in the Boston area.[2] The motifs of the carved shell and the bellflower (on the knee), although long associated with Newport, appear on several chairs with Massachusetts histories.[3]

Between 1735 and 1740, English chairmakers introduced chairs of this shape and with these proportions.[4] Decorative motifs — details such as the claw feet and the carved knees — also have English prototypes and were used by American craftsmen outside New England as well.[5] The side stretchers are especially close to English examples (see chair no. 90).

Yet the exact pattern of this chair design is distinctive to America. Although very elegant by New England standards, it is simple compared with English examples with flashy veneers or gilt and japan. The splat here is a modest modification of the splat found on most related English chairs. The shell, however, is more robust, and unlike those at the center crest of English chairs, it rises above the crest.

At least fifty New England examples similar to this one survive, although some chairs vary in splat contour and knee bracket design. Two slightly different designs traditionally have been attributed to New York and Hartford.[6] This design, however, was apparently made by craftsmen in both Boston and Newport, and the differences are even more subtle than those on the earlier chairs from Boston and Rhode Island (chairs no. 94 and 95). As yet, no one can discern a Massachusetts from a Rhode Island example. When and if such a distinction can be made, this chair will be able to serve as a document of the Newport version of what an Englishman would call "Early Georgian" and what Americans continue to regard as "Queen Anne."

1. Chairs of the type are attributed to Newport by Carpenter, *Arts and Crafts of Newport*, fig. 5, and by Ott, "Some Rhode Island Furniture," fig. 4.

2. Similar chairs having histories in the Boston area include the Vose family chair at the Museum of Fine Arts, Boston, the General Warren chair at the Henry Ford Museum, the Salisbury family chair at the Worcester Art Museum, and the Holyoke family chair in a private collection.

3. Examples include a chair having a history of ownership in the Ellis family of Dedham, at the Winterthur Museum and noted in Hummel, "Queen Anne and Chippendale Furniture," pt. 1, 903; the chair from the Phippen family of Salem, Mass., and a chair purchased in Massachusetts in 1830, Carpenter, *Arts and Crafts of Newport*, figs. 27 and 23 respectively; and a similar chair lacking carved feet and shells on the knees descending in the Haven family of Dedham and owned by the Dedham Historical Society.

4. Gilbert, *Furniture at Temple Newsam*, vol. 1, no. 61.

5. English prototypes include the chair cited in note 4; a chair illustrated in Huth, *Lacquer*, figs. 88, 89; a chair illustrated in Macquoid, *History of English Furniture*, vol. 2, fig. 188; and a set of seating furniture made in 1735, Gilbert, "Newly-Discovered Furniture," 224–25. The motifs were used in Virginia; see Gusler, *Furniture of Williamsburg*, no. 16.

6. Fales, *Historic Deerfield*, 46–47, figs. 79, 80, the former possibly Hartford, the latter New York.

NOTES ON STRUCTURE AND CONDITION: The seat rails (III-29) and seat frame are identical in construction to those on the preceding chair. The medial stretcher is of a block-ended type that is joined with rectangular tenons to the side stretchers. The stiles — broader than those on the preceding examples — are pieced at their widest point, a common feature on chairs of this design. Rear brackets — not part of the preceding designs — are nailed in place. No corner blocks were ever present.

The condition is excellent. The loose seat retains fragments of its original webbing and linen underupholstery. Only reupholstered once before, the seat is covered in a reproduction stamped worsted.

MATERIALS: *Black walnut; soft maple* loose seat frame.

PROVENANCE: The chair apparently shares a provenance with chair no. 97 and descended as did chest of drawers no. 19.

ACCESSION: 1948.152b   A gift of Caroline Barr Wade

100 / Roundabout Chair

1740–1765
Probably Boston
H. 30¾ (78.1); W. 26⅝ (67.6); SEAT D. 23¾ (60.3); SEAT H. 16¹¹⁄₁₆ (42.4)

In 1741 Samuel Grant, a Boston upholsterer, was selling leather chairs (probably like chair no. 91) at 32 shillings each, maple chairs at 43, walnut chairs at 65, compass seat chairs at 80, maple elbow chairs (armchairs) at 90, and "a round about wallnutt Chair" at 115 shillings.[1] This is a roundabout walnut chair or, as more accurately described in a Boston inventory of 1747, "half Round about Chair."[2]

In the middle of the eighteenth century, roundabouts or corner chairs were far fewer than side chairs, fewer than "elbows," fewer even than the very expensive easy chairs. At first they were sold individually; in later years they were often made with matching sets of side chairs (see chairs no. 114 and 115). Designed for men and encouraging a singularly masculine sitting posture, they were used with desks or at tables used for writing.[3]

The painting (100a) of George Wyllys (1710–1796) of Hartford shows Connecticut's secretary of state near his books, his desk behind his elbow, the case with the Royal Charter of 1662 at his fingertips, and his legs straddling the cabriole of a chair much like the Society's.

This chair belonged to a contemporary of Wyllys's, Judge Jonathan Sayward of York, the second richest man in Maine before the Revolution, a representative in the legislature, a man who like Wyllys had his coat of arms on the wall. Although inventory references are not specific, Sayward apparently kept his roundabout in the sitting room, which contained his desk and bookcase (in Sayward's case a unified piece of furniture, not the two separate pieces Wyllys enjoyed).

Sayward's sitting room served as his winter bedchamber, at least when he was elderly. Each November or early December, he moved his bed — "1786, Nov. 17   Snow for

100

the first time this fall — I removed my bed from the bed Room to the Sitting Room"
— and returned it in the spring, sometimes as late as early June.[4] Conveniently, his
roundabout was fitted for a chamber pot. Many midcentury corner chairs, even those
not designed with the typical deep skirt, were so equipped.[5]

With its conventional skirt, this roundabout chair is the epitome of fine chair design;
all the elements are beautifully integrated into the roundabout formula. The splat, for
example, is pleasing and perfectly suited to the squat space it fills. The swelled stretchers,
unknown on comparable examples, enhance the curvilinear outline of the chair.

Sayward's roundabout shows no design similarities to his three sets of side chairs (nos.
96, 112, and 118) made in Portsmouth or York. Sayward bought his easy chair (no.
101) in Boston, where he had strong political and business connections. This chair too
was probably made in Boston.

100a. Portrait of George Wyllys. Attributed to Joseph Steward (1735–1822), Hartford, 1785–1795. Oil on canvas; H. 79¾ (202.6); W. 59¾ (151.8). Connecticut Historical Society.

1. Grant Account Book, American Antiquarian Society, 1741 entries: August 22 (leather), August 21 (maple, walnut, compass seats), November 6 (maple elbows), and November 28 (roundabout).

2. Charles Coffin's inventory, old series, vol. 40, p. 301, Suffolk County (Mass.) Probate. Another term is suggested by John Boydell's 1740 inventory: "2 three Corn.ʳ Chairs & Cushions"; old series, vol. 38, p. 177, Suffolk County (Mass.) Probate.

3. Inventory references make this clear, as in the one-line entry: "Black Walnut desk 60/ round about Chair 30/"; Jabez Hatch's 1763 inventory, old series, vol. 62, p. 112, Suffolk County (Mass.) Probate.

4. Sayward Diary, American Antiquarian Society.

5. A somewhat similar chair, also fitted for a chamber pot, is at the Longfellow National Historic Site.

NOTES ON STRUCTURE AND CONDITION: The roundabout is similar in construction to side chairs except that the stretchers are lap-jointed where they cross and are round-tenoned into the legs, and strips are nailed along the rear seat rails so that the loose seat can rest on them as well as on the rabbeted edge of the two front seat rails. Additional strips nailed inside the seat rails supported a board with a hole for a chamber pot. The board and pot are missing. The loose seat has been recovered for many years with the worsted originally on one of Sayward's Chippendale chairs (see detail 118a).

The crest rail, originally nailed to a two-piece arm, is now joined by eight screws to a three-part arm. The left arm, from the handhold to just inside the splat, is an old replacement. Pieced repairs are at the left end of the crest and the back of the right stile. Splines have been added where the front leg joins the rails. The feet are well worn. The chair has been harshly cleaned and refinished.

MATERIALS: *Black walnut; white pine* supports for the chamber pot board; *soft maple* loose seat frame.

PROVENANCE: The chair came to the Society with the furnishings of Sayward's house in York, Me., and probably shares a provenance with tea chest no. 4.

ACCESSION: 1977.264   A gift of the heirs of Elizabeth Cheever Wheeler

101 / Easy Chair

1759
Boston
Clement Vincent or George Bright, chairmaker
Samuel Grant, upholsterer
H. 46⅛ (117.2); W. 33⅞ (86); SEAT D. 21¾ (55.2); SEAT H. 15¾ (40)

In August 1759, Samuel Grant of Boston finished upholstering this easy chair in green worsted, and on August 15 he billed the Boston shopkeeper John Scollay for "a Green

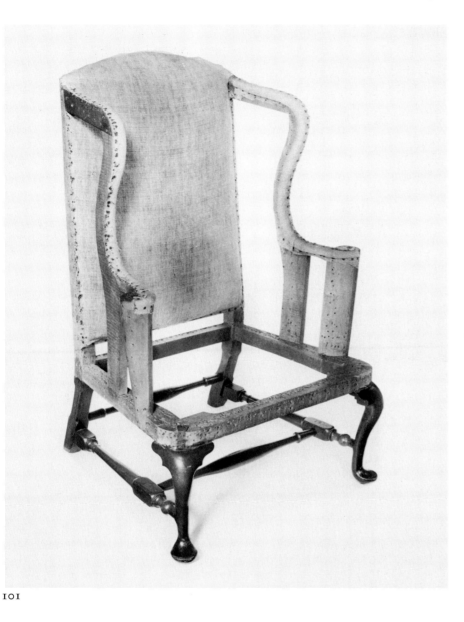

101

Easie Cha^r & packing [£]4:18:6.”[1] The next day Scollay charged Jonathan Sayward the same amount for the chair (bill 4a).

Grant's petty ledgers reveal that in 1759 he was obtaining easy chair frames from two Boston craftsmen: Clement Vincent, who was paid about 14 shillings for each frame, and George Bright, who was paid about 16 shillings each.[2] Vincent supplied three frames, Bright five; and Grant sold five easy chairs during the year.

No other documented Boston cabriole easy chair is known.[3] A superb Newport example at the Metropolitan Museum, New York, signed on the crest rail “Gardner Junr / Newport May / 1758,” has served until now as the only documented cabriole easy chair.[4] The Newport chair retains its splendid original upholstery.

This chair has some of its original upholstery (see *Notes on Structure and Condition*). While its front feet are replacements, the frame serves as a document of Boston construction practices. The precise design of the medial and rear stretchers — especially the unusual contour of the turning at the center — can now be dated and ascribed to Boston.[5] The manner in which the frame is joined (e.g., the crest is set between the stiles, 101a) is here shown to have been current in Boston in 1759. A documented easy chair with all its original upholstery is a prize to be coveted by furniture historians; this chair, revealing all the construction features of the frame, is almost as great a treasure.

1. Grant Account Book, 904, American Antiquarian Society.

2. Grant Petty Ledger, vol. 1, Boston Public Library; for Vincent, see p. 88; for Bright, see p. 95.

3. It is, however, tempting to suppose that the similar easy chair with serpentine crest branded "S.G." (in *Israel Sack Collection*, 5:1335) was upholstered and branded by Grant.

4. Heckscher, "Form and Frame."

5. An easy chair with the same medial stretcher design was sold at auction; George Palmer Collection, American Art Association, sale 2280, October 1928, lot 282.

NOTES ON STRUCTURE AND CONDITION: The rear legs and stiles are of one piece. The side seat rails are tenoned into the front seat rail. The top of each front leg, cut to form a large dovetail, passes through the front seat rail. The maple rear legs and rear stretcher were stained to match the walnut front legs.

Each wing support is tenoned into the seat rail and the wing. The wing is also tenoned into the stile. Each arm support is composed of a vertical element tenoned into the seat rail and a cone-shaped block glued and nailed to it. The arm is nailed to the top of the arm support and wing support. The lower back rail and the arched crest are tenoned into the stiles. All mortise-and-tenon joints are pinned except those of the rear seat rail, lower back rail, and the stretchers.

The surviving upholstery on the back is 1¾-inch webbing covered by a coarse, plain-woven linen, a layer of marsh grass and curled hair stuffing, and an outer layer of linen. Stitches through the back cloth hold the stuffing in place. The edging of the wing is a roll of grass wrapped in linen.

The chair was fitted with casters beneath the feet in the nineteenth century. Because the recent owners considered the upright posture of the back uncomfortable, the casters were removed, the rear feet were cut about ½ inch, and the bottom halves of

101a

the front legs were replaced with new feet and elongated ankles, tilting the chair backward. The original stretchers were retained. The right front knee bracket is replaced.

MATERIALS: *Black walnut* front legs and side and medial stretchers; *maple* rear legs, rear stretcher, and all other secondary wood except for white pine cone-shaped arm supports.

PROVENANCE: Sayward left his widow "the use and improvement of my Easy chair" for her lifetime, after which it shared a provenance with tea chest no. 4.

ACCESSION: 1977.253   A gift of the heirs of Elizabeth Cheever Wheeler

102 / Easy Chair

1755–1770
Probably Newport; possibly New London or Norwich, Connecticut
H. 51⅜ (130.5); W. 35¾ (90.8); SEAT D. 23½ (59.7); SEAT H. 15½ (39.4)

The fabric, not the frame, proved by far the greatest expense in making an easy chair.

1 Easie chair fraim	2: :
6½ y^d chainy @ 6/8	2:13:4
1 y^d ⅛ print 4/	: 4:6
18 y^d silk bind^g 12^d	3:14:4
Tax [tacks] 5/ girt web thred & line 3/	: 8:
4 [lb] curled hair 10/ 4 [lb] feath. 14/	1: 8:
1½ y^d Ticken 9/4 crocus & Ozn^a [2 coarse fabrics] 12/	1: 1:4
mak^g an Easie chair	1:15: 9:18:2[1]

102

The 6½ yards of chainy — a worsted outer fabric — did not cover all the chair; the 1⅛ yards of print — a stamped textile — apparently was used on the outside of the chair back.[2] As a rule, the outer covering (in the instance cited, the chainy, print, and binding) cost about half the total price, the frame about a fifth, the labor even less.

Textiles and stuffing made the chair "easie." The American easy chair descended from English seventeenth-century chairs designed for invalids; these were fitted with small upholstered supports flanking the upper chair backs to cradle dozing heads.[3] By the beginning of the eighteenth century, the wings extended down to the arms, and the seated sleeper was enveloped in upholstered comfort.[4] The upholstered winged chair was known in America in the first quarter of the eighteenth century, but the form did not become popular until after 1725.[5]

In recent years, scholars have stressed that easy chairs were chamber furniture for the elderly. They cite the origin of the form as an invalid's seat, the portraits of elderly sitters in such chairs, and the usual placement of eighteenth-century easy chairs in bedchambers. They even claim that easy chairs were commonly fitted with chamber pots. In their attempt to correct the impressions created by the modern use of easy chairs as parlor furnishings, they overstate their case. None of the easy chairs described (nos. 101, 102, 103, and 104) has a chamber pot fitting because there was no such practice with cabriole easy chairs.

Nor were they solely chairs for the elderly. Jonathan Sayward's easy chair (no. 101) was purchased (according to the bill, 4a) by the judge when he was forty-five years old. He and his wife were living by themselves; their only child had recently married and the judge's elderly mother had died on August 1. Is one to believe that either the judge belatedly ordered the chair for his mother shortly before she died or that he was preparing for his last years while in the prime of life? Easy chairs may have been favorites of the elderly, but the chairs were prestigious items purchased by men of means long before they retired to dozing while seated.

Merchants put the fashionable easy chairs in their best bedchambers. When completely furnishing a chamber, a man had his easy chair upholstered to match the other furnishings. In 1763, the Honorable Benjamin Prat had in the middle chamber of his house in Milton, Massachusetts:

> a Green Harrateen Bed . . .
> Green dᵒ Easy Chair & 8 compass bottom Chairs dᵒ . . .
> Two pʳ Green Harrateen Window Curtains.[6]

Beneath its reproduction worsted damask (102a), this easy chair has much in common with the preceding chair in design and construction. The similarities show that this too is a New England chair and suggests a 1755–1770 date.

The differences in construction may help pinpoint the origin of the chair. The seat rails are lapped at the front corners (102b), a technique common in Philadelphia and used as well in Rhode Island and Connecticut.[7] The quarter-round shape of the leg tenon, which extends through the lapped seat rail, is distinctive. An easy chair at Colonial Williamsburg, believed by Greenlaw to be probably from Newport, and a chair advertised in 1972 have similarly shaped tenons.[8] The three chairs are apparently by the same urban craftsman working in Rhode Island or southeastern Connecticut.

1. Samuel Grant, Account Book, December 3, 1729, p. 32, Massachusetts Historical Society.

2. For an English example with original upholstery including an outside print, see *Golden Age of English Furniture Upholstery,* no. 9.

3. Thornton, *Seventeenth-Century Interior Decoration,* fig. 178.

4. Ibid., figs. 180, 181.

5. Hornor, "Survey of American 'Wing Chairs,'" 29, and Thomas Fitch, Account Book, March 9,

102a

1726, p. 378, and subsequent entries, Massachusetts Historical Society.

6. Cummings, *Inventories*, 201.

7. Heckscher, "Form and Frame," 890.

8. Greenlaw, *New England Furniture*, 76, 77, fig. 68; *Antiques* 102 (September 1972): 369.

NOTES ON STRUCTURE AND CONDITION: The rear legs and rear stiles are of one piece. The construction of the wings is like that of chair no. 101. The arm is screwed to the wing support.

The chair is well worn, the frame chipped and riddled with tack holes. The medial stretcher has broken through the left stretcher mortise. The feet once had casters. The cone-shaped elements of the arm supports originally extended to the bottom of the seat rail.

MATERIALS: *Black walnut* front legs and stretchers; *maple* rear legs and seat rails; *white pine* cone-shaped arm supports; *birch* other secondary wood.

PROVENANCE: The chair was purchased by Mary Thacher apparently at the auction of the Hyman Kaufman Collection, American Art Association, sale 4100, April 1934, lot 147, and descended to the donor.

ACCESSION: 1971.64   A gift of Guido R. Perera

102b

103 / Easy Chair

1760–1775
Newport or Boston
H. 46⅜ (117.8); W. 34 (86.4); SEAT D. 21¹¹⁄₁₆ (55.1); SEAT H. 12¾ (32.4)

This handsome easy chair, the sophisticated work of an urban New England craftsman, features the carved shells, bellflowers, and webbed claw feet that have long been associated with Newport (see chair no. 99). However, of the several related easy chairs, the only one with a history descended in the Phippen family of Salem, Massachusetts.[1]

To attribute this easy chair to Newport solely on the basis of the knee and feet carvings seems too facile. Similar feet and knees appear on chairs with long histories of ownership in Boston.[2] In addition, Boston inventories suggest that chairs with shell-carved knees and claw feet were made there also.[3] This easy chair is constructed exactly like Boston chairs (see a chair attributed to Boston in 104a; compare the seat rail and front leg joints in 103a and 104b with those on the documented Boston chair, no. 101).

103

Although the carved feet and knees attract our attention, an equally notable feature is the crest rail. The crest is mounted on top of the stiles, not between them. The former positioning appears on serpentine-crested chairs and seems to have become a common construction method in about 1760. This mahogany cabriole chair apparently was made in the era when serpentine crests were fashionable.

The flattened shape of the arch, a crest outline seldom seen in New England, perfectly echoes the front seat rail. A chair with the same crest and feet but uncarved knees (103b) is probably by the same maker.

103a

103b. Easy Chair. Newport or Boston, 1760–1775. Black walnut and maple; H. 46 (116.8). Private collection; illustrated in *Antiques,* July 1948. Photograph, courtesy, Israel Sack, Inc., New York. *The chair retains portions of its original stamped worsted upholstery on the back and wings.*

1. The related examples include a chair that also is number 26 in Carpenter, *Arts and Crafts of Newport;* the Phippen family chair, Carpenter, no. 27; and two with different crests, *John Brown House Loan Exhibition,* no. 24, and Heckscher, "Form and Frame," 888, fig. 6.

2. The chairs are listed in entry 99, note 2.

3. The Boston upholsterer Theodore Wheelwright's "Chairs Eagles Foot & Shell on the Knee" cited under chest of drawers no. 22 were probably made by his Boston chairmaker.

NOTES ON STRUCTURE AND CONDITION: The stiles and the rear legs are of one piece. The side seat rails are tenoned into the front seat rail. A dovetail-shaped extension of each front leg fits into a slot in the front seat rail. An ash wedge set through the dovetail tightens the joint. The stiles are tenoned into the crest rail. The wings are dovetailed and nailed to the stiles and crest.

The right front leg was once broken and a screw was added at the repaired joint. The right talon of the right foot is chipped away. The frame is in good condition, with few tack holes and chips, but the cone-shaped element of each arm support originally extended down over the seat rail.

MATERIALS: *Mahogany* front legs and side and medial stretchers; *hard maple* rear legs and rear stretcher; *ash* arms; *white pine* cone-shaped arm supports; *soft maple* other secondary wood.

PROVENANCE: The chair was part of a furniture collection assembled by Mary Thacher in the early twentieth century in Massachusetts and descended to the donor.

ACCESSION: 1976.129   A gift of Guido R. Perera

104 / Easy Chair

1765–1775
Probably Boston
H. 47¾ (121.3); W. 33⅞ (86); SEAT D. 22¼ (56.5); SEAT H. 13 (33)

The construction of this chair is the same as that of the preceding easy chair. (See 104a and 104b; the corner blocks are later additions.) In design, however, differences are apparent: principally the vigorous serpentine crest and the turned feet on thick disks, now well worn.

104

Randall notes that such feet are contemporaneous with furniture of the Chippendale style, and, indeed, examples similar to this easy chair have claw-and-ball feet.[1] Two documented objects with turned feet and similar disks help in dating and placing this easy chair. One, a closely related example at the Old Gaol Museum in York, Maine, contained in its original stuffing a Boston receipt of 1771. The other is the drop-leaf table that George Bright made in Boston in 1770 (no. 63). The several chairs that correspond closely to the Society's and the Old Gaol's examples are probably also from Boston.[2]

The Society's chair was recently reupholstered, following the methods used on chairs that retain original upholstery, emulating the contours evident in eighteenth-century

104a

portraits, and using fabrics that approximate those then in fashion. Crisp contours, often outlined in brass nails or a silk binding, were characteristic of cabriole easy chairs. Seat cushions were thick with down. Most easy chairs were permanently covered with worsteds (see III-34). Others, especially in the last quarter of the eighteenth century, were finished in canvas and had slipcovers of a copperplate print or a checked weave to match the bed hangings. The worsted chosen for this chair is crimson, the most popular color in Boston at the time. Because the frame showed no evidence of brass nails, a binding provides the neat edge.

1. Randall, *American Furniture*, 192; a similar chair is in the Winterthur Museum (G70.71).

2. Related chairs include one in Fales, *Historic Deerfield*, fig. 68, another advertised in *Antiques* 84 (October 1963): 363; and a third in Kane, *American Seating Furniture*, no. 213.

NOTES ON STRUCTURE AND CONDITION: The frame is in good condition. The cone-shaped arm supports are intact. All elements except the front knee bracket for the left front leg are original. The bottoms of the front feet are very worn; they once had casters.

MATERIALS: *Black walnut* front legs and side and medial stretchers; *soft maple* rear legs, rear stretchers, and all other secondary wood except for *white pine* cone-shaped arm supports.

PROVENANCE: The easy chair is part of a collection assembled in the early twentieth century by the donor, who lived in Abington and Salem, Mass.

ACCESSION: 1939.362   A bequest of Eva R. Greeley

104b

105 / Side Chair

1750–1775
Eastern Massachusetts
H. 40⁵⁄₁₆ (102.4); W. 19 (48.3); SEAT D. 13³⁄₈ (34); SEAT H. 17¼ (43.8)

New England chairmakers continued for more than half a century to use the legs and stretcher design that had become established by 1710. They grafted onto their time-honored chair base an overlapping succession of more fashionable chair backs, creating

105

leather chairs such as no. 91; Queen Anne chairs such as nos. 92, 93, and this one; and Chippendale chairs such as nos. 127 and 128.

Elements of both William and Mary and Queen Anne design coexist here. Such chairs were not produced, as was once thought, during a brief transition period but for a longer time and in greater number than either pure William and Mary or Queen Anne chairs.

This chair is a handsome version of a common form. Bold baluster turnings on the front legs, well-carved feet, and a graceful curved splat set it apart from most surviving examples. The skilled craftsman who made it was prolific.[1] Extant chairs from several sets feature the same subtle tapering of the stiles and are identical in every detail, from the simple rear stretcher to the unusual turning on the front legs above the front stretchers. One set of seven chairs descended in the Clark family of Lexington, Massachusetts; a Chippendale chair with a similar base belonged to the Estabrook family of Lexington.[2] This example was probably made just west of Boston.

1. Examples apparently from one shop include a chair (76.6.4) at the Lyme Historical Society, two in *Israel Sack Collection*, 4:1061 and 6:1518, a pair of chairs in a private collection, and a chair on loan to the Society.

2. The Clark chairs are in the collection of the Lexington Historical Society; the Estabrook chair is in the collection of the Arlington Historical Society.

NOTES ON STRUCTURE AND CONDITION: The top of the legs are round-tenoned into the chamfered ends of the front seat rail, and a single pin secures each joint. The side seat rails are round-tenoned into the front seat rail and rear legs. The chair is covered with several layers of paint, the outermost a crackled black. The lower edge of the splat rail is chipped; the crest is cracked.

MATERIALS: *Soft maple; ash* rear seat rail.

PROVENANCE: The chair was collected in the twentieth century by Florence Evans Bushee.

ACCESSION: 1976.232   A gift of the estate of Florence Evans Bushee

106 / Roundabout Chair

1760–1790
Probably Connecticut
H. 30⅝ (77.8); W. 27 (68.6); SEAT D. 24³⁄₁₆ (61.4); SEAT H. 17½ (44.5)

This simple, inexpensive roundabout is unpretentious. The chair has no splats, and the rear stretchers are unadorned. The one carved foot is so minimally modeled that it seems to suggest a Spanish foot more than to be one (compare with the foot on chair no. 86). The arms and crest rail are simple versions of those on more stylish roundabouts (see chairs no. 100 and 115).

The chair is in the same turned-base tradition as chairs no. 92, 93, and 105. But these turnings, attenuated in part because of the late date of the chair, are crude or at best bland. Plain as the chair is, however, an even simpler one is known: a related chair with the legs unturned from the floor to above the stretchers.[1]

Several turned roundabouts without splats are known from Connecticut.[2] One splendid chair from Lyme, at the mouth of the Connecticut River, features a squat version of the back on chair no. 92 mounted on the crest.[3] Chair no. 106 served as a desk chair (photograph 70a) for the Reverend Mr. Myron Dudley in his Nantucket house at the end of the last century.

106

1. A picture of the chair appeared in *Antiques and the Arts Weekly,* June 29, 1979, 52.

2. One is at the Norwalk Historical Society.

3. Myers and Mayhew, *New London County Furniture,* no. 15.

NOTES ON STRUCTURE AND CONDITION: The front leg is round-tenoned into the left side seat rail; the three posts are round-tenoned into the arm rail, made of two lap-jointed boards. Four rose-headed nails secure it to the crest rail. The rear seat rails are round-tenoned to the legs, the right side rail to the right leg and left side rail. The painted rush dates from the late nineteenth century. An old 4-inch chip is under the left arm. The chair is stained a light red. Casters, once present, were removed by about 1890.

MATERIALS: *Soft maple.*

PROVENANCE: The chair was brought from Nantucket to the Marrett House in Standish, Me., by Mary Marrett Dudley, the widow of the Reverend Mr. Myron Dudley (1837–1905), and descended with the house to the donor.

ACCESSION: 1959.394   A bequest of Frances S. Marrett

107 / Settee

ca. 1748
England, probably London
H. 37¾ (95.9); W. 58⅜ (148.3); SEAT D. 22⅛ (56.2); SEAT H. 16½ (41.9)

This English settee (plate 9) was bought with Spanish gold by an American merchant prince, Josiah Quincy (1710–1784).

Although the large-scale importation of English seating, so common during the fashion for cane chairs, had long ended by the middle of the eighteenth century, the goods bought by the colonists continued to include some English furniture.

> *JUST IMPORTED in the Ship* Jupiter, *from* LONDON, *and TO BE SOLD Cheap for Cash by Capt.* SAMUEL BULL,
>   The following GOODS
> NAILS, *Locks, Hinges, and all Sorts of Carpenters Tools — A neat Assortment of Cutlery — Glass Lanthorns, and Tin Ware . . . — Sconce Looking-Glasses of different Sizes — Mahogany Tables and Chairs . . . — Setts of Pictures glazed and framed*
>   *— Boston News-Letter,* December 25, 1760

107

Merchants who traded directly with London acquired English furniture for their houses through their London agents. John Hancock ordered a mahogany cabinet from London in 1767, having already instructed his agent in 1763 that "when any Article is wrote for Family use . . . Send it of the best kind, Cost what it will."[1] Although most wrote that no more than a certain price should be paid for the items they ordered, English furniture imported in this era tended to be, by colonial standards, select objects for select people.

This settee, according to family memoirs, was neither a venture cargo import nor ordered by correspondence: Quincy apparently purchased it while in England in 1748. He went shopping with the profits gained when the small ship he, his brother, and a brother-in-law owned seized a large Spanish vessel carrying 171,000 Spanish dollars in coin alone.[2]

The settee was a well-established form in English furniture. Seventeenth-century couches (see 81a), made en suite with upholstered chairs, had upholstered backs; eighteenth-century settees featured wooden backs that look like two or three chair backs. Although numerous English chair-back settees survive, the form appeared infrequently in America and seldom outside of Boston.

Among the prominent Bostonians owning English settees was Thomas Hancock.[3] His settee, purchased in the early 1740s, may have been the impetus for Quincy's purchase. These examples created a demand, albeit limited, and soon Boston furniture makers were producing their own double-chair-back settees.[4]

The stylish English furniture sought by wealthy Bostonians became the inspirations and models for much of the furniture made in Boston. Hancock's "Settee Crimson bottom" in his "Great Parlour" and Quincy's "Mohogany Settee damask Covering" in his second-floor hall introduced Bostonians to a Georgian style with features such as the carved shell, the curved stiles, the eared crest, the pierced splat, and this claw design.[5] Such stiles and shell-carved crests, both featured on chair no. 99, were popular in England in the 1740s. These beautiful claws are unlike the webbed and tentative claws carved on chairs no. 99 and 103 and presage the crisply delineated talons that became the standard in Boston Chippendale style (see the next chair).

Not all of the design elements of Quincy's settee were adopted in New England. American carvers did not emulate either the oak leaf and acorn motif (107a), only occasionally seen even on English furniture, or the rococo design on the handhold and arm, stylistically the most advanced feature on the settee.[6]

1. Hancock, Letter Book, 1762–83, 33, Hancock Collection, New England Historic Genealogical Society.

2. A letter from Isaac Freemen, master of the "Bethell," to ship owners Edmund and Josiah Quincy and Edward Jackson describing the capture of the Spanish vessel is reproduced in *A Pride of Quincys*.

3. Cooper, "American Chairback Settees," 35, 36.

4. Ibid., figs. 7, 8, 9, 11, 12, 14, 15.

5. The upholstery and locations of the settees are

107a

Each arm support apparently is screwed to the seat rail. The arms, mortised to receive the arm supports, appear to be held at the back by screws through the stiles. The central front foot is pieced, an original feature. The central front leg has a dovetail-shaped tenon at the top that is keyed into a slot in the seat rail. The central rear leg is tenoned into the rear seat rail. Diagonal corner braces, common on English work, are nailed behind the front legs. A medial brace is tenoned into the rear seat rail and dovetailed and nailed to the central front leg. The loose seat also has a medial rail.

The settee is in excellent condition. The brackets of the right rear leg are replacements, one claw is chipped away on the right front foot, and a new block was added to the rear seat rail beneath the medial brace.

MATERIALS: *Mahogany; English walnut* braces; *beech* loose seat frame.

PROVENANCE: In 1790 the settee went to Boston to the Sudbury Street house of a Quincy relative, Mrs. Storer (d. 1826). In 1840 it was taken to Cambridge by Josiah Quincy (1772–1864), then president of Harvard, and later to the Quincy homestead. The settee descended in the family to Josiah Phillips Quincy (1829–1910), to Josiah Quincy (1859–1919), to his widow, and to the donor.

ACCESSION: 1972.48   A gift of Edmund Quincy; conservation funded in part by the Massachusetts Council on the Arts and Humanities

from Hancock's 1794 inventory, old series, vol. 93, p. 11; and Josiah Quincy's 1784 inventory, docket 18158, both Suffolk County (Mass.) Probate.

6. The oak leaf and acorn motif appears on a set of sixteen English side chairs at the Metropolitan Museum of Art (*English Furniture . . . in the Untermyer Collection,* figs. 124–26), on English looking glasses (Gilbert, *Furniture at Temple Newsam,* nos. 260, 262), and on an English or Irish chair (Kirk, *American Furniture,* 255).

NOTES ON STRUCTURE AND CONDITION: The settee is constructed like a chair. The splat shoe and rear rail are of one piece, a common English practice. A strip to support the seat is nailed to the rear seat rail. Each stile is pieced at its broadest point. The bridge between the center stiles is tenoned to them.

108 / Side Chair

1755–1785
Boston-Salem area
H. 37¾ (95.9); W. 23⅜ (59.4); SEAT D. 17⁹⁄₁₆ (44.6); SEAT H. 16¹³⁄₁₆ (42.7)

New England craftsmen reshaped and modified the style introduced by such English seating as the preceding settee into a distinctive version of the Chippendale style. It satisfied the desire of New Englanders for the new while accommodating their reluctance to discard the familiar.

The New England Chippendale chair, exemplified by chair no. 108, takes on the new style from the seat up but maintains an older appearance below. The pierced splat and serpentine crest with prominent ears proclaim the modernization. The seat rails adopt a

108

new straight skirt and a molded upper edge. However, the cabrioles are retained; but in deference to the new trend away from the curvilinear, the knees develop a sharp corner and their flanking brackets are simplified. The chamfered rear legs remain; the stretchers, only somewhat modified (compare with detail 95a), are retained. The claws are of a new pattern — unwebbed and with long, thin nails. (Earlier talons resemble those on chair no. 99.)

This chair is an early version of the new fashion. Its feet and the two tiers of piercings on the baluster-shaped splat owe much to English Georgian chairs of the late 1740s.[1] The splat pattern, derived from English design, was adopted in Newport and Philadelphia but was especially popular in coastal towns north of Boston.[2] The splat is used with various crest patterns. Sometimes leafy carvings ornament the upper scrolls of the splat and are echoed on the knees.[3]

This mahogany chair, somewhat austere because it is uncarved except at the ears and feet, is either from coastal Essex County, Massachusetts, or from Boston. A set of similar chairs in walnut, with pad feet and cut-out skirts, has a history of ownership either in Chelsea, just north of Boston, or in Gloucester.[4] A pad-footed chair with a Marblehead history is also closely related.[5] Chair no. 110, featuring another splat design, a different crest, much more carving, and over-the-rail upholstery, has remarkably similar claw feet. The two chairs, which may well be by the same chairmaker, exemplify the range of options available to a customer.

1. See a British chair, Kirk, *American Furniture*, no. 891; the foot on the preceding settee; and the splat illustrated in Hinckley, *Directory of Furniture*, fig. 98.

2. For a Rhode Island example, see *John Brown House Loan Exhibition*, no. 11; Philadelphia examples appear in *Antiques* 109 (April 1976): 670, and in *Israel Sack Collection*, 3:749. For Massachusetts chairs of similar design, see Downs, *Queen Anne and Chippendale*, nos. 153, 154; a set of six chairs in the Sargent-Murray-Gilman-Hough House; three chairs, originally owned by Nathaniel Silsbee of Salem, Benjamin Flayderman Collection, American Art Association, sale 3908, April 1931, lot 327; and two side chairs in the Lee Mansion, Marblehead Historical Society.

3. See Downs, *Queen Anne and Chippendale*, no. 154.

4. The set of six chairs cited in note 2 apparently descended from Benjamin Hough, who was born in Chelsea, Mass., and moved to Gloucester.

5. The Lee Mansion chair cited in note 2 came from the Turner Farm in Marblehead.

NOTES ON STRUCTURE AND CONDITION: An original slat is nailed to the left seat rail, a modern slat to the right, apparently because the rabbeted edges of the seat rail seemed too shallow to support the seat. Corner blocks were never present. The original loose seat frame is covered with a reproduction worsted damask. The stretcher rings and blocks were, at one time, picked out with gold. The back of the chair shows some charring from fire. The chair has been cleaned and shellacked.

MATERIALS: *Mahogany; cherry* rear seat rail; *hard maple* loose seat frame.

PROVENANCE: The chair shares a provenance with easy chair no. 104.

ACCESSION: 1939.359   A bequest of Eva R. Greeley

109 / Side Chair

1755–1785
Boston
H. 37¹¹/₁₆ (95.7); W. 23½ (59.7); SEAT D. 17⅛ (43.5); SEAT H. 16½ (41.9)

The most popular splat design on Massachusetts chairs of the Chippendale style was the pattern graphically described by the modern term "owl's eye." As with other splat designs, it was based on English examples (109a). This chair is the first in a series of five with the owl's eye splat; they serve to illustrate the range of options still available to the customer who had chosen a splat design.

The traditional base of this example is enhanced by the refinement of handsome baluster turnings on the block-ended medial stretcher. The well-carved feet display the

109

characteristic raked toes that are today regarded as a stamp of coastal Massachusetts chairs. In keeping with standard New England work, the chair is relatively uncarved and delicate in proportions. Its elements (e.g., stretchers and seat rails) are thin. An attenuation of the parts and a delicacy of the whole are so much the hallmark of New England design that it would be hard to mistake a chair such as this for one from New York or Philadelphia.

This particular chair makes the furniture historian's research a joy: the inside of the front seat rail is branded "M·MACKAY" (109b). Two matching side chairs, a blockfront desk and bookcase, and a bowfront chest of drawers are similarly branded.[1] During the period this chair was made, such brands were owners' marks; the probable owner was

Mungo Mackay, a Boston merchant. Mackay (ca. 1740–1811), a mariner when he married in 1763 and captain of a brig by 1766, bought a house in Boston in 1771; after the Revolution he acquired much Boston real estate, including a distillery and two shops on Long Wharf. He was also part owner of the West Bridge, the second to span the Charles River.[2]

Mackay's thirteen children included a namesake. Mungo Jr. (1765–1800) died early and unmarried; his inventory included "10 Mahogany framed Chairs" valued at $50, a desk and bookcase at $20, and a bureau at $12.50.[3] The branded furniture may have belonged to Mungo Jr., passing at his death to his father, who outlived him and in whose parlor were "10 Silk Chairs. 1 Sophy & Cushings."[4]

1. Photographs of the privately owned chairs and desk are in DAPC files, Winterthur Museum, 65.4429, 67.2209, 70.894. The chest sold at auction in 1982; *Antiques and the Arts Weekly,* August 13, 1982, 34.

2. Mackay bought a house on Water Street in 1771 and, in 1782, bought another at the corner of Staniford and Cambridge streets (Thwing file, Massachusetts Historical Society). Harrison Gray Otis, a partner in the bridge corporation, became his neighbor in 1796, when he built his house, now the Society's headquarters.

3. Mungo Mackay [Jr.]'s 1800 inventory, old series, vol. 98, p. 375, Suffolk County (Mass.) Probate.

4. Mungo Mackay [Sr.]'s 1811 inventory, docket 23724, Suffolk County (Mass.) Probate.

NOTES ON STRUCTURE AND CONDITION: The rabbeted edge of the seat rails is extremely thin, so small rectangular mahogany blocks are glued and nailed at the rear corners for additional support for the loose seat. The chair is in excellent condition; all original elements survive except the upholstery. The original loose seat is covered in a yellow reproduction worsted moreen.

MATERIALS: *Mahogany; soft maple* loose seat frame.

PROVENANCE: Nothing is known of the history of the chair before 1942, when it came to the Society with a collection of furniture acquired principally in the Portsmouth area.

ACCESSION: 1942.1208   A gift of Virginia L. Hodge and Katherine D. Parry

109a. Side Chair. England, 1750–1765. Mahogany. Present location unknown. Photograph, courtesy, Hampshires of Dorking, Surrey, England.

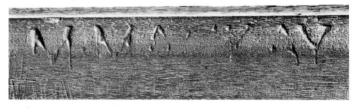

109b

110 / Side Chair

1755–1785
Boston-Salem area
H. 38³⁄₁₆ (97); W. 24 (61); SEAT D. 17⁵⁄₁₆ (44); SEAT H. 16½ (41.9)

This chair closely resembles the preceding example, yet three differences are apparent: over-the-rail upholstery, a medial stretcher of a different pattern, and carved embellishments.

Over-the-rail upholstery was more expensive than loose seats because more stuffing and fabric were required.[1] Thomas Chippendale's *Director* suggests:

110

The Seats look best when stuffed over the Rails, and have a Brass Border neatly chased; but are most commonly done with Brass Nails, in one or two Rows; and sometimes the Nails are done to imitate Fretwork.[2]

This seat is outlined with a single row of brass nails, following the original pattern. Over-the-rail upholstery, common in England, was more popular in New England than elsewhere in the colonies. It grew in vogue during the era of Chippendale design, becoming de rigueur in the Federal period.

The medial stretcher is of a common design, less formal than the block-ended stretcher on the preceding chair. Yet the upholstery and carvings easily dress up the chair. The shell carved on the crest, for example, fills a space that appears to have been created especially for it, and when the space is left uncarved — as in chair no. 109 — the crest seems neglected. The spiral carvings at the center of the splat are a neat finishing touch, sometimes repeated in the similar round spaces just above.

The chair features one of two popular types of leaf-carved knees (110a) seen in the Boston area: leaves with a few deeply notched blades and a long tip. (The other type of leaf — see detail 115a — has multiple blades that are barely notched and a short rounded tip.) The talons here and those on chair no. 108 are so alike that the two chairs may well be the work of one craftsman, as yet unidentified.

Owl's eye splat chairs with shell carving on the crest were fashionable in Boston.[3] But a combined Boston-Salem attribution is necessary because of the migration of craftsmen, as demonstrated by the career of Joseph Goodwin of Charlestown, an urban community across the Charles River from Boston. By 1771, Goodwin had left Charlestown for Salem:

> *Joseph P. Goodwin,* Chair-Maker from CHARLESTOWN . . . *has just set up his Business a little above the Naval-Office in Salem, where he makes the best Sort of Mahogany Chairs, Couches and easy Chairs, Sofa's, and any Thing in the Chair-making Business. . . . Work done in the neatest Manner, and served with Fidelity and Dispatch, N.B. He has got two Sorts of Chairs made by him which are called as neat as any that are made in Boston.*[4]

During the third quarter of the eighteenth century, Salem prospered so well that the second city came to rival Boston as a home for wealthy patrons and as a marketplace for craftsmen.

1. According to the Hartford Price List of 1792, a loose seat chair cost 1:6:0, exclusive of the outer cover, whereas an over-the-rail upholstered chair cost 1:8:0, exclusive of brass nails and the cover cloth, in the latter case, a larger piece; Lyon, *Colonial Furniture,* 3rd ed., 270.

2. These remarks first appeared in the *Director,* 3rd ed. (1762), 3.

3. Related chairs with Boston histories include one formerly belonging to Thomas Hutchinson, number 73 in Warren, *Bayou Bend;* another owned by John Hancock, in the Old State House–The Bostonian Society; a third owned by William Greenleaf, in *Israel Sack Collection,* 1:243; and a settee and eight matching chairs that descended in the Forbes family, numbers 94 and 74 in Warren, *Bayou Bend.*

4. *Essex Gazette,* July 9–16, 1771, as quoted by Anne Farnam in Clunie, Farnam, and Trent, *Furniture at the Essex Institute,* 17.

NOTES ON STRUCTURE AND CONDITION: The construction is the same for an over-the-rail upholstered chair as for a loose-seated chair except that on the former the seat rails are not rabbeted on the inside and finished on the outside. This chair has no corner blocks or braces. It is covered in a red reproduction worsted damask; the brass nails match the originals in size. The chair has been reupholstered several times, and the seat rails are chipped and split along the tack line. The feet show noticeable wear, but the condition is otherwise excellent.

MATERIALS: *Mahogany; birch* front and side seat rails.

PROVENANCE: The chair was owned in Boston early in this century; no earlier history is known.

ACCESSION: 1948.16   A bequest of Harriet Buckingham

110a

111 / Side Chair

1755–1785
Boston-Salem area
H. 38⅜ (97.5); W. 23⁷⁄₁₆ (59.5); SEAT D. 17¹⁄₁₆ (43.3); SEAT H. 16¾ (42.5)

This sophisticated version of the owl's eye splat chair is obviously different from the preceding two. The dated feature of the turned stretchers has been discarded. The rear legs end in club feet much like those on English examples (chair 109a). Small brackets, nailed at the rear corners of the seat rails, complete the elegance of this more fully developed Chippendale chair.

Although the Yankees of Massachusetts and Rhode Island showed an astonishing tenacity in holding on to stretchers, some craftsmen did make chairs without them. These chairs were the most stylish and often the most elaborate examples, featuring ornate carvings.[1]

A pair of chairs, apparently identical to the Society's chair, has a history of ownership in Groton, Massachusetts.[2] A related pad-footed side chair with carved leafage on the crest descended in the Dane family of Andover (I-30). A carved-knee chair otherwise akin to this one was exported to Baltimore.[3]

111

1. Ibid., nos. 114, 115, 116, 117, and 123.

2. The pair in the Groton Historical Society descended in the Dalrymple family of Groton.

3. The chair descended in the Patterson family of Baltimore; "Furniture at the Maryland Historical Society," *Antiques* 109 (May 1976): 971, fig. 3.

NOTES ON STRUCTURE AND CONDITION: The back of the stiles is rounded. A large triangular block is nailed with two rose-headed nails to each corner of the seat frame. The original loose seat is covered in a yellow reproduction worsted moreen. The condition of the chair is virtually perfect.

MATERIALS: Mahogany; white pine corner blocks; *soft maple* loose seat frame.

PROVENANCE: The chair is part of an exceptional furniture collection assembled in the early twentieth century in Massachusetts by Mary Thacher.

ACCESSION: 1949.191   A gift of Mary Thacher

112 / Side Chair

1760–1775
Portsmouth, New Hampshire, or York, Maine
H. 37³/₁₆ (94.5); W. 23³/₈ (59.4); SEAT D. 17⁷/₁₆ (44.3); SEAT H. 16⁹/₁₆ (42.1)

The fourth in this series of owl's eye splat chairs, this chair resembles chairs no. 109 and 110 only at first glance. Placed next to the others, differences become as apparent as similarities. The medial stretcher, for example, is very thin, and the top edge of the seat rails is beveled instead of molded (see chair no. 109), as was common in Massachusetts.[1]

112

Some differences result from the customer's several choices based on taste and purse — turned feet, uncarved knees, uncarved center crest. Others reflect regional tastes, such as the sharp dissolve of the crease on the knees, often associated with Essex County, Massachusetts. Then there are the differences that are more likely the mark of a shop (e.g., the contours of the splat template used).

Small details on this chair — the knees and the seat rail edges — are identical to those on chair no. 96. Both chairs are from sets that furnished the York house of Jonathan Sayward. This chair is from an extant set of six, five of which are in the Society's collections; three retain their original upholstery. A third set of Sayward's chairs, chair no. 118 and its mates, is upholstered in the identical fabric: a green worsted impressed with a meandering line, flowers, and butterflies (detail 118a).

The three sets of chairs apparently come from one shop. The maker obviously emulated Boston designs, but judging from such features as the thin stretchers and the shape of the cabrioles, the shop was not in Boston. Although Salem is suggested by the cabrioles, beveled seat rails are not known on Salem furniture. The history points to the area of York, probably no farther away than Kittery or Portsmouth.

1. A rare Boston example with beveled seat rails displays the very same splat pattern and creased knees as this chair, but its turned feet and stretchers are of different designs; Randall, *American Furniture,* no. 143.

NOTES ON STRUCTURE AND CONDITION: The chair is in excellent condition. The frame shows almost no wear, and the condition of the feet is remarkably fine. The original upholstery, although very worn, survives. The loose seat retains its girt web (two strips from front to back and one from side to side) nailed to the top of the loose seat frame; a layer of plain woven linen similarly nailed; marsh grass stuffing; another linen layer pulled over the loose seat rails and nailed to the underside of the rails; and an outer covering of worsted similarly nailed. Two subsequent layers of modern upholstery covered the original in this century but have been removed.

MATERIALS: *Mahogany; soft maple* loose seat frame.

PROVENANCE: The chair descended like tea chest no. 4, or it may have been in the set of "Six mehogany Chairs Seated with green" that Sayward willed to his wife. It would then share a provenance with chest of drawers no. 21.

ACCESSION: 1977.202.3   A gift of the heirs of Elizabeth Cheever Wheeler

113 / Side Chair

1770
Boston
George Bright
H. 37⅜ (94.9); W. 21⅜ (54.3); SEAT D. 17¼ (43.8); SEAT H. 16¼ (41.3)

The last owl's eye splat chair presented here completes our five interpretations of a motif with a thoroughly documented chair in original condition. We know its maker, first

113

owner, date, and price, and we see it here intact with its original upholstery and brass nails.

This chair and one mate survive from a set of twelve chairs made by George Bright of Boston for Jonathan Bowman of Pownalborough, Massachusetts (now Maine), in 1770 and described in the bill (15a) as "12 Mahogany Chairs with Leather Seats a^t 30/ 18:0:0." (For more history on Bright and Bowman, see entry 15.) The documentation of the Bright-Bowman chairs makes them instrumental in the study of Boston furniture.[1]

Because the chair retains its original upholstery (the name of the upholsterer is the only unknown in its history), it offers an opportunity to study a common brass nailing pattern. At the corners of the seat, the tacks extend vertically to the top of the rails, flanking each corner. The pattern was depicted in Boston portraits (113a) and frequently can be found as the original pattern on chairs from the Boston area.

This owl's eye stands on straight legs, called "Marlborough" legs, with its stretchers in an H pattern, the usual arrangement on stylish Chippendale chairs. Marlborough legs, used in Boston as early as 1746, became increasingly popular during the third quarter of the century and remained fashionable into the Federal era.[2] Most are like these legs — decorated with a beaded edge, a muted echo of the decoratively carved rope edge that embellishes chair no. 117. (Other Marlborough legs are fluted, or stop-fluted [see chair no. 122], or molded [see chair no. 130].) The Marlborough base favored in Boston includes stretchers with a beaded edge matching that on the legs. Brackets beneath the front seat rail often complete the design.

1. A related pair, in *Israel Sack Collection*, 1:147, can now be attributed to Bright.

2. Grant Account Book, 507, American Antiquarian Society; the entry for August 20, 1746, mentions Marlborough chairs.

NOTES ON STRUCTURE AND CONDITION: The medial stretcher is half-dovetailed to the side stretchers. Ogee brackets are glued and nailed to the upper front corners of the front legs; no side brackets were ever attached. A triangular block is secured with two rose-headed nails to each corner of the seat. The chair is in excellent condition, with only minor nicks and some wear.

MATERIALS: *Mahogany; birch* rear seat rail; *maple* front and side seat rails; *yellow pine* (probably pitch pine) corner blocks.

PROVENANCE: The chair shares a provenance with chest of drawers no. 15.

ACCESSION: 1980.74.1   A gift of Florence L. Bixby

113a. Portrait of Joseph Hooper. John Singleton Copley (1738–1815), Boston, 1770–1771. Oil on canvas; H. 58 (127.0); W. 40 (101.6). Baltimore Museum of Art. *The splat pattern is seen on chair no. 123.*

114 / Side Chair

1755–1775
Boston-Salem area
H. 37⅛ (94.3); W. 23⁵/₁₆ (59.2); SEAT D. 16⅞ (42.9); SEAT H. 17¼ (43.8)

Another splat pattern favored for fine New England Chippendale chairs is the pierced vase with an interlaced diamond and figure eight. The intricate design, apparently more expensive to execute than most other patterns, appealed to customers who demanded the most elegant furnishings (plate 10).

114

The top of the splat design features a tassel suspended at the center of a swag. Carvings on English prototypes of the middle of the century and on some Pennsylvania examples clearly delineate drapery and a tassel.[1] All that remains of the tassel on New England examples is the outline; all that remains of the drapery, two indentations, and — on a related example (114a) — the curled outer ends of the swag.

In eastern Massachusetts, two versions of the splat were popular; only subtle differences distinguish them. The one on the Essex Institute chair (114a) is more delicate of line, has an attenuated diamond, and features curls at the crest and base of the splat outline. The other, seen on chair no. 114, has a more solid appearance and a stubby diamond; the curls have disappeared in favor of a smoother outline.

Several chairs are so like this example that they may be by the same craftsman.[2] The only example whose eighteenth-century history is known was given by John Hancock of Boston to Nathan Fessenden of Lexington, Massachusetts.[3] The Essex Institute chair has no history but is of a type traditionally called "Salem" because of the scratched turned feet.[4] For the present, it is impossible to be more specific than to ascribe both versions to the Boston-Salem area (see entry 110).

Although made in Massachusetts, this chair was in Portsmouth by the early nineteenth century. It is one of a set branded "C·STORER" by Clement Storer (1760–1830), a Portsmouth merchant and United States congressman and senator.[5] Storer was too young to have been the first owner of the chairs. The story of the set (six side chairs and roundabout no. 115 survive) continues in the next entry.

1. For English prototypes, see Cescinsky, *English Furniture*, 261, and Kirk, *Chairs*, no. 74; for a Philadelphia example, see Kirk, *Chairs*, no. 75.

2. Examples are at Yale, Kane, *American Seating Furniture*, 100; at the Daughters of the American Revolution Museum (see note 3); at the Rhode Island School of Design, Kirk, *Chairs*, no. 117; and two advertised in *Antiques:* 81 (August 1961): 95 and 97 (May 1970): 683.

3. The chair at the DAR Museum was given to Fessenden after his house was burned by the British in 1775; *Antiques* 102 (July 1972): 31.

4. Others of this type include a set with claw feet owned by Joseph Willard, a minister in Beverly, Mass. (1772–1781), and president of Harvard (1781–1804); *American Art at Harvard*, no. 168.

5. Kaye, "Marked Portsmouth Furniture," 1101, pl. 3.

NOTES ON STRUCTURE AND CONDITION: The brackets at the corners of the side seat rails and rear legs are secured with forged finishing nails. Two rose-headed nails hold each of the large triangular blocks to the corners of the seat. The shoe and the base of the splat are each numbered with a row of four punch marks. (Four of the other chairs are numbered one, six, seven, and eight; the fifth has a replaced shoe and splat.)

Reproduction yellow moreen covers the seat. The original tacking pattern followed the pattern seen on the preceding chair. The tops of the front legs beneath the upholstery have been splintered and are partially pieced. The splat is cracked. Screws reinforce the joints of the rear legs and side seat rails. New nails secure the knee brackets.

MATERIALS: *Mahogany; birch* seat rails; *white pine* corner blocks.

PROVENANCE: The chair descended in the family of Dorothy Cutter Storer (1765–1841), the widow of Clement, to her brother Jacob Cutter (d. 1857), to his daughters, one of whom was Frances Cutter Langdon Bassett, the mother of Woodbury Langdon (1837–1921). Langdon left it to his wife, the donor.

ACCESSION: 1966.294b   A bequest of Elizabeth Elwyn Langdon

114a. Side Chair. Boston-Salem area, 1755–1775. Mahogany; H. 36⅜ (92.4); W. 23¾ (60.3); SEAT D. 17⅝ (44.8); SEAT H. 15¾ (40.0). Essex Institute.

115 / Roundabout Chair

1755–1775
Boston-Salem area
H. 32½ (82.6); W. 30¹/₁₆ (76.4); SEAT D. 25⅜ (64.5); SEAT H. 16⅞ (42.9)

This roundabout was made en suite with the set that includes the preceding side chair. They belonged to Clement Storer of Portsmouth and probably were the "14 Hair bottom Chairs [$]10.50" in his inventory.[1] Storer may have inherited the set (his family had ties to Wells, Maine; Portsmouth; and Boston), acquired it with the elegant house he pur-

115

chased in 1792 from his bride's family (the Treadwells and Cutters of Portsmouth), or purchased it at auction, a favorite method of furnishing households in that era.[2]

Storer's fourteen chairs were probably a parlor set of twelve side chairs (a surviving side chair is numbered eight) and two roundabouts. In the years dominated by Chippendale design roundabouts grew in popularity, especially as parts of parlor suites.

Storer's suite features knees with leaf carving (115a), an ornamentation that, like fluted stiles (see detail 114a), was available at considerable extra cost.[3] The knee carvings are of a many-fronded leaf design popular in coastal Massachusetts. (For the other common leaf pattern, see detail 110a.) Punchwork not only gives texture to the center of the foliage at the crease of the knee, but star punchwork outlines the leaf to add to the depth of the carving.

The curve of the arms and the turning of the stiles, as well as the carving of the knees, contribute to a roundabout design that is superbly planned and handsomely rendered.[4]

1. Storer's 1831 inventory, docket 12121, Rockingham County (N.H.) Probate.

2. *New Hampshire Gazette*, Portsmouth, December 5, 1787, advertised such an auction: "TO BE SOLD *At Public Vendue* . . . at the house of Mr. Jacob Treadwell, late of Portsmouth . . . A variety of *Houshold Furniture* . . ."

3. Whereas Philadelphia chairs with claw feet cost £2 in mahogany and 1:10:0 in walnut, the addition of leaf carving alone made them 2:6:0 and 1:15:0 respectively, while the addition of fluted stiles alone made them 2:10:0 and 1:15:0. Weil, "Price Book," 182.

4. An almost identical roundabout, carved at the knee but with the leaf pattern seen in detail 110a, was advertised in *Antiques* 99 (January 1971): 44.

NOTES ON STRUCTURE AND CONDITION: The side and rear legs extend up to form side and rear stiles that are round-tenoned into the arm rail. The two parts of the arm rail butt above the rear stile. The arm rail is held by six rose-headed nails to the crest rail. The splats are tenoned into the rear seat rails and into the arm rail. A large triangular block was nailed originally with two rose-headed nails to each corner of the seat. All but one of the blocks are now attached with modern nails. Each leg, even the rear one, has flanking brackets. The feet and one splat shoe are cracked. The chair once had casters.

MATERIALS: Mahogany; *soft maple* seat rails; *hard maple* corner blocks.

PROVENANCE: The roundabout chair shares a provenance with chair no. 114.

ACCESSION: 1966.293   A bequest of Elizabeth Elwyn Langdon

115a

116 / Armchair

1760–1790
Coastal Essex County, Massachusetts, probably Salem
H. 36⅝ (93); W. 29⅛ (74); SEAT D. 19⅞ (50.5); SEAT H. 16⁹⁄₁₆ (42.1)

This unusual armchair has no traceable provenance but has two inscriptions. The older, in penciled script, reads: "In the year 1849 I will be married." The future bride or groom added neither name nor town.

The newer inscription seemed, at first, as useless as the prenuptial graffiti. "Bought about 1804 Lord Fairfax Sale in Virginia" was inked onto the rear seat rail after a late-

nineteenth-century dust cover was applied. Written so long after the date cited, the inscription was suspect.

However, a little detective work revealed that the effects of Bryan, the eighth Lord Fairfax, were auctioned in 1803.[1] His family had strong ties to Massachusetts: his mother, the second wife of William Fairfax (1691–1757), was Deborah Clarke of Salem.[2] If Bryan did not have the chair in Virginia by 1799, his son Thomas, eventually the ninth Lord Fairfax, could have purchased it for him that year when he visited family in Salem.

More than inscriptions make this an unusual chair. It is extraordinarily wide. Probably because of its girth, the corner blocks are huge. The simple modeling of the arms is a jarring contrast to the fine molding of the stiles. The rear brackets were designed to be covered with upholstery. Even the leaf carving, an asymmetrical frond emerging above the crossed bands, is distinctive.

Flat, rather awkwardly shaped arms (compare with the more sculptural treatment on armchair no. 119) are seen on chairs generally attributed to Newburyport.[3] A documented chair once owned in Salem similarly juxtaposes unsculptured arms and shaped (stop-fluted) stiles.[4] Upholstered rear brackets are seen on two chairs with Essex County histories: one from Andover, another from Salem.[5]

The splat design was not as popular in Massachusetts as in New York and Connecticut.[6] Similar Massachusetts chairs are few.[7] Yet an exact mate is in the Bayou Bend Collection, identical even to the simple leaf carving and the dimensions of the outsized corner blocks.[8]

1. *Alexandria* (Va.) *Advertiser and Commercial Intelligencer*, March 3, 1803, p. 3.

2. *Vital Records of Salem*, 3:344.

3. *Israel Sack Collection*, 1:163, 4:1069, 5:1298, 6:1444, and Fales, *Historic Deerfield*, fig. 123.

4. *Israel Sack Collection*, 3:614.

5. Greenlaw, *New England Furniture*, no. 55, and Randall, *American Furniture*, no. 144.

6. Kirk, *Chairs*, nos. 139–44 for New York examples, nos. 197–98 for Connecticut examples. For Massachusetts chairs, see Nutting, *Furniture Treasury*, vol. 2, no. 2188; *Israel Sack Collection*, 4:940; 2:378; Randall, *American Furniture*, nos. 151–52.

7. *Antiques* 32 (September 1937): 144; 42 (September 1942): 111; and 56 (October 1949): 247.

8. Warren, *Bayou Bend*, no. 83.

NOTES ON STRUCTURE AND CONDITION: The rear brackets, usually separate pieces, are of one piece with the side seat rails. The front triangular corner blocks measure 5½ inches and the rear ones 7 inches at their widest. The knee brackets are glued, not nailed. The screws that hold the arm and arm support (one and three screws, respectively) are countersunk, the holes capped with wooden plugs. Two pins secure the mortise-and-tenon joint of the arm support to the arm. The upholstery originally was decorated with brass nails following the pattern on chair no. 113. The side knee brackets are replacements.

MATERIALS: *Mahogany; maple* front and side seat rails and rear corner blocks; *birch* rear seat rail and front corner blocks.

PROVENANCE: The armchair is from the early-twentieth-century collection of the donor.

ACCESSION: 1933.6041   A bequest of Julia G. Crocker

117 / Side Chair

1760–1769
Boston
H. 38⅞ (98.7); W. 22⁷⁄₁₆ (57); SEAT D. 18⅝ (47.3); SEAT H. 17¼ (43.8)

This chair is part of a set of eight that reportedly was given in 1769 to Abigail Phillips and her groom, Josiah Quincy, Jr., a son of the first owner of settee no. 107 and high chest no. 36.[1] A desk and bookcase and the chairs passed to Abigail after the death of her young husband in 1775.[2] In 1806 the chairs, which had been used in the dining room, and the desk and bookcase were moved from Boston to the Quincy homestead in nearby Braintree.

117

117a. Photograph of Chair No. 117 in situ in the Josiah Quincy House. Wollaston, Massachusetts, ca. 1880. Photographic Archives, Society for the Preservation of New England Antiquities.

There, three of the set and the desk and bookcase were photographed in the Quincys' west parlor in about 1880 (117a), and a fourth chair appears in a photograph of the east parlor.[3] Five of the set survived into the middle of the twentieth century and were since dispersed. One chair came to the Society, one was purchased by the Winterthur Museum, another by the Metropolitan Museum, and two by the Tryon Palace Restoration.[4]

Quincy's stylish chairs closely resemble English ones in design, ornament, and construction.[5] Few American chairs feature this handsome and complex splat pattern.[6] With the exception of the next chair, probably all of them were made in the Boston area. The small Boston group apparently originated in one shop, for the chairs are in many ways atypical of Boston work.

The crest, splat, and rope carvings are the most ornate to be found on Boston Chippendale chairs. The stretchers lack the bead customary on Boston chair stretchers (see chair no. 113). The corner braces are like those used in English construction. Every aspect of these chairs suggests a craftsman who was either trained in England or, through an imported prototype, became well versed in English chairmaking.

1. Quincy, "Memorandums," 5, 6 (full citation, see entry 36, n. 7).

2. Josiah Quincy, Jr.'s 1775 inventory lists "8

Chairs" at £18 as well as "1 Mohogony Desk & Book Case" at £12; Quincy Papers, 53, Massachusetts Historical Society. Quincy's desk and bookcase, with which the chairs share a nineteenth-century provenance, is now in a private collection and bears an inscription by Eliza Susan Quincy, dated 1846:

> This Secretary was the property of Josiah Quincy jun^r & of Abigail Phillips Quincy/ and [w]as probably purchased at the time of their [marri]age 1768/ It was moved from [Pearl] St Boston to Quincy in 180[6].

3. Photographic Archives of the Society.

4. The Winterthur Museum chair is in Hummel, "Queen Anne and Chippendale, Part II," 903, fig. 5. The other three were sold at auction, Parke-Bernet, sale 3215, May 1971, lot 128.

5. An almost identical English chair belongs to Wendell Garrett of New York.

6. American examples with cabriole legs include a set of three: two at the Winterthur Museum (Hummel, "Queen Anne and Chippendale, Part II," 902, fig. 3); the third at the Metropolitan (Comstock, *American Furniture,* no. 272). Two straight-legged examples, probably of American origin, are in Lockwood, *Colonial Furniture,* 3rd ed., vol. 2, figs. 568 and LXXXIII.

NOTES ON STRUCTURE AND CONDITION: The diagonal corner braces are glued into slots in the seat rails. The rear seat rail is of solid mahogany. The present covering is a reproduction worsted damask. The original pattern of brass nails probably resembled that on chair no. 113. The seat rails are riddled with tack holes. The rope carving on the left stile is chipped; a small portion of the crest rail at the right of the center is broken off. The splat is cracked.

MATERIALS: Mahogany; *soft maple* front and side seat rails; *beech* corner braces.

PROVENANCE: The set, including this chair, was given to Abigail Phillips and Josiah Quincy, Jr., in 1769, and it presumably descended through their granddaughter Abigail Phillips Quincy (1803–1893) to her nephew Josiah Phillips Quincy (1829–1910), to Josiah Quincy (1859–1919), to his widow, and to the donor.

ACCESSION: 1971.227   A gift of Edmund Quincy; conservation funded in part by the Massachusetts Council on the Arts and Humanities

118 / Side Chair

1760–1775
Portsmouth, New Hampshire, or York, Maine
H. 37^{15}/$_{16}$ (96.4); W. 23^3/$_{16}$ (58.9); SEAT D. 17^1/$_{16}$ (43.3); SEAT H. 16^9/$_{16}$ (42.1)

Unlike other American examples with this unusual splat design (including the preceding chair), this chair (plate 11) and its mates were clearly not made in Boston.[1] Cabriole examples of the splat design were produced in Boston, but this chair would not be mistaken for one.[2] The exaggerated knuckles of the feet and the pronounced ridge of the knees are not seen on Boston claws and cabrioles. This chair is from a third set of chairs in Jonathan Sayward's house in York, Maine. All three sets (see the Queen Anne chair no. 96, the owl's eye splat chair no. 112) emulate Boston design. This set, Sayward's best, furnished his best parlor (see the chairs *in situ,* 62a).

Both of Sayward's Chippendale sets retain their original upholstery (118a). The outer covers are a green watered worsted impressed with a meandering line, flowers, and butterflies. Patterned worsteds were popular and green was a common upholstery color, but the use of the very same textile suggests that Sayward's two sets of Chippendale chairs were made at about the same time.

The chairmaker and the upholsterer were probably not the same man. In Boston and

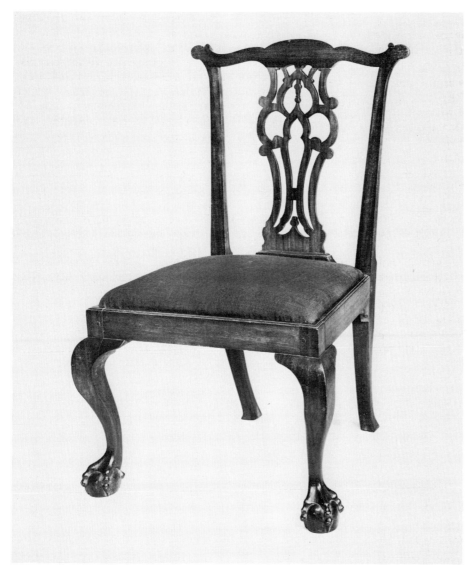

118

at least after 1763 in Portsmouth, the tasks were performed by specialists.[3] If the chairs were made in York — perhaps by Sayward's joiner, Samuel Sewall — the loose seats probably had to be sent elsewhere to be upholstered. Sayward did just that in 1787, when Ziphion Thayer of Boston upholstered six seats for him in leather (see chair no. 96). Perhaps the loose seat frames for chairs no. 112 and 118 also were shipped to Boston and covered either by Thayer or Samuel Grant, who upholstered Sayward's green worsted easy chair (no. 101).[4]

1. The six chairs of the set survive; five are owned by the Society.

2. See entry 117, note 5.

3. In 1763 Henery Golden advertised that he "stuffs all Manner of Chairs, Safoys, Sattees, Couches, &c.," [Portsmouth,] *New Hampshire*

118a

Account Book, 836, American Antiquarian Society.

NOTES ON STRUCTURE AND CONDITION: Four large triangular corner blocks are secured by two rose-headed nails each to the seat rails. Small rear brackets are glued and nailed to the side seat rails at the rear. The original upholstery comprises four narrow webs nailed to the top of the loose seat rails — two running side to side, interwoven with two running front to back; a layer of linen nailed over the webbing; a layer of tow stuffing; another layer of linen; and the outer covering of green worsted, nailed to the underside of the loose seat rails. The chair is in excellent condition; even the scribe lines used for setting off the claws before carving the feet survive on the bottom of the feet.

MATERIALS: *Mahogany; black walnut* front and right loose seat rails; *birch* rear and left loose seat rails; *white pine* corner blocks.

PROVENANCE: The chair descended either as tea chest no. 4 did or it was in the set of "Six mehogony Chairs Seated with green" that Sayward willed to his wife and would then share a provenance with chest of drawers no. 21.

ACCESSION: 1977.201.1   A gift of the heirs of Elizabeth Cheever Wheeler

Gazette, July 29, 1763, as quoted in Orcutt, *Moffatt-Ladd House,* 29–30. In the November 23, 1764, *New Hampshire Gazette,* Joseph Bass advertised "Beds, Easy Chairs, Cushions, and all other sorts of Upholsterer's Work done after the neatest Manner."

4. Grant occasionally upholstered loose seats. On November 9, 1756, he billed John Scollay for "bottom[ing] of 6 Chairs wth gr^n. har^a[teen]"; Grant

119 / Armchair

1760–1790
Portsmouth
H. 38⅞6 (97.6); W. 26⅞ (68.3); SEAT D. 20⅜ (51.8); SEAT H. 17¼ (43.8)

Through inscriptions and comparative examples, this chair makes an interesting contribution to what is known of Chippendale furniture from Portsmouth.

The splat shoe of the chair is inscribed on the inside in pencil: "Admiral Dewey held this / piece in his hand and / examined it Sept 2 1901." On that date, the admiral was apparently in Portsmouth, his home town, visiting Woodbury Langdon, in whose house this chair was photographed by 1897.[1]

An earlier, faded ink inscription on the splat shoe says: "G^{eo} G Brewster / Portsmouth NH / 1832."[2] The signer, George Gains Brewster (1797–1872), was a Portsmouth watchmaker and dentist whose father, Samuel (d. 1834), owned "1 Mahogany arm Chair" and whose family included joiners, chairmakers, and antiquarians.[3]

A late-nineteenth-century inscription on the bottom of the shoe imitates eighteenth-century script; it reads: "1776 / PORTSMOUTH John Langdon." The inscription is spurious, but the armchair is splendid enough to have been owned by the wealthy shipbuilder and eventual governor of New Hampshire, John Langdon (1741–1819).

The chair has several especially handsome features: (1) a carved Gothic arch in the center of the crest and splat; (2) a carved bead on the crest, terminating in spiral-leafed ears (compare with chair no. 120); (3) well-modeled arms (compare with armchair no. 116); (4) neatly scrolled arm supports (119a); and (5) a shaped front seat rail (119b).

Several chairs with this splat and crest are extant, some apparently by the same hand.[4] The splat pattern, based on English examples, was very popular in Portsmouth. It did not gain popularity outside the Piscataqua region and does not appear on any chair that can be documented to Boston, Salem, or Newburyport, Massachusetts.

119

For many years this armchair and others like it have been attributed to Newburyport and to a specific craftsman on the basis of the carved scrolls of the arm supports, which have been cavalierly regarded as the hallmark of Joseph Short.[5] Fales wisely suggests thinking of them "as a regional rather than a personal characteristic."[6] That region may not be Newburyport; it surely includes, and may well center about, Portsmouth.

119a

119b

1. The chair was photographed in the north parlor; Photographic Archives of the Society.

2. The deciphering of this inscription led to the discovery of a phenomenon in Portsmouth — the widespread marking of furniture by owners; Kaye, "Marked Portsmouth Furniture," 1099–1100 and fig. 4.

3. That the hand is Brewster's is verified by his signature on the executor's account for his father's estate; docket 12612, Rockingham County (N.H.) Probate. George G. Brewster is listed as "watchmaker, and surgeon dentist" in the *Portsmouth Directory* of 1827 (Portsmouth: Miller & Brewster). Samuel Brewster's chair is listed in his estate inventory; his occupation is cited as joiner; docket 12612, Rockingham County (N.H.) Probate. Samuel's mother, Mary Gaines, was the daughter of the Ipswich and Portsmouth chairmaker John Gaines (1704–1743). Samuel's son Charles, the author of *Rambles about Portsmouth*, and two daughters of Charles Brewster were antiquarians.

4. Possibly by the same maker are a pair of an assembled set of six side chairs sold at auction (Sotheby Parke Bernet, sale 2604, October 1977, lot 147); an armchair (Cescinsky and Hunter, *English and American Furniture*, 137); a side chair (Nutting, *Furniture Treasury*, vol. 2, no. 2300); another side chair in the Society's collections; and three loose-seated armchairs (in Fales, *Historic Deerfield*, fig. 115, and *Israel Sack Collection*, 3:802, and *Antiques* 70 [September 1956]: inside front cover). A set of four in the Society's collections are related as is an armchair (*Israel Sack Collection*, 4:941).

5. Swan, "Newburyport Furnituremakers"; Downs, *Queen Anne and Chippendale*, no. 58; "Shop Talk," *Antiques* 68 (September 1955).

6. Fales, *Historic Deerfield*, 67.

NOTES ON STRUCTURE AND CONDITION: The medial stretcher is half-dovetailed to the side stretchers. A curved pine block held by four rose-headed nails is added to the straight front seat rail to form the curved shape of the seat. The rear seat rail is veneered with a strip of mahogany, an English practice. Diagonal braces, set into slots in the seat rails and glued, reinforce the seat corners. This, too, is an English technique. The arm construction is unusual. The arms are tenoned into the stiles; each arm support is tenoned into the arm and the seat rail; these tenons are not pinned. While the crest is edged with a carved bead, the stiles are edged (above the arms) with a scratched bead. The backs of the stiles are rounded.

A reproduction worsted damask covers the seat. The brass nails follow the original pattern (see entry 126). The chair is in excellent condition. The front legs and splat shoe are chipped. Wire nails have been added to the corner braces.

MATERIALS: *Mahogany; maple* seat rails and corner braces; *white pine* applied strip to front seat rail.

PROVENANCE: The armchair is part of a collection assembled by the donor and her husband at the end of the nineteenth century.

ACCESSION: 1966.286   A bequest of Elizabeth Elwyn Langdon

120 / Side Chair

1760–1790
Portsmouth
H. 38⅛ (96.8); W. 21⅞ (55.6); SEAT D. 16½ (41.9); SEAT H. 17⅝ (44.8)

This chair, featuring a plain version of the splat seen on the preceding armchair, is part of a large group of related chairs. They further document the splat pattern to Portsmouth and should put to rest a mythical cabinetmaker.

Among the chairs that look exactly like chair no. 120 are two branded "R·HART."[1] The authors examined one of these and found it identical to the Society's chair down to the chairmaker's score marks beneath the stretchers. Apparently the Society's chair, which is unmarked, is not from the R·HART set but was made by the same craftsman.

Over the years, several pieces of furniture marked "R·HART" have been published.[2] The mark was believed to be that of an unknown craftsman. Because of the similarities between the marked chairs and others traditionally ascribed to Newburyport, people began to attribute much furniture to one R. Hart, a "Newburyport cabinetmaker."

He never existed. Richard Hart (ca. 1733–1820), a Portsmouth merchant, was the owner, not the maker, of the furniture.[3] His furniture was probably made in or near Portsmouth. In addition to the R·HART chairs, the other examples of this design that have histories are tied to Portsmouth.[4]

This chair presents another style of Chippendale crest, one with rounded shoulders, without even the restrained ears seen on armchair no. 119. Round-shouldered crests were popular in Portsmouth and were used on chairs with other splat patterns as well, as the next chair illustrates.

120

1. Apparently identical chairs include a pair in the Wentworth-Gardner House, Portsmouth (Howells, *Architectural Heritage of the Piscataqua,* fig. 91); chairs once in the Sarah Orne Jewett House, South Berwick, Me. (Photographic Archives of the Society and Howells, fig. 101); a set of six sold at auction (Joseph Hirshhorn Collection, Sotheby Parke Bernet, sale 4851Y, January 1982, lot 1113); a chair advertised in *Antiques* 104 (October 1973): 539; one owned by Charles R. Yeaton of Andover, Mass. (examined by the authors); and another by Mrs. F. W. Wieder (Comstock, "American Furniture in California," 56, fig. 13). The latter two are stamped "R·HART"; the "R" may not be visible on the Wieder example.

2. A pair of Pembroke tables advertised in *Antiques* 54 (December 1948): 407 (see one, I-37); a chalk-marked easy chair, *Israel Sack Collection,* 3:749; Sheraton stand mentioned in Comstock, "American Furniture in California," 56; another chair, similar to no. 120, owned by Charles Yeaton.

3. Kaye, "Marked Portsmouth Furniture," 1099–1100.

4. Chair no. 119; the first two sets listed in note 1. A chair with this splat design and the crest of 119 appears in an unidentified Portsmouth interior in Elwell, *Colonial Furniture,* pl. 280.

NOTES ON STRUCTURE AND CONDITION: The backs of the stiles and tops of the stretchers are rounded. The medial stretcher is tenoned into the side stretchers. Originally no corner blocks were used;

front corner blocks are now in place and rear corner blocks were once present. The chair was reupholstered by the donor in a modern silk damask and braid; neither is an accurate reproduction. Originally the upholstery was finished with a row of brass nails along the bottom of the seat rail, a vertical row of nails at the rear, and at each front corner a single row nailed to the very edge (see chair no. 126).

MATERIALS: *Mahogany; maple* front and side seat rails; *birch* rear seat rail.

PROVENANCE: The chair came to the Society with a collection of furniture acquired principally in the Portsmouth area.

ACCESSION: 1942.1209   A gift of Virginia L. Hodge and Katherine D. Parry

121 / Side Chair

1760–1790
Portsmouth
H. 38⅛ (96.8); W. 22¼ (56.5); SEAT D. 18¹/₁₆ (45.9); SEAT H. 18 (45.7)

The round-shouldered crest on this chair, reminiscent of that on the preceding chair, sits above another splat design popular in Portsmouth.[1] The splat pattern, like that on chairs no. 119 and 120, was inspired by the English but infrequently used elsewhere in America.[2] This example, skillfully designed and executed, manifests the ability of the chairmaker and illustrates the high quality of Piscataqua furniture.

For many years no particular Chippendale chair or chair patterns were attributed to the Portsmouth area. The elaborate fretwork tea tables (I-36) that were evidently produced in Portsmouth were viewed in isolation as amazing oddities. Now the tea tables no longer seem out of place. Chairs no. 119, 120, 121, and the Portsmouth replica of a London chair (I-15) illustrate the sophisticated seating available to the residents of Portsmouth. Chest of drawers no. 16 further illuminates their taste for elegance.

Portsmouth was an important town in the last half of the eighteenth century. A prosperous port, New Hampshire's capital, it was the home of wealthy people who desired and acquired furniture of beauty and sophistication.

1. Closely related side chairs are a pair owned and branded by Captain William Rice of Portsmouth (Decatur, "George and John Gaines of Portsmouth," 7); chairs at Portsmouth's Moffatt-Ladd House (Giffen, "Moffatt-Ladd House, Part 1," figs. 4, 6); and a set that was in Portsmouth's Cutter Mansion (Howells, *Architectural Heritage*, figs. 107, 108). An armchair with this splat was in the Sarah Orne Jewett House, South Berwick, Me., in a 1931 photograph (Photographic Archives of the Society).

2. For English chairs see Hinckley, *Directory of Furniture*, fig. 282; Kirk, *American Furniture*, nos. 911, 912; and Matthew Pratt's painting of Benjamin West's London studio, figure 13 in Evans, *Benjamin West*. American chairs with related splats are in *Israel Sack Collection*, 2:342 and 374, and attributed to Newburyport.

NOTES ON STRUCTURE AND CONDITION: A scratched bead outlines the crest and the stiles. The backs of the stiles are rounded. The rear seat rail is veneered with a mahogany strip, an English practice. The original diagonal braces at each corner of the seat are half-tenoned and glued to the seat rails; modern screws tighten the joints. The front legs project well above the seat rails, a common Portsmouth technique (see detail 133b). The top edge of the stretchers is gently rounded. The medial stretcher is tenoned into the side stretchers.

The top of the front legs is cracked, the medial stretcher is chipped, and a small pieced repair is visible on the crest. A row of brass nails, similar in pattern to that on chair no. 126, originally ornamented the chair.

MATERIALS: *Mahogany; maple* seat rails and corner braces.

PROVENANCE: The chair came to the Society with a collection of furniture acquired principally in the Portsmouth area.

ACCESSION: 1942.1238   A gift of Virginia L. Hodge and Katherine D. Parry

121

122 / Side Chair

1765–1790
Newport
H. 37¹³/₁₆ (96); W. 21 (53.3); SEAT D. 16¾ (42.5); SEAT H. 16⅞ (42.9)

In urban Rhode Island, where chairs of rectilinear form were not prevalent and pierced splats were slow to win favor, the one rectilinear model and the one pierced splat that did become popular are illustrated by this Newport chair. The splat pattern was not unique to Rhode Island, but the magnificent Newport rendering of the pattern (122a) outshines all others.[1]

122

Numerous chairs of this design and quality survive, some with over-the-rail upholstery, others with loose seats.[2] The group displays outstanding craftsmanship, which is most noticeable in the fine cross-hatching on the crest, in the delicate scrolls and gouge lines on the splat, and in the crisp stop-fluting on the legs.

No chair of this type is labeled, none can be documented to a particular craftsman, yet chairs manifesting this elegant design and workmanship have been attributed to John Townsend. Several of his labeled tables (I-40) do feature similar cross-hatching and stop-fluting, but given the number of accomplished cabinetmakers in Newport, the number of Townsends alone, such an attribution is unsupportable.

1. The splat design is derived from English chairs: see Lyon, *Colonial Furniture,* 3rd ed., fig. 79, an example with a Hartford provenance; also Kirk, *Chairs,* no. 181; and an English oak chair advertised in *Antiques* 39 (March 1941): 184. The design also appears in Philadelphia (*Israel Sack Collection,* 4:879); New York (Kane, *American Seating Furniture,* no. 121); and on a set of Massachusetts chairs at the Museum of Fine Arts, Boston, associated with the Appleton family of Boston.

2. Over-the-rail upholstered chairs include a side chair (*John Brown House Loan Exhibition,* no. 12); a set of chairs, two with typical Rhode Island arm supports sold at auction (King Hooper Collection, part 2, American Art Association, sale 2192, November 1927, lot 214); and a side chair with a carved diamond in the upper center splat (Fales, *Historic Deerfield,* fig. 116). Loose-seated examples are at the Henry Ford Museum (with carved diamond) (Bishop, *American Chair,* no. 202); at the Winterthur Museum (Kirk, *Chairs,* no. 182); Warren, *Bayou Bend,* no. 75; a set at the Hunter House, Preservation Society of Newport; a pair at the Hunter House that are badly stripped but appear to be old; and a pair advertised in *Antiques* 97 (January 1970): 82.

122a

NOTES ON STRUCTURE AND CONDITION: The rear legs, flaring only slightly, are straighter than those on the preceding Marlborough chairs. The backs of the stiles are rounded. The rear seat rail is solid mahogany. Triangular blocks are nailed to the rear corners of the seat with four rose-headed nails each; small blocks, originally glued to the front corners, are missing.

The chair, which was reupholstered only once before, is covered in reproduction yellow moreen; the brass nails follow the original pattern. The medial stretcher is a replacement. The cracked left front leg and broken rear stretcher have been glued. Small pieced repairs were made to the left stretcher and to the top of the right front leg. The seat rails have suffered woodworm damage.

MATERIALS: *Mahogany; soft maple* front and side seat rails; *white pine* corner blocks.

PROVENANCE: The history of the chair is unknown before its acquisition by the donor early in the twentieth century.

ACCESSION: 1933.6044　A bequest of Julia Crocker; conserved through the generosity of Mrs. Oliver F. Ames

123 / Side Chair

1770
Boston
George Bright
H. 36½ (97.8); W. 21⅛ (53.7); SEAT D. 17¼ (43.8); SEAT H. 16⅝ (42.2)

This chair, like no. 113, is one of an extant pair made by George Bright of Boston for Jonathan Bowman of Pownalborough, Maine.[1] In the Bright-Bowman bill (15a), the chair is one of either the "6 Ditto Stufft in Canvis aᵗ 26/8" or the "6 Ditto Stufft in Canvis aᵗ 24/."

123

The two sets of "Ditto Stufft" left Bright's shop without permanent outer covers, either to be finished by someone else — probably with cloth Bowman already owned — or to be used with slipcovers. We do not know how Bowman covered his chairs. The check now on this chair is modern. Beneath the outer cover, however, the chair retains its original web, linen, stuffing, and cover linen; all that made it "Stufft in Canvis" survives.

The handsome splat pattern was popular in Boston on over-the-rail upholstered chairs (see portrait 113a) as well as loose-seated ones, on cabriole chairs as well as Marlborough ones.[2] Like this American chair, English prototypes feature Marlborough legs, H-pattern stretchers, and brackets under the seat rail.[3] Many New England chairs were made with plainer versions of the splat, rushed seats, and legs and stretchers of vernacular design (see the next two chairs).

1. A chair from the set is shown in Allen, *History of Dresden*, 241.

2. Portrait 113a is one of four Copley portraits (Prown, *Copley*, vol. 1, nos. 217, 218, 277, 319) that depict chairs with this splat. Related examples with cabriole legs include a privately owned pair branded "T·BUMSTEAD"; a hairy-paw footed chair (Kirk, *Chairs*, no. 119); a side chair with claw feet (Kane, *American Seating Furniture*, no. 95); a corner chair (*Paul Revere's Boston*, no. 130); and a set of eight (*Israel Sack Collection*, 5:1260, 1261). Marlborough examples include a pair with a crest with rounded ears (*Israel Sack Collection*, 3:611, no. 1391); a pair that was owned in Connecticut but surely was made in Boston, possibly by Bright (Warren, *Bayou Bend*, no. 76); three chairs owned by John Walton of Jewett City, Conn., in 1981; and a walnut example upholstered over the rails with an identical base to chair no. 113 (*Maine Antique Digest*, July 1981, 7-A).

3. An English example is number 73 in Gilbert, *Furniture at Temple Newsam*, vol. 1.

NOTES ON STRUCTURE AND CONDITION: Each fretwork bracket is nailed with two forged finishing nails. The seat never had corner blocks; otherwise the chair is made like chair no. 113. It is in excellent condition.

MATERIALS: *Mahogany; maple* loose seat frame.

PROVENANCE: The chair shares a provenance with chest of drawers no. 15.

ACCESSION: 1980.75.2   A gift of Florence L. Bixby

124 / Side Chair

1760–1785
Salem, Massachusetts, area
H. 36⁷⁄₁₆ (92.6); W. 20³⁄₈ (51.8); SEAT D. 15⁷⁄₈ (40.3); SEAT H. 17¼ (43.8)

A simplified version of the splat seen on the preceding chair was developed in England and copied in America; the New England counterpart is well represented by this chair.[1]

The loose seat was designed to be rushed, its square corners meant to be exposed. The corner blocks beneath the loose seat (124a) are shaped to support the wooden corners of the loose seat without undue pressure on the fragile rushed surface. Rush-

124

covered loose seats are infrequently seen in New England, especially on mahogany chairs of the Chippendale style.[2]

Another unusual feature of this chair is the one-piece splat shoe and rear seat rail. The English settee (no. 107) has the same feature, but this is the only American seat in the book that is so constructed. The one-piece splat shoe and rail is seen on a pair of chairs of identical design at the North Andover Historical Society. That pair and the Society's chair are evidently the work of the same chairmaker, but they are not from the same set; the loose seats on the pair were not designed to be rushed.

The pair, although part of a collection rich in Merrimack Valley objects, has no provenance; a closely related chair has been ascribed to Salem.[3] The Society's chair presents the strongest evidence for attributing the group to the Salem area. It is one of a set of twelve chairs always known to the donor's family as "the Porter chairs." The set descended in the Tileston family from Mary Porter Tileston (1797–1879), a daughter of Dudley Porter of Salem. The splat design was popular throughout Essex County, and the enthusiasm for the pattern is illustrated by a plethora of vernacular examples (see the next chair).

1. See Kirk, *Chairs*, nos. 151 and 152, English and New York examples respectively.

2. Rush-covered loose seats are occasionally seen in Queen Anne chairs: Nutting, *Furniture Treasury*, vol. 2, no. 2104; Sack, *Fine Points*, 19. They seem to have been more common in Philadelphia; see Forman, "Delaware Valley 'Crookt Foot' and Slat-back Chairs," 41–64, for several examples.

3. For the closely related chair, see *Israel Sack Collection*, 1:82.

NOTES ON STRUCTURE AND CONDITION: The medial stretcher is half-dovetailed to the side stretchers. Most of the beaded edge on the medial stretcher has worn away. In 1981 the loose seat frame was rerushed and the broken front tenon of the left stretcher was repaired.

MATERIALS: *Mahogany; maple* loose seat frame; *white pine* corner blocks.

PROVENANCE: The chair descended from Mary Por-

124a

ter Tileston through her daughter Clara Bryce (m. 1849) to the latter's great-granddaughter, the donor.

ACCESSION: 1981.17   A gift of Mary B. Comstock

125 / Side Chair

1760–1795
Salem, Massachusetts, area
H. 36¾ (93.3); W. 20 (50.8); SEAT D. 14¹¹⁄₁₆ (37.3); SEAT H. 17 (43.2)

This chair, one of a birch pair originally stained mahogany, presents a variant of the splat pattern seen on the preceding chair. The heartlike piercing terminates in a point; the upper part of the splat design has been shortened and simplified.

Although the chair is small, the design — bold Spanish feet, a broad compass seat, a stocky splat, a well-proportioned crest with handsome, molded ears — makes a strong impression. No wonder Albert Sack, writing about furniture's fine points, labeled a similar but not quite as fine example "Best."[1]

The chair that Sack illustrated, a somewhat thinner version with attenuated turnings, and a chair in the Essex Institute, Salem, are the only related examples with compass

125

seats found by the authors.[2] However, numerous chairs of this design have the standard trapezoidal seat, and they can be seen in historical collections throughout Essex County, Massachusetts: in Salem, Beverly, Ipswich, Rowley, Boxford, and Andover.[3] Chairs from four sets in the adjoining ports of Salem and Beverly appear most similar to the Society's superb pair.

1. Sack, *Fine Points,* 18.

2. Essex Institute (112,041).

3. Essex Institute: an armchair possibly matching 112,041 (see note 2) and a side chair from another set; Beverly Historical Society: a set of five chairs with the identical back and a chair from another set with a related back; Whipple House, Ipswich Historical Society: a side chair with Marlborough legs; Rowley Historical Society: an armchair and a side chair with solid splats; Boxford Historical Society: a side chair with Marlborough legs and another related chair; Andover Historical Society: two side chairs, one with Spanish feet, one with pad feet.

NOTES ON STRUCTURE AND CONDITION: The rush seat has at least three layers of paint. Black paint now covers both olive paint and red stain. The right side stretcher is replaced. The rear feet have been cut about ¾ inch, causing the chair to lean backward and become more comfortable. Iron L-shaped braces reinforce the joints of the side seat rails and the rear legs.

MATERIALS: *Birch.*

PROVENANCE: The chair was purchased for Florence Evans Bushee from a home in Derry, N.H.

ACCESSION: 1976.231.2   A gift of the estate of Florence Evans Bushee

126 / Side Chair

1755–1790
Portsmouth
H. 37¹³⁄₁₆ (96); W. 21⁵⁄₁₆ (54.1); SEAT D. 17 (43.2); SEAT H. 17¼ (43.8)

The contrast in appearance between this chair (one of a pair) and each of the preceding ones is created by an angular, yokelike crest with pointed ears and enhanced by the simple straightness of the splat. Both crest and splat owe much to Chinese design and its influence on Georgian chairs (see the English settee, no. 107).

Chinese forms and motifs, which had been affecting English design since early in the eighteenth century, inspired Thomas Chippendale and his contemporaries to adopt an especially rectilinear design. This chair is not derived from any of Chippendale's patterns, nor is it at all related to those he dubbed "Chinese," but the same rectilinearity imparts to this chair and to Chippendale's designs their Chinese character.

The stiff, angular lines of this particular version are clean and striking. An oddity of the otherwise sophisticated design is the use of a front stretcher instead of a medial one.[1] Front stretchers, a continuation of an old arrangement (see cane chair no. 84) are, in the Chippendale period, usually associated with vernacular designs.

Similar Marlborough-legged chairs with related splats are known from Virginia, Rhode Island, Boston, and Portsmouth.[2] The fashion was especially popular in Portsmouth, where the merchants Oliver Briard and John Salter branded the related chairs that they owned. Portsmouth's Wendell family owned a similar set.[3]

This example, the Briard, Salter, and Wendell chairs, and other extant chairs from Portsmouth (including chairs no. 119, 120, and 121 and I-15) suggest a preference in that area for over-the-rail upholstery. All but the Salter chair exhibit a distinctive nailing pattern: a single row of brass nails with a single column at each front corner running up the very edge. Apparently a Portsmouth upholsterer favored this economical method, whereas in Boston and elsewhere craftsmen placed a double row at each front corner (see chair no. 113).

126

1. The front stretcher appears on all of the Portsmouth examples cited in note 3 as well as the pair at the Newport Historical Society and the Virginia examples cited in note 2.

2. Virginia examples (Kirk, *Chairs,* nos. 205, 207); a Rhode Island pair at the Newport Historical Society; and a Rhode Island set of seven sold at auction (Duncan A. Hazard Collection, Parke-Bernet, sale 266, November 1940, lot 174); for Portsmouth examples, see note 3; a Boston chair is privately owned. Virginia and Portsmouth examples are remarkably similar.

3. Briard side chair, with original leather upholstery ("Portsmouth Side Chair"); Salter armchair, with original leather upholstery (Kaye, "Marked Portsmouth Furniture," 1103, fig. 6); Wendell chairs are privately owned. Probably from Portsmouth are a side chair with a rush loose seat owned in the late nineteenth century by Ben Perley Poore of West Newbury, Mass.; a side chair at the Billerica Historical Society; and a set of three chairs at the Museum of Early Southern Decorative Arts, identical to the Briard chair.

NOTES ON STRUCTURE AND CONDITION: Large triangular blocks are nailed at the front corners of the seat. The chair was reupholstered for the first time, in 1873, by a Thomas Locke and for the second time, in 1977, in a reproduction yellow moreen. The chair appears to have always been stained a dark reddish brown. The crest is slightly cracked, a leg and stretcher chipped. Screws were added in 1873 through the seat rails into the corner blocks; the blocks were renailed.

MATERIALS: *Birch; hard maple* seat rails; *white pine* corner blocks.

PROVENANCE: The chair apparently belonged to Woodbury Langdon (1837–1921) of Portsmouth and came to the Society with his widow's collection.

ACCESSION: 1974.354.1   A bequest of Elizabeth Elwyn Langdon

127 / Side Chair

1770–1800
Newbury, Massachusetts, area
H. 41⅞ (105.3); W. 19¾ (50.2); SEAT D. 13½ (34.3); SEAT H. 18 (45.7)

In the second half of the eighteenth century and into the first years of the nineteenth, rural New England craftsmen produced a multitude of "Chippendale" chair designs. Although the variations are distinctive, they are clearly derived from and related to the chairs produced in urban centers.

The outline of the splat on this chair resembles that on some Queen Anne chairs (see chair no. 99). However, the piercings derive from those on Chippendale chairs such as chair no. 108 (see also the next two examples). The dip in the center of the crest, a feature shared with Queen Anne chairs, is echoed in the shoulders, which flare to ears in the common Chippendale fashion. The amalgam bespeaks the imagination and taste of the craftsman and his customers, not any ignorance of urban fashion.

The craftsman's production techniques, based on traditional chairmaking skills, dictated the rest of the chair design. The seat construction and the scheme for the front legs, with a front stretcher and paired side stretchers, follow a long-established formula with minor variation (see chair no. 92).

But this is a distinctive chair; its attenuated proportions and especially its crest make it so. The design reflects a localized fashion and probably marks the work of one man, possibly in Newbury or neighboring Byfield, in the northeastern corner of Essex County, Massachusetts. A related crest is seen on a set of chairs from Byfield.[1] A pair of chairs similar to this example came from nearby New Hampshire.[2] The Society's chair has the clearest provenance of the group; it has always belonged to the Coffins of Newbury.[3]

1. The set is owned by Bertram K. and Nina Fletcher Little and illustrated in Watkins, "Highfields," 205.

2. The pair, at the Lyman Allyn Museum, descended in the Clark family of New Hampshire. Related side chairs are at the Yale University Art Gallery (Kane, *American Seating Furniture*, no. 85); in Nutting (*Furniture Treasury*, vol. 2, no. 2097); and three in private collections.

3. The chair appears in a photograph taken in the Coffin House by Wallace Nutting (Bell, *Pathways of the Puritans*, between 118 and 119) as well

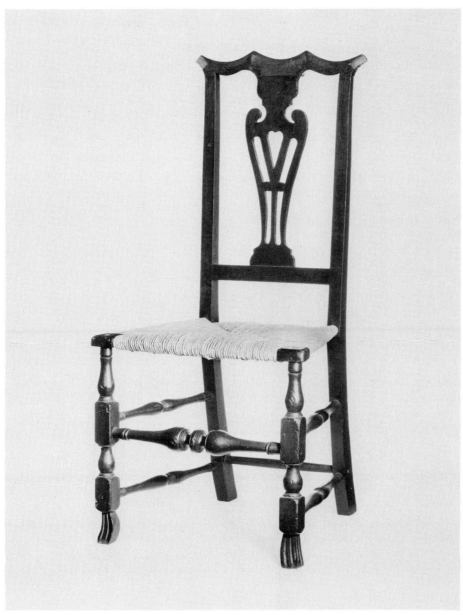

127

as in a ca. 1880 photograph (Photographic Archives of the Society).

NOTES ON STRUCTURE AND CONDITION: The only pins used secure the tenons of the stiles to the crest. In the nineteenth century, the chair was painted black and the seat was upholstered with a woven cloth of a flamestitch pattern. The chair is in excellent condition.

MATERIALS: *Soft maple; ash* rear stretcher and side and rear seat rails.

PROVENANCE: The chair apparently shares a provenance with table no. 64.

ACCESSION: 1963.96   A gift of Mrs. Arthur Merriam

128 / Side Chair

1770–1800
Middleton, Massachusetts, area
H. 39¾ (101); W. 18¼ (46.4); SEAT D. 14 (35.6); SEAT H. 17⅜ (44.1)

More typical than the preceding example — the back design can be found on many city and rural chairs — this chair too has variant features. The blocks, or unturned portions of the front legs, are unusually sharp (compare with chair no. 125). Between the blocks are mirrored turnings, not the usual baluster forms. Nor are the front and side stretchers

128

of common patterns. Such distinctive qualities suggest the hand of a craftsman in a rural community.

The chairmaker probably lived near Middleton, in Essex County. The chair is from a set of six from the Middleton farmhouse that Joseph Symonds built in 1792 and may have been new when it went into Deacon Symonds's house, for the attenuation of the turnings suggests a post-Revolutionary date.

The front legs are carefully turned. The adeptly shaped stiles, crest, and splat (the piercing of the splat is precisely beveled) contrast markedly with the chair back of the same design on the next example.

NOTES ON STRUCTURE AND CONDITION: A pin set through each of the exposed corners of the front seat rail secures the round tenons of the front legs. The chair is in excellent condition. Old mahogany graining, possibly the original finish, covers the chair. The rush seat has had at least three coats of paint: yellow, white, and the current tan. An iron L-shaped brace has been added at the back of the left seat rail.

MATERIALS: *Soft maple.*

PROVENANCE: The chair was purchased from a descendant of Deacon Joseph Symonds (1758–1831) of Middleton.

ACCESSION: 1936.230   Museum purchase

129 / Armchair

1770–1810
Southern New England
H. 40¹⁵/₁₆ (104); W. 24½ (62.2); SEAT D. 16⅜ (41.6); SEAT H. 13½ (34.3)

A third variation of the splat pattern seen on chairs no. 127 and 128 appears on this low armchair. The splat, common on sophisticated chairs as well, is the only ordinary feature of this odd and ungainly armchair.[1]

Even for a chair with a low seat, the space between the seat and the splat rail is inordinately high. The arm supports are distinctively joined through the seat rails to the upper side stretchers.[2] The handholds on the shallow arms are carved on their sides, but not along their handled surface. Turned legs occasionally end in feet of this type, but this foot design is made distinctive by the coved disk beneath it, which is reminiscent of the work of the Dunlap school (page 25). The ears of the crest jut out without shaping or tapering, showing none of the smoothness customary on even rude examples.

A related chair, owned by Captain John Coffin Pinkham (1785–1864) of Nantucket, a packet master, is decorated with paint, paper cutouts, and gold paper banding. The façade of this chair back may have benefited originally from a decorated finish; the flat surfaces certainly seem to invite it.

The maker of the Society's chair was not a carver. He was a turner, and the turned

129

elements are the best features of his chair. The rear and side stretchers are very decorative for such secondary elements; the front stretcher is of a complex pattern, handsomely worked.

There is not sufficient documentation to attribute the work to a particular turner or town. But because the features are so distinctive, several chairs can be attributed to the same shop: a nearly identical armchair, the Pinkham family side chair of almost usual seat height (16¾ inches); a low side chair illustrated by Lockwood; and two low side chairs, apparently from different sets, that were in the collection of Stewart E. Gregory of Connecticut.[3] Low chairs, especially low armchairs, are few. For all the known chairs of this shop to have seats that are lower than usual is truly extraordinary.

1. For a sophisticated version, see the walnut cabriole-legged chair at the Museum of Fine Arts, Boston; Randall, *American Furniture*, no. 147.

2. Trent (*Hearts & Crowns*, 80) notes that this form of arm support became common along the Connecticut coast after the Revolution; see numbers 63 and 64.

3. The somewhat larger but otherwise identical armchair was advertised in *Maine Antique Digest*, May 1982, 6C; the Pinkham chair is at the Peter Foulger Museum; the low side chair in Lockwood, *Colonial Furniture*, rev. ed., vol. 2, fig. 539, belonged to Dwight Blaney; the Gregory chairs were lots 304 and 362, Sotheby Parke Bernet, sale no. 4209, January 1979. A related chair is illustrated *in situ; Antiques* 69 (April 1956): 341.

NOTES ON STRUCTURE AND CONDITION: The arm supports are round-tenoned to the arms and upper side stretchers. The arms are round-tenoned to the stiles. The chair has sustained some woodworm damage. It was refinished in this century and has a new rush seat.

MATERIALS: *Birch; ash* seat rails, stretchers, and arm supports.

PROVENANCE: The chair is from the furniture collection formed in the early twentieth century by Mary Thacher of Massachusetts and descended to the donor.

ACCESSION: 1972.207   A gift of Guido R. Perera

130 / Side Chair

1770–1780
England
H. 37¼ (94.6); W. 21⅞ (55.6); SEAT D. 19⁵⁄₁₆ (49.1); SEAT H. 17 (43.2)

A new style of chair back, one composed of two or three slats that echo the crest, is beautifully exemplified by this English chair, one of a pair with an American provenance. The chair back is invariably seen with a Marlborough base in America although not always in England.[1] A late Chippendale fashion (which owes nothing to any published design of Thomas Chippendale), it was at its height in Massachusetts in the last three decades of the eighteenth century. Numerous interpretations of several patterns were produced.

Some of the very best American slat-back chairs look remarkably like this English chair.[2] For years this chair was assumed to have been made in America because old photographs and a long family history documented it to Newburyport. It apparently belonged to the wealthy William Bartlett (1748–1841) and was among the furnishings he placed in the Newburyport house he built in 1804, possibly for his son Edmund.[3]

The chair is now believed to be English because of three features: the only secondary wood is beech, the only stuffing is curled hair, and the carving is in deep relief. Beech — occasionally used in New England, especially in Essex County, Massachusetts — is seldom the sole secondary wood. Curled hair — generally used in New England in small amounts to augment marsh grass or flax — is the sole stuffing in this chair, which retains all of its original upholstery except for the outer cover. The carving of the chair back is deeper than that on New England examples. The anthemions at the center of the slats

130

are completely pierced; on almost all related New England chairs, the anthemions are either unpierced or open merely in the center.[4] The four tiny decorative holes through each slat are almost never seen on New England examples.[5] The design of the precisely cut leafage on the ears is distinctive, although two known Massachusetts chairs emulate the pattern.[6]

A chair at the Arlington Historical Society is so very similar (it also has a serpentine front seat rail) that, aside from the presence of typical New England secondary woods, only flatter carving differentiates it from the Society's chair. The New England chair-maker copied a chair so like this one that it may have been this very chair.

New fashions — chair forms such as the Chippendale slat-back, motifs such as the neoclassical anthemion — were transported from England to America in furniture such as this. Because so many New England examples resemble it, this chair proves valuable for the comparative study of European and American furniture.

1. An English example with this chair back has cabriole legs; Hinckley, *Directory of Furniture*, fig. 311. An American cabriole example (Nutting, *Furniture Treasury*, vol. 2, no. 2253) is probably the one at Historic Deerfield (Fales, *Historic Deerfield*, fig. 119); Philip Zea of Deerfield says that the legs are old but not original to the chair.

2. Three-slat examples include a chair at the Arlington Historical Society; a pair at the Concord Antiquarian Museum; a chair at the Winterthur Museum (58.2353); another chair and a set of four also at Winterthur (Montgomery, *American Furniture*, nos. 13, 11); and a set of three, one at Colonial Williamsburg and two at the Essex Institute (one of the latter appears in an illustration in Fales, "Crowninshield-Bentley House," 489). Two-slat chairs are a set of eleven at the American Antiquarian Society; a side chair at the Winterthur Museum (Montgomery, *American Furniture*, no. 12); a pair sold at auction (Mrs. J. Amory Haskell Collection, pt. 2, Parke-Bernet, sale 570, May 1944, lot 568); and one of a pair illustrated in *Israel Sack Collection*, 2:314.

3. Hale, *Old Newburyport Houses*, caption for figure 16. One chair of the pair appears in figure 18.

4. The exception is the Arlington Historical Society chair (see note 2).

5. A chair at the Winterthur Museum (Mont-

gomery, *American Furniture*, no. 12) and the one at the Arlington Historical Society have the small holes.

6. The Arlington Historical Society and American Antiquarian Society chairs.

NOTES ON STRUCTURE AND CONDITION: The serpentine front seat rail is made of one piece of wood. The rear seat rail is veneered with a strip of mahogany. The shoe is the thin, flat strip common on Chippendale slat-back chairs. Diagonal braces are glued into slots in the front corners of the seat. The medial stretcher is half-dovetailed to the side stretchers. The outer upholstery, a reproduction worsted damask, covers the original layers of webbing, linen, stuffing, and linen. The original brass nailing pattern has been followed.

MATERIALS: Mahogany; *beech* seat rails and braces.

PROVENANCE: The chair apparently descended with the Bartlett-Atkinson house in Newburyport from William Bartlett to his son Edmund (d. 1853), to his daughter Hannah Bartlett Atkinson (1806–1872), to her son William Bartlett Atkinson (d. 1895), and to his stepsisters, aunts of the donor.

ACCESSION: 1934.574a   A bequest of Alice A. Stevens

131 / Armchair

1770–1790
Boston-Salem area
H. 36½ (92.7); W. 23⅛ (58.7); SEAT D. 18⅜ (46.7); SEAT H. 17⅞ (45.4)

This armchair and its six matching side chairs (131a) have "two cross slats and top rail."[1] The set makes an interesting comparison with the preceding chair, with carved anthemions and serpentine seat. Instead of anthemions, leafage decorates the crest and slats. Instead of the graceful serpentine front seat rail, the seat is fashionably "hollowed," to use an eighteenth-century term for this concave surface.[2] Both slat-back designs are elaborate and pierced. This chair is American but closely related to English prototypes; the pattern was made in both two- and three-slat versions.[3]

131

This chairback design was very popular in the last quarter of the eighteenth century. The admiration for the sophisticated model can be appreciated by the number and variety of simplified chairs that it inspired (see the next chair).

1. The term was used in the Hartford Price List of 1792, quoted in Lyon, *Colonial Furniture,* 3rd ed., 270.

2. Montgomery, *American Furniture,* no. 11.

3. For an English prototype, see Gilbert, *Furniture at Temple Newsam,* vol. 1, no. 81. For related two-slat American chairs, see *Israel Sack Collection,* 3:612; and *Antiques* 77 (February 1960): back cover. Three-slat examples include a pair at the Museum of the American China Trade with a Milton, Mass., history in the Robbins family; and an armchair with carving apparently identical

to that on this chair; *Israel Sack Brochure*, no. 34 (May 1980): 37.

NOTES ON STRUCTURE AND CONDITION: The hollowed seat is created with concave seat rails. The shoe is the thin, flat strip common on Chippendale slat-back chairs. No corner braces or blocks were ever used. The medial stretcher is half-dovetailed to the side stretchers. Each arm support fits into a dovetail-shaped slot in a side seat rail; each arm fits into a dovetail-shaped slot in a stile. The upholstery is modern silk damask. Originally the chair was ornamented with a double row of brass nails like that on chair no. 130. It is in excellent condition.

MATERIALS: *Mahogany; soft maple* front and side seat rails; *birch* rear seat rail.

PROVENANCE: The armchair and matching side chairs came to the Society from the collection of Mary Thacher and are probably the set sold at auction, King Hooper, Inc., Hyman Kaufman, and Herbert Lawton Collections, National Art Galleries, sale 22, December 1931, lot 473.

ACCESSION: 1948.131   A gift of Mary Thacher

131a. Side Chair. Boston-Salem area, 1770–1790. *Mahogany, soft maple,* and *birch;* H. 36 (91.4); W. 21⅛ (53.6); SEAT D. 17½ (44.4); SEAT H. 18 (45.7). Society for the Preservation of New England Antiquities.

132 / Side Chair

1780–1815
Eastern Massachusetts
H. 36¹¹/₁₆ (93.2); W. 18⅞ (47.9); SEAT D. 14¼ (36.2); SEAT H. 17¼ (43.8)

This simplified version of the preceding chair design is almost its opposite in stylishness. The crest and slats are not carved; not even a scribed line outlines the crest and stiles. The rushed seat is the converse of the modish hollowed seat in elegance. The front stretcher, standard on common chairs, replaces the medial stretcher of the stylish H pattern. The stretchers are not even molded at the edge. However, the corners of the front legs are bead-molded, a popular modeling that seems simple when compared with the ogee-molded outer surfaces on more fashionable Marlborough legs.

This chair is the humblest imitation of the design epitomized by chair no. 131; many chairs strike a middle level of decoration.[1] One can appreciate the group better by knowing how basic a version can be made without losing the essence of the design.

1. In the middle range of decoration are a privately owned set of loose-seated cherry chairs with a scratched bead on the crest and stiles, and a side chair at the Essex Institute (130,090) that is upholstered over the rails. A rush-seated example at Old Sturbridge Village, very similar to chair no. 131, is attributed to Essex County; Fales, *American Painted Furniture*, no. 19.

NOTES ON STRUCTURE AND CONDITION: This chair, in excellent condition, has traces of white paint and red stain beneath the present coat of black paint. The rush seat is modern.

MATERIALS: *Birch.*

PROVENANCE: No history is known.

ACCESSION: 1956.M4   Donor unknown

132

133 / Side Chair

1775–1805
Portsmouth
H. 38 (96.5); W. 21⅞ (55.6); SEAT D. 17¹/₁₆ (43.3); SEAT H. 17⅞ (45.4)

The particular slat-back design of this chair was especially popular in Portsmouth.[1] Daniel Austin, a merchant, owned an identical chair,[2] and a set with hollowed seats

133

belonged to the Peirces.[3] A rush-seated common version (133a) descended in the Lord family.[4]

This chair, one of a pair in the Society's collection, is from a set owned by George Washington's personal secretary, Tobias Lear (1760–1816), of Portsmouth. Five of the set are extant.[5] According to mid-nineteenth-century reports, the chairs were made from cherry trees that grew in Lear's garden.[6]

Historic associations are only part of what makes this chair interesting. The original underupholstery (layers of webbing, linen, and marsh grass and curled hair stuffing) clearly illustrates old methods. The raised corners on top of the front legs create stable endings for the roll of straw that pads the front edge of the seat (133b). The upholsterer used the roll to create a straight, firm edge for the stuffing.

No brass nails ever decorated this chair; the random holes on the side rails are from the iron tacks that secured the outer linen. Apparently the chair was originally upholstered in linen alone (see entry 123) and was covered with a slipcover (such as that in 133c) when it was in Lear's west parlor.[7]

133b

133a. Side Chair. Portsmouth, 1785–1810. *Birch* and *maple;* H. 39½ (100.3); W. 21 1/16 (53.5); SEAT D. 14⅞ (37.8); SEAT H. 17⅝ (44.8). Society for the Preservation of New England Antiquities.

133c. Chair No. 133 with a Reproduction Slipcover. *The cover is a copy of one made in the 1760s, now at Colonial Williamsburg.*

1. It is based on English sources; Hinckley, *Directory of Furniture*, 180, no. 304.

2. Kaye, "Marked Portsmouth Furniture," 1098–99.

3. Photograph of the Peirce dining room; Howells, *Architectural Heritage*, fig. 32. Possibly the same set appears in the Wentworth-Gardner dining room; figs. 84, 89.

4. The pair in the Society's Rundlet-May House, Portsmouth, photographed *in situ* when upholstered in leather (Howells, *Architectural Heritage*, fig. 128), came from the Portsmouth house of Samuel Lord (1788–1871).

5. Three of the set, now at Strawbery Banke, were still owned by the family in 1940. One was illustrated by Decatur, then the owner, in "The Lear House," 15. An article in the *Portsmouth Herald*, August 30, 1934, about the Tobias Lear House cites Decatur as "heir to the family papers, relics and portraits of Colonel Lear." Fragments of a clipping of the article were affixed under the seat of chair no. 133.

6. Brewster, *Rambles about Portsmouth*, 270. See also Decatur, "The Lear House," 11, and Decatur, "George and John Gaines," 7.

7. The chairs were in the west parlor when Washington visited Lear's house; *Portsmouth Herald*, August 30, 1934.

NOTES ON STRUCTURE AND CONDITION: The medial stretcher is tenoned into the side stretchers. The top of each stretcher is rounded. The chair never had corner blocks or braces. The angled corner projections of the front legs are neatly rounded.

Except for a missing splat shoe, the chair is in excellent condition. It retains its original reddish stain. The modern slipcover, a copy of a late-eighteenth-century cover in the collections of Colonial Williamsburg, was made of a reproduction copperplate-printed cotton.

MATERIALS: *Cherry.*

PROVENANCE: By 1940, the Society's pair was no longer with the rest of the set that descended in the family of Tobias Lear and was apparently in the collection of the donors.

ACCESSION: 1942.1236   A gift of Virginia L. Hodge and Katherine D. Parry

134 / Side Chair

1785–1805
Essex County, Massachusetts, probably Newbury
H. 37⁵⁄₁₆ (94.8); W. 19³⁄₁₆ (48.7); SEAT D. 16¹⁄₈ (41); SEAT H. 16⁷⁄₁₆ (41.8)

An interesting comparison to the preceding chair and its common cousin (133a) is seen in this slat-back chair and its close relation, chair no. 135. The latter two, the simplest Chippendale slat-back designs included here, are each from an extant pair that descended in the Coffin family of Newbury (see tables no. 60 and 64) and typify a design popular throughout Essex County.

The wavy slat design appears on stylish as well as simple chairs in the Essex County area.[1] The two simple examples owned by the Society (chairs no. 134 and 135) are actually very different. This three-slat one has nicely rounded ears, and the back of its crest rail is also rounded. Yet its plain front legs lack even a beaded edge at the corners. In contrast, the little two-slat chair has none of the above characteristics; it is much thinner and holds some interesting surprises (see the next entry).

1. Mahogany examples with over-the-rail upholstery are a side chair with molded legs, owned by Josiah Bartlett (1728–1795) of Kingston, N.H. (*Decorative Arts of New Hampshire*, no. 51); two owned by Ben Perley Poore of West Newbury, Mass., ca. 1900 (photograph of interior of his house, Indian Hill, Photographic Archives of the Society); and a side chair with plain legs in the Henry Ford Museum (Bishop, *American Chair*, no. 233). Simpler rush-seated versions include a grain-painted maple side chair privately owned (Fales, *American Painted Furniture*, no. 110); a maple pair and a set of four at the Cape Ann Historical Association; a chair at the North Andover Historical Society; and one at the Ipswich Historical Society.

NOTES ON STRUCTURE AND CONDITION: The front corners of the seat are noticeably small. The chair, in excellent condition, has a modern rush seat and shows traces of original red stain.

MATERIALS: *Birch; soft maple* side and rear seat rails.

PROVENANCE: The pair of chairs either descended from Edmund Coffin (1764–1825) with table no. 60 or from his brother Joseph (1762–1805) to his son Joshua (1792–1864), to his daughter Anna (b. 1838), to Edmund Colman (d. 1915), a cousin, and to his sister, the donor.

ACCESSION: 1963.97b   A gift of Mrs. Arthur Merriam

135 / Side Chair

1785–1810
Essex County, Massachusetts, probably Newbury
H. 38 (96.5); W. 19¼ (48.9); SEAT D. 14½ (36.8); SEAT H. 17⅛ (43.5)

Although of a common sort, this is an unusual chair.[1] It is one of a pair in the Society's collection and shares a history with another pair (see the preceding chair). The chairs also share a similar basic design and at a glance may appear to be merely two- and three-slat versions of the same pattern, but they are not.

This is a much thinner, lighter chair. The elements of the back — the crest, slats, and stiles — are measurably slighter (see *Notes on Structure and Condition*). The back of the crest is not rounded as on the preceding chair, nor are the ears round. The front legs

135

have a beaded edge not present on the preceding example. But it is the rear legs, which are very slender when viewed from the front (compare with chair no. 134), that are especially different.

It is almost an axiom of chair construction that rear stretchers are set above the side stretchers. Yet here the chairmaker set the rear stretcher below. The rearrangement was made structurally sound by broadening the rear feet (135a). Thus, this design incorporates a most attractive feature, a flare at the rear legs reminiscent of the club rear feet on elegant furniture such as chair no. 111.

1. Related two-slat rush-seated examples are: Garrett, "Living with Antiques," 192; *Antiques and the Arts Weekly,* April 7, 1978, 89; a set of at least four with a Newbury history in the Spencer-Pierce-Little House, Newbury (Photographic Archives of the Society).

NOTES ON STRUCTURE AND CONDITION: This chair lacks the ¼-inch chamfers seen on the inside edge of all four legs of chair no. 134. It has rectangular, not square, front corners of the seat, and its slats are ¼ inch, not 7⁄16 inch, thick. The seat is covered with modern rush. The rear stretcher was broken and repaired.

MATERIALS: *Birch; white oak* side and rear seat rails.

PROVENANCE: The chair shares a provenance with the preceding chair.

ACCESSION: 1963.97D   A gift of Mrs. Arthur Merriam

135a

Cradles and Bedsteads

136 / Cradle

1665–1685
Barnstable-Yarmouth area, Massachusetts
H. 33⅜ (84.8); W. 25¼ (64.1); D. 33⅝ (85.4)

This cradle is a tour de force of joinery and turning. Stiles, rails, and muntins abound, each decoratively molded. The horizontal lines of the rails continue around the enclosure, creating a headboard of eight panels (136a), a cradle of twenty-two. Turned finials and screens of spindles complete this remarkable seventeenth-century American cradle, the finest one known.[1]

Cradles — some joined, some nailed, some upholstered, many of wicker — were generally used in the lower rooms of houses. Inventories imply that they were not as numerous as their representation in historic houses suggests.[2]

In the nineteenth century, early cradles, like spinning wheels, became cherished symbols of our colonial heritage. This cradle was illustrated and its history narrated in a book on Yarmouth published in 1884:

> Col. [John] Thacher's descendants still preserve a cradle made . . . more than two centuries ago, and a blanket, brought . . . from England, by Anthony Thacher. . . . The cradle was made of rifted oak, in most ingenious style, and must have been in great request, Col. Thacher being the father, by his two marriages, of twenty-one children.[3]

Anthony Thacher (ca. 1589–1667), the colonel's father, immigrated in 1635, settling in Yarmouth on Cape Cod. His son John (1639–1713) was prominent in the militia and in government, serving both town and province for about twenty years.[4] In his will, John bequeathed "to my son Peter Perkins . . . my Cradle and bearing blanket which he has in [his] possession."[5]

Thacher's bearing blanket may have come across the Atlantic, but his cradle did not. The use of American woods, red oak and white pine, shows that it was made here. It is possible almost to pinpoint its origin because a related cradle (136b) belonged to the Hinckley family of neighboring Barnstable.

The Hinckley and Thacher cradles are apparently by the same maker. Barnstable, a prosperous town, supported several turners and joiners.[6] One joiner, John Gorham

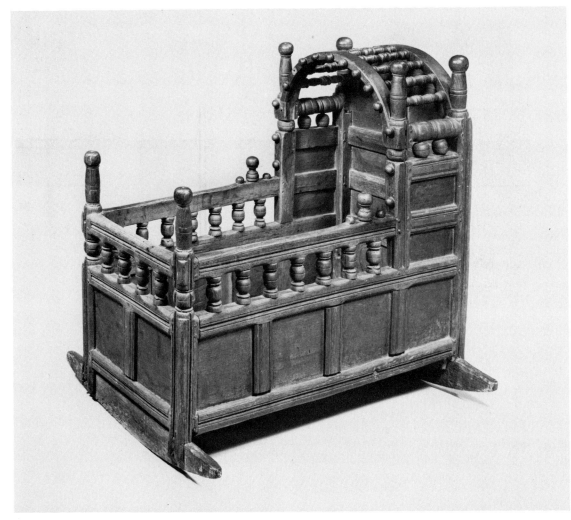

136

(1621–1675), lived on the border of the two towns and had close connections with John Thacher. He too was in the militia and his daughter, Lydia, became Thacher's second wife.[7]

1. Several other joined New England cradles are extant. The second most elaborate one is the cradle (136b) that descended in the Hinckley family of Barnstable. Other examples are the Noyes and Cushman family cradles (St. George, *The Wrought Covenant*, nos. 39 and 53 respectively); a cradle at the Museum of Art, Rhode Island School of Design, with an Abington, Mass., history (Banks, "The Radeke Collection," 27); the Minot family cradle at the Old State House–The Bostonian Society; and a cradle at the Massachusetts Historical Society with a Salem history.

2. In 109 inventories of rural Suffolk County, from 1675 to 1775, there are 15 references to cradles and 278 references to beds; Cummings, *Inventories*, 273, 279.

3. Swift, *Old Yarmouth*, 135.

4. Ibid., 133–34.

5. John Thacher's will, vol. 3, p. 296, Barnstable County (Mass.) Probate.

6. St. George, *The Wrought Covenant*, 72–102.

7. A tale tells of Thacher, on his wedding trip with his first wife, seeing the infant Lydia at her father's house; Swift, *Old Yarmouth*, 58, 134–35.

136a

136b. Photograph of the Hinckley Family Cradle in situ. Barnstable, Massachusetts, ca. 1890. Photographic Archives, Society for the Preservation of New England Antiquities.

NOTES ON STRUCTURE AND CONDITION: The small turned spools and round buttons are round-tenoned into place. The bottom is nailed. The rockers, eighteenth-century replacements, are set into grooves in the bottoms of the corner stiles and held tight with nails.

The cradle is in remarkably good condition. A turned button is missing on the face of the hood. The knobs on the top of the side rails are replacements. Woodworm damage is evident throughout.

MATERIALS: *Red oak; white pine* bottom and rockers.

PROVENANCE: The chair descended in the Thacher family of Yarmouth to the donors.

ACCESSION: 1958.100   A gift of Elizabeth T. Acampora, Dorothy Armour, L. Hope Carter, Guido R. Perera, Henry C. Thacher, Louis B. Thacher, Jr., and Thomas C. Thacher

137 / Cradle

1735
Boston
H. 28³⁄₁₆ (71.6); W. 22¹³⁄₁₆ (57.9); D. 42³⁄₄ (108.6)

This cradle has a far simpler form than the preceding one. It is the product not of a joiner but of a carpenter, who nailed the frame together, and an upholsterer, who covered it with black leather and decorated it with brass nails.

137

Upholstered board construction was commonly used for trunks and coffins and seems to have been popular for making cradles as well in the early eighteenth century. Cradles upholstered in leather survive from New York as well as from New England.[1] Three Boston leather cradles have been preserved because of their historical associations. One, dated 1730, belonged to the family of a governor; another, from 1731, was made by an upholsterer for one son and survives because of the patriotic actions of another son; the third, marked 1735 (137a), supposedly rocked a future general. The Society owns the latter two cradles; the one from the family of Governor Joseph Dudley (d. 1720) of Massachusetts belongs to the Massachusetts Historical Society.

This 1735 cradle, descended in the family of General William Heath (1737–1814) of Roxbury, a delegate to the Provincial Congress, the commander of a brigade during the Revolution, a member of the convention that ratified the federal Constitution, a state senator, and a judge.[2] The Heath and Dudley cradles are almost identical and probably were upholstered by the same craftsman.

The more modestly decorated 1731 cradle (137b) descended in the family of Samuel Grant, a Boston upholsterer, having been made by Samuel for his first child, Samuel Jr.

Young Samuel's initials and year of birth are inscribed with brass nails on the headboard. Grant's cradle was exhibited in 1876 at an exhibition of Revolutionary relics at the Old South Meeting House and described as having belonged "to Samuel Grant [Sr.], Father of Moses Grant who assisted in throwing the Tea overboard in Boston Harbor, Dec. 16, 1773."[3]

Such are the historical associations that have preserved three dated products of Boston upholstery. Made in the same shops as Boston leather chairs (see chair no. 91), the cradles illustrate an aspect of the upholsterer's craft that is rarely noted, the handsome decoration achieved with brass nails.

137a

137b. Cradle. Upholstered by Samuel Grant (1705–1784), Boston, 1731. White pine; H. 27¾ (70.5); W. 24¹⁄₁₆ (61.1); D. 40½ (102.9). Society for the Preservation of New England Antiquities.

1. New York examples are the Sanders family cradle dated 1749 (Blackburn, *Cherry Hill*, no. 35); the Brinckerhoff family cradle dated 1762 (Metropolitan Museum of Art); and a cradle owned by Robert Livingston (1746–1813) (*Israel Sack Collection*, 1:67).

2. Drake, *Dictionary of American Biography*, 424.

3. *Catalogue of Revolutionary Relics*, 5, no. 41.

NOTES ON STRUCTURE AND CONDITION: The sides are nailed to the foot, headboards, and hood crest. The two-board hood is nailed to the top edges of the sides, headboard, and crest. The black leather is nailed with iron tacks to the underside of the bottom. Small sections of leather have been lost. The interior is lined with two layers of nineteenth-century wallpaper. The rockers have been moved and renailed but appear to be original.

MATERIALS: *White pine*. Original brass handles on foot and headboards.

PROVENANCE: The cradle was probably first owned by William Heath, the father of General William. It was inherited by the general's nephew and namesake, sold to a neighbor, Peter Brigham (d. 1852), given by him to William and Mary Ann Day Lingham (m. 1848), and inherited by their daughters Sarah Emerson and Lucy and Emma Lingham, from whom it was purchased by the donor.

ACCESSION: 1924.47   A gift of Francis H. Bigelow

138 / Cradle

1790–1810
Boston area
H. 27⁷⁄₁₆ (69.7); W. 22³⁄₄ (57.8); D. 41¹⁄₈ (104.5)

The most common form of cradle in New England in the eighteenth and nineteenth centuries was the board cradle. Many are nailed; others have dovetail joints as well. This mahogany example, more finely constructed than most (see *Notes on Structure and Condition*), is dovetailed at the footboard but otherwise joined with nails.

Board cradles were made in this traditional form well into the nineteenth century. Based on the simple arch of its hood, this example would probably be dubbed Queen Anne. The next example, featuring serpentine cutouts on the hood, would be associated with the Chippendale style. Yet this Queen Anne cradle could not have been made before about 1790, for it was made with cut nails.

When it came to adopting new styles, the form of furniture least susceptible to change, the form that stood still for over a century, was the cradle.

NOTES ON STRUCTURE AND CONDITION: Except for the joined cradle (no. 136), this one has the most sophisticated construction of those in the book.

The top edge of each row of dovetails joining the footboard and the sides is mitered. A quarter-round vertical block, glued at each inside corner of the

138

headboard and extending through the bottom of the cradle, strengthens the nailed joints. Similar blocks reinforce the hood crest. Nails, passing through the sides, footboard, and headboard, secure the bottom. A double-arched bead covers the nailheads. Screws through the bottom hold the rockers. Six glue blocks originally flanked each rocker; five, at the foot rocker, are missing.

Part of the foot rocker has been replaced. Small chips in the base molding and hood have been filled. The cradle was refinished in 1976.

MATERIALS: Mahogany; *maple* rockers; white pine bottom and support blocks. Replaced brass handles on footboard and headboard.

PROVENANCE: The cradle came to the Society with many items from the Beal family of Boston. No further history is known.

ACCESSION: 1920.67   A gift of the estate of Mrs. James H. Beal

139 / Cradle

1795–1805
Portsmouth
H. 25¹¹/₁₆ (65.2); W. 19 (48.3); D. 37 (94)

Unlike the preceding cradle, this one is entirely of nailed construction. Made of pine, it is a humble object. Nevertheless, it is in excellent condition; even the original red stain finish is well preserved.

139

The cradle belonged to James Rundlet (1772–1852), a Portsmouth merchant. Rundlet married Jane Hill on January 1, 1795; their daughter Harriet, the first of thirteen children, was born that November. The cradle probably was made the same year. Cut nails are used throughout, so it could not have been made much earlier.

A Rundlet bed and the crib into which the Rundlet babies graduated are seen in entry 141.

NOTES ON STRUCTURE AND CONDITION: The bottom, nailed to the headboard, sides, and footboard, protrudes to simulate a base molding. Nails pass through the bottom into the rockers, and a cleat, screwed to the underside of the bottom, is tenoned through the rockers.

MATERIALS: *White pine.*

PROVENANCE: The cradle shares a provenance with table no. 71.

ACCESSION: 1971.726   A gift of Ralph May

140 / Bedstead

1745–1755
England, probably London
H. 89⅛ (226.4); W. 54⅛ (137.5); D. 78 (198.1)

During the seventeenth and eighteenth centuries, the most important and valuable furnishing in a house was the fully dressed high-post bed. It formed the focal point of a chamber; in grand houses, the chair upholstery and window curtains matched the bed hangings.

The hangings, of imported materials, were assembled by American upholsterers or acquired complete from England. Bedsteads, however, were rarely imported. This example, the most elaborate piece of furniture in the book, is the only known English bedstead with a New England provenance. Though its original owner is unknown, it was an heirloom that descended in the Cambridge, Massachusetts, family of Erastus Forbes Brigham (b. 1807) and Sophia De Wolf Homer Brigham (d. 1881), who married in 1832. As with cane seating (no. 81–84), settee no. 107, and Chippendale slat-back chair no. 130, it illustrates the use of English furniture in New England houses and illuminates our understanding of elegant American interiors.

Generally, the bedstead was by far the least expensive part of a bed, the textiles and feathers being very dear, but in this case, because of the great amount of carved work, the bedstead itself must have been exceedingly costly.

The beautiful carvings — the hairy paw feet (140a), the acanthus leaves on the balusters (140b), the spiraled and stop-fluted posts, the baskets of fruit and flowers (140c), the vine-covered and diaper-patterned rails — are unequaled on American bedsteads.[1] Although New England craftsmen ornamented bedsteads with some carvings, such skillfully created detail as the overlapping leaves on these balusters was not copied.

140

Construction peculiarities make this bedstead even more interesting. Mortise-and-tenon joints are used instead of bed bolts at the carved footposts, and each corner post has two parts — the footposts separate just above the spiral turnings, the headposts just above the brass collar. Two-part posts (see *Notes on Structure and Condition*) are rarely seen on English or American bedsteads.[2]

The bedstead retains only a bit of evidence of how it was originally draped. Cloak-pin holes in the footposts show that festooned curtains (140d) hung from the tester frame and were drawn up with cords passing through pulleys in the frame and wrapped in place over the cloak pins.[3] The carved rails probably were left uncovered (140d, left side) so that the graceful vines could be seen.

The original headboard was probably carved. The missing cornice, if not decoratively carved on the surface, at least was cut out like that on bedstead no. 141 and covered with cloth. The bedstead as shown — without cornice, original headboard, and hangings — only hints at the elaborate appearance it had when fully outfitted.

1. A chair made in Charleston, S.C., has similar knee carvings and was evidently based on an English model; Rauschenberg, "Royal Governor's Chair," figs. 1, 12.

2. A Connecticut bed in the Deane House, Wethersfield, Conn., has two-part posts, mortise-and-tenon joined just above the urns.

3. Montgomery, *Printed Textiles*, 55.

NOTES ON STRUCTURE AND CONDITION: On most beds with cabriole legs, the knee carving is placed on detachable caps that cover bed bolts; here the carving is directly on the knees, bed bolts were not used, and the footposts and rails were joined with mortises and tenons. Standard bed bolts were used at the headposts. The upper portion of each post is round-tenoned into the lower portion. A brass insert reinforces the mortise for each footpost; a brass collar surrounds each headpost mortise. The bed once had casters. Strips, nailed to the headposts, form slots for the headboard.

The bed was originally 58 to 60 inches wide. It was cut before the present tester and headboard were attached more than a century ago. The pins, around which the original canvas bottom was laced, have been cut off. One of the vertical strips edging the headboard is replaced. The old shellac finish is crazed, the carvings are chipped in many places, and the footrail has a 6-inch pieced repair.

MATERIALS: *Mahogany*; *white pine* tester and headboard; *red oak* vertical strip nailed to headboard.

PROVENANCE: The bedstead descended from Erastus F. and Sophia Brigham to their son Joseph Lincoln Brigham (1840–1923), to his daughter Emmeline Brigham Agnew (b. 1870), and to her daughter, the donor.

ACCESSION: 1975.152   A bequest of Janet M. Agnew

140a   140b   140c

140d. Design for a Bed with a Festoon Curtain. Chippendale, *The Director*, 1st ed., 1754, pl. 27. Society for the Preservation of New England Antiquities Library.

141 / Bedstead

1795–1810
Portsmouth
H. 80⅝ (204.8); W. 56⁷⁄₁₆ (143.4); D. 78¾ (200)

During the last quarter of the eighteenth century and the early years of the nineteenth, the most common form of New England bedstead featured the standard footpost design

141

— turned pillar, baluster, and Marlborough leg — seen on this example. This bedstead was made for the Portsmouth merchant and mill owner James Rundlet, who married in 1795 and built a new house in 1806–1807.

At about the time Rundlet had this bedstead made, he ordered a crib (141a) for whoever of his thirteen children was then of suitable size. (Cradle no. 139 was also used by Rundlet's children.) The birch crib completes our knowledge of the birch bedstead, for the crib retains the original reddish-brown stain that the bedstead has lost. Unfortunately, the crib's posts, which probably ended in finials, have been cut.

The bed, missing its original headboard and headrail, retains its pine cornice, an often damaged or discarded portion of a high-post bed. The undulating shape of the cornice is typical of Rundlet's day. This cornice was probably covered with a printed cotton; the same fabric would have been used for the bed hangings.[1]

Painted pine cornices were also common. A related bedstead with an identically shaped painted cornice came from Dover, New Hampshire, and is attributed to Rundlet's neighbor, the cabinetmaker Langley Boardman.[2] In 1802 Boardman supplied Rundlet with a mahogany bedstead.[3] No accounts or bills, however, refer to bedstead no. 141 or to the crib.

1. Rundlet's accounts for May 12, 1808, present a tantalizing clue to the textile used in one of his bedchambers: he bought 114 yards of "Drab & Green Furnitures" from T. & J. Wiggin of Boston; Invoice Book B, Rundlet Papers, Society for the Preservation of New England Antiquities.

2. The bed is in the Society's collections; Nylander, "First Harrison Gray Otis House," 1141. Attribution is made on the basis of the fan inlay that matches that on a chest of drawers Boardman made for Rundlet in 1802; *Plain & Elegant*, no. 2.

3. Ledger B, 271, Rundlet Papers. The same page lists bedrails, cornice, and bedcaps on December 10, 1803.

NOTES ON STRUCTURE AND CONDITION: Four sections of unmitered molding are nailed and glued to each footpost to create the foot. The headposts are mortised for the headboard. The rails and posts are warped and have been severely cleaned and refinished. Pins, around which the original canvas bottom was laced, are mounted in a slot on the foot and side rails. Except for the replaced right side of the tester frame, the tester and cornice are original. The tops of the posts have been cut somewhat. The brass caps covering the bed bolts are replacements.

MATERIALS: *Birch;* white pine tester and cornice.

141a. Crib. Portsmouth, 1795–1810. Birch; H. 29⁹⁄₁₆ (75.1); W. 26⁷⁄₈ (68.3); D. 42³⁄₈ (107.6). Society for the Preservation of New England Antiquities.

PROVENANCE: The bedstead shares a provenance with table no. 71.

ACCESSION: 1971.735   A gift of Ralph May

Looking Glasses

142 / Dressing Glass

1740–1760
England, probably London
H. 27⅞ (70.8); W. 20¹/₁₆ (51); D. 8½ (21.6)

Dressing glasses — a London manufactory called them "Dressing Boxes & Swingers"; a Bostonian advertised "swinging glasses with draws and without" — were elegant appointments for eighteenth-century bedchambers.[1] As early as 1711, the inventory of Thomas Lanyon of Boston listed "dressing box and glass."[2] In 1725, the front chamber of Henry Franklin's Boston house included:

> 1 fine Green Camblet Bed Curtains & Silk Quilt [£]15
> 1 large Looking Glass £12   One handsome Dressing Ditto £3
> 1 Buroe £5   1 fine Glass Escrutore the Glass broke   £8.[3]

Franklin's "handsome" dressing glass was almost certainly imported. It probably stood on the bureau that was mentioned next in the inventory.

This dressing glass shares a history with a bureau. It is listed with chest of drawers no. 14 in the inventory of Samuel Allyne Otis of Boston.[4] The glass may predate the chest of drawers, but once the chest was made, the English glass and the American chest remained together.

The most stylish attribute of this glass, and of many English looking glasses of the era, is the swelled, or shaped, façade. It is quite possible that the Boston fashion for blocked and bombé shapes on large cases arose from the familiarity with imported dressing glasses. At the least, swelled English dressing glasses led Boston craftsmen to adopt shaped façades for the dressing boxes they produced.[5]

1. Trade card of Lake Young, more fully quoted in entry 143, illustrated in Heal, *London Furniture Makers*, 208. Advertisement in *Boston News-Letter*, September 22–29, 1737, as quoted in Dow, *Arts and Crafts*, 127.

2. Thomas Lanyon's inventory, old series, vol. 17, pp. 354–55, Suffolk County (Mass.) Probate.

3. Henry Franklin's inventory, old series, vol. 24, p. 415, Suffolk County (Mass.) Probate.

4. Samuel Allyne Otis's inventory, old series, vol. 112, p. 320, Suffolk County (Mass.) Probate.

5. Boston blockfront examples are in Wick, "Gore Place" (missing its glass); and in *Paul Revere's Boston*, no. 60. Bombé examples appear in *Boston Furniture*, figs. 122, 123, and in Nutting, *Furniture Treasury*, vol. 2, nos. 3206, 3210.

NOTES ON STRUCTURE AND CONDITION: The back of the box is nailed to the rabbeted edges of the mahogany-veneered top and sides. The drawer partitions extend to the back of the case. The bracket feet are nailed and glued to the base molding; each rear foot is but a single side element. Each drawer front is of two pieces of mahogany. The vertical supports for the looking glass frame are tenoned through the top of the box. All of the façade of the frame except the inner border is veneered. The crest is glued to the top rail and has no support blocks. Blocks that originally separated the glass from the four-piece backboard have been removed, and the backboard rests against the glass, held by twelve wedge-shaped blocks.

The glass, the drawer bottoms, and the wooden ball finials are old replacements. In 1977, the veneered surfaces were cleaned, and damaged areas of the gilt were restored.

MATERIALS: Mahogany veneer on *spruce;* mahogany; *beech* drawer sides and back; *spruce* secondary wood. Replaced pulls and escutcheon; original brass lock.

PROVENANCE: The dressing glass shares a provenance with chest of drawers no. 14.

ACCESSION: 1933.1507   A bequest of Mina Mason Van Sinderen; conserved through the generosity of J. Peter Spang III

142

143 / Looking Glass

1748
England, probably London
H. 72³⁄₁₆ (183.4); W. 33 ⅛ (84.1)

This is the largest of six looking glasses presented here, all owned in New England, most if not all of European manufacture. The English looking glass business, centered in London, relied upon a wide market, as the trade card of Lake Young makes clear. Young conducted business

in James Street, Covent-Garden:
or at his Warehouse near the Pump in
WATLING STREET, LONDON.
Where Merchants, Captains of Ships, Country Chap-
men &c, may be supply'd on reasonable Terms with
all Sorts of Looking Glasses, Viz^t Sconces, Pier &
Chimney Glasses, Dressing Boxes & Swingers,
in Mahogany, Walnut-tree, & Painted, or in rich Carv'd
& Gilt Frames in the neatest Taste & newest fashion.
All Sorts of Window Glass,
Wholesale and Retail, or for
Exportation.[1]

Large shipments of looking glasses arrived regularly in Boston. Virtually every merchant, upholsterer, and japanner, and several other tradesmen as well, sold imported glasses. Before the Revolution, few Americans attempted the expensive and complicated manufacture of glass.[2] One who did, Stephen Whiting of Boston, advertised in 1767:

Said Whiting does more at present towards manufacturing Looking-Glasses than any one in the Province, or perhaps on the Continent, and would be glad of Encouragement enough to think it worth while to live.[3]

This looking glass, neither domestically made nor part of a large shipment, was, according to family legend, purchased by Josiah Quincy during a trip to England in 1748. Like settee no. 107, which was purchased at the same time, the expensive looking glass was an obvious symbol of affluence. Quincy selected one of massive size; the lower piece of glass alone is 42 inches high.[4] The design, from the broad base to the three gilt feathers on the crest, is characteristic of the early Georgian style.[5]

Quincy apparently hung the huge glass over a marble-top table in the principal parlor of the house he built in 1770.[6] It would have been similarly placed in his earlier two houses. In spite of its size and fragility, the looking glass was moved often and even was rescued from two fires during Quincy's lifetime. The original glass plates miraculously survive. In the nineteenth century, when Quincy's furniture was deemed "very much injured by time and wear," the looking glass was "new silvered & repaired & regilt."[7]

1. The card is illustrated in Heal, *London Furniture Makers*, 208.
2. The complicated procedures for making glasses are discussed in Wills, *English Looking-Glasses*, 47–48, 54–55, 61–63.
3. *Boston News-Letter*, November 12, 1767, as quoted in Dow, *Arts and Crafts*, 129.
4. On July 10, 1739, Thomas Hancock ordered an even larger glass from his London agent: "1 Looking Glass the Lower plate four foot Long & 22 Inches wide the top plate in proportion to the bigness of ye Lower plate. The frame to be Veneer'd Eng^h Walnutt Dark van'd with a handsome Carved Gilt Edge"; Hancock Letter Book, 1738–40, New England Historic Genealogical Society.
5. Edwards and Jourdain, *Georgian Cabinetmakers*, fig. 35.
6. Josiah Quincy's 1784 inventory, docket 18158, Suffolk County (Mass.) Probate.
7. The history of the looking glass is recorded in

143

Eliza S. Quincy, "Memorandums," 31–32 (see entry 36, n. 7).

NOTES ON STRUCTURE AND CONDITION: The rails and stiles are lap-jointed and glued. Modern nails strengthen the joints of the bottom rail. The crest, glued to the front of the top rail, is additionally supported by the stiles, which continue to the top of the crest. The only block for the crest is glued behind the carved feathers. Walnut veneer covers the façade (except for the carved areas) and the outer edges of the sides of the frame. The carved feathers and gilt border (except for an applied outer gilt border on the crest) are cut from the solid secondary wood. The upper glass rests on a rabbet cut in each stile. A series of wedge-shaped blocks glued and nailed to the stiles separate the glass from the backboards. The backboards follow the inner border in outline. The two-board upper section of the back and the three-board lower section are separated by a horizontal strip dovetailed and nailed to the stiles. Cut brads reinforce the backboard.

MATERIALS: English walnut veneer on *spruce; spruce* secondary wood.

PROVENANCE: The looking glass shares a provenance with high chest no. 36.

ACCESSION: 1972.44   A gift of Edmund Quincy; conservation funded in part by the Massachusetts Council on the Arts and Humanities

144 / Looking Glass

1750–1758
England
Sold in Boston by Joseph Grant, Jr.
H. 39⅞ (101.3); W. 16⁵⁄₁₆ (41.4)

The importance of this plain looking glass lies in the old inscription inked on its back: "Joseph Grant jun^r / at ye head of ye Town Dock."[1]

Joseph Jr. (b. 1716), a Boston upholsterer, apparently operated a shop on the town dock during the 1750s. He probably served an apprenticeship with his uncle, the upholsterer Samuel Grant (see entry 137), and had begun to work on his own by November 1738, when he billed Thomas Richardson, Jr., of Worcester County, Massachusetts, for "30 yds Print," "1 Blankett," 30 yards of lace, and "5 Doz: Brass Rings."[2]

Grant expanded his business to general retailing and shipping, a common practice among upholsterers, and by the late 1740s he had at least one apprentice.[3] His patrons included the wealthy Thomas Hancock, who bought a looking glass that, at £39, must have been far grander than this one.[4] In the 1750s, while continuing his mercantile trade, Grant began insuring vessels. This risky activity proved a mistake. In 1758 he went bankrupt, his effects were sold to satisfy creditors, and his business career in Boston ended.[5]

This walnut-veneered looking glass is of a standard design. Glasses like it, veneered or japanned, were apparently imported in large quantities into the several colonies. A closely related japanned looking glass belonged to a New York family.[6] In the 1760s, a glass identical in pattern to the Society's was sold by John Elliot of Philadelphia.[7]

1. When this glass appeared in "Collector's Notes," *Antiques* 107 (May 1975): 984, Grant's location was misread and published as "ye Lion Lock."

2. The 1738 bill was attached to a summons dated November 9, 1743, Grant Junr vs Richardson Junr, no. 502, Court of Common Pleas, Suffolk County, Mass.

3. Samuel Holyoke signed for his master on a bill dated August 9, 1746, from Grant to Thomas Hancock; Hancock Personal Bills 1735–64, vol. 3, Hancock Papers, New England Historic Genealogical Society.

4. Ibid.

5. Notice of bankruptcy appeared in the *Boston Post Boy,* November 13, 1758; notice of the sale, the same day in the *Boston Gazette and Country Journal;* the latter is excerpted in Dow, *Arts and Crafts,* 118.

6. Glen-Sanders Collection, Colonial Williamsburg (1964-267).

7. Reginald M. Lewis Collection, Parke-Bernet, sale 2026, March 1961, lot 247.

NOTES ON STRUCTURE AND CONDITION: The lower rail of the frame is mitered and glued to the stiles; the upper rail butts against the stiles and is nailed. The crest, glued to the front of the upper rail and the stiles, never had support blocks. Walnut veneer covers the façade and outer edges at the sides and bottom. The upper glass rests on a rabbet cut in each stile. Original wedge-shaped blocks separate the glass from the four-piece backboard. The glass originally hung by a cord or wire strung through two holes in the upper rail. The upper 1½ inches of the crest volutes are replaced, as is some veneer on the outer edges.

MATERIALS: English walnut veneer on red pine; *red pine* rails; *spruce* backboard.

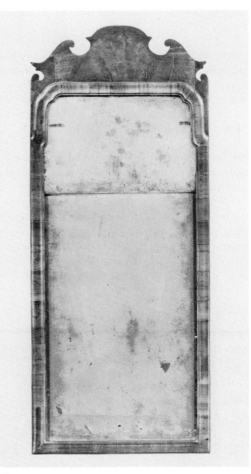

144

PROVENANCE: The looking glass was purchased in New York in 1974.

ACCESSION: 1981.54   A gift of Mr. and Mrs. David Thomas

145 / Looking Glass

1750–1770
England
H. 53¹⁵⁄₁₆ (137); W. 26⅞ (68.3)

This elaborate glass, like the preceding plain example, is important because of an eighteenth-century inscription inked on the backboard: "For / Mr Charles Treadwell."

In 1724, Charles Treadwell (1705–1793) moved from Ipswich, Massachusetts, to Portsmouth, New Hampshire, where he enjoyed a successful career as a merchant and store owner. He married Mary Kelley of nearby New Castle, and they lived in the large house he built in Portsmouth in 1728.[1] The glass, which could have been purchased by Treadwell either for resale or for his own use, is of a design worthy of the elegant house the prosperous Treadwells enjoyed.

The frame is ornate, decorated with wildly scalloped crest and volutes and beautifully carved side pieces of gilt leaves and fruit. It originally had a gilt ornament mounted in the center of the crest.[2] Applied cartouches are more unusual than those carved into the crest (see the next looking glass).

145

1. Brewster tells the story of the Treadwells in *Rambles,* 133–36.

2. An applied ornament can be seen on an almost identical glass in Nutting, *Furniture Treasury,* vol. 2, no. 2930.

NOTES ON STRUCTURE AND CONDITION: The lower rail of the frame is mitered and glued to the stiles; the upper rail butts against the stiles and is nailed. The crest is glued to the front of the upper rail and the stiles. Five vertical blocks were glued to the back of the crest to retard warpage. Two survive. The volutes are glued to the stiles; small glue blocks help secure the joints. The carved foliage is glued and nailed to the stiles. Walnut veneer covers the façade (except for the carved areas) and the outer edges of the stiles. The upper glass rests on a rabbet cut in each stile. Original wedge-shaped blocks separate the glass from the rectangular backboard, which, except for the area with the inscription, is covered by nineteenth-century wallpaper. Original brass hanging plates are still screwed to the stiles. Except for the missing cartouche and support blocks, the glass is in excellent condition.

MATERIALS: English walnut veneer on spruce; *spruce* secondary wood.

PROVENANCE: The looking glass came to the Society with a collection of furniture principally acquired in the Portsmouth area.

ACCESSION: 1942.1218   A gift of Virginia L. Hodge and Katherine D. Parry

146 / Looking Glass

1755–1770
England
H. 54⁷⁄₁₆ (138.3); W. 27⅛ (68.9)

While all six looking glasses included here are in very good condition, retaining their original glass and backboards, this one stands out as exceedingly well preserved. It remains in its original position, screwed through its brass plates onto horizontal boards set in the plaster wall, a common eighteenth-century method of mounting a looking glass.[1]

This glass was acquired by Jonathan Sayward, the York, Maine, trader and judge who owned a number of objects illustrated here.[2] He probably purchased the glass about the time he was enlarging his house (1761–1767) and acquiring additional furniture. The looking glass is clearly in the mainstream of pre-Revolutionary design. Although simpler than the preceding one, this frame features more ornate scalloping on the inner edge.

1. The looking glass can be seen *in situ* in Nylander, "The Jonathan Sayward House," pl. 5.
2. See entry 4, note 2.

NOTES ON STRUCTURE AND CONDITION: The crest and frame are basically joined as is looking glass no. 144, except that original splines are inserted in the mitered joints of the base rail and stiles, and the crest was backed by three horizontal and two vertical blocks (the latter are missing). The volutes are glued and nailed to the stiles; small glue blocks help secure the joints. Walnut veneer covers the façade (except for the carved areas) and the outer edges of the stiles; the bottom edge is not veneered. The bottom edge of the upper glass, which rests on a rabbet in each stile, is the only beveled glass edge. Original wedge-shaped blocks separate the glass from the rectangular five-piece backboard. The backboard is beveled along its outer edge and held in place with L-headed forged nails. Remnants of the paper that originally covered the seam between the backboard and frame survive. The damage is minor: a chip on the gilt shell and another in the veneer.

MATERIALS: English walnut veneer on spruce; *spruce* secondary wood.

PROVENANCE: The looking glass shares a provenance with tea chest no. 4.

ACCESSION: 1977.272   A gift of the heirs of Elizabeth Cheever Wheeler

146

147 / Looking Glass

1770
England
Sold in Boston by William Jackson
H. 54½ (138.4); W. 24 (61)

This looking glass (plate 12), dated by its 1770 bill of sale (147a), is an example of a new style that remained popular into the nineteenth century. It features a single plate of glass and a unified frame whose scalloped skirt echoes the form of the crest. The crests on such looking glasses were often architectural. Crowned by a pediment and finial, they resemble the tops of case furniture (see the pediment of a desk and bookcase, I-24).

Few looking glasses of the period display as spectacular a play of gold against walnut veneer. Gilt abounds. A gilt bird sits atop a gilt pediment from whose rosettes spill gilded leaves. Carved leaves and acorns glisten along the sides. And carved and golden sprigs, the most unusual feature of the frame, fill the crest and skirt.[1]

147

This is the "1 ditto Ornamented with Side peices and Bird on the top" listed with a sconce looking glass on the 1770 bill. The glasses were sold and shipped by the Boston merchant William Jackson (147b) to Jonathan Bowman after he had moved from the Boston area to Pownalborough, Maine, to administer the Kennebec region for the Boston merchants who were developing it (see entry 15).[2] Bowman acquired, at £42:10–, a splendid looking glass for his house on the frontier.

The glass bears on the backboard several inked inscriptions that probably were placed there before it was shipped from England: "30.17" designated the dimensions of the glass; "Sham Pediment / flewer pott & Sprigs" further described the merchandise; "Inv° 8" and "Case 16" facilitated shipping.

1. Related glasses without sprigs are: Nutting, *Furniture Treasury*, vol. 2, no. 2911; Downs, *Queen Anne and Chippendale*, no. 263; and Lockwood, *Colonial Furniture*, rev. ed., vol. 1, fig. 343. An example with some sprig ornamentation was advertised in *Antiques* 116 (December 1979): 1271.

2. Jackson's insignia (147b) is the reverse of a 1770 bill to Jonathan Bowman for a warming pan, metal dish, and iron firedogs. The bills (147a and 147b) are in Box 1, 2, folder 4, Lincoln County (Me.) Cultural and Historical Association.

NOTES ON STRUCTURE AND CONDITION: The crest and frame are basically joined as is looking glass no. 144, except that originally two horizontal and three vertical blocks (one of the latter is missing) backed the crest and one vertical and two horizontal blocks (the former is missing) backed the skirt.

147a. Bill. William Jackson to Jonathan Bowman. Lincoln County Cultural and Historical Association.

147b. Trade Insignia. Engraved by Paul Revere (1735–1818), Boston, 1770. Engraving; H. 7⅞ (20.0); W. 6⅞ (17.5). Lincoln County Cultural and Historical Association.

Walnut veneer covers the façade (except for the carved areas). The floral sprigs are cut into the secondary wood. The pediment, rosettes, and leaves are applied. The bird fits into a slot in the crest. The volutes are glued to the stiles; a single block helps secure each volute. The side foliage is glued and nailed to the stiles. Original wedge-shaped blocks separate the glass from the rectangular four-piece backboard.

MATERIALS: English walnut veneer on *spruce;* spruce secondary wood.

PROVENANCE: The looking glass shares a provenance with chest of drawers no. 15.

ACCESSION: 1980.80   A gift of Florence L. Bixby

148 / Looking Glass

1794–1800
Holland or New England
H. 47⅛ (119.7); W. 23½ (59.7)

Were it not for pieces of Dutch newspaper between the blocks and the back of the glass plate, this looking glass would be assumed to be an American product because all of the secondary wood is white pine. The newspaper suggests that this is a Dutch import.

New England inventories often mention Dutch looking glasses, generally meaning small, inexpensive, early-eighteenth-century glasses.[1] This one, however, is not small, or inexpensive, or pre-Revolutionary. Inked on the backboard is the size of the glass, "28 by 17," and the price, "£9 pair / 16 dollar single." The newspaper is dated 1794 in several places. The glass probably was framed that year or shortly thereafter, and the newspaper lining will help date closely related examples.[2]

The post-1793 looking glass is in the same style as the 1770 looking glass (no. 147), yet an end-of-the-century appearance can be discerned in the streamlining of the gilt leaves on the side, the simplicity of the cuts on the gilt border, and the oval shape of the opening behind the bird. The oval was the favorite shape of the neoclassical design of the new Federal era.

1. Hughes, "North European Export Mirrors," 856–60, and "More about 'Dutch Looking Glasses,'" 693.

2. An identical glass is at the Rhode Island Historical Society. Related examples include one at the Marblehead Historical Society, and one sold by Parke-Bernet, sale 1771, October 1957, lot 322.

NOTES ON STRUCTURE AND CONDITION: The stiles and rails of the frame are lap-jointed and glued. Molded mahogany veneer covers the façade of the stiles and rails except at the gilt border. The crest, skirt, and volutes are glued to the edge of the stiles and rails; small glue blocks help secure the joints. Gilt leaves are glued and nailed to each side of the frame. Original wedge-shaped blocks separate the glass from the one-piece backboard. Small glazier's points hold the backboard in place.

The looking glass was originally hung with a cord or wire strung through two holes in the top rail. A horizontal split in the skirt and a replaced right crest volute are the only damage and repair.

MATERIALS: *Mahogany* crest, volutes, and skirt; mahogany veneer on *white pine;* white pine secondary wood.

PROVENANCE: The looking glass came from the Philbrick family, cousins of the donor.

ACCESSION: 1959.318   A bequest of Frances S. Marrett

148

Acknowledgments / Bibliography / Collections and Institutions / Index

Acknowledgments

Throughout our country, artifacts and documents lie unstudied and little known, even though they are the treasures of our past, the expressions of our culture, the very stuff of which American history was made and through which it can be relished. We are privileged to be able to illuminate one trove, the New England furniture in the collection of the Society for the Preservation of New England Antiquities, and proudly acknowledge that the impetus was the generous financial support of the National Endowments.

Grants from the National Endowment for the Humanities for research and writing and grants from the National Endowment for the Arts and the Ford Foundation for printing and photography provided the initial funding. Additional funds were received from William Banks and Roland Hammond. The generosity of Mr. and Mrs. George Kaufman and the Mifflin Trust made it possible for us to complete the task of writing.

The dedicated researchers who volunteered their efforts to make this endeavor as thorough and extensive as possible are: Alison Butler; Olga Dalton; Karen D. Fischer, who excelled in checking obscure provenances; Charles Garland, who brought expertise in antiques to cataloguing; Phebe Goodman, who checked almost every footnote; Sally Johnson; Sandra Landow; Alice MacCarthy; Marilee Meyer; Nancy Muldoon, who checked some footnotes and wrote others; Rolce Payne; Elizabeth Redmond; Barbara Rittel, who did our research in Plymouth and Barnstable counties; Clinton Savage; Luciene Schroeder, whose plight it was to repeatedly organize the files; Priscilla Sloss; Nancy Smith, who brought her expertise in furniture to our comparative studies; Jayne Stokes; Patricia Warner, who made Portsmouth research her forte and led a courthouse staff; and Natalie Zook.

From the beginning we were assisted by Philip Zea, who did much more than write the essays on rural furniture and on furniture methods and materials. He was always available as a consultant on rural objects and on clocks and was a prop or a pillar during every phase of the study and writing.

Much of the expertise found here is not ours but that of scholars whose help we received in abundance. Those generously sharing their knowledge were: Michael Brown, Edward Cooke, Wendy A. Cooper, Dean Failey, Dean A. Fales, Martha G. Fales, Charles A. Hammond, Roland B. Hammond, Morrison H. Heckscher, William Hosley, Philip Johnston, Patricia E. Kane, John T. Kirk, Bernard and S. Dean Levy, Nina Fletcher Little, Robert Mussey, Jane C. Nylander, Charles S. Parsons, Albert, Donald, Harold, and Robert Sack, Robert Blair St. George, Robert F. Trent, Dorothy Vaughan, John Walton, Gerald Ward, Charles Yeaton, and Philip Zimmerman. The assistance of the late Benno M. Forman merits special citation. His was the largest role of all. He was both inspirational and supportive, sending up to ten-page responses to our one-paragraph requests. His knowledge of colonial American furniture was vast, and his enthusiasm is already greatly missed.

We are indebted to these museums, whose curators opened their doors and files to us as we looked for and examined comparable objects: Adams National Historic Site, Quincy, Mass; Alden House, Duxbury, Mass.; American Antiquarian Society, Worcester, Mass.; Andover Historical Society, Andover, Mass.; Arlington Historical Society, Arlington, Mass.; Bayou Bend Collection, Houston, Tex.; Beverly Historical Society, Beverly, Mass.; Billerica Historical Society, Billerica, Mass.; Boston Athenaeum, Boston, Mass.; Boxford Historical Society, Boxford, Mass.; Braintree Historical Society, Braintree, Mass.; Brookline Historical Society, Brookline, Mass.; Cape Ann Historical Association, Gloucester, Mass.; Chelmsford Historical Society, Chelmsford, Mass.; Cohasset Historic House, Cohasset, Mass.; Colonial Williamsburg Foundation, Williamsburg, Va.; Concord Antiquarian Museum, Concord, Mass.; Connecticut Historical Society, Hartford, Conn.; Currier Gallery of Art, Manchester, N.H.; Danvers Historical Society, Danvers, Mass.; Dedham Historical Society, Dedham, Mass.; Dorchester Historical Society, Boston, Mass.; Duxbury Rural and Historical Society, Duxbury, Mass.; Elizabeth Perkins House, Society for the Preservation of Historic Landmarks in York County, York, Me.; Essex Institute, Salem, Mass.; Fairbanks House, Dedham, Mass.; Fall River Historical Society, Fall River, Mass.; Falmouth Historical Society, Falmouth, Mass.; Fogg Art Museum and Harvard University, Cambridge, Mass.; Fruitlands Museum, Harvard, Mass.; Gore Place Society, Waltham, Mass.; Groton Historical Society, Groton, Mass.; Henry Francis du Pont Winterthur Museum, Winterthur, Del.; Historic Deerfield, Inc., Deerfield, Mass.; Historical Society of Old Newbury, Newburyport, Mass.; Historical Society of Santuit and Cotuit, Cotuit, Mass.; Ipswich Historical Society, Ipswich, Mass.; Lexington Historical Society, Lexington, Mass.; Lincoln County Cultural and Historical Association, Wiscasset, Me.; Longfellow National Historic Site, Cambridge, Mass.; Lyman Allyn Museum, New London, Conn.; Lyme Historical Society, Old Lyme, Conn.; Lynn Historical Society, Lynn, Mass.; Marblehead Historical Society, Marblehead, Mass.; Massachusetts Historical Society, Boston, Mass.; Mead Art Gallery, Amherst College, Amherst, Mass.; Metropolitan Museum of Art, New York, N.Y.; Moffatt-Ladd House, Portsmouth, N.H.; Museum of the American China Trade, Milton, Mass.; Museum of Art, Rhode Island School of Design, Providence, R.I.; Museum of Fine Arts, Boston, Mass.; Nantucket Historical Association, Nantucket, Mass.; New Bedford Whaling Museum, New Bedford, Mass.; New Hampshire Historical Society, Concord, N.H.; Newport Historical Society, Newport, R.I.; Nichols House Museum, Boston, Mass.; North Andover Historical Society, North Andover, Mass.; Old Chelmsford Garrison

House, Chelmsford, Mass.; Old Gaol Museum, York, Me.; Old Ordinary, Hingham, Mass.; Old South Meeting House, Boston, Mass.; Old State House–The Bostonian Society, Boston, Mass.; Old State House in Newport, Newport, R.I.; Old Sturbridge Village, Sturbridge, Mass.; Pilgrim Hall Museum of the Pilgrim Society, Plymouth, Mass.; Portland Museum of Art, Portland, Me.; The Preservation Society of Newport County, Newport, R.I.; Quincy Historical Society, Quincy, Mass.; Rhode Island Historical Society, Providence, R.I.; Rowley Historical Society, Rowley, Mass.; Sargent-Murray-Gilman-Hough House, Gloucester, Mass.; Saconesset Homestead, West Falmouth, Mass.; Scituate Historical Society, Scituate, Mass.; Stoughton Historical Society, Stoughton, Mass.; Strawbery Banke, Portsmouth, N.H.; Topsfield Historical Society, Topsfield, Mass.; Wadsworth Atheneum, Hartford, Conn.; Warner House, Portsmouth, N.H.; The Webb-Deane-Stevens Museum, Wethersfield, Conn.; Wenham Historical Association and Museum, Wenham, Mass.; Wentworth-Gardner House, Portsmouth, N.H.; Willard House and Clock Shop, Grafton, Mass.; Women's City Club of Boston, Boston, Mass.; Worcester Art Museum, Worcester, Mass.; Yale University Art Gallery, New Haven, Conn.

We are grateful to Donna J. Christensen at the Center for Wood Anatomy Research, U.S. Department of Agriculture, Madison, Wis., for all of the wood analysis. Graham Hood, director of the Department of Collections at Colonial Williamsburg, kindly permitted his curator of exhibition buildings, Brock Jobe, to take two-month sabbaticals in the summers of 1975, 1976, and 1977. We wish to thank the directors of the Society, Nancy R. Coolidge and Abbott Lowell Cummings. Our overwhelming job was made easier by the support of the Society's staff, especially that of Richard C. Nylander, who throughout willingly contributed his time and expertise.

For their typing, retyping, and patience, we thank Helen Grady, Germaine Juneau, and Carolyn Parsons; for their dogged dedication to keeping the text readable, Joan Lautman, Barbara Mende, Sabra Morton, Shirley Moskow, Jeri Quinzio, and Janet Tassel; for their outstanding skills and patient understanding, our editor, Linda Glick Conway, and copy editor, Luise M. Erdmann. Our greatest debt is to our families for their sacrifices, forbearance, and, when we flagged, encouragement.

Bibliography

The substantial literature on New England furniture was a resource and an inspiration to us. It begins with Irving Lyon's landmark volume, *The Colonial Furniture of New England* (1891). In about 1877, Lyon began to collect antique furniture in Hartford and its environs, and by 1880 he had embarked on a study of where his items were made and how they were originally used. He consulted collectors, investigated hundreds of pieces of furniture, and scrutinized colonial documents, particularly household inventories in county probate records. He concluded that "much, perhaps most, of the carved oaken furniture found in New England was made here," although at the time many had suspected it to be of European origin. Later work has verified Lyon's view, and, on the whole, his findings have become a cornerstone for subsequent research.

Lyon's book is organized by form: chests, cupboards, chests of drawers, desks, chairs, tables, and clocks. In a clear, succinct manner, he discusses the origin of each form and its use in New England households. He identifies the original names of most items, noting, for example, that a "Turkey work chair" was upholstered with a carpet-like covering on the seat and back. He carefully reports the evidence for each of his conclusions. "The reader is not told," one commentator notes; "he moves along with the author in his discoveries."[1]

Lyon's work is not without fault, but errors are minor. He believed, for instance, that the coverings on turkeywork chairs were imported from the Orient; in fact, they were woven in England. He refrained from a detailed analysis of style, choosing instead to speculate on the introduction of a few specific motifs like the cabriole, or "bandy" leg, as he called it. His investigation was limited by and large to furniture from Hartford, Boston, and Salem, and of the hundred and thirteen illustrations in the book, only one depicts a Rhode Island object. Nevertheless, Lyon's work represents an exceptional achievement for its day and remains an essential guide to the subject. His areas of research, particularly household inventories, continue to be excellent sources for students of furniture history.

Several general works on furniture appeared during the first decade of this century. The three best — Esther Singleton, *The Furniture of Our Forefathers* (1900–1901), Luke Vincent Lockwood, *Colonial Furniture in America* (1901), and Frances Clary Morse, *Furniture of the Olden Time* (1902) — are valuable for their hundreds of illustrations and histories of ownership of New England furniture. None equals Lyon in scholarship.

Wallace Nutting published two useful compendiums of photographs, *Furniture of the Pilgrim Century* (1921), illustrating over fifteen hundred items, and *Furniture Treasury* (1928), containing five thousand drawings and photographs. Nutting, a devoted antiquarian, collected, sold, and wrote about antique furniture and oversaw a reproductions firm specializing in "the oak and maple cabinet and turned work of the 17th Century ... and the pine and maple cupboards, tables and Windsor chairs of the 18th Century, with some articles in walnut."[2] Apparently his greatest pleasure came from the discovery of important examples of early furniture, for he often recounted his efforts to locate major objects and the condition in which he found them. Today it is easy to criticize the self-aggrandizing tone of Nutting's texts, yet his publications are the best pictorial archive of New England furniture.

Nutting, Lockwood, and other early writers occasionally commented on the artistic merits of individual pieces of furniture. However, trained connoisseurship of furniture did not begin until 1951, with the publication of Albert Sack, *Fine Points of Furniture, Early American*. This work, which divides furniture into three categories — good, better, best — has served as the basic reference in evaluating American antiques. More recent efforts in this vein include Charles Montgomery's "Some Remarks on the Practice and Science of Connoisseurship," written for the Walpole Society in 1961, and the publications of John Kirk, especially *Early American Furniture* (1974).

In recent years, few surveys of American furniture have been published and, until now, none has been devoted exclusively to the products of New England. In *American Furniture* (1962), Helen Comstock presents an extensive chronological review that organizes the furniture by style. Her designations — Jacobean, William and Mary, Queen Anne, and Chippendale — had become well established long before she wrote the book. Edgar Miller uses the same nomenclature in *American Antique Furniture* (1937); however, Comstock's desire to write a "history of style" is indicative of the changing fashion in furniture studies. Several publications, such as Jonathan L. Fairbanks and Elizabeth Bidwell Bates, *American Furniture, 1620 to the Present* (1981), and Oscar Fitzgerald, *Three Centuries of American Furniture* (1982), take the same approach, though with some changes in terminology. Fairbanks and Bates drop Jacobean in favor of "the beginnings" and add early Georgian between Queen Anne and Chippendale.

The construction of furniture has failed to receive the careful attention accorded to style. Fairbanks and Bates include diagrams of the construction of certain objects to help the reader understand the techniques of colonial craftsmen. Another work, Nancy Smith, *Old Furniture, Understanding the Craftsman's Art* (1975), provides useful information on construction methods as well as what happens to furniture over time.

In addition to these surveys, many specialized works have been written within the past twenty-five years, some published separately, others issued in periodicals such as *Antiques* and the *Winterthur Portfolio*. These works fall chiefly into two categories: catalogues and regional studies. In 1941, Edwin Hipkiss wrote the first catalogue of a museum furniture collection, *Eighteenth-Century American Arts: The M. and M. Karolik Collection.* His learned remarks and the excellent illustrations established a standard of excellence that, happily, has been maintained in several subsequent catalogues. The best are, in chronological order: Joseph Downs, *American Furniture, Queen Anne and Chippendale Periods in the Henry Francis du Pont Winterthur Museum* (1952); Richard H. Randall, Jr., *American Furniture in the Museum of Fine Arts, Boston* (1965); Barry A. Greenlaw, *New England Furniture at Williamsburg* (1974); Dean A. Fales, Jr., *Furniture of Historic Deerfield* (1976); and Patricia E. Kane, *300 Years of American Seating Furniture* (1976).

Regional studies include a range of topics, from the furniture of an entire colony to the output of a single craftsman. During the 1920s, articles appeared on such figures as Benjamin Frothingham of Charlestown, Massachusetts, and John Goddard and John Townsend of Newport.[3] The next decade brought Irving P. Lyon's splendid series on the oak furniture of Ipswich and Clair Franklin Luther's classic on a distinctive regional form, *The Hadley Chest* (1935). However, most regional studies are more recent. These include book-length treatments of the colonial furniture of Connecticut and Rhode Island as well as shorter studies of smaller areas.[4] The most complete ones present an analysis of the furniture of a region — chiefly its relationship to the products of other areas and its distinctive design and construction features. These works also identify a region's craftsmen and discuss their background, shop output, and standing in the community. Among the best Connecticut studies are Patricia Kane's on seventeenth-century New Haven and Hartford, Robert Trent's on chairs of coastal Connecticut, Edward Cooke's on eighteenth-century Woodbury and Southbury, and Minor Myers's and Edgar Mayhew's on New London County. For Rhode Island, most work has centered on the craftsmen of Newport and Providence, with emphasis on the products of masters like John Townsend. The most useful material has been compiled by Morrison Heckscher, Liza and Michael Moses, and Joseph Ott. Many of the best publications on Massachusetts have been devoted to seventeenth-century settlements. In 1960, Helen Park wrote two illuminating articles on Essex County furniture; one introduced new evidence on the career of the Ipswich joiner Thomas Dennis. Benno Forman and two of his students, Robert Trent and Robert St. George, followed with superb studies of eastern Massachusetts. Forman's efforts centered on Boston and Salem, Trent's on Middlesex County and the upholstered furniture of Boston and Salem, and St. George's on southeastern Massachusetts. In addition, Trent prepared the furniture entries for *New England Begins: The Seventeenth Century* (1982), which, with his accompanying essays on mannerism and New England joinery and turning, are milestones in scholarship on seventeenth-century furniture. A prominent work on eighteenth-century Massachusetts is *Boston Furniture of the Eighteenth Century* (1974), a compilation of papers presented at a conference sponsored by the Colonial Society of Massachusetts. The colonial furniture of northern New England has received scant treatment, aside from a few publications on Portsmouth and on the Dunlaps of southern New Hampshire. The Society's catalogue is the first to investigate the area of coastal New Hampshire and Maine, but there is still much fertile ground for subsequent research.

The following bibliography provides complete entries for published sources, theses, and dissertations cited with short titles in the notes and text. Newspapers, unpublished records, and auction catalogues are not included but receive full citation when they appear in the notes.

1. Fales, introduction to Lyon, *Colonial Furniture*, xiii.

2. Nutting, *Checklist*.

3. See Spaulding, "Benjamin Frothingham of Charlestown"; Isham, "John Goddard and His Work"; and Cornelius, "John Townsend."

4. Kirk, *Connecticut Furniture*; Carpenter, *Arts and Crafts in Newport*; and Ott, *John Brown House Loan Exhibition*.

Allen, Charles Edwin. *History of Dresden, Maine.* Augusta, Me.: Katahdin, 1931.

Allen, David Grayson. "*Vacuum Domicilium:* The Social and Cultural Landscape of Seventeenth-Century New England." In *New England Begins: The Seventeenth Century,* vol. 1, 1–10. Boston: Museum of Fine Arts, 1982.

American Antiques from the Israel Sack Collection. 6 vols. Washington, D.C.: Highland House, 1969–79.

American Art at Harvard. Cambridge: Harvard University Press, 1972.

American Queen Anne Furniture, 1720–1755. Dearborn, Mich.: Edison Institute, 1976.

Americana, Midwest Collectors Choice. Dearborn, Mich.: Henry Ford Museum, 1960.

Andrews, Charles M. *The Colonial Period of American History.* New Haven: Yale University Press, 1934, 1964.

Andrus, Vincent D. "American Furniture from the Blair Collection." *Antiques* 61 (February 1952): 164–67.

"Antiques in Domestic Settings: New England Farmhouse." *Antiques* 37 (June 1940): 292–94.

Arnold, James N. *Vital Record for Rhode Island, 1636–1830: Births, Marriages and Deaths.* 1st ser., vol. 7, *Friends and Ministers.* Providence: Narragansett Historical Publishing Company, 1895.

Banks, Charles E. *History of York, Maine.* Vol. 2. Boston, 1935.

Banks, Miriam A. "Art in Primitive Americana: The Radeke Collection." *Fine Arts* 18 (January 1932): 27–29, 56.

Barry, John S. *A Historical Sketch of the Town of Hanover, Mass.* Boston: Samuel G. Drake, 1853.

Belknap, Henry Wyckoff. *Artists and Craftsmen of Essex County, Massachusetts.* Salem, Mass.: Essex Institute, 1927.

Belknap, Jeremy. *The History of New Hampshire. . . .* Dover, N.H.: J. Mann & J. K. Remick, 1812.

Bell, Mrs. N. S., compiler. *Pathways of the Puritans.* Framingham, Mass.: Old America Company, 1930.

Benes, Peter. *Two Towns: Concord & Wethersfield, A Comparative Exhibition of Regional Culture, 1635–1850.* Vol. 1. Concord, Mass.: Concord Antiquarian Museum, 1982.

———, and Philip D. Zimmerman. *New England Meeting House and Church: 1630–1850.* N.p.: Boston University and the Currier Gallery of Art, 1979.

Biddle, James. *American Art from American Collections.* New York: Metropolitan Museum of Art, 1963.

Birket, James. *Some Cursory Remarks Made by James Birket in His Voyage to North America, 1750–1751.* Edited by Charles M. Andrews. New Haven: Yale University Press, 1916.

Bishop, Robert. *American Furniture, 1620–1720.* Dearborn, Mich.: Edison Institute, 1975.

————. *Centuries and Styles of the American Chair.* New York: Dutton, 1972.

Bjerkoe, Ethel Hall. "The Booth Family of Newtown and Southbury, Connecticut." *Old-Time New England* 48 (Summer 1957): 8–11.

————. *The Cabinetmakers of America.* New York: Doubleday, 1957.

Blackburn, Roderic H. *Cherry Hill: The History and Collections of a Van Rensselaer Family.* Kinderhook, N.Y.: Historic Cherry Hill, 1976.

Boston Furniture of the Eighteenth Century. Boston: Colonial Society of Massachusetts, 1974.

Brazer, Esther Stevens. "The Early Boston Japanners." *Antiques* 43 (May 1943): 208–11.

Brewster, Charles W. *Rambles about Portsmouth.* 1st and 2nd ser., 1859 and 1869. Reprint. Somersworth, N.H.: New Hampshire Publishing Company, 1971, 1972.

Bridenbaugh, Carl. *The Colonial Craftsman.* Chicago: University of Chicago Press, 1950, 1974.

————. *Fat Mutton and Liberty of Conscience: Society in Rhode Island, 1636–1690.* Providence: Brown University Press, 1974.

————. *Peter Harrison, First American Architect.* Chapel Hill, N.C.: University of North Carolina Press, 1949.

Bulkeley, Houghton. "George Belden and Erastus Grant: Cabinetmakers." In *Contributions to Connecticut Cabinetmaking,* 72–81. Hartford: Connecticut Historical Society, 1967.

Burnaby, Andrew. *Travels through the Middle Settlements in North America. In the Years 1759 and 1760.* 2nd ed., 1775. Reprint. New York: Cornell University Press, 1960.

Burroughs, Paul H. "Furniture Widely Made in New Hampshire." *American Collector* 6 (June 1937): 6–7, 14–15.

Cabinet-Maker's Guide: or Rules and Instructions in the Art of Varnishing, Dying, Staining, Japanning, Polishing, Lackering and Beautifying Wood, Ivory, Tortoise-shell and Metal. 1818. Reprint. Greenfield, Mass.: Ansel Phelps, 1825.

Cabinet-Makers' London Book of Prices and Designs of Cabinet Work. London: W. Brown and A. O'Neil, 1793.

Candee, Richard M. "Merchant and Millwright: The Water Powered Sawmills of the Piscataqua." *Old-Time New England* 90 (Spring 1970): 131–49.

Cappon, Lester J., ed. *Atlas of Early American History: The Revolutionary Era, 1760–1790.* Princeton: Princeton University Press, 1976.

Carpenter, Ralph E., Jr. *The Arts and Crafts of Newport, Rhode Island, 1640–1820.* Newport: Preservation Society of Newport County, 1954.

————. "Discoveries in Newport Furniture and Silver." *Antiques* 68 (July 1955): 44–49.

Catalogue of the Loan Collection of Revolutionary Relics Exhibited at the Old South Church, November, 1876. 5th ed. Boston: Press of George H. Ellis, 1876.

A Century of Population Growth from the First Census of the United States to the Twelfth, 1790–1900. Washington, D.C.: Government Printing Office, 1909.

Cescinsky, Herbert. *English Furniture.* New York: Dover, 1968.

————, and George Leland Hunter. *English and American Furniture.* Garden City, N.Y.: Garden City Publishing Company, 1929.

Chase, Ada R. "Old Clocks in Norwich, Connecticut." *Antiques* 27 (March 1935): 99–101.

Cheek, Mary Tyler Freeman. "Rare Gift to Stratford Hall." *Delaware Antiques Show Catalogue.* 1977.

Chippendale, Thomas. *The Gentleman and Cabinet-Maker's Director.* London: Thomas Chippendale, 1754.

————. *The Gentleman and Cabinet-Maker's Director.* 3rd ed., 1762. Reprint. New York: Dover, 1966.

Clark, Charles E. *The Eastern Frontier: The Settlement of Northern New England, 1610–1763.* New York: Knopf, 1970.

Clunie, Margaret Burke, Anne Farnam, and Robert Trent. *Furniture at the Essex Institute.* Salem, Mass.: Essex Institute, 1980.

Coffin, Edward M. *Merrimac River Shipping.* Newburyport, Mass.: Historical Society of Old Newbury, 1926.

Cogswell, Leander W. *History of the Town of Henniker.* 1880. Reprint. Somersworth, N.H.: New Hampshire Publishing Company, 1973.

Comstock, Helen. "American Furniture in California." *Antiques* 65 (January 1954): 52–61.

————. *American Furniture, Seventeenth, Eighteenth and Nineteenth Century Styles.* New York: Viking, 1962.

————. "Frothingham and the Question of Attributions." *Antiques* 63 (June 1953): 502–5.

————. "An Ipswich Account Book, 1707–1762." *Antiques* 66 (September 1954): 188–92.

"Connecticut Cabinetmakers." Parts 1–2. *Connecticut Historical Society Bulletin* 32 (October 1967): 97–144, 33 (January 1968): 1–36.

Connecticut Chairs in the Collection of the Connecticut Historical Society. Hartford: Connecticut Historical Society, 1956.

Cooke, Edward S., Jr. *Fiddlebacks and Crookedbacks: Elijah Booth and Other Joiners in Newtown and Woodbury, 1750–1820.* Waterbury, Conn.: Mattatuck Historical Society, 1982.

————. "The Selective Conservative Taste: Furniture in Stratford, Connecticut, 1740–1800." Master's thesis, University of Delaware, 1979.

Cooper, Wendy A. "American Chairback Settees: Some Sources and Related Examples." *American Art Journal* 9 (November 1977): 34–45.

————. *In Praise of America.* New York: Knopf, 1980.

————. "The Purchase of Furniture and Furnishings by John Brown, Providence Merchant, Part 1: 1760–1788." *Antiques* 103 (February 1973): 328–39.

Cornelius, C. O. "John Townsend: An Eighteenth-Century Cabinetmaker." In *Metropolitan Museum Studies* 1: 72–80. New York: Metropolitan Museum of Art, 1928.

Cornforth, John. *English Interiors, 1790–1848.* London: Barrie and Jenkins, 1978.

Crafts, J. M. *History of the Town of Whately, Mass., 1661–1889.* Orange, Mass.: D. L. Crandall, 1889.

Crunden, John. *The Carpenter's Companion for Chinese Railings and Gates.* London: Henry Webley, 1765.

————. *The Joyner and Cabinet-Maker's Darling or Pocket Director.* London: Henry Webley, 1765.

Cummings, Abbott Lowell. *The Framed Houses of Massachusetts Bay, 1625–1725.* Cambridge: Harvard University Press, 1979.

————. *Rural Household Inventories.* Boston: Society for the Preservation of New England Antiquities, 1964.

Daniell, Jere R. *Experiment in Republicanism: New Hampshire Politics and the American Revolution, 1741–1794.* Cambridge: Harvard University Press, 1970.

Daniels, Bruce C. *The Connecticut Town: Growth and Development, 1635–1790.* Middletown, Conn.: Wesleyan University Press, 1979.

DAPC. Decorative Arts Photographic Collection, Winterthur Museum.

Dartmouth, Massachusetts, Vital Records to 1850. Boston: New England Historic and Genealogical Society, 1929.

Decatur, Stephen. "George and John Gaines of Portsmouth." *American Collector* 7 (November 1938): 6–7.

————. "The Lear House and Its Furnishings." *American Collector* 9 (October 1940): 11, 15.

Decorative Arts of New Hampshire, 1723–1825. Manchester, N.H.: Currier Gallery of Art, 1964.

Dibble, Ann W. "Major John Dunlap: The Craftsman and His Community." *Old-Time New England* 68 (Winter–Spring 1978): 50–58.

Diderot, Denis, ed. *Recueil de Planches, sur les Sciences, les Arts Libéraux, et les Arts Méchaniques.* Vol. 9. Paris, 1771.

Dow, George Francis. *The Arts and Crafts in New England, 1704–1775.* Topsfield, Mass.: Wayside Press, 1927.

Downing, Antoinette F., and Vincent J. Scully, Jr. *The Architectural Heritage of Newport, Rhode Island.* 2nd ed., rev. New York: Bramhall House, 1967.

Downs, Joseph. *American Furniture: Queen Anne and Chippendale Periods in the Henry Francis du Pont Winterthur Museum.* New York: Viking, 1967.

————. "American Japanned Furniture." *Old-Time New England* 28 (October 1937): 61–67.

Drake, Francis S. *Dictionary of American Biography.* Boston: James R. Osgood, 1872.

The Dunlaps & Their Furniture. Manchester, N.H.: Currier Gallery of Art, 1970.

Dwight, Timothy. *Travels in New England and New York.* Edited by Barbara M. Solomon. Cambridge: Harvard University Press, 1969.

Edwards, Ralph, and Margaret Jourdain. *Georgian Cabinet Makers c. 1700–1800.* Rev. ed. London: Country Life, 1955.

Ellesin, Dorothy E., ed. "Collectors' Notes." *Antiques* 107 (May 1975): 952–53.

Ellis, L. B. *History of New Bedford and Its Vicinity, 1602–1892.* Syracuse: D. Mason, 1892.

Elwell, Newton W. *Colonial Furniture and Interiors.* Boston: George H. Polley, 1896.

Emerson, George B. *A Report on the Trees and*

Shrubs Growing Naturally in the Forests of Massachusetts. 2nd ed. 2 vols. Boston: Little, Brown, 1875.

English Furniture, with Some Furniture of Other Countries in the Irwin Untermyer Collection. London: Thames and Hudson, 1958.

Evans, Dorinda. *Benjamin West and His American Students.* Washington, D.C.: Smithsonian Institution Press for the National Portrait Gallery, 1980.

Evans, Nancy Goyne. "The Genealogy of a Bookcase Desk." In *Winterthur Portfolio 9*, edited by Ian M. G. Quimby, 213–22. Charlottesville, Va.: University Press of Virginia, 1974.

———. "Unsophisticated Furniture Made and Used in Philadelphia and Environs, ca. 1750–1800." In *Winterthur Conference Report 1969: Country Cabinetwork and Simple City Furniture,* edited by John D. Morse, 151–203. Charlottesville, Va.: University Press of Virginia, 1970.

Failey, Dean F. *Long Island Is My Nation.* Setauket, N.Y.: Society for the Preservation of Long Island Antiquities, 1976.

Fairbanks, Jonathan L. "American Antiques in the Collection of Mr. and Mrs. Charles L. Bybee." Parts 1–2. *Antiques* 92 (December 1967): 832–39, 93 (January 1968): 76–82.

———, and Elizabeth Bidwell Bates. *American Furniture, 1620 to the Present.* New York: Richard Marek, 1981.

Fales, Dean A., Jr. *American Painted Furniture, 1660–1880.* New York: Dutton, 1979.

———. "Boston Japanned Furniture." In *Boston Furniture of the Eighteenth Century,* 49–69. Boston: Colonial Society of Massachusetts, 1974.

———. The Crowninshield-Bentley House in Salem." *Antiques* 88 (Ocobter 1965): 486–93.

———. *Essex County Furniture: Documented Treasures from Local Collections, 1660–1860.* Salem, Mass.: Essex Institute, 1965.

———. *The Furniture of Historic Deerfield.* New York: Dutton, 1976.

———. Introduction to *The Colonial Furniture of New England: A Study of the Domestic Furniture in Use in the Seventeenth and Eighteenth Centuries,* by Irving Whitall Lyon. 3rd ed., 1925. Reprint. New York: Dutton, 1977.

Fede, Helen Maggs. *Washington Furniture at Mount Vernon.* Mount Vernon, Va., 1966.

Fitzgerald, Oscar P. *Three Centuries of American Furniture.* Englewood Cliffs, N.J.: Prentice-Hall, 1982.

Forman, Benno M. "Continental Furniture Craftsmen in London: 1511–1625." *Furniture History* 7 (1971): 94–120.

———. "The Crown and York Chairs of Coastal Connecticut and the Work of the Durands of Milford." *Antiques* 105 (May 1974): 1147–54.

———. "Delaware Valley 'Crookt Foot' and Slatback Chairs: The Fussell-Savery Connection." In *Winterthur Portfolio 15* (Spring 1980): 41–64.

———. "Mill Sawing in Seventeenth-Century Massachusetts." *Old-Time New England* 60 (Spring 1970): 110–30, 149.

———. "Origins of the Joined Chest of Drawers." In *Nederlands Kunsthistorisch Jarrboek,* 169–83. Leyden, 1980.

———. "Salem Tradesmen and Craftsmen Circa 1762: A Contemporary Document." *Essex Institute Historical Collections* 107 (January 1971): 62–81.

———. "The Seventeenth-Century Case Furniture of Essex County, and Its Makers." Master's thesis, University of Delaware, 1968.

———. "Urban Aspects of Massachusetts Furniture in the Late Seventeenth Century." In *Winterthur Conference Report 1969: Country Cabinetwork and Simple City Furniture,* edited by John D. Morse, 1–33. Charlottesville, Va.: University Press of Virginia, 1970.

Fowler, John, and John Cornforth. *English Decoration in the Eighteenth Century.* Princeton: Pyne Press, 1974.

Furniture History, Journal of the Furniture History Society 16 (1980).

Garrett, Wendell D. "The Goddard and Townsend Joiners of Newport." *Antiques* 111 (May 1982): 1153–55.

———. "Living with Antiques, The Home of Mr. & Mrs. Charles Montgomery." *Antiques* 101 (January 1972): 185–92.

———. "The Newport Cabinetmakers: A Corrected Check List." *Antiques* 73 (June 1958): 558–61.

———. "Providence Cabinetmakers, Chairmakers, Upholsterers and Allied Craftsmen, 1756–1838." *Antiques* 90 (October 1966): 514–19.

Garvin, Donna-Belle. "Two High Chests of the Dunlap School." *Historical New Hampshire* 35 (Summer 1980): 178–85.

Geer, Walter. *The Geer Genealogy*. New York: Brentamas, 1923.

George Dudley Seymour's Furniture Collection in the Connecticut Historical Society. Hartford: Connecticut Historical Society, 1958.

Giffen, Jane C. "The Moffatt-Ladd House at Portsmouth, New Hampshire." Parts 1–2. *Connoisseur* 175 (October, November 1970): 113–22, 201–7.

Gilbert, Christopher. *Furniture at Temple Newsam House and Lotherton Hall*. 2 vols. Leeds: National Art-Collections Fund and the Leeds Art Collections Fund, 1978.

———. *The Life and Work of Thomas Chippendale*. 2 vols. London: Studio Vista, 1978.

———. "Newly Discovered Furniture by William Hallett." *Connoisseur* (December 1964): 224–25.

———. "Regional Traditions in English Vernacular Furniture." In *Winterthur Conference Report 1974: Arts of the Anglo-American Community in the Seventeenth Century*, edited by Ian M. G. Quimby, 43–77. Charlottesville, Va.: University Press of Virginia, 1975.

Girl Scouts Loan Exhibition. See *Loan Exhibition of Eighteenth and Early Nineteenth Century Furniture and Glass. . . .*

Gloag, John. *Georgian Grace: A Social History of Design from 1660–1830*. New York: Macmillan, 1956.

The Golden Age of English Furniture Upholstery, 1660–1846. Leeds: Temple Newsam, 1973.

Goyne, Nancy A. "The Bureau Table in America." In *Winterthur Portfolio 3*, edited by Milo M. Naeve, 24–36. Winterthur, Del.: Winterthur Museum, 1967.

Greenlaw, Barry. *New England Furniture at Williamsburg*. Williamsburg, Va.: Colonial Williamsburg Foundation, 1974.

"The Greenwood Gift." *Antiques* 57 (February 1950): 120–22.

Gusler, Wallace B. *Furniture of Williamsburg and Eastern Virginia, 1710–1790*. Richmond, Va.: Virginia Museum, 1979.

Haas, Robert Bartlett. "The Forgotten Courtship of David and Mary Spear, 1785–1787." *Old-Time New England* 52 (Winter 1962): 61–74.

Hale, Albert, compiler. *Old Newburyport Houses*. Boston: W. B. Clarke, 1912.

[Hamilton, Alexander.] *Gentleman's Progress: The Itinerarium of Dr. Alexander Hamilton, 1744*. Edited by Carl Bridenbaugh. Chapel Hill, N.C.: University of North Carolina Press, 1948.

Harlow, Henry J. "The Shop of Samuel Wing, Craftsman of Sandwich, Massachusetts." *Antiques* 93 (March 1968): 372–77.

Harrison, Molly. *People and Furniture*. London: Ernest Berin, 1971.

Harvard Tercentenary Exhibition: Catalogue of Furniture, Silver, Pewter, Glass, Ceramics, Paintings, Prints together with allied arts and crafts of the period 1636–1836. Cambridge: Harvard University Press, 1936.

Hayden, Arthur. *Chats on Old Furniture, A Practical Guide for Collectors*. London: T. Fisher Unwin, 1913.

Hayward, J. G. *English Desks and Bureaux*. London: Her Majesty's Stationery Office, 1968.

Heal, Ambrose. *The London Furniture Makers from the Restoration to the Victorian Era, 1660–1840*. London: B. T. Batsford, 1953.

Heckscher, Morrison H. "Form and Frame: New Thoughts on the American Easy Chair." *Antiques* 100 (December 1971): 886–93.

———. "John Townsend's Block-and-Shell Furniture." *Antiques* 121 (May 1982): 1144–52.

Hedges, James B. *The Browns of Providence Plantations: Colonial Years*. Cambridge: Harvard University Press, 1952.

Hendrick, Robert E. T. "John Gaines II and Thomas Gaines I, 'Turners' of Ipswich, Massachusetts." Master's thesis, University of Delaware, 1964.

Henretta, James A. "Economic Development and Social Structure in Colonial Boston." *William and Mary Quarterly*, 3rd ser., 22 (January 1965): 75–92.

Hill, John H. "The History and Technique of Japanning and the Restoration of the Pimm Highboy." *American Art Journal* 8 (November 1976): 59–84.

Hinckley, Lewis. *A Directory of Queen Anne, Early Georgian and Chippendale Furniture*. New York: Crown, 1971.

Hipkiss, Edwin J. *Eighteenth-Century American Arts: The M. and M. Karolik Collection*. Cambridge: Harvard University Press, 1941.

Hitchings, Sinclair. "Thomas Johnston." In *Boston Prints and Printmakers, 1670–1775*, 83–131. Boston: Colonial Society of Massachusetts, 1973.

Hornor, William M., Jr. "A Survey of 'American Wing Chairs.'" *International Studio* 99 (July 1931): 28–30, 71–73.

Hosley, William N., Jr., and Philip Zea. "Decorated

Board Chests of the Connecticut River Valley." *Antiques* 119 (May 1981): 1146–51.

Household Furniture in Genteel Taste for the Year 1760. By a Society of Upholsterers, Cabinet-Makers, etc. London: Robert Sayer, 1760.

Howard, Cecil H. C. *Genealogy of the Cutts Family in America.* Albany: Joel Munsell's Sons, 1892.

Howells, John Mead. *The Architectural Heritage of the Piscataqua.* N.p.: Architectural Book Publishing Company, 1965.

Hughes, Judith C. "North European Export Mirrors." *Antiques* 89 (June 1966): 856–61.

Hummell, Charles F. "Queen Anne and Chippendale Furniture in the Henry Francis du Pont Winterthur Museum." Parts 1–2. *Antiques* 97 (June 1970): 896–903, 98 (December 1970): 900–909.

"Huntington Papers." *Connecticut Historical Society Collections* 20 (1923): 159–60.

Huth, Hans. *Lacquer of the West, 1550–1950.* Chicago: University of Chicago Press, 1971.

Ince, William, and John Mayhew. *The Universal System of Household Furniture.* London: Robert Sayer, 1762.

Ingate, Margaret Rose. "History in Towns: Mobile, Alabama." *Antiques* 81 (March 1964): 294–309.

Isham, Norman. "John Goddard and His Work." *Rhode Island School of Design Bulletin* 15 (April 1927): 14–24.

Israel Sack Collection. See American Antiques from the Israel Sack Collection.

Jobe, Brock. "The Boston Furniture Industry, 1720–1740." In *Boston Furniture of the Eighteenth Century,* 3–48. Boston: Colonial Society of Massachusetts, 1974.

———. "The Boston Furniture Industry, 1725–1760." Master's thesis, University of Delaware, 1976.

———. "A Desk by Benjamin Frothingham of Charlestown." *Currier Gallery of Art Bulletin* (1976): 3–23.

———. "New Discoveries in New England Furniture." In *Ellis Memorial Antiques Show 1978,* 45–52. Boston: Ellis Memorial Antiques Show Committee, 1978.

———. "The Upholstery Trade of Colonial Boston." In *Proceedings from the Conference on Historic Upholstery and Drapery.* Boston: Museum of Fine Arts, forthcoming.

John Brown House Loan Exhibition of Rhode Island Furniture. Providence: Rhode Island Historical Society, 1965.

Jorgensen, Neil. *A Guide to New England's Landscape.* Chester, Conn.: Pequot Press, 1977.

Jourdain, Margaret. *English Decoration and Furniture of the Early Renaissance: 1500–1650.* London: B. T. Batsford, 1924.

Judd, Sylvester. *History of Hadley.* Springfield, Mass.: H. R. Huntting, 1905.

Kane, Patricia E. *Furniture of the New Haven Colony: The Seventeenth-Century Style.* New Haven: New Haven Colony Historical Society, 1973.

———. "The Joiners of Seventeenth-Century Hartford County." *Connecticut Historical Society Bulletin* 35 (July 1970): 65–85.

———. "The Seventeenth-Century Furniture of the Connecticut Valley: The Hadley Chest Reappraised." In *Winterthur Conference Report 1974: Arts of the Anglo-American Community in the Seventeenth Century,* edited by Ian M. G. Quimby, 79–122. Charlottesville, Va.: University Press of Virginia, 1975.

———. *300 Years of American Seating Furniture.* Boston: New York Graphic Society, 1976.

Kaye, Myrna. "Concord Case Furniture: Cabinetry Twenty Miles from the Bay." In The Dublin Seminar for New England Folklife Annual Proceedings: 1981. *The Bay and the River: 1600–1900,* edited by Peter Benes, 29–42. Boston: Boston University Scholarly Publications, 1982.

———. "Eighteenth-Century Boston Furniture Craftsmen." In *Boston Furniture of the Eighteenth Century,* 267–302. Boston: Colonial Society of Massachusetts, 1974.

———. "Marked Portsmouth Furniture." *Antiques* 113 (May 1978): 1098–1104.

Kettell, Russell Hawes. *Pine Furniture of Early New England.* New York, 1929.

Keyes, Homer Eaton. "A Study in Differences." *Antiques* 22 (July 1932): 6–7.

Kirk, John T. *American Chairs: Queen Anne and Chippendale.* New York: Knopf, 1972.

———. *American Furniture and the British Tradition to 1830.* New York: Knopf, 1982.

———. *Connecticut Furniture: Seventeenth and Eighteenth Centuries.* Hartford: Wadsworth Atheneum, 1967.

———. "The Distinctive Character of Connecticut Furniture." *Antiques* 92 (October 1967): 524–29.

———. *Early American Furniture.* New York: Knopf, 1974.

———. "Sources of Some American Regional Furniture." *Antiques* 88 (December 1965): 790–98.

Kirkham, P. A. "Samuel Norman: A Study of an Eighteenth-Century Craftsman." *Burlington Magazine* 111 (August 1969): 500–11, 513.

Kurath, Hans. *Handbook of the Linguistic Geography of New England.* 2nd ed. New York: AMS Press, 1973.

Landman, Hedy B. "The Pendleton House at the Museum of Art, Rhode Island School of Design." *Antiques* 112 (May 1975): 923–38.

Litchfield County Furniture, 1730–1850. Litchfield, Conn.: Litchfield Historical Society, 1969.

Loan Exhibition of Eighteenth and Early Nineteenth Century Furniture & Glass . . . For the Benefit of the National Council of Girl Scouts, Inc. New York: American Art Galleries, 1929.

Lockwood, Luke Vincent. *Colonial Furniture in America.* New York: Scribner's, 1901.

———. *Colonial Furniture in America.* Rev. ed., 2 vols. New York: Scribner's, 1913.

———. *Colonial Furniture in America.* 3rd ed., 2 vols. Reprint (2 vols. in 1). New York: Castle Books, 1951.

Lovell, Margaretta Markle. "Boston Blockfront Furniture." In *Boston Furniture of the Eighteenth Century,* 77–135. Boston: Colonial Society of Massachusetts, 1974.

Luther, Clair F. *The Hadley Chest.* Hartford: Case, Lockwood & Brainard, 1935.

Lyon, Irving P. "The Oak Furniture of Ipswich, Massachusetts." Parts 1–6. *Antiques* 32 (November, December 1937): 230–33, 298–301; 33 (February, April, June 1938): 73–75, 198–203, 322–25; 34 (August 1938): 79–81.

Lyon, Irving Whitall. *The Colonial Furniture of New England: A Study of the Domestic Furniture in Use in the Seventeenth and Eighteenth Centuries.* Boston: Houghton Mifflin, 1891.

———. *The Colonial Furniture of New England: A Study of the Domestic Furniture in Use in the Seventeenth and Eighteenth Centuries.* 3rd ed., 1925. Reprint. New York: Dutton, 1977.

McCusker, John J. *Money and Exchange in Europe and America, 1600–1775.* Chapel Hill, N.C.: University of North Carolina Press, 1978.

Macquoid, Percy. *A History of English Furniture.* Vol. 1, *The Age of Oak;* vol. 2, *The Age of Walnut.* London: Lawrence & Bullen, 1904–1905.

———, and Ralph Edwards. *The Dictionary of English Furniture.* Rev. ed., 2 vols. London: Country Life, 1954.

Manwaring, Robert. *The Cabinet and Chair-Maker's Real Friend and Companion; or, The Whole System of Chair-Making Made Plain and Easy.* London: Henry Webley, 1765.

———. *The Chair-Maker's Guide.* London: Robert Sayer, 1766.

Maverick, Samuel. "A Brief Description of New England and the Severall Townes Therein, Together with the Present Government Thereof." *Proceedings of the Massachusetts Historical Society,* 2nd ser., 1 (1884–1885): 231–39.

Miller, Edgar G. *American Antique Furniture: A Book for Amateurs.* 2 vols. Baltimore: Lord Baltimore Press, 1937.

Minsheu, Iohn. *A Dictionarie in Spanish and English.* London: Edm. Bollifant, 1599.

Montgomery, Charles F. *American Furniture: The Federal Period in the Henry Francis du Pont Winterthur Museum.* New York: Viking, 1966.

———. "Some Remarks on the Practice and Science of Connoisseurship." In *Walpole Society Notebook.* Litchfield, Conn.: The Walpole Society, 1961.

Montgomery, Florence M. *Printed Textiles.* New York: Viking, 1970.

"More about 'Dutch Looking Glasses.'" *Antiques* 90 (November 1966): 693.

Morison, Samuel Eliot. *The Oxford History of the American People.* New York: Oxford University Press, 1965.

Morse, Frances Clary. *Furniture of the Olden Time.* New York: Macmillan, 1902.

———. *Furniture of the Olden Time.* Rev. ed. New York: Macmillan, 1936.

Moses, Liza and Michael. "Authenticating John Townsend's and John Goddard's Queen Anne and Chippendale Tables." *Antiques* 121 (May 1982): 1130–43.

———. "Authenticating John Townsend's Later Tables." *Antiques* 119 (May 1981): 1152–63.

Mussey, Robert. "Transparent Furniture Finishes in New England, 1700–1820." In *1980 Proceedings of the Furniture and Wooden Object Symposium,* 77–101. Ottawa: Canadian Conservation Institute, 1981.

Myers, Minor, Jr., and Edgar deN. Mayhew. *New*

London County Furniture: 1640–1840. New London, Conn.: Lyman Allyn Museum, 1974.

Nash, Gary B. *The Urban Crucible: Social Change, Political Consciousness, and the Origins of the American Revolution.* Cambridge: Harvard University Press, 1979.

Nelson, Lee H. "Nail Chronology as an Aid to Dating Old Buildings." Technical Leaflet 15. *History News* 19 (December 1963).

New England Begins: The Seventeenth Century. 3 vols. Boston: Museum of Fine Arts, 1982.

Norman, Diane A., ed. *Meet Our Craftsmen: A Presentation of 18th Century Preston Cabinetmakers.* Preston: Preston Historical Society, 1976.

Norman-Wilcox, Gregor. "American Furniture, Noteworthy and Unrecorded." *Antiques* 36 (December 1939): 282–85.

Nutting, Wallace. *Checklist of Early American Reproductions.* 1930. Reprint. Watkins Glen, N.Y.: American Life Foundation and Institute, 1969.

———. *Furniture of the Pilgrim Century, 1620–1720.* Boston: Marshall Jones, 1921.

———. *Furniture of the Pilgrim Century (of American Origin) 1620–1720.* Rev. ed. Framingham, Mass.: Old America Company, 1924.

———. *Furniture Treasury.* 3 vols. Framingham, Mass.: Old America Company, 1928.

Nylander, Richard. "The First Harrison Gray Otis House." *Antiques* 107 (June 1975): 1130–41.

Oedel, Howard T. "Portsmouth, New Hampshire: The Role of the Provincial Capital in the Development of the Colony, 1750–1775." Ph.D. diss., Boston University, 1960.

Orcutt, Philip D. *The Moffatt-Ladd House.* Norwood, Mass.: Plimpton Press, 1935.

Ott, Joseph K. "Exports of Furniture, Chaises, and Other Wooden Forms from Providence and Newport, 1783–1795." *Antiques* 102 (January 1975): 135–41.

———. "More Notes on Rhode Island Cabinetmakers and Their Work." *Rhode Island History* 28 (Spring 1969): 49–52.

———. "Recent Discoveries among Rhode Island Cabinetmakers and Their Work." *Rhode Island History* 28 (Winter 1969): 3–25.

———. "Some Rhode Island Furniture." *Antiques* 107 (May 1975): 940–51.

———. "Still More Notes on Rhode Island Cabinetmakers and Allied Craftsmen." *Rhode Island History* 28 (Fall 1969): 111–21.

Palmer, Brooks. *The Book of American Clocks,* New York: Macmillan, 1950.

Park, Helen. "The Seventeenth-Century Furniture of Essex County and Its Makers." *Antiques* 78 (October 1960): 350–55.

———. "Thomas Dennis, Ipswich Joiner: A Reexamination." *Antiques* 78 (July 1960): 40–44.

[Parkman, Ebenezer.] "The Diary of Ebenezer Parkman." Edited by Francis G. Walett. *Proceedings of the American Antiquarian Society* 72 (April 1962): 31–233.

Parsons, Charles S. "The Dunlap Cabinetmakers." In *The Dunlaps & Their Furniture,* 1–74. Manchester, N.H.: Currier Gallery of Art, 1970.

———. *New Hampshire Clocks & Clockmakers.* Exeter, N.H.: Adams Brown, 1976.

Parsons, Usher. *The Life of Sir William Pepperrell, Bart.* Boston: Little, Brown, 1855.

Paul Revere's Boston, 1735–1818. Boston: Museum of Fine Arts, 1975.

"Pepperrell Manuscripts." *New England Historic and Genealogical Register,* 19 (1865): 141–48, 222–30.

Perley, Sidney. "Marblehead in the Year 1700, No. 3." *Essex Institute Historical Collections* 46 (July 1910): 221–46.

Phillips, Daniel L. *Griswold — A History.* N.p.: Tuttle, Morehouse & Taylor, 1929.

Plain & Elegant, Rich & Common: Documented New Hampshire Furniture, 1750–1850. Concord, N.H.: New Hampshire Historical Society, 1979.

"Portsmouth Side Chair Presented to Museum." New Hampshire Historical Society *Newsletter* 17 (Spring 1979): 4.

A Pride of Quincys. Boston: Massachusetts Historical Society, 1967.

Probate Records of the Province of New Hampshire 1 (1635–1717). *State Papers Series,* 31. Concord, N.H.: Rumford Printing Company, 1907.

Prown, Jules David. *John Singleton Copley.* 2 vols. Cambridge: Harvard University Press, 1966.

Pye, David W. *The Nature and Art of Workmanship.* New York: Van Nostrand–Reinhold, 1971.

Randall, Richard H., Jr. *American Furniture in the Museum of Fine Arts, Boston.* Boston: Museum of Fine Arts, 1965.

———. "Boston Chairs." *Old-Time New England* 54 (Summer 1963): 12–20.

———. "George Bright, Cabinetmaker." *Art Quarterly* 27 (1964): 134–49.

———. "William Randall, Boston Japanner." *Antiques* 105 (May 1974): 1127–31.

Rauschenberg, Bradford L. "The Royal Governor's Chair: Evidence of the Furnishing of South Carolina's First State House." *Journal of Early Southern Decorative Arts* 6 (November 1980): 1–32.

Rhoades, Elizabeth, and Brock Jobe. "Recent Discoveries in Boston Japanned Furniture." *Antiques* 105 (May 1974): 1082–91.

Richards, Nancy E. "Furniture of the Lower Connecticut River Valley, The Hartford Area, 1785–1801." In *Winterthur Portfolio 4*, edited by Richard K. Doud, 1–25. Charlottesville, Va.: University Press of Virginia, 1968.

Roe, Albert S., and Robert F. Trent. "Robert Sanderson and the Founding of the Boston Silversmiths' Trade." In *New England Begins: The Seventeenth Century*, vol. 3, 480–89. Boston: Museum of Fine Arts, 1982.

Roth, Rodris. "Tea Drinking in 18th-Century America: Its Etiquette and Equipage." *Contributions from the Museum of History and Technology*. United States National Museum Bulletin 225. Washington, D.C.: Smithsonian Institution, 1961.

Rutman, Darrett B. *Winthrop's Boston: A Portrait of a Puritan Town, 1630–1649*. Chapel Hill, N.C.: University of North Carolina Press, 1965.

Sack, Albert. *Fine Points of Furniture: Early American*. New York: Crown, 1950.

St. George, Robert Blair. "The Staniford Family Chest." *Maine Antique Digest* 11 (February 1983): 16B–18B.

———. "Style and Structure in the Joinery of Dedham and Medfield, Massachusetts, 1635–1685." In *Winterthur Portfolio 13: American Furniture and Its Makers*, edited by Ian M. G. Quimby, 1–46. Chicago: University of Chicago Press, 1979.

———. *The Wrought Covenant: Source Material for the Study of Craftsmen and Community in Southeastern New England, 1620–1700*. Brockton, Mass.: Brockton Art Center, 1979.

Saltar, Gordon. "New England Timbers." In *Boston Furniture of the Eighteenth Century*, 251–64. Boston: Colonial Society of Massachusetts, 1974.

Schwartz, Marvin D. *American Furniture of the Colonial Period*. New York: Metropolitan Museum of Art, 1976.

Scott, Kenneth, and Russell H. Kettell. "Joseph Hosmer, Cabinetmaker." *Antiques* 73 (April 1958): 356–59.

Scotti, N. David. "Notes on Rhode Island Cabinetmakers." *Antiques* 87 (May 1965): 572.

The IIᵈ Edition of Genteel Household Furniture in the Present Taste with an Addition of Several Articles Never before Executed, by a Society of Upholsterers, Cabinet-Makers, & c. London: Robert Sayer, probably 1762.

[Sewall, Samuel.] *The Diary of Samuel Sewall, 1674–1729*. Edited by M. Halsey Thomas. 2 vols. New York: Farrar, Straus & Giroux, 1973.

———. *Letter-Book of Samuel Sewall. Collections of the Massachusetts Historical Society*. 6th ser., vol. 2. Boston, 1888.

Seymour Collection. See George Dudley Seymour's Furniture Collection . . .

Shattuck, Lemuel. *Report to the Committee of the City Council Appointed to Obtain the Census of Boston for the Year 1845*. Boston: John H. Eastburn, 1846.

Sheldon, George. *A History of Deerfield, Massachusetts . . . 1636–1886*. Greenfield, Mass.: Press of E. A. Hall & Company, 1895.

Sheraton, Thomas. *The Cabinet Dictionary*. 1803. Reprint. New York: Praeger, 1970.

Shipton, Clifford K. *Sibley's Harvard Graduates*. Vol. 13. Boston: Massachusetts Historical Society, 1965.

Shy, John. "The American Revolution: The Military Conflict Considered as a Revolutionary War." In *Essays on the American Revolution*, 121–56, edited by Stephen G. Kurtz and James H. Hutson. New York: Norton, 1973.

Siddons, G. A. *The Cabinet-maker's Guide*. 5th ed. London: Sherwood, Gilbert and Piper, 1830.

Singleton, Esther. *The Furniture of Our Forefathers*. 2 vols. New York: Doubleday, Page, 1901.

Smith, H. Clifford. *Catalogue of English Furniture and Woodwork*. Vol. 2, *Late Tudor and Early Stuart*. London: Victoria and Albert Museum, 1930.

Smith, Nancy. *Old Furniture: Understanding the Craftsman's Art*. Indianapolis: Bobbs-Merrill, 1975.

Spalding, Dexter E. "Abner Toppan, Cabinetmaker." *Antiques* 15 (June 1929) 493–95.

———. "Benjamin Frothingham of Charlestown, Cabinetmaker and Soldier." *Antiques* 14 (December 1928): 535–37.

Spring, James W. "The Coffin House in Newbury, Massachusetts." *Old-Time New England* 20 (July 1929): 2–29.

Stackpole, Everett S. *Old Kittery and Her Families*. Lewiston, Me.: Lewiston Journal Company, 1903.

Swan, Mabel Munson. "Furnituremakers of Charlestown." *Antiques* 46 (October 1944): 203–6.

———. "John Goddard's Sons." *Antiques* 57 (June 1950): 448–49.

———. "Major Benjamin Frothingham, Cabinetmaker." *Antiques* 62 (November 1952): 392–95.

———. "Newburyport Furnituremakers." *Antiques* 47 (April 1945): 222–25.

———. "Some Men from Medway." *Antiques* 17 (May 1930): 417–21.

Swift, Charles F. *History of Old Yarmouth*. 1884. Reprint. Yarmouth Port, Mass.: Historical Society of Old Yarmouth, 1975.

Symonds, R. W. "English Cane Chairs." Parts 1–2. *Connoisseur* (April, June 1951): 8–15, 83–91.

———. "Turkey Work, Beech and Japanned Chairs." *Connoisseur* (April 1934): 221–28.

Temple, J. H. *History of the Town of Whately, Mass.* Boston: T. R. Marvin, 1872.

Thirtieth Report of the Record Commissioners. Boston Marriages, 1752–1809. Boston: Municipal Printing Office, 1903.

Thornton, Peter. *Seventeenth-Century Interior Decoration in England, France, and Holland*. New Haven: Yale University Press, 1978.

Trent, Robert F. "The Concept of Mannerism." In *New England Begins*, vol. 3, 368–79. Boston: Museum of Fine Arts, 1982.

———. *Hearts & Crowns: Folk Chairs of the Connecticut Coast, 1720–1840*. New Haven: New Haven Colony Historical Society, 1977.

———. "The Joiners and Joinery of Middlesex County, Massachusetts, 1630–1730." In *Winterthur Conference Report 1974: Arts of the Anglo-American Community in the Seventeenth Century*, edited by Ian M. G. Quimby, 123–48. Charlottesville, Va.: University Press of Virginia, 1975.

———. "New England Joinery and Turning before 1700." In *New England Begins*, vol. 3, 501–10. Boston: Museum of Fine Arts, 1982.

Van Deventer, David E. *The Emergence of Provincial New Hampshire: 1623–1741*. Baltimore: Johns Hopkins University Press, 1976.

Vibert, Jean Arthur. "The Market Economy and the Furniture Trade of Newport, Rhode Island. The Career of John Cahoone, Cabinetmaker: 1745–1765." Master's thesis, University of Delaware, 1981.

Vincent, Gilbert T. "The Bombé Furniture of Boston." In *Boston Furniture of the Eighteenth Century*, 137–96. Boston: Colonial Society of Massachusetts, 1974.

Vital Records of Ipswich, Massachusetts, to 1849. Vol. 2. Salem, Mass.: Essex Institute, 1910.

Vital Records of Salem, Massachusetts, to 1850. Vol 3. Salem, Mass.: Essex Institute.

Warren, David B. *Bayou Bend, American Furniture, Paintings and Silver from the Bayou Bend Collection*. Houston: Museum of Fine Arts, 1975.

Warren, William L. "Were the Guilford Painted Chests Made in Saybrook?" *Connecticut Historical Society Bulletin* 23 (January 1958): 1–10.

Waters, Thomas F. *Ipswich in the Massachusetts Bay Colony*. Vol. 2. Ipswich, Mass.: Ipswich Historical Society, 1917.

Watkins, Lura W. "Highfields and Its Heritage." *Antiques* 90 (August 1966): 204–7.

Weeks, Edward. *The Lowells and Their Institute*. Boston: Little, Brown, 1966.

Weil, Martin Eli. "A Cabinetmaker's Price Book." In *Winterthur Portfolio 13: American Furniture and Its Makers*, edited by Ian M. G. Quimby, 175–92. Chicago: University of Chicago Press, 1979.

Wells-Cole, Anthony. "An Oak Bed at Montacute: A Study in Mannerist Decoration." *Furniture History* 17 (1981): 1–19.

———. "Oak Furniture in Dorset: Some Introductory Materials." *Furniture History* 12 (1976): 24–28.

Wendell, William G. "The Macpheadris-Warner House in Portsmouth, New Hampshire." *Antiques* 77 (June 1965): 712–15.

Whinney, Margaret. *Sculpture in Britain*. Harmondsworth, Middlesex: Penguin Books, 1964.

Wick, Peter A. "Gore Place, Federal Mansion in

Waltham, Massachusetts." *Antiques* 110 (December 1976): 1250–61.

Wills, Geoffrey. *English Looking-Glasses.* New York: A. S. Barnes, 1965.

Wood, William. *New England's Prospect.* Edited by Alden T. Vaughan. Amherst, Mass.: University of Massachusetts Press, 1977.

Wyman, Thomas B. *The Genealogies and Estates of Charlestown.* 2 vols. Boston: David Clapp, 1879.

Yonge, Ena L. *A Catalogue of Early Globes: Made Prior to 1850 and Conserved in the United States.* New York: American Geographical Society, 1968.

Young, M. Ada. "Five Secretaries and the Cogswells." *Antiques* 88 (October 1965): 478–85.

Zea, Philip. "A New Hampshire Grant Town, 1760–1815." Master's thesis, Wesleyan University, 1974.

————. "William Mather: A Specialist in Specialies." Paper presented for the Historic Deerfield Summer Fellowship Program, 1973.

Zuckerman, Michael. *Peaceable Kingdoms: New England Towns in the Eighteenth Century.* New York: Knopf, 1970.

Collections and Institutions

Adams National Historic Site, Quincy, Massachusetts

Albany Institute of History and Art, Albany, New York

American Antiquarian Society, Worcester, Massachusetts

Andover Historical Society, Andover, Massachusetts

Antiquarian and Landmarks Society, Inc., of Connecticut, Hartford, Connecticut

Archives of American Art, Washington, D.C.

Arlington Historical Society, Arlington, Massachusetts

Art Institute of Chicago, Chicago, Illinois

Baker Library, Graduate School of Business Administration, Harvard University, Boston, Massachusetts

Baltimore Museum of Art, Baltimore, Maryland

Bayou Bend Collection, Museum of Fine Arts, Houston, Texas

Beverly Historical Society, Beverly, Massachusetts

Billerica Historical Society, Billerica, Massachusetts

Boston Athenaeum, Boston, Massachusetts

Boston Public Library, Boston, Massachusetts

Bowdoin College Museum of Art, Brunswick, Maine

Boxford Historical Society, Boxford, Massachusetts

The Brooklyn Museum, Brooklyn, New York

Cape Ann Historical Association, Gloucester, Massachusetts

Cincinnati Art Museum, Cincinnati, Ohio

Colonial Williamsburg Foundation, Williamsburg, Virginia

Colorado Springs Fine Arts Center, Colorado Springs, Colorado

Concord Antiquarian Museum, Concord, Massachusetts

Connecticut Historical Society, Hartford, Connecticut

Currier Gallery of Art, Manchester, New Hampshire

Danvers Historical Society, Danvers, Massachusetts

Daughters of the American Revolution Museum, Washington, D.C.

Dedham Historical Society, Dedham, Massachusetts

The Detroit Institute of Arts, Detroit, Michigan

Diplomatic Reception Rooms, U.S. Department of State, Washington, D.C.

Duxbury Rural and Historical Society, Duxbury, Massachusetts

Elizabeth Perkins House, Society for the Preservation of Historic Landmarks in York County, York, Maine

Essex Institute, Salem, Massachusetts

Fairbanks House, Dedham, Massachusetts

Golden Ball Tavern, Weston, Massachusetts

Gore Place Society, Waltham, Massachusetts

Groton Historical Society, Groton, Massachusetts

Ham House, Victoria and Albert Museum, London

Henry Ford Museum and Greenfield Village, Dearborn, Michigan

Henry Francis du Pont Winterthur Museum, Winterthur, Delaware

Historic Cherry Hill, Albany, New York

Historic Deerfield, Inc., Deerfield, Massachusetts

Historical Society of Old Newbury, Newburyport, Massachusetts

The Historical Society of York County, York, Pennsylvania

Home Sweet Home Museum, East Hampton, New York

Ipswich Historical Society, Ipswich, Massachusetts

Jonathan Trumbull House, Lebanon, Connecticut

Lexington Historical Society, Lexington, Massachusetts

Lincoln County Cultural and Historical Association, Wiscasset, Maine

Longfellow National Historic Site, Cambridge, Massachusetts

Lyman Allyn Museum, New London, Connecticut

Lyme Historical Society, Old Lyme, Connecticut

Lynn Historical Society, Lynn, Massachusetts

Macpheadris-Warner House, Portsmouth, New Hampshire

Marblehead Historical Society, Marblehead, Massachusetts

Massachusetts Historical Society, Boston, Massachusetts

Metropolitan Museum of Art, New York, New York

Milwaukee Art Center, Milwaukee, Wisconsin

Moffatt-Ladd House, Portsmouth, New Hampshire

Museum of the American China Trade, Milton, Massachusetts

Museum of Art, Carnegie Institute, Pittsburgh, Pennsylvania

Museum of Early Southern Decorative Arts, Winston-Salem, North Carolina

Museum of Fine Arts, Boston, Massachusetts

New England Historic Genealogical Society, Boston, Massachusetts

New Hampshire Historical Society, Concord, New Hampshire

New Hampshire State Archives and Record Management Division, Concord, New Hampshire

New-York Historical Society, New York, New York

New York Public Library, New York, New York

Newburyport Public Library, Newburyport, Massachusetts

Newport Historical Society, Newport, Rhode Island

Newport Restoration Foundation, Newport, Rhode Island

North Andover Historical Society, North Andover, Massachusetts

Norwalk Historical Society, Norwalk, Connecticut

Old Gaol Museum, York, Maine

Old Ordinary, Hingham, Massachusetts

Old South Meeting House, Boston, Massachusetts

Old State House–The Bostonian Society, Boston, Massachusetts

Old Sturbridge Village, Sturbridge, Massachusetts

Peter Foulger Museum, Nantucket Historical Association, Nantucket, Massachusetts

Philadelphia Museum of Art, Philadelphia, Pennsylvania

Porter-Phelps-Huntington House Museum, Hadley, Massachusetts

The Preservation Society of Newport County, Newport, Rhode Island

Rhode Island Historical Society, Providence, Rhode Island

Rhode Island School of Design, Museum of Art, Providence, Rhode Island

Rowley Historical Society, Rowley, Massachusetts

Sargent-Murray-Gilman-Hough House, Gloucester, Massachusetts

Scituate Historical Society, Scituate, Massachusetts

Smithsonian Institution, Washington, D.C.

Strawbery Banke, Portsmouth, New Hampshire

Wadsworth Atheneum, Hartford, Connecticut

Wayside Inn, Sudbury, Massachusetts

The Webb-Deane-Stevens Museum, Wethersfield, Connecticut

Wentworth-Gardner House, Portsmouth, New Hampshire

Wilton, Richmond, Virginia

Winslow House, Historic Winslow House Association, Marshfield, Massachusetts

Winterthur Museum. *See* Henry Francis du Pont Winterthur Museum.

Worcester Art Museum, Worcester, Massachusetts

Yale University Art Gallery, New Haven, Connecticut

Index